## CONTRIBUTORS

**Prof. Dr Abdul Latiff Mohamad**
*Universiti Kebangsaan Malaysia*

**Assoc. Prof. Dr Aishah Salleh**
*Universiti Malaya*

**Dr S. Appanah**
*Forest Research Institute Malaysia (FRIM)*

**Dr P. N. Avadhani**
*National University of Singapore (retired)*

**Dr Cheksum Supiah Tawan**
*Universiti Malaysia Sarawak*

**Emeritus Prof. Dr Chin Hoong Fong**
*Universiti Putra Malaysia*

**Dr Lillian Chua Swee Lian**
*Forest Research Institute Malaysia (FRIM)*

**R. C. K. Chung**
*Forest Research Institute Malaysia (FRIM)*

**Prof. Dr Ghazally Ismail**
*Universiti Malaysia Sarawak*

**Dr Hadzim Khalid**
*Malaysian Agricultural Research and Development Institute*

**Assoc. Prof. Dr Halijah Ibrahim**
*Universiti Malaya*

**Dr Hoi Why Kong**
*Forest Research Institute Malaysia (FRIM)*

**Dr Hsuan Keng**
*National University of Singapore (retired)*

**Assoc. Prof. Dr Isa Ipor**
*Universiti Malaysia Sarawak*

**Dr Ruth Kiew**
*Singapore Botanic Gardens*

**K. M. Kochummen**
*Forest Research Institute Malaysia (FRIM)*

**Prof. Dr Laily Din**
*Universiti Kebangsaan Malaysia*

**Dr Lee Su See**
*Forest Research Institute Malaysia (FRIM)*

**Dr N. Manokaran**
*Forest Research Institute Malaysia (FRIM)*

**Prof. Dr Haji Mohamed bin Abdul Majid**
*Universiti Malaya*

**Dr Noorma Wati Haron**
*Universiti Malaya*

**Assoc. Prof. Dr Ong Hean Chooi**
*Universiti Malaya*

**Dr Othman Omar**
*Malaysian Agricultural Research and Development Institute*

**Dr N. Rajanaidu**
*Palm Oil Research Institute of Malaysia*

**Dr Salma Idris**
*Malaysian Agricultural Research and Development Institute*

**Dr Saw Leng Guan**
*Forest Research Institute Malaysia (FRIM)*

**Dr Shamsudin Ibrahim**
*Forest Research Institute Malaysia (FRIM)*

**Dr Tan Swee Lian**
*Malaysian Agricultural Research and Development Institute*

**Dr Hugh Tan Tiang Wah**
*National University of Singapore*

**Dr Chris K. H. Teo**
*Universiti Sains Malaysia*

**Dr Ian Turner**
*Kyoto University*

**Dr Wee Yeow Chin**
*National University of Singapore (retired)*

**Assoc. Prof. Dr Wong Khoon Meng**
*Universiti Malaya*

**Zabedah Mahmood**
*Malaysian Agricultural Research and Development Institute*

THE ENCYCLOPEDIA OF
# MALAYSIA

Volume 2

# PLANTS

Volume Editor
## Dr E. Soepadmo

ARCHIPELAGO PRESS

# Contents

# Classification of selected Malaysian plants and fungi

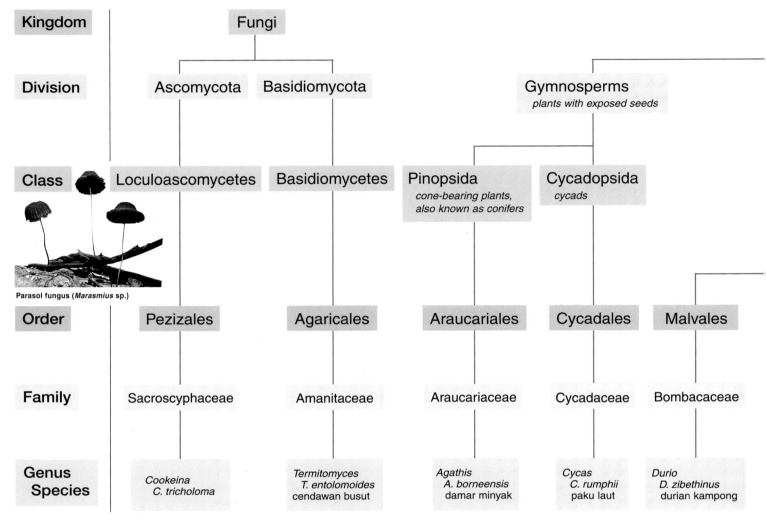

| | | | | | | |
|---|---|---|---|---|---|---|
| **Kingdom** | | Fungi | | | | |
| **Division** | Ascomycota | Basidiomycota | | Gymnosperms *plants with exposed seeds* | | |
| **Class** | Loculoascomycetes | Basidiomycetes | Pinopsida *cone-bearing plants, also known as conifers* | Cycadopsida *cycads* | | |
| **Order** | Pezizales | Agaricales | Araucariales | Cycadales | Malvales | |
| **Family** | Sacroscyphaceae | Amanitaceae | Araucariaceae | Cycadaceae | Bombacaceae | |
| **Genus Species** | *Cookeina* *C. tricholoma* | *Termitomyces* *T. entolomoides* cendawan busut | *Agathis* *A. borneensis* damar minyak | *Cycas* *C. rumphii* paku laut | *Durio* *D. zibethinus* durian kampong | |

Parasol fungus (*Marasmius* sp.)

## Plant classification

All plants are members of the plant kingdom, except for fungi which have their own kingdom. A kingdom is further subdivided into different taxanomic groups comprising divisions, classes, orders, families, genera and species. Taxa that are not featured in this table include subspecies, varieties, forms and cultivars, which all come after the species level. In the hierarchy of plant classification, each taxon consists of more components than the one above it. Species form the largest number of taxa and are grouped into genera which are, in turn, grouped into families and so on, until the division level. The divisions of the plant kingdom comprise algae and bryophytes (non-vascular plants) and pteridophytes, gymnosperms and angiosperms (vascular plants). Whilst bryophytes and pteridophytes reproduce by minute spores, gymnosperms and angiosperms do so through seeds. In gymnosperms, the seeds are exposed and organized in cone-like structures, whereas in angiosperms they are concealed within fruit walls.

Examples of the different taxa have been selected from plants that are characteristic of Malaysian flora. Hence, durian, pitcher plants, *Rafflesia* and *kapur* are used to illustrate the dicotyledons, while gingers, orchids and palms represent the monocotyledons. Similarly, conifers and cycads are typical components of the gymnosperms which are found in Malaysia.

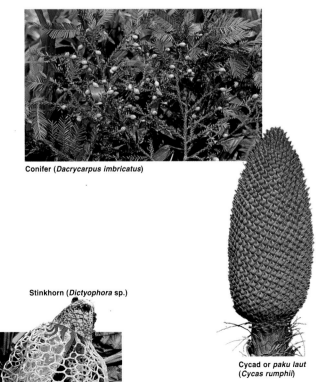

Conifer (*Dacrycarpus imbricatus*)

Stinkhorn (*Dictyophora* sp.)

Cycad or *paku laut* (*Cycas rumphii*)

6

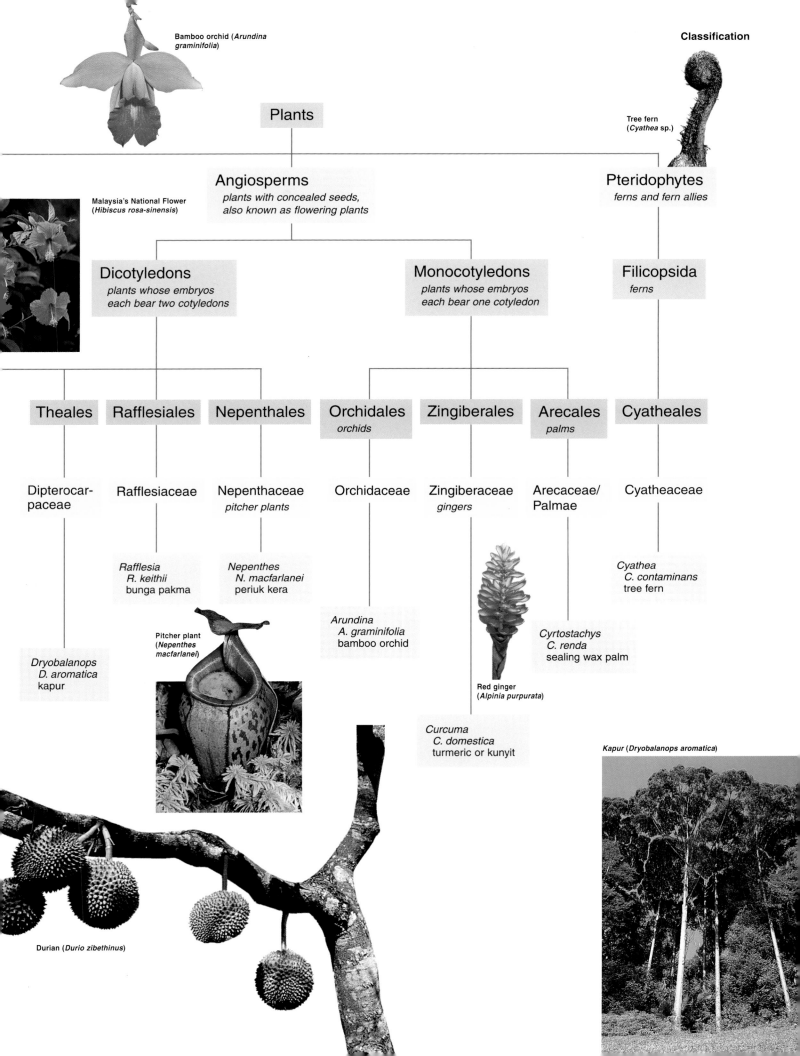

Bamboo orchid (*Arundina graminifolia*)

**Classification**

Tree fern (*Cyathea* sp.)

Plants

Angiosperms
*plants with concealed seeds, also known as flowering plants*

Pteridophytes
*ferns and fern allies*

Dicotyledons
*plants whose embryos each bear two cotyledons*

Monocotyledons
*plants whose embryos each bear one cotyledon*

Filicopsida
*ferns*

Malaysia's National Flower (*Hibiscus rosa-sinensis*)

Theales

Rafflesiales

Nepenthales

Orchidales
*orchids*

Zingiberales

Arecales
*palms*

Cyatheales

Dipterocar-
paceae

Rafflesiaceae

Nepenthaceae
*pitcher plants*

Orchidaceae

Zingiberaceae
*gingers*

Arecaceae/
Palmae

Cyatheaceae

*Rafflesia*
  *R. keithii*
  bunga pakma

*Nepenthes*
  *N. macfarlanei*
  periuk kera

*Cyathea*
  *C. contaminans*
  tree fern

Pitcher plant (*Nepenthes macfarlanei*)

*Arundina*
  *A. graminifolia*
  bamboo orchid

*Cyrtostachys*
  *C. renda*
  sealing wax palm

*Dryobalanops*
  *D. aromatica*
  kapur

Red ginger (*Alpinia purpurata*)

*Curcuma*
  *C. domestica*
  turmeric or kunyit

*Kapur (Dryobalanops aromatica)*

Durian (*Durio zibethinus*)

# Introduction

*The 'Plants volume' focuses mainly on the wealth of plant life forms found in Malaysia, from unicellular algae to 81-metre-tall* **Koompassia excelsa** *trees, and the socioeconomic impact of these plant resources. Underlying the discussion of man's exploitation of plant resources is the driving theme of conservation and sustainable forest management. Also highlighted in this volume are the relationships between plants and the physical environment. In the physical environment, plants are primary producers, forming vital and complex relationships with animals, the elements and other plants, whilst in the human world they fulfil both ecological and economic functions.*

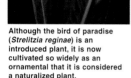

Although the bird of paradise (*Strelitzia reginae*) is an introduced plant, it is now cultivated so widely as an ornamental that it is considered a naturalized plant.

This rhododendron growing on Mount Kinabalu is one of 24 species found in that locality. The mountain is home to about 4,000 species of vascular plants, making it one of the most species-rich localities in the world.

Lowland and hill mixed dipterocarp forests are the most extensive natural habitats found in Malaysia. Although Malaysia has lost some of its dipterocarp forests as a result of development, sizable areas still remain, the largest being in Taman Negara, the National Park.

## Malaysia's rich flora

Malaysia is located in the western part of the Malay Archipelago, which as a geographical entity was formed about 10–15 million years ago. It is part of the tropics, the most diverse floristic region in the world. Many plant species, genera and families have their centre of diversity in the tropics, meaning that they exhibit a greater genetic variation here than in any other part of the world. The majestic Mount Kinabalu, for example, with its unique assemblage of plants and habitats, is the centre of diversity for many plant species.

Malaysia is also home to a wide variety of plant life forms and species. Trees are the most physically dominant life form in the rainforest, but coexisting with them are shrubs, climbers, stranglers, epiphytes, parasites, saprophytes and a multitude of smaller, non-vascular plants such as lichens, fungi and bryophytes. In Malaysia's streams, rivers and wetlands dwell a host of aquatic flowering plants as well as microscopic algae. Certain life forms are exceptionally interesting because of their unique habits, such as the carnivorous pitcher plants (*Nepenthes*), or because of their extraordinary appearance, as in the case of *Rafflesia*, the world's largest flower.

A Kelabit rattan collector wears a rattan knapsack while he mimes the action of rattan harvesting in a longhouse. These performances are acted out during informal gatherings of the community.

## A land of many habitats

The number of different habitats that are found in Malaysia is high in proportion to the size of the country's landmass. Covering the most extensive area are the lowland and hill mixed dipterocarp forests, whose vegetation is also the most species rich in the world. These forests start at sea level and go up to an altitude of about 1200 metres. Peppering the forests are limestone hills. They cover only 0.2 per cent of Malaysia's landmass, but are home to a disproportionately high number of plant species, including many endemics. Above an altitude of 1200 metres to about 1800 metres are lower montane forests and from 1800 to 2900 metres upper montane forests, which are found in places such as Fraser's Hill and Cameron Highlands. Beyond the 2900-metre mark is subalpine vegetation, which becomes alpine vegetation above 3500 metres. Only one locality in Malaysia, Mount Kinabalu, has altitudes high enough to allow subalpine and alpine vegetation to flourish.

A brightly coloured fungus on a dead log. Fungi decompose dead organic material, absorb the nutrients and return the inorganic substances to the ecosystem.

Along the coasts of Peninsular Malaysia, Sabah and Sarawak are mangrove forests, sandy beaches and rocky shores. Perhaps the most remarkable characteristic of these habitats is the adaptive features displayed by the plants that live there. These features have evolved so that the plants can cope with the high saline and low rainfall conditions. Some mangrove plants, for example, have developed pneumatophores, or breathing roots, which protrude from the ground instead of penetrating it. On sandy beaches, where there is a dearth of fresh water, some plants have special roots that plunge deep into the sand to reach sources below. Also occurring near the coasts are freshwater and peatswamp forests, which are waterlogged environments. Here too are plants with adaptive roots, such as trees with aerial, knee, stilt and buttress roots.

## Major agricultural and horticultural industries

As Malaysia has developed economically, native plant resources have been tapped and new plants introduced to support certain industries. Rubber and oil palm, for example, are both introduced but are now the two most commercially important crops in Malaysia. The country is the world's third largest producer of natural rubber and the largest exporter of palm oil. The rubber industry in Malaysia started in the late 19th century, but boomed in the 1930s and continues to be a significant contributor to Malaysia's economy. It has expanded to include rubber products that are manufactured in Malaysia and rubber wood timber which is used primarily for making furniture. The oil palm industry, on the other hand, matured in the 1960s, much later than rubber. It has, however, grown dramatically since then with the benefit of new technologies and agricultural and processing methods.

Palms are commonly found in Malaysia's forests and are also grown ornamentally. With their big and attractive, fan-shaped leaves, *Licuala* palms are popular as ornamentals in gardens and parks.

Timber has always been a valuable plant resource in Malaysia. Dipterocarp trees, which dominate Malaysia's rainforests, are the main source. Because the timber business is so lucrative, indiscriminate logging has been carried out in some forested areas. This is extremely destructive to the habitat, and many other plants besides the felled trees are also killed. Besides making such logging operations illegal, the Malaysian Government has also set up what are called productive forests. Licences are issued for the harvesting of timber from these forests, which are part of forest reserves. In these ways, the government is ensuring that one of Malaysia's most valuable natural resources is being managed in a sustainable manner.

Ornamental plants are seen growing in gardens, parks and along roadsides all across the country. Many of these are native plant species, such as *angsana* (*Pterocarpus indicus*) and *ixora* (*Ixora javanica*), while others are introduced, such as frangipani (*Plumeria obtusa*) and mussaenda (*Mussaenda philippica*). The National Flower, *Hibiscus rosa-sinensis*, is an introduced plant, but is now so widely cultivated that it has become naturalized. In the cut flower industry, orchids are a major component. Orchid hybrids are cultivated on a large scale in farms. Malaysia is a world-class centre for orchid hybridization, owing much of its credibility to the efforts of the Penang group of orchid growers in the 1960s who created well-known hybrids such as *Aranda*.

The contribution made by plants to Malaysia's development cannot be underestimated. Aside from the major industries, there are also others of lesser proportions but no less significance. Vegetables, spices, tea, coffee and cocoa are all cultivated in Malaysia both for domestic use and for export.

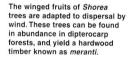
The winged fruits of *Shorea* trees are adapted to dispersal by wind. These trees can be found in abundance in dipterocarp forests, and yield a hardwood timber known as *meranti*.

The size of the pitcher of *Nepenthes rajah* is apparant as this boy holds the plant to his chest. It is one of Malaysia's 30 species of pitcher plants which devour insects who, attracted by the sugary secretions at the mouth of the pitcher, fall into the base of the pitcher where they are trapped and eventually drown.

Malaysia is host to hill mixed dipterocarp forest, the most species-rich forest vegetation in the world, seen here, in the foreground, in Ulu Gombak. The mountain in the background, covered with upper montane forest, is Gunung Bunga Buah.

*BELOW*: *Rafflesia keithii*, endemic to Sabah, is a species with the largest flower in the world.

Seen from a distance, this *tualang* tree (*Koompassia excelsa*), one of the tallest species in Malaysia, stands out from other plants.

*INSET*: At its tallest, the *tualang* tree is 35 times the height of an adult human being.

The Malesian phytogeographical region is in brown, and part of it, namely Peninsular Malaysia, Sabah and Sarawak, is in red. This region is superimposed here on Europe and a northern corner of Africa to indicate its comparative land size.

# BIOGEOGRAPHICAL SETTING OF MALAYSIAN FLORA

Malaysia is an integral part of the Indo-Malayan or Malesian phytogeographical zone extending from the Kra Isthmus in peninsular Thailand in the northwest, to Papua New Guinea and its adjacent islands in the southeast. In this zone, more than 40,000 species of vascular plants have been recorded. Of these, slightly more than 36,000 are flowering plants, 3,600 are ferns and fern allies, and 87 are conifers. The total number of lower plants, such as fungi, algae, liverworts and mosses, and lichens, is not yet known. In comparison to this magnificent array, Europe, with a total land area of about 9 million square kilometres, is home to only 11,500 species of vascular plants—approximately one-quarter of those found in the much smaller Malesian zone of 3 million square kilometres.

This terrestrial orchid, *Corybas comptus*, is one of the smallest rainforest plants in Malaysia. It has a single leaf that lies flat on the ground, and a solitary, proportionately large flower.

By unit area, the flora of Malaysian lowland and hill mixed dipterocarp rainforests is also much richer in species than any other type of vegetation in the world. Many species are endemic, such as the dipterocarp tree, *Dipterocarpus lamellatus*; the largest pitcher plant, *Nepenthes rajah*; one of the smallest flowering plants, the orchid *Corybas comptus*; and a bamboo, *Yushania tesellata*. This high species diversity is attributed to the prevailing moist and warm climatic conditions, and to the availability of diverse types of microhabitats resulting from past and recent geological history. The ability of indigenous and introduced species to adapt, compete and invade newly formed habitats, and the existence of different reproductive strategies among plants of different taxa growing in the same habitat, are also reasons for the high species diversity.

The rainforests of Malaysia are very complex in structure. Many trees, such as kapur (*Dryobalanops aromatica*) and tualang (*Koompassia excelsa*), attain a height of 81 metres, while a few species of orchids and aquatic plants reach a maximum size of only a few centimetres. Between these extremes is a variety of plant groups, including many herbs, shrubs and trees, and species of climbers, stranglers, epiphytes and parasitic as well as saprophytic plants. Both the complex structure and the diversity of the rainforest have a direct bearing on its ecological role in maintaining and stabilizing nutrient cycles, food chains, energy flows and heat and water balance. The elimination of these forests may have a pronounced effect on the climate and ecological balance at local, regional and global levels.

Malaysia's forests also provide useful products, such as timbers, rattans, fruits, vegetables, medicines, spices and ornamentals, and habitats for a range of wildlife. To sustain its ecological and economic functions, the conservation and wise utilization of the Malaysian rainforest and its resources are extremely important. To this end, a sizable amount of forest has been put aside as national parks, wildlife sanctuaries, and other such areas of conservation.

# Geological history and geographical affinity

*The species diversity and pattern of geographical distribution of present-day Malaysian flora have their roots in the geological history of the region. Fossil records strongly suggest that many species of Malaysian flora first appeared as long ago as 60–70 million years. Located at the heart of the western part of the Malay Archipelago, Malaysia also has a unique flora that displays both differences and affinities to those of continental Asia and Australia.*

Matonia pectinata is a montane fern whose ancestors date back about 395 million years. It is one of the living fossils surviving in Malaysia's forests.

### Geological history

The drifting of continental plates about 180 million years ago, caused by the spreading ocean floor, was a geological event that gave rise to today's continents, islands and other landmasses.

More recent global climatic changes associated with glacial and interglacial episodes have also exerted a profound influence on the geographical distribution of tropical flora. These episodes took place in the polar regions, beginning about 2 million years ago. During the glacial periods, the tropical climate was cooler and drier than it is today, with a lower and more seasonal rainfall. About 18,000 years ago, the sea level was lower by as much as 180 metres, because most of the earth's surface water was frozen in polar icecaps. Both the Sunda Shelf, which stretched from the Asian continent to the western part of the Malay Archipelago, and the Sahul Shelf, which reached from Australia to New Guinea, were exposed.

Peninsular Malaysia has had a relatively more stable geological history than Sabah and Sarawak. This, together with the continental drifts and the climatic changes, may explain the presence of a unique assemblage of plant species of the present-day natural vegetation of Malaysia.

This species, *Gymnostoma sumatrana*, is a member of the *rhu* family. The family's centre of distribution is in the eastern part of the Malay Archipelago, New Guinea and Australia.

### Living fossils

A number of plant groups found in tropical forests have a long geological history. The ancestors of ferns, cycads and conifers first appeared on the earth's surface some 395 million years ago, becoming dominant about 195 million years ago. Hence, present-day relatives of these ancient plants, such as the ferns *Cyathea contaminans*, *Dipteris conjugata* and *Matonia pectinata*, and the cycad *Cycas rumphii*, are considered living fossils surviving in the Malaysian rainforest.

Flowering plants, or angiosperms, are relatively young in geological terms. Early flowering plants or their ancestors appeared only 140 million years ago, and as a group became dominant only 70–80 million years ago. Among the Malaysian flowering plants with a long geological history are members of the *karas* (Thymelaeaceae), *medang* (Lauraceae), *cempaka* (Magnoliaceae), lily (Liliaceae) and elm (Ulmaceae) families.

### Regional affinities and differences

As an integral part of the Malesian phytogeographical region, Malaysia is the meeting point of two major floristic zones, those of continental Asia and Australia. Because of this, components of

## Floristic characteristics of tropical rainforests

There are three major blocks of tropical rainforest in the world, namely the South American block, the Indo-Malayan block in Southeast Asia and the African block. All three attain their grandest luxuriance in a humid and warm climate, and are species rich and complex in structure. These shared characteristics stem from an intertwined geological history of the different regions, as well as from the evolution of rainforest plants. Africa, South America and Southeast Asia originated from the same geological region, Gondwanaland, where major developments in the evolution of flowering plants had occurred before the landmass broke up into several fragments. As a result, there are 334 genera in 59 families of flowering plants that are pantropical, including members of the Annonaceae, Leguminosae and Myristicaceae.

Not all characteristics are shared among the three major rainforest blocks. Differences have arisen due to local geological developments, topography and climate. The rainforests of Southeast Asia are for the greater part evergreen, whereas those of Africa are almost entirely semi-evergreen, and those of South America are a combination of both forest types. In semi-evergreen rainforest, some emergent tree species may be deciduous, and one or a few tree species dominate. In evergreen rainforests, on the other hand, none of the emergent trees are completely deciduous, and a single species is never dominant.

Members of two pantropical families—*mempisang* (left) belonging to the Annonaceae and *Canavalia microcarpa* (right), a member of the Leguminosae.

### Distribution and area of tropical rainforests

Tropic of Cancer

African rainforest (1.8 million km²)

South American rainforest (4 million km²)

Equator

Indo-Malayan rainforest (2.5 million km²)

Tropic of Capricorn

Source: After Whitmore (1990)

## Fossil records of Malaysian flora

The fossil records of a few plant families in Malaysia date back 60–70 million years. Examples are the mango (Anacardiaceae), durian (Bombacaceae), mangosteen (Clusiaceae), *jambu* (Myrtaceae) and rambutan (Sapindaceae) families. Going back about 30 million years are the fossil records of the dipterocarp (Dipterocarpaceae), *kedondong* (Burseraceae) and *limau* (Rutaceae) families.

In Sabah and Sarawak, pollen fossils of mangrove plants belonging to the nipa palm (*Nypa fruticans*) have been found in deposits that are about 70 million years old. Fossils of *bakau* (*Rhizophora* spp.) date back roughly 50 million years, and those of *beremban* (*Sonneratia* spp.) approximately 36 million years.

Several components of Malaysia's peatswamp forests have fossil records that are about 35 million years old. Examples are *nibong* (*Oncosperma tigillarium*), *ramin* (*Gonystylus bancanus*) and *terentang* (*Campnosperma* spp.). Some other plants, such as *minyak berok* (*Xanthophyllum* spp.) and the pitcher plants (*Nepenthes* spp.), have fossils that are 18 million years old.

*Durio kutejensis*, a durian species endemic to Borneo. Fossil records of the genus *Durio* go back about 60–70 million years.

### RECORD OF FOSSILIZED POLLEN GRAINS OF MANGROVE GENERA IN BORNEO

*Avicennia* type
*Sonneratia* type
*Rhizophora* type
*Nypa* type

80 70 60 50 40 30 20 10 0
Cretaceous | Paleocene | Eocene | Oligocene | Miocene | Pliocene | Quaternary

million years ago and geological subdivisions

INSET: Fruits of the nipa palm, one of the oldest components of Malaysia's mangrove forests, whose fossils date back about 70 million years.

## The geological history of the Malay Archipelago

**180 MILLION YEARS AGO** During the mid-Jurassic period, the supercontinent Pangea broke up into its northern half, Laurasia, and its southern half, Gondwanaland. These two continental fragments were separated by the great Tethys Ocean.

**100 MILLION YEARS AGO** In the lower Cretaceous period, Gondwanaland split into several continental plates, namely South America, Africa and a landmass comprising India, Antarctica, Australia and New Guinea.

**40 MILLION YEARS AGO** During the late Eocene period, first Africa followed by India drifted northwards and closed the Tethys Ocean. Further east, the continental plate comprising Antarctica, Australia and New Guinea moved northwards and broke into two, leaving Antarctica behind.

**10–15 MILLION YEARS AGO** The Australia–New Guinea plate collided with the southeastern extremity of Laurasia, resulting in the formation of the Malay Archipelago.

Source: After Whitmore (1984 and 1990)

present-day Malaysian flora have a definite affinity with and yet differ from those of the other two floristic zones.

Widespread genera, such as those of the rubber (Euphorbiaceae) and orchid (Orchidaceae) families, do not have a distinct centre of distribution in the Old World tropics. Others, such as the rhododendrons and *mempening* (*Lithocarpus* spp.), have their centre of distribution in the Asian continent, but are poorly represented in Australian flora. The centre of distribution of rattans, dipterocarps and pitcher plants is in the Indo-Malayan region. The centre of development of the *damar minyak* (Araucariaceae), and *jambu* or *kelat* (Myrtaceae) families is in the Australian continent, and they are not well represented in Asia. On the other hand, there are genera and families with their centre of distribution in the Pacific-subantarctic region, such as *Hebe* (Scrophulariaceae), *Nothofagus* (Fagaceae) and the sedges *Oreobolus* (Cyperaceae).

Besides these similarities, there are significant differences. At the Malaysian–Thai border, for example, 200 genera of Asiatic flora do not cross south of the border and 375 genera of Indo-Malayan flora do not occur north. This has resulted in a demarcation knot of 575 genera.

## Floristic variation within Malaysia

The tropical rainforests of Peninsular Malaysia and Sabah and Sarawak are similar in terms of the complexity of structure and diversity of life forms. However, species diversity and the occurrence of endemic species in a given forest formation differ from place to place. In lowland and hill mixed dipterocarp forest, for example, there are more

genera and species of dipterocarps in Sabah and Sarawak than in Peninsular Malaysia. On the other hand, there are genera in either region that are not found in the other. For example, the genus *Upuna* is not present in Peninsular Malaysia, while *Neobalanocarpus* or the *chengal* tree is not known in Sabah and Sarawak. While the dominant tree species in the peatswamp forests of Peninsular Malaysia are *mersawa paya* (*Anisoptera marginata*), *meranti paya* (*Shorea uliginosa*) and *kempas* (*Koompassia malaccensis*), in Sarawak they are *alan bunga* (*S. albida*), *semayur* (*S. inaequilateralis*) and *kapur paya* (*Dryobalanops rappa*). Some timber species, however, such as *ramin* (*Gonystylus bancanus*), are common to both regions.

The montane flora of Mount Kinabalu is richer in species and has more endemic species than any other mountain in Peninsular Malaysia and Sarawak. For example, 15 species of rhododendrons are found in the mountains of Peninsular Malaysia, of which 9 are endemic, whereas Mount Kinabalu has 24 species, of which 5 are endemic. Mount Kinabalu's flora is also unique because it harbours species and genera that are related to flora in other parts of the world. Members of the rose and rhododendron families are related to the Sino-Himalayan species; the Kinabalu buttercup and eyebright and the conifers bear an affinity with Australian flora; whilst the climbing madder or *Rubia* has European relatives.

*Cempaka putih* (*Michelia alba*) belongs to the family Magnoliaceae, one of the oldest flowering plant families in Malaysia.

# Species richness and endemism

*Malaysia is counted among the plant biodiversity hot spots of the world because of its tropical rainforests, which exhibit species richness not only at the community level but also at the family and genus levels. The flowering plant flora of Peninsular Malaysia is estimated to comprise over 8,500 species, while Borneo is even richer with about 12,000 species. The proportion of endemic species is also high, reaching 100 per cent in the Didissandra herbs.*

**The most species-rich plant families in Peninsular Malaysia**

| Dipterocarpaceae | Myrtaceae | Lauraceae | Euphorbiaceae | Rubiaceae | Orchidaceae |
|---|---|---|---|---|---|
| 155 species | 209 species | 212 species | 344 species | 362 species | 850 |

A common native orchid, member of the Orchidaceae.

*Homalanthus* belongs to the Euphorbiaceae.

*Jambu mawar* is a member of the Myrtaceae.

## Species-rich forest types

In the Pasoh Forest Reserve in Negeri Sembilan, a 1-hectare plot of lowland mixed dipterocarp forest harbours about 200 tree species with a stem diameter of 10 centimetres or larger.

At Fraser's Hill, at least 950 flowering plant species are known from the lower montane forest, of which 31 species are endemic to the area.

### SPECIES COMPOSITION OF THE MAJOR PLANT GROUPS ON FRASER'S HILL

| PLANT GROUP | NO. OF SPECIES |
|---|---|
| Orchids | 148 |
| Laurels | 42 |
| Figs | 30 |
| Oaks | 27 |

## Plants as species-rich habitats

Some plants are in themselves species-rich habitats as they are home to a variety of other plants. The trunks and branches of trees are home to epiphytic ferns and orchids, climbers and stranglers, as well as non-vascular plants, such as fungi, mosses and algae, which also grow on leaves and roots.

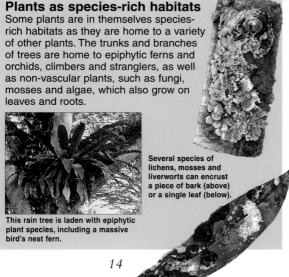

Several species of lichens, mosses and liverworts can encrust a piece of bark (above) or a single leaf (below).

This rain tree is laden with epiphytic plant species, including a massive bird's nest fern.

## Causes of species richness

Malaysia's species richness is attributed to several factors. The first is the great age of the forests, which are estimated to have existed continuously for 150 million years without any devastating climatic changes, such as ice sheets during the Ice Ages (except for the summit of Mount Kinabalu), that would have caused widespread extinctions. The second is the equatorial climate, free of droughts and frosts, which is optimum for plant growth. The third is the complexity of habitats that allow many species to coexist in a particular area. Thus, for example, the intricacy of the tropical rainforest is in part due to its many-layered structure comprising three tree layers, the shrub and herb layers and, in addition, shade and sun climbers and epiphytes. On limestone hills or on Mount Kinabalu, for example, each habitat or microhabitat supports its own suite of species. The fourth factor is the lack of any single dominant species, which means that it is common in lowland mixed dipterocarp forest to encounter in a 1-hectare plot more than 100 tree species with a stem diameter greater than 10 centimetres. Instead, forests are dominated by families, such as the lowland mixed dipterocarp forests by the Dipterocarpaceae and the lower montane forest by the oak and laurel families.

## Species-rich plant communities

At the community or ecosystem level, species richness is reflected by the number of species found in a specific area. Isolated limestone hills and montane forests, for example, are biodiverse. The lower montane oak-laurel forest at Fraser's Hill comprises at least 950 species in 404 genera and 120 families. Well represented in this forest are orchids, oaks or Fagaceae, laurels or Lauraceae, and figs. Nothing, however, can match the species richness of Mount Kinabalu, which is home to about a third of all species known in Borneo.

Even a single tree species, such as *neram* (*Dipterocarpus oblongifolius*), can provide a habitat for a biodiverse flora of 87 species of epiphytes. A palm leaf provides a microhabitat for a variety of lichens, cyanobacteria, green algae and leafy liverworts.

Even though the flora of Peninsular Malaysia is relatively well known, new species continue to be discovered. For Sabah and Sarawak, many groups of plants have never been studied in detail and much remains to be learnt. For example, a recent study of the Bornean species of *Fagraea* (Loganiaceae) added 20 new species to the 22 already known.

## Endemism and its causes

Endemic plants are those that are confined in their occurrence to a specific area or habitat. Thus, taxa may be endemic to a particular plant geographical region, such as the Malesian region, which covers Malaysia, Singapore, Indonesia, Brunei, the Philippines and Papua New Guinea; to an island, such as Borneo; to a single state, such as Melaka; or in the case of narrow endemics, to a mountain peak or even a single rock face.

Endemism is the result of several evolutionary processes. One such process is isolation, which prevents genetic mixing between populations. Over long periods of time, isolated populations diverge and become distinct and can eventually be recognized as separate taxa. Plants can be isolated by physical barriers, such as the sea or the lowland forest, the latter preventing the dispersal of highland taxa; or by adaptation to specific soil types or conditions; or by the pollinating agent. Soil types, such as ultramafic and limestone soils, or waterlogged conditions, such as swamp forest, challenge the plants' physiology and has led to the evolution of specially adapted taxa. This has resulted in certain habitats, such as mountain peaks, islands, limestone hills and ultramafic soils, having higher than average levels of endemism.

14

## Species richness by plant family and genera

The Dipterocarpaceae dominates lowland and hill mixed dipterocarp forests and is one of the most important sources of tropical hardwood timber in Malaysia. In Peninsular Malaysia, it is represented by 155 species, and in Sabah and Sarawak by 267 species of which 183 species (47 per cent) are endemic to Malaysia. However, the Dipterocarpaceae is by no means the largest tree family in Peninsular Malaysia, being outstripped in species number by the *jambu* family (Myrtaceae), laurel family (Lauraceae), rubber tree family (Euphorbiaceae) and coffee family (Rubiaceae). These families are, however, eclipsed by the Orchidaceae, which has 850 species, which in Borneo number between 2,500 and 3,000 species.

*Dryobalanops oblongifolius* belongs to the Dipterocarpaceae, the most species-rich family in the Peninsula.

Richness of species is also seen at the generic level, with three genera—the figs (*Ficus*), the orchids (*Bulbophyllum*) and the jambu (*Syzygium*)—in Peninsular Malaysia having more than a hundred species each. Species richness in *Bulbophyllum* and *Ficus* is probably the result of pollinator isolation. For instance, the majority of *Ficus* species are pollinated by a single species of fig wasp.

## Endemism in the Malaysian flora

Among flowering plants there are no families endemic to Peninsular Malaysia and only one in Borneo, the Scyphostegiaceae, which comprises a single tree species, *Scyphostegia borneensis*. There are 88 genera endemic to Malaysia, of which 62 (70 per cent) occur only in Borneo. Many of these are extremely small in species number, with 76 per cent consisting of a single species (they are monotypic), only 7 per cent having between four and six species, and none having more than six species. This has implications for conservation because, if the single species becomes extinct, so does the genus.

It is, however, difficult to be certain of the exact figures for endemism at the species level, especially for Sabah and Sarawak where the flora is still incompletely known. Levels of endemism for certain groups of plants in Peninsular Malaysia that have been studied in detail show that species endemism stands at 23.9 per cent for orchids and 26.4 per cent for trees. The highest levels for trees are 57 per cent for the tea family (Theaceae) and 60 per cent for the holly family (Aquifoliaceae), both predominantly montane families.

For many groups of herbaceous plants, the level of endemism is much higher. For example, in Peninsular Malaysia it is 97 per cent for begonia species and 100 per cent for *Didissandra* species (Gesneriaceae).

The much higher level of endemism in Borneo compared with Peninsular Malaysia is not only seen at the generic level but also at the species level. Exceptions are a few groups of plants, such as the balsam family, which have their centre of diversity in mainland Asia. In Peninsular

Malaysia, for tree families with at least 20 species, about a quarter are endemic compared with about a third in Sabah and Sarawak. This higher endemism in Sabah and Sarawak can be attributed to the isolation of the island of Borneo, the presence of much higher mountains, and a wider range of soil types, in particular the ultramafic soils.

As yet, there is little detailed information on the flora of specific areas or habitats in Malaysia, but the little there is confirms that some habitats are particularly high in endemic species, notably montane or limestone habitats. In the lower montane forest at Fraser's Hill, 36 per cent (319 species) of seed plants are endemic to Peninsular Malaysia, of which 31 are endemic to Fraser's Hill itself. On Mount Kinabalu, where the montane vegetation is home to nearly 4,000 species of vascular plants, the level of endemism is extremely high, with 40 per cent of these species being known from a single locality on the mountain.

Limestone hills also harbour a large number of endemic species. In Peninsular Malaysia, of the 261 endemic species of vascular plants that live on limestone, half are confined to this habitat. The same is probably true for the flora of ultramafic soils but information is still lacking, although data for the flora of Mount Kinabalu indicate that about a third of the species that grow on ultramafic soils are confined to it.

With rapidly changing land use occurring on a large scale in Malaysia, the possibility of endemic plant taxa becoming extinct and special types of plant communities being destroyed is a reality.

### Habitats with high species endemism

Mountain peaks, such as Gunung Kajang on Tioman Island, have a high degree of endemism because of their isolation.

In being cut off from other habitats, islands, such as Pulau Silingan in Sabah, shown here, often harbour unique plant species.

Limestone hills possess a very specific soil type in which only a selection of plant species can thrive.

### Endemic herbaceous plant genera

1. and 2. Both *Orchadocarpa lilacina* (Gesneriaceae) and *Klossia montana* (Rubiaceae), endemic to Peninsular Malaysia, belong to genera consisting of only one species.

3. All 16 species of *Didissandra* in Malaysia, which includes *Didissandra kiewii*, are endemic.

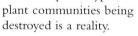

# Growth and reproductive seasonality

*In spite of the equable tropical climate without any unfavourable season for plant growth, in Malaysia there are only a small number of plants which produce leaves and flowers regularly throughout the year. Many of these aseasonal trees are found along the coasts or in secondary forests. Examples are the* simpoh ayer (Dillenia suffruticosa) *among the dicotyledons, and many species of palms among the monocotyledons. Most Malaysian plants periodically produce new leaves or flowers, the latter followed by fruits. If this happens regularly at the same time of the year, then these plants are considered seasonal.*

### The wild cinnamon tree: Leafing and flowering

A common roadside tree, the wild cinnamon tree is not only tolerant of pollution but also produces a spectacular display in young leaf.

Profuse seasonal flowering of the wild cinnamon tree follows the expansion of new leaves.

## Leafing

Although the difference between deciduous and evergreen trees is striking, it is really just a matter of timing of leaf exchange. Leaves have a fixed but short life—for trees it is about 6 or 12 months—after which they have no further function, and are shed. If they are shed before the new ones expand, the tree is then bare. This is the deciduous state. However, if the new leaves expand before the old ones are shed, then the tree remains evergreen.

The great majority of tropical forest trees, shrubs and herbs are evergreen. There are trees that produce new leaves once or, for the majority, twice a year, or even three or more times a year. The main seasons when most forest trees produce new leaves in Peninsular Malaysia are between February and April, when rain follows a dry period, and again later in the year between September and October. This is when the forest is at its most colourful as the flushes of new leaves may be red, white or even metallic purple or blue. On the forest floor, this growth flush is mirrored by some herbs and shrubs, occurring a little later, between March and May and again between September and December. A profusion of toadstools also appears 2–4 weeks after heavy rain between March and May, and again between August and October.

The deciduous habit of trees is sometimes seasonal, such as in the *kerayong* tree (*Parkia javanica*) in Peninsular Malaysia, which loses its leaves once a year following the dry spell in January and February. In contrast, the *ketapang* or sea almond tree (*Terminalia catappa*) sheds its leaves twice a year between January and February and again between July and August. In aseasonal deciduous trees, such

as the Bohd tree (*Ficus religiosa*), the timing of leaf shedding is less regular and the trees are never quite completely bare.

The deciduous habit may be considered disadvantageous in the tropics, where climatic conditions are ideal for growth throughout the year. However, in the wild *kapok* tree or *Bombax valetonii* (Bombacaceae), such a growth habit is advantageous. This habit allows the tree to display its flowers on the bare crown, making it easy for potential pollinators to detect and for the fluffy seeds to waft away unimpeded by leaves.

*Top*: During the leafing season, the forest canopy is brightened with splashes of colour. *Above*: The wild *kapok* tree is one of the few deciduous species in Malaysia.

## Flowering

In Malaysian forests, there are very few tree species that produce flowers continuously. In most cases, trees produce flowers periodically, and the pattern of flowering is not precisely timed, either in terms of the exact date or the regularity of flowering between years. This is due to climatic variability between years. The classic example of this flowering behaviour is shown by the dipterocarps, which in some years see most species flowering heavily, followed by 2–5 years without flowering. The heavy flowering year of the dipterocarps also coincides with abundant flowering in other trees. This strongly indicates that climatic factors are responsible. The stimulus for such heavy flowering has, therefore, been sought in climatic records but no single parameter, such as a dry period or duration of sunshine, has convincingly been shown to correlate with flowering.

On an annual basis, the main flowering season for most trees begins at the onset of the drier months, which are January and July in Peninsular

### The secret of synchronous flowering

A few plant species are conspicuous because, within a particular area, they flower on the same day—synchronously. The secret of how they do this was discovered for the pigeon orchid (*Dendrobium crumenatum*) when experiments revealed that a sudden drop in temperature of 4 °C, caused by the onset of a tropical storm, stimulates flower bud development, which results in flowers maturing and blooming simultaneously exactly nine days later.

The pigeon orchid is a common epiphyte on wayside trees, and displays an interesting synchronous flowering habit.

Malaysia, with the first season being the heavier. However, some trees produce flowers just once a year, for example, the *angsana* (*Pterocarpus indicus*) and *tualang* (*Koompassia excelsa*). For several species, such as the rambutan (*Nephelium lappaceum*), flowers develop on shoots that have produced a new flush of leaves, while in others, such as the durian (*Durio zibethinus*), flowers are borne on older branches. While the actual date of the commencement of flowering may vary from year to year, the sequence in which species produce flowers remains the same. This sequence is clearly seen for species which are visited by the local honeybee (*Apis cerana*). Seasonal flowering begins in January with wild cinnamon trees (*Cinnamomum iners*), reaching a peak in February and March, when many species, such as rambutan and several types of *jambu* (*Syzygium*) start flowering, followed by durian. This continues until May, when *tembusu* (*Fagraea fragrans*) and angsana begin to flower. A dearth of flowering in June is followed by a second smaller and less synchronized flowering season between July and October.

Closely related dipterocarp species growing in the same habitat are a good example for demonstrating the close interaction between plant species and their pollinators. In *Shorea* section *Mutica* or the red *meranti* group of dipterocarps, for example, species that use the same pollinators flower in sequence, which means their flowering periods scarcely overlap. This behaviour has been interpreted as a strategy to maintain the advantage of large pollinator populations, and at the same time to avoid competition for the pollinator as well as the chance of cross-pollination between trees of the same species. Sequential flowering among species of the same genus appears to be a general phenomenon, as it is also observed in other forest trees, such as the aglaias and parkias, as well as in the epiphytic medinillas.

The stimulus for bud formation and flowering development is extremely complex and varied. It is understood for very few species, mostly temperate crop plants. Dry periods and hours of bright sunshine have been suggested as stimuli, but day length is not a factor in Malaysia. Even within the forest, where climatic factors are dampened and temperature and relative humidity are much more constant, several species of herbs and shrubs exhibit strongly seasonal flowering patterns, which are the same as those for trees. The flowering of the forest water lily (*Barclaya motleyi*), for example, takes place between May and August and again between October and December, even though its shallow water habitat never dries out. Some parasitic plants, such as *Balanophora fungosa*, flower seasonally with the main season occurring at the end of August to September, and in some years also in April to May.

## Fruiting

Fruiting naturally follows flowering. In some dipterocarps, like the illipe nut or *engkabang* trees, an extraordinary fruiting occurs at 2–5 yearly intervals and is called a mast year. It has been suggested that this superabundance in fruiting is beneficial to the species, as not all seeds will be attacked by pests and diseases.

Fruiting seasons are well known in Malaysia as many of the most popular local fruits, such as the durian, mangosteen, rambutan and *langsat* (*Lansium domesticum*), are seasonal. It is equally well known that the July–August season is heavier than the one at the end of the year, and that a lean year will follow a bumper one.

However, in the forest, some tree species can be found in flower and fruit throughout the year. A good example of such trees are the figs or *ara* (*Ficus* spp.), some of which fruit continuously, others four times a year, three times a year, twice or just once a year.

Durians are a seasonal fruit, with the main season in July and August, and a smaller season in December and January in Peninsular Malaysia.

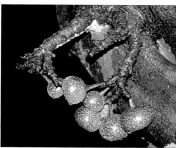

The apple fig, *Ficus oligodon*, is in season throughout the year.

Illipe nuts or *engkabang* of *Shorea* trees, which are famous for producing a profusion of fruits at 2–5 yearly intervals.

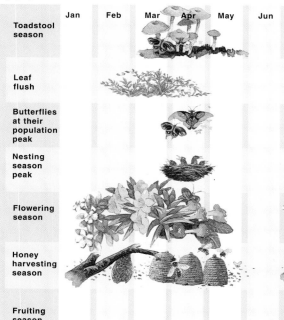

| | Jan | Feb | Mar | Apr | May | Jun | July | Aug | Sept | Oct | Nov | Dec | Jan |
|---|---|---|---|---|---|---|---|---|---|---|---|---|---|
| Toadstool season | | | | | | | | | | | | | |
| Leaf flush | | | | | | | | | | | | | |
| Butterflies at their population peak | | | | | | | | | | | | | |
| Nesting season peak | | | | | | | | | | | | | |
| Flowering season | | | | | | | | | | | | | |
| Honey harvesting season | | | | | | | | | | | | | |
| Fruiting season | | | | | | | | | | | | | |

## The relationship between plant seasons and animal life

Leafing, flowering and fruiting have a profound effect on animal life in the forest. New leaves provide a banquet for insects, whose populations greatly increase in the new leafing season with, for example, butterflies being most abundant in April and September. These protein-rich insects and their larvae in turn feed nestling birds. The flowering season provides a rich source of nectar and pollen for honeybees, resulting in an accumulation of honey for harvest. Fruits support many species of birds and mammals, and the diverse genus of figs, with its variety of fruiting patterns, is particularly important in supplying a continuous source of fruits throughout the year.

Limestone hills cover only 0.3 per cent of Peninsular Malaysia's land surface, but are home to a disproportionately large number of plant species. Seen here are the jagged pinnacles of Bukit Takun.

LEFT: Mangrove forests are found at Malaysia's river estuaries. They are easily recognizable at low tide, when the characteristic roots of some mangrove tree species are revealed, such as those of the genus *Rhizophora*.

MIDDLE: Montane forest covers much of Malaysia's highlands, as in Fraser's Hill. Oaks, laurels, conifers and epiphytic ferns and orchids are typical of the vegetation found in this forest type.

RIGHT: Sparse alpine vegetation is found near the summit of Mount Kinabalu. It consists of shrubby, tufted plant species that are able to withstand the adverse conditions in this harsh environment.

# HABITATS AND VEGETATION TYPES

Sandy beaches cover much of Malaysia's coastline, which boasts an interesting and unique array of plant species.

Malaysia is richly endowed with a variety of natural habitats. From sandy beaches to alpine forests, these habitats are conducive to plant growth and vegetation development. The country's tropical rainforests are categorized in 14 different forest formations, each one possessing a unique set of floristic characteristics and fulfilling specific ecological functions.

Climate is one factor, amongst others such as altitude, water table and water quality, rainfall and soil type, that determines the development and species distribution and composition of the forests. The Malaysian climate is wet and warm, with rainfall evenly distributed throughout the year. It is also strongly influenced by the winds that blow over the Indian Ocean in the southwest and the Pacific Ocean in the northeast. These wind systems are, respectively, the southern and northern monsoons. In most parts of the country, there is only a very short dry season, and the average temperature in the lowlands is 24–26 °C. Along the Malaysian–Thai border, however, a short but pronounced dry season is experienced annually, resulting in the development of semi-evergreen forest, where deciduous trees are present.

The quantity and quality of moisture in the soil is reflected in the location and distribution of dryland and wetland forests. Drylands comprise sandy beach and rocky shore vegetation and hill and mountain forests, whereas wetlands are made up of mangrove, freshwater and peatswamp forests. By far the most extensive dryland forest formation in Malaysia is the lowland and hill mixed dipterocarp forest. Up to 1990, this forest formation covered a total area of about 17.29 million hectares, but this has been considerably reduced as a result of conversion of forested land for other uses. Timber harvesting has also drastically altered the structure and floristic composition of this forest type.

Soil type greatly affects the vegetation that grows on it. Heath forest, for example, develops on highly acidic soil that is poor in base minerals. The Malaysian name given to heath forest, *kerangas*, is an Iban word that means 'land on which rice will not grow'. Ultramafic soil, on the other hand, is high in base metals and carries a distinct forest formation, which contains a high number of endemic plant species. On limestone, soil is hardly formed except in fissures and crevices and at the foot of slopes and tops of ridges, thus limiting the number of plant species that can thrive in this habitat.

As altitude increases and the atmosphere becomes cooler and moister, a shift from lowland to montane forest is observed. Montane forest is found in the highlands, in places such as Cameron Highlands and Fraser's Hill. Beyond the altitude of montane forests are subalpine and alpine forests, which occur in only one location in Malaysia—the spectacular Mount Kinabalu.

The subalpine region of Mount Kinabalu is home to Low's buttercup.

# Sandy beach and rocky shore vegetation

*Malaysia has a long coastline estimated to be about 4800 kilometres. Sandy beaches and rocky headlands and cliffs are the habitats that predominate. Plants inhabiting these coastal habitats show remarkable adaptive morphological and physiological features that enable them to withstand prevailing, harsh environmental conditions, such as strong winds and solar radiation, constant salt spray, a shortage of fresh water and nutrient-deficient substrates. Some plant species are used for food, whilst others are harvested for timber or grown as ornamentals.*

Fruits of *Pittosporum ferrugineum*, a tree found growing on Tioman Island's rocky shores.

In between Malaysia's sandy beaches and rocky shores are other types of coastal habitats, such as mangroves and cliffs.

## Sandy beach vegetation

In Malaysia, there are two major types of vegetation that develop on a coastal, sandy substrate. In flat or gently undulating coasts, where sand is deposited continuously, a low vegetation cover known as the *Ipomoea pes-caprae* association is found. The majority of species that constitute this plant community have tough, long, creeping stems or stolons, and include *Canavalia microcarpa* (Leguminosae), *Cyperus stoloniferus* (Cyperaceae) and *Ipomoea pes-caprae*, or morning glory (Convolvulaceae). Grasses are also present, such as *Ischaemum muticum*, *Spinifex littoreus* and *Zoysia matrella* (all Graminae). Most *Ipomoea pes-caprae* association species are restricted almost entirely to the sandy beach habitat, but are pantropical in distribution.

On the ridges, or *permatang*, of sandy beaches, which are flooded only during high tide, a plant community known as the *Barringtonia* association thrives. It is not uncommon for this vegetation type to occur behind a stretch of *Ipomoea pes-caprae* association, except on abraded coasts where sand either does not accumulate or is constantly removed by the retreating tide. Here, the *Barringtonia* association is found without the *Ipomoea pes-caprae* association in front. Instead, the narrow beach, which is inundated during high tide, is shaded by the low, much-branched crowns of *Barringtonia* association trees. The width of this seaward forest fringe is seldom more than 50 metres, and on steep rocky shores it is confined to an even narrower strip.

Plants that colonize the *Barringtonia* association are trees, shrubs and tall herbs. They belong to different families and have a wide geographical distribution—from the African coasts, across Southeast Asia to the Pacific. Trees typical of this forest fringe are *Barringtonia asiatica* or *putat laut* (Lecythidaceae), *Calophyllum inophyllum* or *bintangor laut* (Clusiaceae) and *Casuarina equisetifolia* or *rhu* (Casuarinaceae). Among the small and

medium-sized much-branched shrubs are *Ardisia elliptica* or *mata pelandok* (Myrsinaceae), *Cycas rumphii* (Cycadaceae) and *Guettarda speciosa* (Rubiaceae). Herbaceous plants frequently found at the edges of the *Barringtonia* association are *Kalanchoe pinnata* (Crassulaceae), which originates from tropical Africa, and *Crinum asiaticum* or *bakung* (Amaryllidaceae) and *Tacca leontopetaloides* (Taccaceae), both native to the Indo-Pacific region.

*Terminalia catappa* has fruits that are well adapted to dispersal by water currents. This tree flourishes on rocky shores.

## Rocky shore vegetation

On islands and in coastal areas that are subjected to constant, strong tidal waves, such as headlands or cliffs, rocky shore vegetation is found. It develops either into a narrow zone along the base of a cliff, or a band of a few metres wide on a steep slope, or occurs on the tops of large, offshore rocks and very small islands that are never completely submerged. This type of vegetation comprises tufted, small-branched, dense shrubs, such as *Arthrophyllum rubiginosum*, *Schefflera havilandii* (both Aralliaceae), *Ficus deltoidea* or *ara* (Moraceae), and a few species of ferns. *Rhododendron brookeanum* is found only in the rocky shore vegetation of Sarawak.

### Distribution of sandy beaches and rocky shores

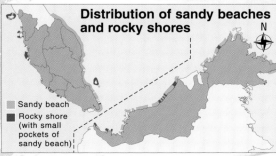

N

- Sandy beach
- Rocky shore (with small pockets of sandy beach)

### Plant species typical of sandy beach vegetation

1. *Ipomoea pes-caprae*, the dominant species of the *Ipomoea pes-caprae* association, which is the low vegetation of creeping plants that occurs on the flat and broad stretches of sandy beaches.

2. A tough grass, *Spinifex littoreus* is typical of an *Ipomoea pes-caprae* association. The structures resembling sea urchins are the fruits, which easily detach from the plant when ripe and are blown by the wind for considerable distances.

3. *Canavalia microcarpa*, a common component of the *Ipomoea pes-caprae* association.

4. A fruit of the tree *Barringtonia asiatica*. This tree is found on the ridges of sandy beaches in a vegetation type known as the *Barringtonia* association.

5. The flowers, fruits and dark green, shiny leaves of *Guettarda speciosa*, a shrub of the *Barringtonia* association. The spherical fruits are hard and woody, and are dispersed by sea currents.

6. Fruits of the Tahiti arrowroot or *Tacca leontopetaloides*, a herb that grows in the *Barringtonia* association. The edible, starchy tubers have a bitter taste.

7. A woody climber found in the *Barringtonia* association is *Abrus precatorius*.

## Adaptive features

The plants that inhabit sandy beaches and rocky shores often possess a set of adaptive features that allow them to flourish in these habitats.

A notable adaptive feature exhibited by plants in the *Ipomoea pes-caprae* association are deep and spreading roots arising from the nodes of creeping stems. Such a root system enables the plants to reach fresh water and serves as an anchor in the loose and unstable sand. Because of this, the plants also act as efficient sand binders when fully established, thus helping to reduce coastal erosion.

Loss of water through evapotranspiration in some plant species is reduced by special features of the leaves. For example, in *Canavalia microcarpa*, *Euphorbia atoto* and *Ipomoea* spp., the leaves are dark green, fleshy or thick and leathery, while those of grasses are stiff, narrow and sharply pointed, and curl in on a hot, dry day. Trees of the *Barringtonia* association have thick and leathery leaves that are covered with a waxy cuticle, as well as thick bark and spreading roots. If the leaves are broad and thin, they are covered with either a dense layer of hairs or scales on their lower surface. These features also help to overcome a shortage of fresh water. To facilitate buoyancy when dispersed by sea currents, the fruits and seeds of these trees are protected by a thick and hard or fibrous or spongy outer covering.

## Ecological and economic importance

Apart from playing their ecological roles as sand binders and preventers of coastal erosion, many plant species of sandy beach and rocky shore vegetation also serve a number of economic purposes.

Timber for boat building and construction is harvested from a few tree species, such as *bintangor laut* and *dungun* (*Heritiera littoralis*). Other species, like *Cycas rumphii*, *Casuarina equisetifolia* and *Hibiscus tiliaceus*, are commonly planted as ornamentals in cities. *Casuarina* trees are also useful windbreaks because of their lofty height, and are a good source of high-grade firewood. In addition, the roots are able to fix nitrogen in the air into nitrates, thus fertilizing the nutrient-poor sandy soil.

The leaves of *pandan* are used to make mats and baskets, while the fruits of *mengkuang* and the seeds of *paku pakis* are eaten as a source of carbohydrate. One species of pandan is used as a traditional flavouring for Malay cakes and desserts, adding to them a vanilla-like taste. *Bakung*, *kemunting* (*Rhodomyrtus tomentosus*) and *mengkudu* (*Morinda citrifolia*) are cultivated for their medicinal properties by villagers.

*Wedelia biflora* (also known as *Wollashtonia biflora*), found on sandy beaches, is known for its medicinal qualities. It is used by the Malays to treat skin diseases, and the young leaves also have a diuretic effect.

A bunch of *Pandanus odoratissimus* or *mengkuang* fruits. The plant is commonly found on sandy beaches, and in some areas the fruits are gathered for food.

21

# Mangroves

*'Mangrove' is the name for the plant community that colonizes the muddy shores of sheltered coasts and river estuaries. A mangrove forest is divided into three vegetation zones, and is home to plant species with unique adaptive features, such as pneumatophores, or breathing roots. Once abundant in Malaysia, much of the area covered by mangroves has been converted into land for other uses. Nonetheless, mangroves continue to be important to the country's fishing and timber industries.*

Mangrove forests line this meandering river in Sarawak.

### Mangrove forest

Sandwiched between land and sea or river, mangroves are subjected to tidal flooding at least once a day. The soil is composed of silt, sand, clay and decomposing organic matter. The constant movement of tides and overflow from rivers make mangrove soils waterlogged, unstable, anaerobic and subjected to a high salinity and pH. In addition to poor soil conditions, mangrove plants are also exposed to a higher than average annual air temperature and solar radiation, stronger winds, constant salt spray, and lower rainfall and humidity than vegetation located further inland.

### Vegetation zones

Where mangroves are well developed and extensive, about 20–30 species of typical mangrove trees and shrubs are found. In an established mangrove, these plants are distributed in three distinct zones: the *Avicennia–Sonneratia* zone, the *Bruguiera–Rhizophora* zone and the back mangrove zone.

### Zonation and species composition

The *Avicennia–Sonneratia* zone (1) is densely colonized by *api api* (*Avicennia alba* and *A. marina*) and *perepat* (*Sonneratia alba*), while the *Bruguiera–Rhizophora* zone (2) is dominated by *berus* (*Bruguiera cylindrica*), *tumu* (*B. gymnorrhiza*) and *bakau kurap* (*Rhizophora mucronata*). In between the crab mounds of the back mangrove zone (3) grow trees and shrubs, such as *jeruju* (*Acanthus ebracteatus* and *A. ilicifolius*), *kacang kacang* (*Aegiceras corniculatum*) and *api-api merah* (*Avicennia intermedia*). In nipa swamp forest (4), nipa palms (*Nypa fruticans*) are interspersed with *penanchang* (*Allophylus cobbe*), *buta buta* (*Excoecaria agallocha*) and *dungun* (*Heritiera littoralis*).

A fruit of *Sonneratia alba*, with 6–7 calyx lobes that help it to float when washed away by sea currents.

The bright red flowers of *Lumnitzera racemosa* attract nectarivorous birds to this species in the back mangrove zone.

### Distribution of mangrove fore[st]

■ Mangrove forests

Up to 1990, there were about 675 000 hectares of mangrove forests in Malaysia, of which 365 000 hectares were in Sabah, 200 000 hectares in Sarawak and 110 000 hectares in Peninsular Malaysia. However, the greater part of these mangroves fell outside Permanent Forest Estates and thus were not spared destruction when development took place.

The hanging seedlings of *Rhizophora mucronata*. The one in the middle is ready to drop and begin establishment.

The *Avicennia–Sonneratia* zone is the most seaward fringe of the mangrove, where the soil is soft and loose and flooded by both low and high tides. Immediately behind that is the *Bruguiera–Rhizophora* zone, which is on higher ground and flooded only by the high tide. The soil here is more compact than in the previous zone. The back mangrove zone has soil that is inundated by equinoctial and other exceptionally high tides. It contains more clay and is the most compact of the three zones. Ground level is kept on the increase by the activities of mound-building crabs, such as species of *Thassalina* and *Uca*, on whose·mounds thickets of *piai* (*Acrosticum aureum*) grow.

Further inland and beyond the tidal influence, a unique brackish-water plant community, known as nipa swamp forest, usually develops. This swamp forest is dominated by nipa palm (*Nypa fruticans*), which forms pure stands along the banks of meandering rivers. At the landward fringe of a nipa swamp, clumps of *nibong* (*Oncosperma filamentosum*) may be found.

## Reproduction and dispersal

Most mangrove plant species produce a large number of flowers and fruits at frequent intervals, if not throughout the year. This reproductive habit compensates for the high seed mortality rate during dispersal and establishment. Seeds of species of *Avicennia*, *Bruguiera* and *Ceriops* increase their chances of survival by germinating while they are still enclosed by the fruit wall and while the fruits are still attached to the parent trees. The primary root of the seedling pierces through the seed coat and fruit wall to protrude from the distal end of the fruit. The long and pointed hypocotyles may fall in the mud directly below the parent trees or be transported by water currents and take root a distance away.

Many fruits, seeds and seedlings of mangrove plants are adapted to dispersal by water currents. The seedling contained in a mature fruit of *Avicennia*, for example, has dense, fine, fibrous, air-filled rootlets that facilitate buoyancy. Fruits of other mangrove species are equipped with spongy, air-filled fruit walls.

## Ecological and economic importance

In their prime, mangroves play important ecological roles in the coastal and estuarine areas. Their dense stands and extensive root systems reduce coastal and river bank erosion and prevent flooding. Moreover, mangroves are the spawning and nursing grounds for many species of fish and prawns. The detritus and nutrients exported from the mangrove ecosystem form the base of the food chain for many marine organisms, including fin fish, shellfish and crustaceans. Mangroves are also the habitats for some rare and endangered species of wildlife, such as the proboscis monkey or *orang belanda* (*Nasalis larvatus*), found in Sabah and Sarawak.

The root systems of *Avicennia marina* exposed during low tide.

Cross section of an *Avicennia marina* breathing root, showing the numerous air spaces.

An enlarged section of the lower surface of an *Avicennia* leaf reveals salt glands surrounded by scales.

This *Avicennia* leaf is covered with salt crystals, excreted by the salt glands in the leaf cells.

### Special roots, stems and leaves

To withstand the extreme and harsh environmental conditions of a mangrove habitat, mangrove plant species have developed a unique set of adaptive features.

The submerged parts of mangrove plants face a shortage of fresh water and oxygen from the substrate. To cope, they have special root systems consisting of anchorage, breathing and absorptive roots. Species of *Avicennia* and *Sonneratia*, for instance, have extensive cable roots that are buried 20–50 centimetres below the mud's surface. These then produce anchorage roots that extend further downwards, and peg-shaped pneumatophores that grow upwards. From the pneumatophores develop a large number of absorptive roots, which penetrate the mineral-rich subsurface soils.

The aerial parts, on the other hand, such as the stems and leaves, face a high rate of water loss through transpiration and a high salt content in their tissues. To overcome these problems, stems of species of *Rhizophora* and *Lumnitzera* have an osmotic pressure that is higher than the ground water's, thus enabling the roots to absorb water from the substrate. The leaf cells of *Acanthus ilicifolius* and *Avicennia* species have glands that excrete excessive salt. To counter water loss from transpiration, the leaves of some plants are succulent and thick and leathery, while others are covered with either a waxy cuticle or dense and matted hairs and scales. In most cases, the stomata are sunken and confined to the lower leaf surface. Some species also have water storage cells in their leaves.

A village woman shearing leaflets of nipa palm (right) for the manufacture of cigarette wrappers (above).

Wood from mangrove trees is made into charcoal.

Both plant and animal products are harvested from mangroves. The wood of *Bruguiera* and *Rhizophora* is used for firewood and to make poles and charcoal. Wood chips for producing rayon are obtained from mangrove species. The bark of *Rhizophora* species is a source of tannin, and the leaves of *Nypa fruticans* make good thatching material. Sugar and alcohol are processed from the sap of inflorescences of the nipa palm. Commercial crustaceans, such as mud crabs (*Scylla serrata*) and cockles (*Anadora granosa*), which constitute the main produce of near-shore and estuarine fisheries, are native to mangroves.

A young boy (right) holding a mangrove crab he caught using a wire loop attached to one end of a stick. After being cleaned, mangrove crabs (above) are ready for sale in a local market.

# Freshwater and peatswamp forests

*Freshwater and peatswamp forests occur on the coastal or riverine plains, on different soil types, along the east and west coasts of Peninsular Malaysia and in Sabah and Sarawak. Displaying a similar forest structure across Malaysia, they are home to a unique flora dominated by tree species. The production of high-quality timber is a source of revenue for the country, while local communities depend on these forests for minor forest products. Conservation of these forest types is extremely important as they play a significant role in the hydrological and carbon cycles.*

There are good-sized, edible fish to be caught in freshwater swamps.

### Tree roots in a waterlogged environment

Trees that grow in freshwater and peatswamp forests often develop special types of roots to adapt to the waterlogged conditions.

1. The aerial roots of *bintangor* trees.
2. The knee roots of *perupuk* trees.
3. The stilt roots of *kelat* and *merbulan* trees.
4. The buttresses of *meranti* trees.

## Characteristic features of swamp habitats

On the west coast of Peninsular Malaysia and in Sabah and Sarawak, freshwater and peatswamp forests develop on a peat layer that overlays clay soil. However, on the east coast of Peninsular Malaysia, the underlying subsoil (the layer of soil between the surface soil and the bedrock) is coarse white sand.

Freshwater swamp forests occur on shallow peat and a fertile subsoil that is regularly or occasionally inundated by mineral-rich fresh water. The soil and drainage water have a pH value that is higher than 4.0. Peatswamp forests, on the other hand, develop on deep peat that is nutrient deficient and which receives water only from rainfall. Therefore, water levels in peatswamp forests fluctuate drastically between the wet and dry seasons. During the wet season, most of the forest floor is submerged but is exposed when the rains abate. The peat is composed of a dark brown to black, amorphous, soupy medium which is held together by a dense, woody mass comprising roots, stumps, trunks and branches of trees in various stages of decomposition. Having a pH of less than 4.0 shows that the deep peat soil and water of a peatswamp forest are more acidic than those of a freshwater swamp forest.

## Forest structure

Although freshwater and peatswamp forests develop on different peat depths, they share certain tree species, such as *meranti* (*Shorea* spp.), *kempas* (*Koompassia malaccensis*) and *pulai* (*Alstonia spathulata*). This results in the two forest types having an identical forest structure. The structure is characterized by three vegetation layers—the canopy, the understorey and the shrub layers.

In Peninsular Malaysia, the upper or canopy layer is discontinuous and dominated by a few tree species, such as *ramin* (*Gonystylus bancanus*), *durian paya* (*Durio carinatus*) and a few species of meranti. The middle or understorey layer is composed of a mixture of small to medium-sized tree species, particularly those of *kelat* (*Syzygium* or *Eugenia* spp.), *kayu arang*

## Distribution of freshwater and peatswamp forests

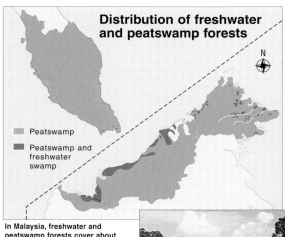

- Peatswamp
- Peatswamp and freshwater swamp

In Malaysia, freshwater and peatswamp forests cover about 2 500 000 hectares or 8 per cent of the total land area. Of this amount, about 830 000 hectares occur in Perak, Selangor, Pahang and Johor; 170 000 hectares in Sabah, mainly on the east coast; and 1 500 000 hectares in Sarawak, chiefly in the Baram, Lupar and Rajang deltas.

*INSET*: While most of Peninsular Malaysia's peatswamp forests are concentrated in Pahang, a fair area occurs in Selangor, such as along the Bernam–Tengi canal in north Selangor.

(*Diospyros* spp.) and *merbulan* (*Blumeodendron tokbrai*). The lower shrub layer is colonized mainly by the *kelubi* (*Eleiodoxa conferta*) and *pinang raja* (*Cyrtostachys renda*) palms.

In Sarawak, on the other hand, *sepetir paya* (*Copaifera palustris*), ramin, *jongkong* (*Dactylocladus stenostachys*) and six species of meranti (*Shorea* spp.), are the dominant species in the canopy layer. The middle layer includes many species of the *medang* (Lauraceae), mangosteen (Clusiaceae), *kedondong* (Burseraceae) and *mempisang* (Annonaceae) families. In addition to kelubi and pinang raja, the shrub or undergrowth layer is occupied by *jejarum* (*Ixora pyrantha*), *Tarenna fragrans*, and thickets of *pandan* (*Pandanus andersonii*, *P. brevifolius* and *P. redleyi*).

*Ramin*, a light hardwood, is harvested from *Gonystylus bancanus* trees. This commercially valuable wood is used for making furniture.

## Species composition

Tree species make up the majority of freshwater and peatswamp forests. In the same geographical location, the total number of tree species does not differ much between freshwater and peatswamp forests. In different geographical locations, however, tree species composition is less uniform, even within the same forest type. For instance, *Durio carinatus*, a species of durian, is found in the peatswamp forests on the east coast of Peninsular Malaysia and in Sarawak, but is absent on the west coast of Peninsular Malaysia. Likewise, out of the total of

289 known tree species occurring in the peatswamp forests of Malaysia, 71 species are confined to Peninsular Malaysia, 169 species to Sarawak, and only 49 species are common to both localities.

## Economic importance

Freshwater and peatswamp forests produce high-quality timber trees, although harvesting is restricted to only a few species. In Peninsular Malaysia, the principal peatswamp forest timbers are ramin, kempas, meranti (*Shorea teysmanniana* and *S. uliginosa*) and *punah* (*Tetramerista glabra*), while in Sarawak they are ramin, six species of meranti, jongkong, sepetir paya and *kapur paya* (*Dryobalanops rappa*). These species comprise about 70–80 per cent of all trees reaching a diameter of 60 centimetres or more.

A number of minor forest products are harvested regularly by local communities. Among these are kelubi fruits, pinang raja for use as ornaments, and pandan leaves for making mats and other types of handicrafts. The rivers and canals are popular fishing grounds, which also function as thoroughfares for people living along the waterways further inland. Hornbills and kingfishers, which inhabit peatswamp forests, are a great attraction for bird-watchers.

## Ecological role and conservation

During the wet season, peatswamp forests absorb and store water, which they then release during the dry season. In this way, flooding is prevented. This function of peatswamp forests has been employed by the Drainage and Irrigation Department to protect agricultural land from flood damage. In the Bernam River in Selangor, for example, flood waters are diverted to feeder canals in peatswamp forests, thereby preventing the flooding of vast areas of paddy fields in nearby Tanjung Karang.

Organic matter stored in the substrate of a peatswamp forest may not decompose for a very long period of time, because fungi and other decomposing agents do not funtion as well in the acidic and oxygen-deprived soil. Parts of the organic matter eventually break down into hydrocarbon compounds, otherwise known as fossils. Over millions of years, fossils turn into coal, gas and oil—fuel reserves that are tapped by man. The burning of these fossil fuels and large-scale clearance and burning of peatswamp forests release a huge amount of carbon dioxide back into the atmosphere. A high concentration of carbon dioxide and a few other gases in the atmosphere is one of the main factors contributing to the rise of global temperature, a phenomenon better known as global warming.

Therefore, it is important that freshwater and peatswamp forests are protected and conserved through sustainable forest management. To this end, the Malaysian Government has formulated the National Wetlands Policy, aimed at protecting and sustaining these fragile ecosystems by maintaining the natural links, such as rivers, canals and forests, and regulating the harvest of timbers and other forest products.

### Canopy layers of a peatswamp forest

A few emergent trees constitute the uneven topmost canopy layer (1). Below this are the small and medium-sized understorey trees (2), with an even and continuous canopy. The shrub layer (3) is dominated by the *kelubi* (inset) and *pinang raja* palms. The forest floor is flooded by rain water during the wet season.

canopy layer

understorey

shrub layer

# Limestone, quartzite and ultramafic vegetation

*Within Malaysia's tall, luxuriant tropical rainforest, strikingly different forest types can be found, which are adapted to specific soil conditions. In these forests, the dipterocarp and fruit tree families typical of rainforests are largely absent. Instead, the forest is made up of smaller trees, often quite spindly, and the canopy is more open. These vegetation types include many endemic species which are adapted to nutrient-poor conditions and, in the case of limestone and quartzite vegetation, to periodic drought and, for ultramafic conditions, to tolerance of heavy metal toxicity.*

The sharp, rugged and steep slopes of Bukit Takun, a limestone outcrop just outside Kuala Lumpur.

## Limestone vegetation

Limestone in Malaysia is found in the form of spectacular, towering, sheer-sided hills with jagged summits. A small amount of coral limestone is found on the coasts and islands of Sabah.

In Peninsular Malaysia, limestone hills are concentrated in the northern parts (mostly north of the Batu Caves outside Kuala Lumpur), while in Sarawak they are found in three main regions, namely Bau near Kuching, Niah and the Gunung Mulu National Park. In Sabah, isolated hills occur scattered throughout the state.

In Malaysia, most limestone hills attain a height of about 500 metres, with Gua Peningat in Taman Negara reaching 713 metres, and Gunung Api and Gunung Benarat in the Gunung Mulu National Park, which are the highest limestone outcrops in Malaysia, reaching 1700 metres.

Compared with the land area they occupy, limestone hills are disproportionately rich in plant species. For example, in Peninsular Malaysia, 1,216 species (13–14 per cent of all known species of flowering plants and ferns) are found on just 0.3 per cent of the land surface occupied by limestone hills. Of these, 262 are endemic and 130 are confined to limestone. This high biodiversity is partly the result of the many different microhabitats packed onto a single limestone hill.

High biodiversity is also due to regional differences—the limestone flora of the Langkawi islands and Perlis share many species with those in peninsular Thailand and are not found elsewhere in Malaysia. Likewise in Sarawak, the floras of the Bau, Niah and Gunung Mulu limestone hills also show distinct differences in species composition. The isolation of individual hills has encouraged this floristic difference and several species, particularly herbs such as paraboeas (*Paraboea* spp.) and balsams (*Impatiens* spp.), are only found on a single hill.

There is no study in Malaysia that explains physiological adaptations of limestone plants to alkaline conditions or high levels of calcium carbonate. Indeed, some species are not fussy and grow both on granite or limestone rocks. Examples are *Monophyllaea horsfieldii* and *Epithema saxatile* (members of the Gesneriaceae). No species has yet been shown to require a limestone substrate for its

## Microhabitats on a limestone hill

The many microhabitats stacked on a single limestone hill is one reason it can support such a biodiverse flora. The damp, deeply shaded base of the hill supports balsams (*Impatiens* spp.) and peperomias (*Peperomia* spp.); the lightly shaded cliff face is home to chiritas; paraboeas are adapted to the hot, dry conditions of the exposed cliff faces; and perched on the crest of the high cliffs are cycads. In deep crevices, the palm *Maxburretia rupicola* is found. Gullies, cave mouths and streams issuing from the hills all support their own assemblage of plant species.

1. This palm species, *Maxburretia rupicola*, is endemic to limestone habitats in Selangor, Peninsular Malaysia.

2. The herbaceous *Paraboea paniculata* is adapted to living on exposed limestone cliffs.

3. *Chirita viola*, a delicate plant confined to the damp and shaded parts of limestone outcrops, is found mainly on the Langkawi Islands.

4. The white-flowered, terrestrial orchid *Paphiopedilum niveum* is a rare species confined to limestone habitats.

**Quartzite vegetation**
The 10-kilometre quartzite dyke, the Klang Gate Ridge, provides a scenic backdrop to Kuala Lumpur. The Kuala Lumpur side of the ridge has since been burnt and is now a grass wasteland. The crest of the ridge is dominated by *Rhodoleia championi* (Hamamelidaceae) (inset) and *Baeckea frutescens* (Myrtaceae).

survival, and only a few show adaptations to it, notably two paraboeas that have special glands which secrete excess calcium carbonate.

## Quartzite vegetation

Compared with the flora that grows on limestone, vegetation on quartzite is very little studied, the best known being that of the Klang Gate Ridge near Kuala Lumpur. The longest quartzite ridge in Malaysia, it is about 10 kilometres long and on average 120 metres high but reaches 289 metres in places. The substrate of this specialized habitat comprises resistant glass-like quartz that scarcely weathers and becomes exposed as cliffs or narrow ridges. Under such conditions, soil formation is extremely poor and infertile conditions prevail. Furthermore, such a habitat is also susceptible to severe drought. It does not, therefore, support tall trees. The dominant shrubs include *Baeckea frutescens* (Myrtaceae) and *Rhodoleia championi* (Hamamelidaceae). Another unusual feature of this vegetation type is the occurrence of normally epiphytic species, such as the fig *Ficus deltoidea* and the fern *Davallia denticulata*, that grow directly on quartzite rocks.

Although the flora on quartz ridges remains poorly known, several endemic species are confined to this particular habitat. For example, 6 of the 175 plant species recorded from the Klang Gate Ridge are endemics, including one of the rarest species in Peninsular Malaysia, the holly *Ilex praetermissa*, known only from fewer than 20 individual plants.

Although quartzite habitats share the nutrient-poor and drought-prone conditions with limestone, their floras have very few species in common and these are mostly climbers. One striking difference is the almost total absence of orchids on quartzite compared with limestone habitats.

A species of *Arisaema*, an aroid confined to limestone.

## Ultramafic vegetation

Most of the ultramafic habitats in Malaysia occur in Sabah where they are found over a wide range of altitudes—from sea level to 3000 metres (on Mount Kinabalu). Ultramafic soil, also called ultrabasic or serpentine soil, is characterized by being poor in most of the major mineral nutrients required for plant growth. It is, however, rich in heavy metal elements, such as chromium, cobalt, iron, magnesium and nickel, that are toxic to most plant species. Therefore, only plants that are physiologically adapted to such conditions can grow on ultramafic soils.

The difference in appearance between forest growing on ultramafic and non-ultramafic soils is striking and often abrupt. Thus, walking up the trail to the summit of Mount Kinabalu, one will notice that the forest changes over just 10 metres from the multilayered oak-laurel forest to the open vegetation of stunted trees on ultramafic soil. In the latter, *Leptospermum recurvum* and *Dacrydium gibbsiae* predominate above a ground layer of sedges and pitcher plants.

On a per area basis, ultramafic flora is extremely species rich. For example, on Gunung Silam in Sabah at an altitude of 884 metres, 91 species of broad-leaved trees of 10 centimetres or more in diameter were recorded from a 0.24 hectare plot.

The flora on ultramafic soil is also rich in endemic species and other species that are specially adapted and confined to this special habitat. In Sabah, notable examples of such endemic species are several of the most spectacular pitcher plants, including the largest, *Nepenthes rajah*, as well as *N. burbidgeae*, *N. edwardsiana*, *N. macrovulgaris* and *N. villosa*. The rare *rhu* tree *Ceuthostoma terminalis* (Casuarinaceae), though not endemic to Sabah (it also occurs in Palawan Island, Philippines), is a good example of a species confined to ultramafic soil.

## Conservation

Because of high species endemism, or because many of their components are restricted to the habitats and are rare or have very localized distributions, the floras of limestone, quartzite and ultramafic soils are of great conservation importance. Their vegetation is particularly sensitive to habitat disturbance. In addition, because these habitats are nutrient poor, the vegetation is slow to recover after disturbance. Limestone flora is particularly vulnerable, because it is susceptible to burning when the surrounding area is cultivated, or being destroyed by quarrying for cement and marble, and in the past by mining for gold and antimony in Bau and iron in Ipoh. Quartzite ridges, in particular the Klang Gate Ridge, are also susceptible to burning, and then suffer from being rapidly invaded by aggressive weedy species. Ultramafic vegetation is threatened by logging, fires, deforestation, and road construction. At present, most of these unique and rich floras are not legally protected and are endangered by man's activities.

**Ultramafic vegetation**
*ABOVE*: Undisturbed forest with an even canopy on ultramafic soil on Bukit Tawai in Sandakan, Sabah.

*INSET*: A rare *rhu* tree, *Ceuthostoma terminalis* is only found in forests on ultramafic soils.

## The destruction of limestone hills

The summit vegetation of Gunung Tempurung, Ipoh, has not recovered from being burnt, even after 10 years.

In Langkawi, limestone has been cut into slabs for the manufacture of marble. Quarrying for marble and cement is one of the major causes of the destruction of limestone hills.

# Lowland and hill dipterocarp forests

*Dipterocarp forests are so-called because of the dominance of the timber family Dipterocarpaceae. Lowland, hill and upper dipterocarp forests are the most complex and species-rich forests that flourish on the well-drained soils of the plains, undulating lands and foothills of Malaysia. They occur from sea level to about 1200 metres. Until 1990, dipterocarp forests in Malaysia constituted about 85 per cent of all forested land, which itself covered about 58 per cent of the total landmass. Apart from being the country's main source of valuable timber, dipterocarp forests play a vital role in providing habitats for wildlife and in maintaining the ecological balance of the surrounding areas.*

Over half of the area of Taman Negara, Peninsular Malaysia's only National Park, is covered with dipterocarp forest.

A *keruing* tree (*Dipterocarpus lamellatus*) loaded with fruits following a mast flowering period in 1996 at the Pasoh Forest Reserve.

## Recent history

Dipterocarp forest once covered almost the entire length and breadth of Malaysia. The significant conversion of lowland dipterocarp forest to other land use began with the advent of tin-mining activities in the western parts of Peninsular Malaysia in the mid-19th century, followed by intensive rubber cultivation in the beginning of the 20th century. When rubber prices dropped sharply on the world market in the 1960s, lowland forests were further cleared to make way for the planting of oil palm.

The conversion of forest to agricultural land, mainly for rubber and oil palm plantations, intensified during the years 1971–90 when government-supported land development schemes were established, mostly in Peninsular Malaysia. There, forested land area decreased by 31.4 per cent by 1990, while in Sabah it fell 29.9 per cent and in Sarawak 10.5 per cent. Malaysia on the whole lost 22.7 per cent or 5.39 million hectares of its forested land area by 1990. Almost all the cleared forest was lowland dipterocarp forest, so much so that in

Peninsular Malaysia the only remaining sizable area of this forest type is Taman Negara, the National Park. This park covers 434 300 hectares, of which 58 per cent is lowland dipterocarp forest below an altitude of 300 metres. The rest comprises other forest types, such as hill and upper dipterocarp forests and lower and upper montane forests.

The fruits of *rambai hutan* (*Baccaurea* sp.), an understorey tree common in the lowland dipterocarp forest of Malaysia.

## Species composition and richness

Foresters classify this forest type as 'dipterocarp' because of the dominance of dipterocarp trees, which in dipterocarp forests constitute the highest number of individuals and the largest timber volume. In the Jengka Forest Reserve in Pahang, for instance, surveys covering an area of about 3200 hectares showed that about 30 per cent of trees with a diameter of 30 centimetres or more, and 55.5 per cent of trees by volume, were those of the dipterocarp family.

Biologically, the Malaysian lowland and hill dipterocarp forests are among the most species-rich terrestrial ecosystems in the world. For example, in the Pasoh Forest Reserve in Negeri Sembilan, a total of 820 species in 294 genera and 78 families of woody plants with a diameter of 10 centimetres or more were enumerated in a 50-hectare plot. This number is almost one-third of the total number of tree species found in Peninsular Malaysia, and is more than the combined number of woody plant species known in the whole of the United States of America and Canada.

The Malaysian dipterocarp forest is also a world centre of species diversity for a number of tropical tree families, such as the Bombacaceae, Clusiaceae, Dipterocarpaceae, Euphorbiaceae, Myristicaceae and Myrtaceae. For example, of the 507 known species of dipterocarp trees in the world, no fewer than 270 species occur in Malaysian dipterocarp forests. Similarly, of the 30 species of durian trees known worldwide, 24 are recorded from this forest type.

### Plant species typical of lowland and hill dipterocarp forests

1. *Gapis* (*Saraca thaipingensis*) has a cauliflorous habit and is common along streams and river banks in lowland dipterocarp forests.

2. The wild ginger (*Etlingera* sp.) is a common herbaceous plant in the hill dipterocarp forests, especially along streams and in shaded gullies.

3. Reaching up into the canopy of the forest is *Shorea longisperma*, a dipterocarp.

Within Malaysia, lowland and hill dipterocarp forests are home to 50–90 per cent of all known tree species that belong to these families: dipterocarp, durian (Bombacaceae), *kelat* (Myrtaceae), *langsat* (Meliaceae), legume (Leguminosae), mango (Anacardiaceae), mangosteen (Clusiaceae), *nangka* (Artocarpaceae), *nyatoh* (Sapotaceae), palm (Arecaceae), *penarahan* (Myristicaceae), rambutan (Sapindaceae), *tongkat ali* (Simaroubaceae) and rubber (Euphorbiaceae). Similarly, more than 75 per cent of all known species of wild gingers (Zingiberaceae) and woody climbers are found in this forest type. The main difference between lowland and hill dipterocarp forests is a shift in their floristic composition. A number of the common lowland forest species are found in hill forests, albeit less frequently, but many species which occur in the hills are absent in the lowlands. Striking examples are *seraya* trees (*Shorea curtisii*), which are confined to hill dipterocarp forests.

## Unique features of dipterocarp forests

The frequent occurrence of trees with compound leaves and a cauliflorous habit (bearing flowers and fruits on the tree trunk), as well as the presence of a large number of both woody and herbaceous climbing plants, is a unique feature of lowland and hill dipterocarp forests. Another remarkable feature is the gregarious flowering habit of the dipterocarp trees, which takes place at irregular intervals from two to five years. During the mast flowering period, nearly all adult dipterocarp trees produce flowers. Concurrently, many trees belonging to non-dipterocarp families also flower outside their usual flowering season. Heavy fruiting of the dipterocarp and other trees follows intense flowering and adds colourful patches of pink, red and brown to the dull, greyish green colour of the forest canopy, a truly breathtaking sight.

## Economic importance

Apart from the well-known tropical timbers and rattans, lowland and hill forests are also home to many useful or potentially useful plant species. These include fruit trees, medicinal plants, ornamental plants and vegetables. In addition, this forest type plays an important ecological role. Lowland and hill forests are crucial for sustaining a number of life-support processes essential for the maintenance of the environmental quality and ecological stability of the surrounding areas. For these reasons, Malaysia is one of the few tropical countries which has successfully formulated and implemented national forestry policies aimed at conserving and managing forest resources on a sustainable basis.

### Fruits of the forest

The lowland dipterocarp forest is especially rich in wild fruit trees. Roughly 9 per cent of the tree flora of this forest type in Peninsular Malaysia bears edible fruits, including *durian beludu* (*Durio oxleyanus*), *kandis* or *manggis* (*Garcinia* spp.), *petai* (*Parkia speciosa*) and *rambai* or *tampoi* (*Baccaurea* spp.).

Strands of *petai* fruit pods for sale in a market stall in Sungai Buloh, Selangor.

*Durian beludu* is one of the six wild durian species with edible fruits.

## Stratification of forest vegetation

In both lowland and hill dipterocarp forests, the vegetation is characteristically stratified into five more or less distinct canopy layers: the emergent layer, main storey, understorey, shrub layer and forest floor.

The **emergent layer (1)** consists of the biggest and tallest trees whose crowns appear broad and spreading above the main canopy layer of the forest. This discontinuous canopy layer, which reaches an average height of 40–45 metres, is dominated by members of the dipterocarp family, such as *keruing* (*Dipterocarpus costulatus* and *D. crinitus*), *chengal* (*Neobalanocarpus heimii*) and *meranti* (*Shorea acuminata*, *S. macroptera* and *S. leprosula*), and by those of a few other families such as *jelutong* (*Dyera costulata*) and *kempas* (*Koompassia malaccensis*).

The **main storey (2)** is continuous, with trees varying in height from 20 to 30 metres and comprising species from a range of families, all with deep crowns. In the more or less continuous **understorey (3)**, trees seldom reach above 20 metres and the crowns tend to be narrow and deep. Many young individuals of trees of the emergent and main storey layers are found here. The **shrub layer (4)** grows up to 5 metres and is fairly open. It is composed of many species of palms, members of the Euphorbiaceae and Rubiaceae, and saplings of trees of the emergent, main and understorey layers. On the **forest floor (5)**, tree seedlings and herbs are the main components of the vegetation.

In addition to the presence of five canopy layers, many species of epiphytes, hemiparasitic plants and woody as well as herbaceous climbers also occur, adding to the complexity of the forest structure. The stratification and complex structure of the forest provide a diversity of niches for plants and animals. The niches may be separated by physical space, such as nesting and feeding grounds, or segregated by the timing of the animals' activities. The forest is thus inhabited by diurnal or nocturnal animals as well as by animals that are active during both day and night.

A woody climber belonging to the family Connaraceae, common in lowland dipterocarp forests.

*RIGHT*: A *tualang* tree (*Koompassia excelsa*) emerging from the main storey from unlogged lowland dipterocarp forest in the Danum Valley Field Centre in Sabah.

# Montane forests

*The forests on mountains in Malaysia differ, according to altitude, in their appearance, structure and floristic composition. At about 1200–1500 metres, hill dipterocarp forest merges into lower montane forest, which in turn becomes upper montane, and on Mount Kinabalu, subalpine and alpine vegetation. However, on isolated mountains, such as Gunung Jerai in Peninsular Malaysia, the vegetation zones are telescoped, and the transition from hill dipterocarp forest directly into upper montane is abrupt, occurring at an altitude of about 800 metres.*

The tree branches in an upper montane forest are usually festooned with mosses and other bryophytes.

The acorns of a tropical oak of the genus *Lithocarpus*, which grows in lower montane forest.

*Rhododendron scortechinii*, a species that is confined to the upper montane forests of Peninsular Malaysia.

## Lower montane forest

In lower montane forest, the tree canopy (15–33 metres tall) is much lower than those of lowland and hill dipterocarp forests (25–45 metres), and emergent trees are either unusual or absent. Trees with buttresses, pinnately compound leaves and those that bear flowers on their trunks or branches are uncommon. Large woody climbers are also largely absent. However, vascular epiphytes, particularly orchids and ferns, are found in great abundance.

Lower montane forest is also distinguished by the predominance of species belonging to the oak (Fagaceae) and laurel (Lauraceae) families. Hence, it is often called oak-laurel forest. Also common are tree ferns, conifers and members of the tea (Theaceae), magnolia (Magnoliaceae), oil-fruit (Elaeocarpaceae) and root-parasite balanophora (Balanophoraceae) families. Characteristic too is the absence of species common in lowland forest, such as most dipterocarps and members of fruit tree families, such as the durian (Bombacaceae), jackfruit (Artocarpaceae), mango (Anacardiaceae) and nutmeg (Myristicaceae) families.

## Upper montane forest

In terms of structure and species composition, upper montane forest is strikingly different from lower montane forest. Its canopy is much lower (1.5–18 metres tall), it is single-layered and, because of constant exposure to wind, the crowns of the trees tend to be flat. The leaves of most trees are also smaller and thicker. Although epiphytic orchids and ferns are less common than in the lower montane forest, trees are frequently festooned with epiphytic lichens, mosses and leafy liverworts, the latter giving the forest its mossy appearance. The ground layer is spongy, consisting of a deep layer of sphagnum moss growing on peat soil.

Upper montane forest is also known as ericaceous forest because members of the Ericaceae, such as the rhododendrons, are conspicuous.

Pitcher plants are also common, and frequently several species and their hybrids grow in close proximity. Conifers are a characteristic component. Temperate genera, such as anemones, gentians and violets, also make their appearance.

On summits and weathered ridges, the trees are gnarled and dwarfed. Here, the *gelam gunung* tree (*Leptospermum flavescens*) is characteristic, with its twisted bonsai trunk and assemblage of ant-plant epiphytes. Other trees are equally stunted, spindly and twisted and, in addition, are draped with the old man's beard lichen (*Usnea* spp.) and a variety of other epiphytic lichens and bryophytes.

## Subalpine vegetation

In Malaysia, subalpine vegetation grows only on Mount Kinabalu. It comprises a windswept, shrubby forest intermixed with open, grassy, waterlogged vegetation. In the windswept forest, the endemic *Leptospermum recurvum* (Myrtaceae) and conifer *Phyllocladus hypophyllus*, and species of *Syzygium* (Myrtaceae) and *Schima* (Theaceae) are common. In the grassy, waterlogged vegetation, several endemic species of temperate genera, such as the Low's buttercup (*Ranunculus lowii*), Bornean eyebright (*Euphrasia borneensis*), gentian (*Gentiana borneensis*) and red sanicle (*Trachymene saniculifolia*) are common.

## Alpine vegetation

Above the tree line on Mount Kinabalu, at an altitude of about 3350 metres, alpine vegetation occurs. The vegetation is sparse and confined to cracks in the granite dome where a little soil collects. A few dwarfed shrubs, such as the heather-leaved rhododendron (*Rhododendron ericoides*) and the honey-scented rhododendron (*Rh. buxifolium*), provide shade for some grasses and rock-dwelling orchids.

## Factors affecting vegetation zonation

The changes in vegetation associated with increasing altitude are due to the different environmental conditions under which the plants grow. At higher altitudes, the climate is cooler and moister because of the 0.67 °C drop in temperature with each 100 metres ascended. At an altitude of about 1200–1500 metres, the cooler temperature results in the condensation of atmospheric humidity,

**ALTITUDINAL ZONATION OF MONTANE VEGETATION IN MALAYSIA**

Altitude (m)

alpine vegetation
3500
subalpine vegetation
2900
upper montane forest
1800
1200
lower montane forest
hill dipterocarp forest

Forest type

Alpine vegetation on the exposed, exfoliated granite near the summit of Mount Kinabalu.

Subalpine vegetation, with the Donkey's Ears Peak in the background.

The majestic Mount Kinabalu in Sabah. Apart from having lower and upper montane vegetation, it is the only mountain in Malaysia high enough to support subalpine and alpine vegetation.

## The montane flora of Mount Kinabalu

The flora of this majestic mountain has been described as the richest and most remarkable assemblage of plants in the world. Covering about 700 square kilometres, it is home to nearly 4,090 species of vascular plants, accounting for about a quarter of all species found in Borneo. It is particularly rich in orchid species (over 1,000 species), ferns (579 species), figs (98 species), rhododendrons (24 species, of which five are endemic to Mount Kinabalu), and pitcher plants (nine species, including the largest pitcher plant in the world, *Nepenthes rajah*). One of the reasons for this extraordinary biodiversity is that Mount Kinabalu is the highest mountain between the Himalayas and Papua New Guinea. Not only are lower and upper montane forests well developed but also above upper montane forest are subalpine and alpine vegetation, types not found elsewhere in Malaysia.

The dwarfed *Rhododendron ericoides* can grow on bare rock, and is found in alpine vegetation from the Paka Cave to the summit plateau.

## Species richness

As on other mountains, individual species have specific altitudinal ranges and, therefore, on ascending Mount Kinabalu there is a series of species, one replacing another. For example, among the pitcher plants, *Nepenthes stenophyllum* grows between 1000 and 2500 metres, *N. lowii* between 2000 and 2500 metres, and *N. villosa* between 2500 and 3125 metres. Another reason for the high biodiversity is the wide range of habitats and soil types, including ridges, deep gullies, exposed rocks, rocky streams and ultramafic soil. The flora of ultramafic soil is particularly biodiverse and includes many endemic species, such as the striking conifer *Dacrydium gibbsiae* and the pitcher plants *Nepenthes rajah* and *N. burbidgeae*.

Besides the largest pitcher plant in the world, Mount Kinabalu harbours many other fascinating plants. Examples are two species of *Rafflesia*; plants with ancient ancestry that are considered living fossils, such as the conifer *Phyllocladus hypophyllus* and the trig oak *Trigonobalanus verticillata*; the stunning slipper orchid *Paphiopedilum rothschildeanum*; and the enigmatic *Scyphostegia borneensis*, alone in its family Scyphostegiaceae.

which is seen as mist or cloud. This cloud line roughly marks the transition between hill dipterocarp and lower montane forest.

The transition from lower to upper montane forest, which occurs at about 1800 metres, is marked by a change in soil type. In upper montane forest, the soil is a deep, acidic peat layer, which is often waterlogged and is poor in nutrients. Constant wind blowing over exposed summits and ridges accounts for the flatter tree crowns and more stunted tree growth. The lower temperature at high altitude explains the presence of temperate genera in tropical montane forest, and the moist conditions allow delicate liverworts, mosses and filmy ferns to flourish. The high level of ultraviolet radiation is thought to be responsible for montane plants having thick leathery leaves, red or pink young leaves, and more intense colours of the flowers.

## Conservation

The major threat to the montane flora is habitat destruction, whether for telecommunication stations, holiday resorts, vegetable and flower gardens, golf courses or roads. Montane vegetation plays an important ecological role. Its canopy breaks the impact of tropical downpours, while the tangled

root mass holds the soil in place when waterlogged. Together with the thick layer of mosses, liverworts and organic debris clothing the tree trunks and branches, the waterlogged soil acts as a sponge, releasing clear water steadily throughout the year. Removing this protective forest therefore results in landslides, soil erosion, siltation of waterways, floods, and even climatic changes leading to the increase in air temperature. In addition, the beauty of many montane plants, particularly orchids and pitcher plants, also makes them vulnerable to unsustainable commercial collecting.

Because mountains are centres of endemism of rare and endangered plant species, several are totally protected as national parks, including Gunung Tahan in Peninsular Malaysia; Mount Kinabalu, the Crocker Range and the Tawau Hills in Sabah; and Gunung Mulu in Sarawak. However, because many endemic species are confined to a single mountain summit, only a fraction of species lives in totally protected areas. In order to protect a larger network of peaks, Sarawak has proposed national park status for several other areas with lower and upper montane forests, such as Usun Apau, Pulong Tau and the Hose Mountains. Elsewhere, however, montane forests remain without legal protection.

Low's buttercup grows in subalpine vegetation and is endemic to Mount Kinabalu.

*Elaeocarpus* or oil fruit trees are common constituents of the lower montane forests of Malaysia.

# Man-made vegetation

*The conversion of Malaysia's forests and other natural habitats into land for agriculture, mining, industrial purposes and urban development has resulted in the creation of various types of man-made vegetation. These are less complex in structure and poorer in species composition than natural vegetation, but nevertheless contribute towards the diversity and uniqueness of Malaysia's flora. Examples of man-made vegetation are vegetation in urban areas, village orchards and gardens, paddy fields and rubber, oil palm and tea plantations.*

The beautifully landscaped Lake Gardens, or Taman Tasik Perdana, in Kuala Lumpur. The gardens were set up in the 1880s and now provide the city with 91.6 hectares of greenery.

*Kayu rajah*, or *bereksa* (*Cassia fistula*), a native of India and Myanmar (Burma), is popularly grown in the parks and along the avenues of towns and cities in Malaysia.

### Vegetation in urban areas

In Malaysia, there are three main areas of urban vegetation: parks and roadsides, arboreta and botanical gardens, and private gardens. In almost all the major cities, nicely landscaped and well-tended parks and roadside are a common sight. They are home to about 600 species and varieties of indigenous and exotic plants, such as *pinang raja* (*Cyrtostachys renda*) and the Indian laburnum (*Cassia fistula*).

Malaysia has well-established arboreta, of which the ones at the Forest Research Institute Malaysia (FRIM) in Kepong, the Sepilok Forest Research Centre in Sabah and the Semenggok Arboretum in Sarawak are good examples. In these arboreta, hundreds of economically important species of native and introduced timber trees are planted for research. The arboreta also include plantations of a particular timber species, which may be surrounded by pockets of natural forest. The different habitats allow arboreta to play a significant role in the *ex situ* and *in situ* conservation of Malaysia's biodiversity.

Although there is no national botanical garden in Malaysia, there are large and well-maintained gardens in Penang, Taiping and Kuala Lumpur. Indigenous and exotic plant species are planted in these beautifully landscaped gardens. Together with adjacent forest reserves, the Penang and Taiping botanic gardens are also important sites for the conservation of Malaysian flora.

Within the compounds of homes, hotels, shopping centres, corporate buildings and

The vegetation grown in this business precinct in the centre of Kuala Lumpur offsets the harshness of the concrete jungle, and provides a soft and soothing effect.

government offices, gardens and small parks are often maintained. Many native and introduced plant species are cultivated in these compounds, thus adding to the species diversity of urban flora.

### Paddy fields, vegetable farms and tea plantations

Where wetland paddy fields are cultivated, many introduced and weedy plant species establish themselves. Exotic and naturalized grasses, sedges, herbs and woody, dwarf shrubs make up the 250 species of weeds common in this habitat.

In the highlands, vegetable farms and tea plantations are invaded by weeds that originate from subtropical and temperate regions. There are no fewer than 100 species of such weeds, comprising mainly members of the sunflower (Compositae), mint (Labiatae) and foxglove (Scrophulariaceae) families. Occasionally, local weedy and pioneer species, such as *Trema tomentosa*, invade and colonize neglected plantations.

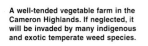

A well-tended vegetable farm in the Cameron Highlands. If neglected, it will be invaded by many indigenous and exotic temperate weed species.

## TYPES OF PLANTS IN URBAN AREAS

| PLANT GROUP/ CHARACTERISTIC | NATIVE SPECIES | INTRODUCED SPECIES |
|---|---|---|
| Trees with a spreading crown | *Pterocarpus indicus* | *Delonix regia, Samanea saman* |
| Trees with a compact, rounded crown | *Cinnamomum iners, Cerbera odollam* | *Filicium decipiens, Khaya sinegalensis, Spathodea campanulata* |
| Trees with a conical crown | *Fagraea fragrans, Podocarpus polystachyus* | *Araucaria cunninghamii, Polyalthia longifolia* |
| Trees with a pagoda-like crown | *Terminalia catappa, Dyera costulata* | *Araucaria excelsa* |
| Palms | *Cyrtostachys renda, Oncosperma tigillarium* | *Chrysalidocarpus lutescens, Veitchia merrillii, Roystonea regia* |
| Shrubs with brightly coloured flowers | *Rhodomyrtus tomentosus, Clerodendron paniculatum* | *Allamanda, Bougainvillea, and Ixora spp.* |
| Shrubs with colourful foliage | *Pisonia alba* | *Acalypha, Codiaeum and Dracaena spp.* |
| Herbaceous plants | *Alpinia, Asplenium and Zingiber spp.* | *Agave, Aglaonema and Heliconia spp.* |
| Ground covers | *Ipomoea pes-caprae, Nephrolepis biserrata* | *Alternanthera, Zebrina and Portulaca spp.* |
| Climbers and vines | *Bauhinia kockiana, Tristellateia spp.* | *Bignonia magnifica, Mucuna bennetii* |
| Bamboos | – | *Bambusa vulgaris, Schizostachyum brachycladum, Thyrsostachys siamensis* |

## Rubber and oil palm plantations

Rubber and oil palm plantations are the most extensive man-made habitats in Malaysia. Because plantations comprise a single species, they require rigorous and intensive tending to get rid of weeds; if neglected, they are quickly invaded. In some plantations, as many as 200 species of herbaceous and woody weeds have been found. Of these, at least 75 are considered serious weeds, including grasses, such as *lalang*, sedges and broad-leafed monocotyledons like the wild banana, dicotyledons such as *sendudok* (*Melastoma malabathricum*), and ferns such as *resam* (*Drecanopteris linearis*).

## Ecological significance

Apart from adding to the species richness of Malaysian flora, many components of man-made vegetation also perform useful ecological functions. In an urban environment, the presence of parks, gardens and roadside plantings softens the otherwise rigid and sterile surroundings. By intercepting rainfall, plants minimize surface soil run off, soil erosion and siltation of drainage systems which can cause frequent flooding. Water is also conserved in the soil and plant tissues, and gradually released back into the environment through natural processes, such as evapotranspiration. This process helps to lower the ambient temperature and raise the relative humidity of the atmosphere. In addition, the greenery filters out airborne pollutants, controls noise pollution by buffering sound waves and provides habitats for small wildlife, thus allowing mini ecosystems to develop.

## Rubber and oil palm plantations: Well-established man-made habitats

A neglected rubber plantation soon becomes densely colonized by various species of weeds.

### AREA UNDER RUBBER CULTIVATION IN MALAYSIA (1993) (ha)

1 479 900 Peninsular Malaysia
91 200 Sabah
210 100 Sarawak

Total area = 1 781 200

Of all the forms of man-made vegetation in Malaysia, oil palm plantations occupy the largest area.

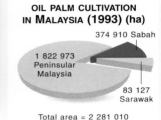

### AREA UNDER OIL PALM CULTIVATION IN MALAYSIA (1993) (ha)

374 910 Sabah
1 822 973 Peninsular Malaysia
83 127 Sarawak

Total area = 2 281 010

## Village orchards and gardens

Throughout Malaysia, village or kampong houses have their own orchards and gardens filled with different types of plants. These include fruit trees, spices, vegetables, ornamental and medicinal plants and plants used in ceremonies. A number of these plants are rare native species, making this type of man-made vegetation a valuable site of conservation.

A typical Malay house in peaceful surroundings. Fruit trees and vegetable gardens are often planted to the rear or the sides of such houses.

Rambutan trees are frequently grown in village gardens for their sweet, red fruits.

## PLANTS CULTIVATED IN VILLAGE ORCHARDS AND GARDENS

| TYPE OF PLANT | EXAMPLES OF SPECIES |
|---|---|
| Fruit trees | asam jawa or tamarind (*Tamarindus indica*), rambutan (*Nephelium lappaceum*), pisang (*Musa* spp.) |
| Medicinal plants | akar saga (*Abrus precatorius*), bintangor (*Calophyllum inophyllum*), cekur manis (*Sauropus androgynus*) |
| Plants used in ceremonies | kelapa (*Cocos nucifera*), kenanga (*Cananga odorata*), melati (*Jasminum sambac*) |
| Ornamental plants | bunga kertas (*Bougainvillea* spp.), bunga raya (*Hibiscus rosa-sinensis*), jejarum (*Ixora* spp.) |
| Spices | bunga kantan (*Etlingera elatior*), cabai (*Capsicum annuum*), lengkuas (*Alpinia galanga*), serai (*Cymbopogon citratus*) |
| Vegetables | bayam (*Amaranthus spinosus*), kangkong (*Ipomoea aquatica*), petai (*Parkia speciosa*) |

# THE DIVERSITY OF LIFE FORMS

The Malaysian jewel orchid has beautifully coloured and patterned leaves.

The Malaysian rainforest is a complex ecosystem that is made up of mainly tree species. However, within the forest, a variety of other plants flourish, including climbers, epiphytes, herbs, parasites, saprophytes, shrubs and stranglers. In waterlogged areas, specialized habitats occur, such as freshwater and peatswamp forests, mangroves, rivers and lakes, where various types of aquatic plants can be found.

Plants can be classified into two major groups: autotrophic and heterotrophic. Most plants are autotrophic, that is, they possess chlorophyll and are able to perform photosynthesis. Heterotrophic plants, on the other hand, are devoid of chlorophyll and therefore unable to photosynthesize. These include the holoparasites, such as *Balanophora* and *Rafflesia*, and the saprophytes, like fungi and a few orchid species.

Herbs are well represented in Malaysia in families of both dicotyledons and monocotyledons. In size, they range from a minute plant of a few centimetres, such as the *Corybas* orchids, to lofty herbs a few metres tall, like the banana plants. Climbers are weak-stemmed plants whose long, slender and fast-growing shoots require other plants or firm objects for support. Epiphytes are plants that grow on other plants, perching on the branches and other exposed parts of the host in order to obtain adequate sunlight and rainwater. Plants that start life as epiphytes but later send roots down to the ground are called stranglers. On reaching the ground, the roots increase in number and size and eventually encase and strangle the host tree. Many species of figs have adopted this growth habit and are frequently seen in the lowland forests of Malaysia.

Most species of fungi and a few species of vascular plants have evolved into a saprophytic way of life. They do not possess structures that enable them to obtain nutrients directly from the environment, and are entirely dependent on decomposing organic material for their growth and reproduction. Lichens are organisms comprising fungi and blue-green algae in a symbiotic relationship. In Malaysia, they are found in damp habitats at all altitudes, and on rocks, walls of old buildings, tree trunks, branches and leaves.

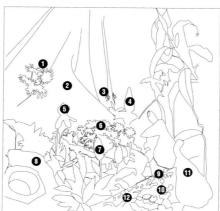

**Plant diversity in the Malaysian rainforest**
1. Stemless palm (*Licuala glabra*)
2. Strangling fig (*Ficus callosa*)
3. Tree (*Baccaurea racemosa*)
4. Herb (*Amorphophallus prainii*)
5. Orchid (*Paphiopedilum barbatum*)
6. Fern (*Dipteris conjugata*)
7. Ginger (*Zingiber spectabile*)
8. Parasite (*Rafflesia pricei*)
9. Fungus (*Phallus indusiatus*)
10. Fungus (*Cookeina tricholoma*)
11. Pitcher plant (*Nepenthes rafflesiana*)
12. Lichen (*Rigidoporus lineatus*)

# Fungi

*Fungi are a diverse group of saprobic (living on dead organic matter), symbiotic or parasitic organisms that help to ensure the continued existence of Malaysian forests by decomposing organic matter and recycling nutrients. They are found in a wide range of habitats, and the edible varieties are food for both animals and humans. They can be both beneficial, when used in industrial processing, and destructive, as they cause disease in humans, animals and economically important plants.*

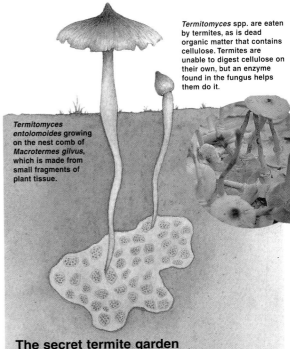

Termitomyces spp. are eaten by termites, as is dead organic matter that contains cellulose. Termites are unable to digest cellulose on their own, but an enzyme found in the fungus helps them do it.

Termitomyces entolomoides growing on the nest comb of Macrotermes gilvus, which is made from small fragments of plant tissue.

A colony of orange fungi lends a splash of colour to a rotting log.

## Structure and classification

Most fungi, or *kulat*, are composed of microscopic tubular filaments called hyphae which contain protoplasm. Hyphae grow by tip elongation and branching, and the resulting mass of hyphae is called the mycelium. In some species, the mycelium may become organized into structures such as mushrooms and puffballs. Fungi differ from green plants in that they do not possess chlorophyll, and thus they do not photosynthesize. To obtain nourishment, they excrete enzymes that dissolve food that is then absorbed through their thin cell walls, and is distributed by simple circulation or streaming of the protoplasm.

Reproduction is both sexual and asexual. They reproduce by fragmentation, fission or budding, as with yeast, or by the production of asexual or sexual spores. Spores are mainly dispersed by wind and sometimes by water, insects and small mammals.

Fungi are classified into the following five groups—Oomycota, Zygomycota, Ascomycota, Basidiomycota and Deuteromycota—based on their reproductive structures. Members of these five groups are found in Malaysia. Among members of the first three are many agents of plant diseases and common food moulds. The Basidiomycota are a large group and include many varied and colourful mushrooms, puffballs, stinkhorns, rusts and brackets. Deuteromycota are distinguished by not having a sexual stage, and a genus of this group is *Penicillium*.

**Three substrates on which fungi grow: Bark, forest litter and soil**

The stinkhorn fungus (*Dictyophora* sp.) grows on tree bark or soil, and is so-called for the unpleasant odour it emits. The foul smell attracts flies that help in spore dispersal.

These small mushrooms, a species of *Marasmius*, help to break down forest litter on which they grow.

*Cookeina tricholoma* is found on twigs and branches, and has tiny trichomes or hairs. It is a common cup fungus in tropical rainforests. These were seen on the trail to Gunung Mulu in Gunung Mulu National Park.

## Varied habitats

Fungi can be found in a wide range of habitats because they secrete enzymes that enable them to act on a variety of substrates. Some species of fungi live in water, such as the chytrids, water moulds and several members of Ascomycota and Deuteromycota. These fungi decompose sewage and other organic matter, and some can cause diseases in fish and humans. *Saprolegnia parasitica*, for example, causes fish

## The secret termite garden

Certain species of *Termitomyces* are cultivated by some species of termites as sources of food in underground fungal gardens. One such species, *Termitomyces entolomoides*, grows out of the ground from a fungus comb made by the termite *Macrotermes gilvus*. The fungus only grows from abandoned termite nests and it is one of several species of *Termitomyces* found in Malaysia.

and fish egg diseases. In Malaysia's mangrove areas, many polypores, resupinate fungi (which recline on the substratum) and small agarics occur on dead wood and tree bark.

Soil is the most common habitat for fungi, and is a reservoir for many species of saprophytes and parasites. In the forest, the mycelia of the fungi can be easily seen branching through the forest floor litter. Together with insects, other small invertebrates and bacteria, these fungi participate in the decomposition and recycling of nutrients essential for the continued existence of the forest. This process is particularly rapid in the tropics because of favourable environmental conditions and the high diversity of microorganisms. Many fungi produce small fruiting bodies, often in large clusters, such as species of the genera *Marasmius* and *Mycena*. Some fungi prey on organisms like rhizopods, which include amoebae and nematodes.

Many fungi are able to successfully colonize wood because they can tolerate the substrate's low nitrogen level. Most of the wood-decay fungi in Malaysia, such as the bright orange *Pycnoporus sanguineus*, produce a white rot. While most wood rotters are saprophytes, some species, like the bracket fungus *Ganoderma*, can colonize and attack living host trees.

In humid forests, hammock-forming fungi are a notable feature. These fungi, mainly species of *Marasmius* and related forms, produce threads of rhizomorphs which trap debris falling from the forest canopy. The fruiting bodies of these fungi develop as small mushrooms directly from these threads.

## Symbiosis

Certain fungi live in close symbiotic relationships with green or blue-green algae, and together create lichens. These are common on tree trunks, stems and leaves. The alga provides carbon compounds and vitamins to the fungus, and in return the fungus supplies the alga with minerals and water, and protects it from desiccation and intense sunlight.

Another widespread phenomenon is the symbiotic association between soil fungi and plant roots, called mycorrhizas. In this interdependent relationship, the host plant receives mineral nutrients from the fungus, while the fungus obtains carbon compounds through the host's photosynthesis. At least seven types of mycorrhizal associations, involving different groups of fungi and host plants, have been identified. The benefits of mycorrhizas to agriculture and forestry have been amply demonstrated elsewhere, but have yet to be fully exploited in Malaysia.

## Fungal diseases

Fungi are responsible for many of the diseases that affect crops and other agricultural produce. Examples are the powdery mildews which attack rubber trees and vegetables; leaf spots and anthracnose, rusts, tomato wilt, pod rots, root and heart rots. Some fungi are human pathogens, causing diseases such as athlete's foot, ringworm, barber's itch, and respiratory diseases such as aspergillosis, which also affect insects and birds. Several fungi are parasites of insects, and others are mycoparasites, meaning they live as parasites only on other fungi. While fungi do cause disease, they can also potentially be used to control weeds, insects and plant disease, for example, species of the genera *Trichoderma*, *Colletotrichum* and *Entomophthora*.

## Fungi as food and medicine

Fungi are important in a number of industrial processes. Yeasts cause the fermentation of carbohydrates and are used in brewing beer and as a rising agent in baking. The enzymes of another fungus are used to ferment sugar cane molasses or hydrolyzed starch to produce industrial ethyl alcohol. Many species of *Penicillium* are capable of producing organic acids, and are important in the manufacture of cheeses and antibiotics, such as the well-known penicillin. Some fungi are known to produce anti-tumour agents, while others, like the magic mushrooms, are hallucinogenic. Although *Gibberella fujikuroi* is the cause of a serious rice disease, it also produces a plant growth promoting substance, gibberellic acid.

Fungi serve as sources of food for a wide variety of animals, from arthropods to snails, flies, tortoises, pigs and deer. Humans also eat fungi, and use them in food preparation. In Malaysia, fungi have long been used as a fermentation agent in the production of a range of food products, such as *tapai*, *tempe* and *taucu*. Several species are used in cooking, namely the paddy straw mushroom (*Volvariella* spp.), oyster mushroom (*Pleurotus* spp.), cendawan kungkur (*Schizophyllum commune*) and cendawan busut (*Termitomyces* spp.).

*Phellinus* sp. growing on a tree trunk.

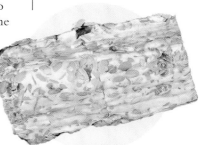

*Tempe*, an important food product in Malaysia, is made from soya beans fermented using the fungus *Rhizopus oligosporus*.

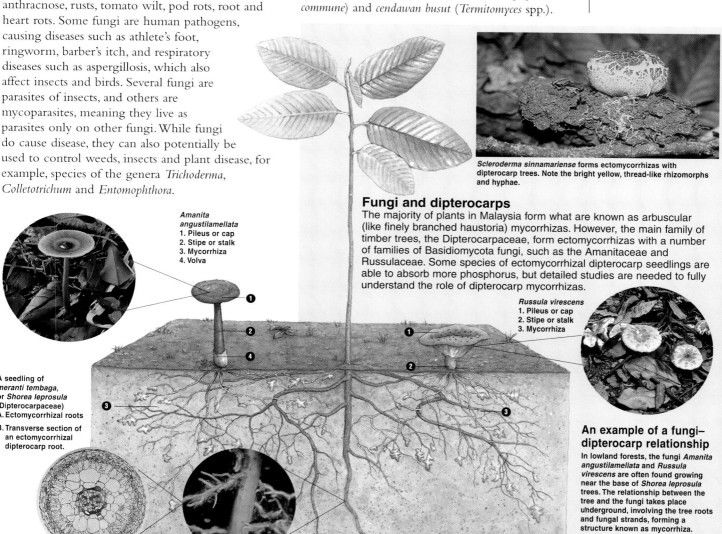

*Scleroderma sinnamariense* forms ectomycorrhizas with dipterocarp trees. Note the bright yellow, thread-like rhizomorphs and hyphae.

### Fungi and dipterocarps

The majority of plants in Malaysia form what are known as arbuscular (like finely branched haustoria) mycorrhizas. However, the main family of timber trees, the Dipterocarpaceae, form ectomycorrhizas with a number of families of Basidiomycota fungi, such as the Amanitaceae and Russulaceae. Some species of ectomycorrhizal dipterocarp seedlings are able to absorb more phosphorus, but detailed studies are needed to fully understand the role of dipterocarp mycorrhizas.

*Amanita angustilamellata*
1. Pileus or cap
2. Stipe or stalk
3. Mycorrhiza
4. Volva

*Russula virescens*
1. Pileus or cap
2. Stipe or stalk
3. Mycorrhiza

A seedling of
meranti tembaga,
or *Shorea leprosula*
(Dipterocarpaceae)
A. Ectomycorrhizal roots
B. Transverse section of an ectomycorrhizal dipterocarp root.

### An example of a fungi–dipterocarp relationship

In lowland forests, the fungi *Amanita angustilamellata* and *Russula virescens* are often found growing near the base of *Shorea leprosula* trees. The relationship between the tree and the fungi takes place underground, involving the tree roots and fungal strands, forming a structure known as mycorrhiza.

37

# Algae

*Malaysia's rivers, ponds, lakes, mangroves and seas harbour a very rich and fascinating group of plants called algae. These are photosynthetic, non-vascular plants that contain chlorophyll and have simple reproductive structures. This vast array of organisms is diverse in its range of habitat, size, organization, physiology, biochemistry and reproduction. In Malaysia, about 600 genera with 2,000 species of algae have been recorded. Laymen refer to algae by various names, such as 'pond scum', 'frog spittle', 'water moss' and 'seaweed'.*

**Freshwater algae habitat**
*Spirogyra zygnema* grows in clean, fast-flowing water that is exposed to plenty of sunlight, as in this freshwater stream in Endau-Rompin.

### Aquatic algae

There are various forms of algae. Aquatic algae may be planktonic, that is, suspended in water, or benthic, living on the floor of water bodies. Planktonic algae, or phytoplanktons, comprise a wide range of sizes, from the largest forms visible to the naked eye to the smallest that are microscopic. Those that receive the necessary nutrients will increase in number and form water blooms, as is the case with the species of *Scenedesmus, Euglena, Navicula, Oscillatoria, Microcystis* and *Cosmarium*. The species composition of planktonic algae found in a locality depends on whether the habitat is freshwater or seawater, clean or polluted. In general, more species are found in freshwater than in seawater habitats, and the dominant species are those of Chrysophyta and Cyanobacteria, or blue-green algae, respectively.

The algae of the open ocean are called pelagic, and are microscopic floating species. In coastal waters, the dominant algae are the microscopic Rhodophyta, Phaeophyta and Chlorophyta, which are attached to rocks. Coral reefs are home to the highest number, about 35 per cent, of

**Marine algae habitats**
*Top: Halimeda opuntia* grows in coral reefs, as in Barracuda Point, off Pulau Sipadan in Sabah.

*Bottom: Catenella* sp. is a red alga that grows in seawater habitats, such as mangroves and rocky shores, as shown in this example from Port Dickson.

marine algae species in Malaysia, followed by rocky shores which harbour 27 per cent, and sandy beaches, muddy coastal areas and mangroves, which have less than 10 per cent each. Marine algae vary in their ability to adjust to degrees of salinity, which affects their distribution. For example, *Laminaria, Navicula* and *Nitzschia* are genera that can adapt to different degrees of salinity, whereas *Odontella, Chaetoceros* and *Tabellaria* are confined to a high degree of salinity.

Marine algae habitats are easily destroyed by pollutants such as industrial waste, oil emissions from ships, oil spills and silt from land reclamation. The coral reefs at Pulau Besar in the Strait of Melaka, for example, have seen a huge decline in their algae population due to land reclamation. While the more resilient species were able to recover, others such as *Microdictyon* sp. were eliminated.

### Subaerial algae

Non-aquatic algae are categorized according to the various substrates on which they grow. Edaphic species grow in and on soil, and studies in Malaysia have shown a great abundance of Cyanobacteria. Epilithic algae occur on the surface of exposed rocks and stones, especially in mountainous regions, by river banks, at the edges of lakes and along the coast. Their population is often massively developed because they are in a habitat where nutrients are continually supplied and waste products removed.

## Algal diversity in a Malaysian freshwater ecosystem

Ankistrodesmus falcatus
Volvox tertium
Ceratium hirundinella
Scenedesmus quadricauda
Tabellaria
Gomphonema
Cocconeis
Cosmarium globosum
Navicula
Frustulia
Cymbella
Blyxa echinosperma
rock
Bulimus tentaculatus
Ulothrix
Lyngbya

Malaysia's freshwater ecosystems support a wide range of algal life, from free-floating species to those that live on a variety of substrates. Algae play an important role in the ecosystem as primary producers in the food chain. Epiphytic algae (1) grow on aquatic plants, like *Blyxa echinosperma*, a completely submerged, common flowering plant. Planktonic algae (2) live suspended near the surface of the water. Epilithic algae (3) live on the surface of exposed rocks and stones, either on land or, as in this case, submerged in water. Epizoic algae (4) attach themselves to animals, such as this freshwater snail, *Bulimus tentaculatus.*

# Classification of algae

Most current systems of classification place algae into seven or eight divisions. These are based on the pigmentation, the storage products, the chemical nature of the cell wall and the number and form of flagella—the long, whip-like outgrowths that act as agents of locomotion.

**Cyanobacteria**, or cyanophyta, also known as blue-green algae, contain chlorophyll and are photosynthetic autotrophs.
This means they are capable of manufacturing their own food, like most green plants. They also fix nitrogen in the soil through their rounded cells called heterocysts, and these can be used as a natural soil fertilizer. Examples of Malaysian species are *Oscillatoria limosa* and *Anabaena flos-aquae*, which are found in paddy fields and rivers.

**Chlorophyta**, or green algae, exhibit diverse forms and methods of reproduction. Their body structures range from single cells to multicellular filaments and sheets. Common in Malaysian habitats are *Cosmarium bioculatum*, *Spirogyra schmidtii* and *Scenedesmus quadricauda*. Green algae share a number of chemical characteristics with higher plants, and it is a generally accepted theory that higher plants have evolved from green algae-like ancestors.

**Euglenophyta**, also known as euglenoids, are unicellular, flagellate organisms. About one-third of them are photosynthetic. Euglenoids change shape continually as they move through the water because their outer covering, known as the pellicle, is flexible. As inhabitants of freshwater ponds, particularly those with large amounts of organic material, they are useful indicators of organic pollution. If a body of water has an unusually large number of euglenoids, it is probably polluted. Malaysian examples of this group are *Euglena acus*, *Phacus caudatus* and *Trachelomonas hispida*.

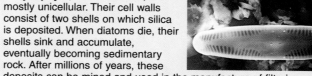

**Chrysophyta**, or the diatoms, are mostly unicellular. Their cell walls consist of two shells on which silica is deposited. When diatoms die, their shells sink and accumulate, eventually becoming sedimentary rock. After millions of years, these deposits can be mined and used in the manufacture of filtering, insulating and soundproofing materials. Examples of species occurring in Malaysia are *Cymbella ventricosa* and *Navicula mutica*.

**Pyrrophyta**, or the so-called dinoflagellates, are unicellular. Their cells are often covered with shells of interlocking cellulose plates. Some of the dinoflagellates form 'red tides', turning the sea to a reddish brown colour with their presence. They produce a toxin that attacks the nervous system of fish, and which is also poisonous to humans, causing a paralytic effect when ingested.

**Rhodophyta**, or red algae, are multicellular organisms. Their body structure is usually composed of complex, interwoven filaments that are delicate and feathery. The cell walls often contain polysaccharides that are of commercial value, like *Gelidium*, *Eucheuma* and *Chondrus* from which agar and carrageen are obtained.

**Phaeophyta**, or brown algae, are multicellular, and range in length from several centimetres to approximately 60 metres. The largest are called kelps. Many possess leaf-like blades, stipes, root-like anchors and gas-filled vesicles (bladder-like cavities) that provide buoyancy. Their cell walls contain alginate that is used as a thickening agent in ice cream and cosmetics. Examples of brown algae found in Malaysia are *Sargassum siliquosum*, *Padina commersonii* and *Turbinaria dentata*.

Corticolous algae live on tree bark. In Malaysia, 11 species have so far been found and identified. Epizoic algae are attached to animals, especially to the hard shells of many species of molluscs, like the snail *Bulimus tentaculatus* (see illustration on previous page), and epiphytic algae grow on other plants. Some algae are parasitic, although these are relatively rare. However, in Malaysia *Cephaleuros virescens* has been found on rubber trees, attacking the leaves, petioles, branches and stems.

## Ecological and economic importance

Algae are extremely important as primary producers of organic matter and oxygen in aquatic environments because of their photosynthetic activities. The filamentous Cyanobacteria, which form mucilaginous sheets, are the primary stabilizers of bare, eroded soils, and act as a pioneer community. The mucilage binds the soil particles, thus reducing water loss and removal by wind. The excretion of organic compounds also fertilizes the soil and provides a substrate for other organisms.

Algae play a major role in the sciences of limnology (study of freshwater ecosystems), oceanography and physiology. Information pertaining to the physiology of protoplasm in higher plants has come from algal studies.

Seaweeds (marine algae) are an important marine resource. Apart from their vital role in primary production, they provide essential spawning habitats for many fish, shellfish and other marine organisms. Several species of seaweed genera, such as *Laminaria*, *Gracilaria* and *Eucheuma*, are highly valued as food, whilst others are sources of gels and chemicals used in various types of household commodities such as agar jelly.

Some algae are considered problem-causing organisms in eutrophic (polluted) waters. Such waters are rich in nutrients and support an abundance of algal communities, which in the process of decaying deplete the oxygen supply for any animals living in the water. If algae reproduction is allowed to proceed unchecked for too long, all animal life in these waters will eventually die. Particular groups of algae have been used to indicate the quality of water, and studies have been carried out in the Gabai and Langat rivers in Ulu Langat, Selangor. Results show a predominance of *Meridion circulare* in Sungai Gabai, meaning that the river is clean. In contrast, Sungai Langat shows the presence of several species of diatoms, such as *Navicula cryptocephala*, *Gomphonema parvulum* and *Cymbella ventricosa*, strongly indicating that the river is polluted.

*Sargassum, a brown alga, dominates coral reefs in Port Dickson, and is collected for use in local cooking and Chinese herbal medicine. In the paper industry, it is used as a smoothing agent.*

# Lichens

*A lichen is composed of two completely different organisms in a symbiotic relationship: colourless, fungal threads called hyphae, and a colony of microscopic, green or blue-green algae. Together they form a thallus, which bears no resemblance to either a fungus or an alga and behaves as a single independent plant. In Malaysia, the wide diversity of lichen flora has led to numerous studies in Peninsular Malaysia and Sabah. Only a few studies have been conducted in Sarawak. Lichens were once a source of fabric dye, and a few species are used as food and medicine, and as a source of essential oils.*

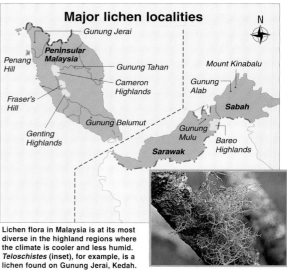

**Major lichen localities**

Lichen flora in Malaysia is at its most diverse in the highland regions where the climate is cooler and less humid. *Teloschistes* (inset), for example, is a lichen found on Gunung Jerai, Kedah.

This highland tree in the Kinabalu Park is laden with lichens.

### Habitat

Almost any stable surface in the forest is an adequate substrate for lichens. They are found on rocks, tree trunks, the surface of leaves and even on the backs of hard-shelled animals. What lichens look for is a smooth surface that is exposed to plenty of sunlight. A moist habitat is also preferred, although lichens are able to survive periods of drought by becoming dormant. In Malaysia, lichens are predominantly found in the highland areas.

### Structure

Lichens lack true roots, stems and leaves. However, their spore-containing structures, or ascocarps, are commonly termed 'fruits'. The whole lichen, except for the spore-containing organs, is referred to as the thallus. In a stratified thallus, the algae are scattered more or less evenly throughout, whereas the algae in an unstratified thallus occur in a single layer. Just below the upper cortex of a stratified thallus are some algal cells, followed by a medulla of fungal filaments. Loose fungal hyphae may grow on the lower cortex, as may root-like hyphae which form compact strands.

The upper surface of the thallus bears structures that are unique to lichens. For instance, there are tufts of hyphae that are covered with fine granules. Each granule comprises a few algal cells enmeshed in fragments of fungal hyphae, which are capable of developing into new individuals. Finger-like protuberances enclosed in the cortex are also able to generate new plants.

Some lichens have their fruiting organs at the tips of the main 'stems' or 'branches'. Whether these organs are

Lichens grow slowly, but will eventually encrust the surface on which they have taken root.

## Structural composition of lichens

The relationship between the two lichen partners is an intimate one, in which the green alga manufactures food via photosynthesis, and the fungus envelops the alga with its protective hyphae. However, while the algal partner is able to survive on its own, the fungus cannot, as it relies entirely on the alga for nutrients.

| | |
|---|---|
| Vegetative propagules, or soredia, are found on the upper surface. If they occur in localized clusters, they are called soralium. | **upper surface** |
| The fungal partner forms a protective layer of hyphae, preventing water loss, shielding the alga from harmful ultraviolet rays and providing a stable environment for growth. | **upper cortex** |
| Beneath the upper cortex lie the algal cells, which perform photosynthesis for the lichen. | **photobiant layer** |
| This layer of loose tissue is provided by the fungus, and is where food and water are kept. | **medulla** |
| Securing the lichen to the substrate are thick strands of hyphae on the lower cortex. | **lower cortex** |

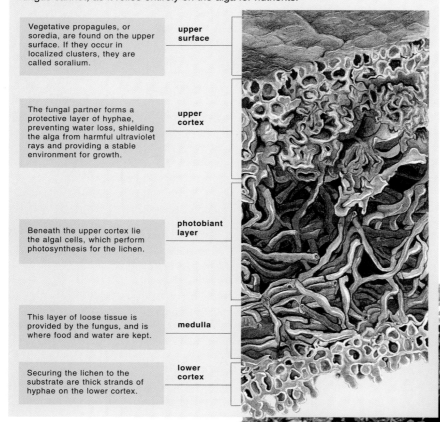

## The forms of lichens

Three growth forms of lichens—foliose, fruticose and crustose—are found in Malaysia.

**Foliose lichens** are always leafy in appearance. The thallus looks like a flattened sheet, and its upper surface is significantly different from its lower, in terms of colour, surface structure and texture. Lying flat on the substrate, the thallus is held down by root-like growths. Some foliose lichens lack these growths, but are instead fastened to the substrate by a central cord, as in species of *Parmotrema* (1).

The thallus expands outwards from the centre as it grows, reaching diameters ranging from 1 to 30 centimetres. Forked, elongated lobes, whose margins may be smooth or indented, dissected or lacerated, are characteristic. The size of the lobes varies from a narrow 0.1–0.3 millimetre to a broad 3–20 millimetres. Some species of foliose lichens, such as *Parmotrema crinitum*, possess hair-like structures called cilia along the margins of the lobes.

Pores occur on the lower surface of several genera. In *Sticta*, they appear in the form of sunken pits scattered on the tomentum, a hyphal structure that mats over the lower surface. On the other hand, in *Pseudocyphellaria* and *Parmelia*, the pores are simple indentations in the cortex of the thallus and are filled with white hyphae.

**Fruticose lichens** are erect or pendulous. The thallus consists of simple or divided branches that are round. Unlike the foliose lichens, there is no clear distinction between the upper and lower surfaces of the thallus. Generally, a fruticose thallus is bushy, hairy or strap-shaped, and attached to the substrate at the base only. Growth occurs at the tips of branches and is profuse, with some species reaching up to 2 metres in length. Examples of fruticose lichens are *Usnea*, *Ramalina* and *Heterodermia* (2).

**Crustose lichens** form a crust on the surface of the substrate. They lack a lower cortex, root-like structures, and certain reproductive parts, such as the hyphae tufts on the thallus and the finger-like protuberances in the cortex. An example of this type of lichen is *Chrysothrix* (3).

circular, cup-shaped, globular or linear depends on the species of the lichen. In other lichens the fruiting organs develop within the thallus, releasing the mature spores through a tiny opening in the thallus surface.

### Growth and reproduction

Among all the classes of plant life, lichens are the slowest growing. The average lichen increases its diameter by only a few millimetres each year. One of the faster growing, *Peltigera*, shows an annual increase of just 2–3 centimetres. Fruticose lichens exhibit rapid growth at their tips, while crustose lichens appear to be the slowest growers. Despite the sluggish growth, some lichens attain a fair size. In the rainforest, for example, *Usnea* can reach a length of 2 metres or more.

Both sexual and vegetative modes of reproduction exist in lichens. A union of male and female gametes occurs prior to the next spore formation. Reproduction by sexual means through true spores is a rare occurrence in foliose and fruticose lichens, while vegetative reproduction through diaspores (lichen fragments) is more common. Crustose lichens, on the other hand, rely totally on spores as their means of reproduction. The granules that occur on the tufts of hyphae on a thallus' upper surface are dispersed by wind. Under the right conditions, these will grow into new plants. When brittle diaspores break off from the parent plant, they develop into separate individuals. The short, finger-like outgrowths in the cortex detach themselves from the thallus surface and are immediately established as new plants.

### Ecological role

Lichens are very sensitive to atmospheric pollutants, such as heavy metals and sulphur dioxide. These airborne substances are absorbed into the surface of the lichen. With this facility, lichens can be used as indicators of air pollution. Ironically, prolonged exposure to these same pollutants will end up killing the lichens.

## Major uses of lichens

Over 600 substances, including pigments, toxins and antibiotics, are found in lichens, making them a useful source of dye, medicine and essential oils. These substances are collectively known as lichenic acids.

### Dye

Before synthetic dyes were invented, lichens were the principal source of colouring for fabrics, especially wool and silk. The source of the dye is the myriad of acids found only in lichens, although the colour of the lichen does not give an indication of the dye. Some of these acids include erythrinic, lecanoric, gyrophoric, salazanic and evernic acid. Dye extraction is carried out by soaking the lichen in an ammonia-rich solution, such as urine! Crustose lichens are more feasible as dyes than the larger foliose or fruticose lichens.

In Malaysia, the use of vegetable dyes is the traditional way to colour fabric. Today, however, most textiles are treated with synthetic dyes, which give more vibrant and longer lasting colours.

| LICHENS USED FOR DYE | |
| --- | --- |
| **LICHEN SPECIES** | **COLOUR OF DYE** |
| Candelariella vitellina | red |
| Ochrolechia parella | yellow |
| O. tartarea | purple |
| Parmelia conspersa | brown |
| P. omphalodes | yellow |
| P. perlata | brown |
| P. saxatilis | red |
| Roccella tinctoria | red |
| Ramalina scoparium | red |
| Teloschistes chrysopthalmus | red |
| T. flavicans | yellow |
| Umbilicaria deusta | red |
| Usnea barbata | yellow |
| Xanthoria parietina | yellow |

### Medicine and essential oils

A small number of lichens have medicinal properties and are used to treat illnesses such as tuberculosis, rabies and whooping cough. *Usnea* works as an antibiotic. Essential oils are extracted from lichens belonging to the genera *Parmelia* and *Ramalina* for the manufacture of soap and perfume.

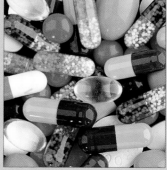

It is not uncommon for modern medicines to include lichen extracts as one of their many ingredients.

| LICHENS USED FOR MEDICINE | |
| --- | --- |
| **LICHEN SPECIES** | **AILMENT TREATED** |
| Lobaria pulmoneria | tuberculosis |
| Peltigera camina | rabies |
| Cladonia pyxidata | whooping cough |
| Usnea spp. | used as an antibiotic |

# Bryophytes

*Bryophytes are the simplest of all land-dwelling plants. Comprising 16,000 species, they are the second most diverse plant group after flowering plants. They are divided into three classes: liverworts (Hepaticae), hornworts (Anthocerotae) and mosses (Musci). Their centres of greatest diversity are the tropical rainforests of South America and Southeast Asia. In Peninsular Malaysia and Borneo, there are an estimated 1,800 species, with over 1,000 on Mount Kinabalu alone.*

The female reproductive organs of a species of *Marchantia*, a thallose liverwort. The yellow organs are the sporophyte capsules, which are already broken, and the spores released.

### Growth habits

Bryophytes are a group of small, green plants, mostly less than 2 centimetres long. On rare occasions they exceed 20 centimetres. While some are aquatic, none are found in the sea. They do not possess many of the complex structures, such as flowers, seeds, xylem and phloem tissue, seen in higher plants. Nor do they have true roots, but instead have root-like structures called rhizoids. These structures help to anchor the plant and absorb and retain water.

Most bryophytes are restricted to moist and sheltered areas, and are therefore not conspicuous in lowland forests except on the banks of forest streams. Above an altitude of 1500 metres, however, bryophytes form a significant part of the flora.

Bryophytes are found on all substrates in upper montane forest above 1500 metres, as in Gunung Berinchang in Cameron Highlands. Although this forest type is commonly known as mossy forest, the majority of the bryophytes that grow in it are in fact liverworts.

INSET: One of the many species of *Bazzania*, a leafy liverwort that is found in the upper montane forests of Malaysia's highlands.

Trunks and branches of trees in montane ericaceous forests are often smothered with a thick covering of bryophytes. The forest floor is also covered with bryophytes, the majority of them *Sphagnum* species.

The three classes of bryophytes—liverworts, hornworts and mosses—differ from each other in many ways. However, they share one important fundamental characteristic, which is their life cycle. It consists of an alternating gamete-producing generation (gametophyte) and a spore-producing generation (sporophyte).

### Liverworts (Hepaticae)

There are two main groups of liverworts: leafy and thallose. Leafy liverworts constitute the majority of liverworts. They bear leaf-like structures arranged horizontally on the substrate on which they grow. Oil bodies are found in these structures that are often only one cell thick. Thallose liverworts, on the other hand, consist of a thallus, which is a flattened tissue of several cells, with numerous scales and rhizoids on its underside. Their sporophytes disappear soon after the spores are dispersed. All liverworts possess a thickened filament—an elater—that twists and turns as it dries, and which helps in the dispersal of spores.

### Hornworts (Anthocerotae)

Hornworts can be identified by their narrow, elongated sporophyte that protrudes from the flat, green thallus tissue. Were it not for the upright sporophyte, hornworts would be hardly noticeable, since the rest of the plant is just a blue-green patch on wet soil and stream banks.

The thallus has chambers that harbour blue-green algae. The algae have a symbiotic relationship with the hornwort, whereby the algae fix nitrogen for the plant, and in return secure a suitable habitat. Unlike in other bryophytes, the sporophyte of a hornwort remains attached to the parent gametophyte throughout its life and will continue to grow as long as there are nutrients available.

### The life cycle of a bryophyte

In the life cycle of a bryophyte, a gametophyte, or gamete-producing generation, alternates with a sporophyte, or spore-producing generation. The gametophyte produces the sperm and egg, and is the dominant generation, whereas the sporophyte is dependent on the gametophyte for nutrients.

The sexual organs of the bryophytes are contained in small, hidden structures called gametangia. Sperm from the antheridium (1) fertilizes the egg in the female organ or archegonium (2). To do this, the sperm requires a film of water, which is why bryophytes only live in moist habitats. After fertilization, the fertilized egg, or zygote (3), in the archegonium undergoes repeated divisions to form the sporophyte (4), which now consists of a spore-containing capsule (5) and a stalk, or seta (6). Microscopic spores are produced by a process called meiosis, and are released by various mechanisms and dispersed by the wind (7). Those spores that fall on to a suitable substrate will germinate and develop into a mass of green filaments, or protonema (8). After some time, the filaments grow into leafy plants and the cycle repeats itself.

**Gamete-producing generation**

sperm — 1
antheridium
male gametophyte
egg — 2
archegonium
zygote — 3
developing sporophyte — 4
female gametophyte

**Spore-producing generation**

developing gametophore
capsule — 5
rhizoid
seta — 6
protonema — 8
mature sporophytes
spores germinate — 7
spores released

42

## Diversity in form, colour and habit in mosses

There are a wide variety of mosses. Some are delicate or hardy, whilst others are weedy. They can grow upright or creep along the substrate. Both terrestrial and epiphytic mosses are found.

1. A hardy moss, *Hypophila involuta* is commonly found along drains and on damp walls. On its rhizoids are produced numerous vegetative tubers, which are washed away and dispersed by running water. During a dry spell, the leaves roll in to conserve water.

2. *Dawsonia superba* is the tallest upright moss on Mount Kinabalu. Unlike other bryophytes, it has a relatively advanced vascular system. In addition, the leaves are modified to retain water and prevent drying.

3. A silver moss, *Bryum argentum* is widespread and often seen in crevices of buildings in the highlands.

4. *Lopidiun trichocladon* is a fan-shaped moss that grows on rocks and trees.

5. A creeping moss, the velvety *Macromitrium* sp. grows on exposed rock.

6. *Meteorium miquelianum* is an epiphytic moss that grows in the montane areas of Malaysia.

7. Along stream banks and on forest trails, *Campylopus umbellatus* is found. It is a weedy moss that grows between altitudes of 1300 and 2300 metres.

## Mosses (Musci)

Although mosses come in a wide variety of forms, they are basically symmetrical and possess stems and leaves. The stems are many-branched and the leaves have a midrib or costa. A primitive vascular system is found in some families, such as Polytrichaceae, which allows mosses to colonize areas uninhabitable to liverworts.

Mosses absorb water through their surface cells. Some hardy species can go without water for long periods without suffering any damage. They do this by lowering their metabolic rate during a dry spell, so that they survive in a dormant state. When the rains return, their metabolism returns to normal. In a hydrated condition, mosses contain many times their own weight and volume of water.

## Ecological and economic importance

Habitats that are hostile to most plant groups are habitable by bryophytes. Tree bark and rocks, for example, are readily colonized by bryophytes, algae and lichens, but not most other types of plants. By acting as pioneer species, bryophytes form the habitat for other plants as well as small animals. Some plants, such as *Corybas* orchids, rely on the presence of a bryophyte cover for their survival. The importance of these tiny plants in intercepting rainfall, and thereby preventing landslides and erosion, has been overlooked. It has only been given attention recently, when the detrimental effects of large-scale destruction of montane forests for tourist developments began to emerge. Because bryophytes grow in blankets, huge quantities of them are eliminated in one fell swoop when a patch of forest is razed.

As most of the bryophytes in Malaysia are found at high altitudes, they are not easily harvested and have not been much utilized by man. An exception is a species of *Leucobryum*, or *lumut putih*, which also occurs in the lowlands. Lumut putih forms a spongy mass when dry, and is traditionally used by the Malays as a pillow stuffing. Liverworts were used to treat ailments of the liver, although their effectiveness has now been disproved. Species of *Sphagnum* are best known for their use in horticulture as a medium for raising small seedlings, especially those of orchids. The extraordinary absorbency and antiseptic qualities of *Sphagnum* have also led to their use in the manufacture of nappies.

In a nursery, seedlings are often raised using a layer of *Sphagnum* moss as a substrate.

# Ferns and fern allies

*Malaysia is home to more than 650 species of ferns and fern allies, about 5.4 per cent of the world's population. Of these, just over 500 are found in Peninsular Malaysia alone. This richness in species can be attributed to an abundance of rainfall and sunshine, the presence of large areas of pristine forest, and the existence of varying vegetation zones. Ferns grow in a wide range of habitats, but are found in greatest diversity in Malaysia's lowland and montane forests.*

A grove of tree ferns, *Cyathea contaminans*, in an open patch of forest at Maxwell's Hill.

INSET: The lower surface of *Cyathea* leaflets showing the sporangia arranged in rows.

The fern ally *Lycopodium cernuum* growing among other weeds in an area with nutrient-poor soil.

The elephant fern is a common upright fern in Malaysia's lowland forests.

## What are ferns?

Ferns and their allies are collectively known as pteridophytes. As non-flowering plants, they do not produce fruits or seeds. Instead, they propagate by tiny, dust-like spores which are contained in sporangia or spore cases. In most ferns, these are grouped together on the lower surface of leaves, while in fern allies they are found in cone-like structures at the tips of branches or shoots. Fern leaves are also large and complex. The largest tree fern, *Cyathea contaminans*, has leaves as long as 4 metres or more. Some ferns, however, do have small leaves. The filmy fern *Trichomanes exigum*, for example, has leaves shorter than 1 centimetre. All fern allies have minute leaves, like the common nodding club moss *Lycopodium cernuum*, whose leaves are only 1.5 millimetres long. Most ferns are terrestrial or epiphytic, but there are a few that grow on the surface of water, and these are found in rice fields, fish ponds and swamps.

## Ferns in lowland forests

Lowland forest, like that in Endau-Rompin, is home to a very wide variety of ferns, such as upright, filmy, climbing, thicket-forming and epiphytic ferns.

The forest floor is the habitat for *Tectaria singaporeana*, an upright fern that has simple leaves. Another upright fern, the elephant fern or *Angiopteris evecta*, has leaves that depend entirely on turgor pressure to remain firm, and any water loss will immediately cause them to wilt.

Creepers abound on large rocks on the forest floor and by forest streams. Many of these are filmy ferns belonging to the family Hymenophyllaceae. These extremely delicate ferns have leaves that are translucent, only one cell thick, and whose entire leaf surface is capable of absorbing moisture from the air. A mere slight drying is sufficient for these sensitive leaves to curl up, unfolding later when conditions improve.

Climbing ferns grow upward with the help of creeping stems whose roots anchor them to the bark of trees. *Teratophyllum*, *Lomariopsis* and *Lomagramma* are high climbers. They start life on the forest floor, creeping along the ground until they make contact with the base of a tree. As the plants climb, the leaves become increasingly dissected, but turn into larger leaflets at a higher level, and only when the plant reaches the canopy will fertile leaves develop.

The upper branches of tall trees are where epiphytic ferns grow, each uniquely adapted for survival away from ground water. Species of *Pyrrosia*

## *Dipteris conjugata*: A primitive fern

This is a terrestrial fern with a stout rhizome located just under the surface of the ground. Its leaves are large and umbrella-like, and it grows in thickets in forest clearings and steep banks in mountainous areas. There is evidence from Mesozoic fossils that this fern has primitive ancestors. Today, it grows well on hills and mountains throughout Malaysia. For years botanists believed that its presence in Malaysia was confined to an altitudinal range of between 350 and 1700 metres. However, an expedition by the Malayan Nature Society into Endau State Park in 1985 brought back information that the fern grows luxuriantly at less than 50 metres above sea level on Pulau Jasin in the Jasin River area.

Fronds of *Dipteris conjugata*. This fern is sometimes seen growing in areas where the forest has been disturbed.

*Dipteris conjugata* in the wild. It is valued as a medicinal plant in Pahang.

store water in their fleshy leaves, which also have a layer of hairs to reduce moisture loss. Oak leaf fern (*Drynaria* spp.), bird's nest fern (*Asplenium nidus*) and stag's horn fern (*Platycerium coronarium*) develop leaf baskets to catch falling leaves from the host tree to keep as nutrient reserves.

In areas where the trees have been felled and the ground exposed to the full blast of the sun, only hardy thicket–forming ferns grow. *Resam* (*Dicranopteris linearis*) and bracken (*Pteridium aquilinum*) may form pure thickets that persist for years, if not decades, as no other plants are able to grow under their thick growth. Fires might eradicate a resam thicket, but not bracken because of its underground stems.

## Ferns in montane forests

With increasing altitude, lowland rainforest gives way to montane forest. With this comes changes in climatic factors—light intensity and humidity increase while temperature decreases. Under these conditions, upright, epiphytic and thicket-forming ferns are found growing more commonly and luxuriantly than their lowland counterparts.

A young frond of *Matonia pectinata*, a thicket-forming fern, found on mountains.

Tall, tree–like, upright ferns like species of *Cyathea* are prominent because of their long, columnar stem with a mass of large, dissected leaves at the top. They are also found in lowland forest, but flourish in the montane region.

Epiphytic species become more spectacular, covering the trunks and branches of the dwarfed trees. Species of *Hymenophyllum* and *Trichomanes* are very common in montane habitats, as found on Gunung Tahan and Mount Ophir. Small epiphytic ferns include species of *Belvisa*, *Selliguea* and members of the Grammitidaceae.

### *Azolla pinnata*: An aquatic fern
Few ferns are aquatic, but those that are play a useful role for man. The submerged leaves of *Azolla pinnata* contain *Anabaena*, a blue-green alga (inset) which traps atmospheric nitrogen and transforms it into nitrates. The increased nitrate level makes this fern useful as manure or fodder.

blue-green alga (*Anabaena*)

leaves of *Azolla pinnata*

### *Lecanopteris carnosa*: An ant-fern
*Lecanopteris carnosa* is an interesting epiphytic ant-fern (see 'Ant-plants'). It has a swollen rhizome, whose branches grow profusely and compactly. In this way, the entire surface of the host branch may be covered with the rhizomes, which are also hollow and inhabited by ants. The rhizomes provide the ants with shelter, and the fatty bodies around the sporangia are a source of food. In return, the ants bring minerals up from the ground, and the nitrogen given off by their excretions is absorbed by the fern. The ants also carry small seeds of other plants into the nest, which then germinate and grow. Old rhizome pieces turn black and fall onto the forest floor, where they look deceptively fungus-like. This fern grows in mountainous areas like Maxwell's Hill, Fraser's Hill, Cameron Highlands and Gunung Tahan.

sporangium

frond

rhizome inhabited by ants

The stem of *Lecanopteris carnosa* forming a crust over the trunk of a tree in Cameron Highlands.

Thicket-forming ferns, like *Matonia pectinata* and *Dipteris conjugata*, are frequently seen on isolated mountain peaks throughout Malaysia.

## Ecological and economic significance
Ferns have important functions in their natural habitat and the human domain. Thicket-forming ferns serve as an effective ground cover, preventing serious soil erosion of denuded land. Young leaves and shoots of *paku tanjong* (*Diplazium esculentum*) and *paku miding* (*Stenochlaena palustris*) are eaten as vegetables, and species of maidenhair (*Adiantum* spp.) and bird's nest ferns are popular ornamentals.

## Conservation
Malaysia's natural forests are being threatened by rapid urbanization, agricultural development and widespread logging. Ferns and fern allies are in desperate need of conservation. Their chances of survival have increased with the establishment of nature reserves and national parks like Taman Negara. These efforts are commendable, but may not be enough to save the endangered species if deforestation continues at the present rapid rate.

At Universiti Kebangsaan Malaysia, fern conservation started in 1988, when 9 hectares of the Bangi Forest Reserve were allocated for use as a fern garden. The garden is divided into three main sections—commercial, rare and endangered, and ornamental ferns. The endangered species collection consists of plants whose natural habitats are being destroyed by tourist developments, such as in Pulau Langkawi and Pulau Tioman. A new species, *Platycerium platylobium*, was discovered on Pulau Langkawi in 1986, and is now growing in the fern garden.

Collecting young leaves and shoots of *paku miding* for food. These ferns are found growing on mud flats in mangrove, freshwater and peatswamp forests.

Ferns are often used decoratively, like this bird's nest fern to the left.

# Cycads

*Millions of years ago, cycads ruled the plant kingdom. They are less prominent today, although they are distributed around the world. Together with conifers and maidenhair trees, cycads are classed as gymnosperms. Reminiscent of palms in their growth habit, Malaysian cycads, or* paku gajah *or* paku laut, *are small to medium-sized trees. Only three native and one introduced species are found in Malaysia, all belonging to the genus* Cycas.

Cycads belong to one of the oldest plant groups in the world, having come into existence about 180 million years before flowering plants, the most dominant flora today.

An old, much branched tree of *Cycas rumphii*, growing among sandy beach vegetation in Desaru, on the east coast of Johor.

## Cycad cones

A male cycad cone. Each tiny protrusion on the cone is a modified leaf, or microsporophyll, to which pollen sacs are attached.

A young female cone. Its megasporophylls bear the ovules, which are hidden from view but will emerge as they mature.

## Geological history and distribution

Cycads are a very ancient group of plants, which have been in existence since the early Permian period, about 280 million years ago. Around the time that dinosaurs and other reptiles began to appear on the earth, about 240 million years ago, cycads and conifers became the principal components of terrestrial vegetation. By the mid-Mesozoic era, 130 million years ago, cycads had become the most dominant floristic element on planet earth, giving rise to the term the 'Age of Cycads'. However, their reign ended some 100 million years ago when they were replaced by the New World flora, which has been dominated by flowering plants up to the present time.

Modern cycads comprise about 123 species in 11 genera, distributed in tropical and subtropical Africa, Asia, Australia, the western Pacific Islands and North, Central and South America. However, in Malaysia, only one genus, *Cycas*, with three native species is found.

## Characteristic features

Although the growth habit of Malaysian cycads resembles palms, cycads do not grow at the same rate. In fact, compared to the fast-growing palms, cycad growth is extremely sluggish. The erect cycad trunk, which consists of a mass of pith, is always covered with persistent leaf bases, with the pinnate leaves forming a crown at the apex of the trunk. It is thought that the number of leaf bases is a clue to the approximate age of an individual tree, and plants have been dated back hundreds of years.

The reproductive organs, called cones or strobili, are borne terminally in the centre of the leaf crown, with male and female parts on separate structures on different plants. Male cones, or microstrobili, consist of numerous spirally and compactly arranged microsporophylls (modified leaves), each with pollen sacs on the lower surface. At maturity, the male cones are orange and scented. The megasporophylls of the female cones are loosely assembled, with 4–6 pairs of ovules each, which develop into large, globular and drupe-like seeds.

## Life cycle

From the time it takes for the reproductive organs of a *Cycas* species to mature to the germination of the fertilized seed, well over two years would have passed. The actual time involved varies from species to species, with *C. rumphii* taking more than two years but *C. revoluta* less than a year.

This lengthy process begins with the male cones and the tips of their megasporophylls becoming visible. At this stage, the ovules on the female cones

### Starch from cycad seeds as food: A rare example

Cycad seeds are not used for food in most parts of Malaysia. One exception is in Padang Mulud on the east coast of southern Johor where they are a source of starch. In their raw state, the presence of neurotoxins and carcinogenic compounds render cycad seeds very poisonous. If ingested, the poisons cause a paralysis that starts in the limbs before moving to other parts of the body. However, the toxins are also highly water soluble and can be removed by soaking or boiling the seeds.

The local community in Padang Mulud harvest the seeds of the dense clumps of *Cycas rumphii* that grow along the sandy beaches. After the seeds are collected, they are cut in half and the kernel removed. Then comes the tedious process of detoxification. For three days, the kernels are left in the sun to dry. Once properly dried, they are boiled and then left to cool. This process of boiling and cooling is repeated several times to ensure that all the poisons are broken down and made harmless before the starch is extracted. From the starch, an edible paste is made.

Although cycads are generally thought of as a source of food that people turn to only during famine or war, it is likely that cycad starch is a part of the daily diet of people of the Padang Mulud area. Interestingly, there is no evidence to suggest that other parts of the cycad plant are eaten by this community, while in the rest of Malaysia young cycad leaves are consumed as a vegetable.

*Cycas rumphii* loaded with mature seeds that are ready to be harvested.

Because of its likeness to tree ferns (inset) or *paku*, and because it grows by the sea or *laut*, *Cycas rumphii* is called *paku laut*.

## Cycads in Malaysia

In Malaysia, there are three native species—*Cycas rumphii*, *C. macrocarpa* and *C. pectinata*—and a single introduced species, *C. revoluta*.

### C. rumphii

This species, known as *paku laut*, grows on the sandy shores and in the beach forests along the coast of Peninsular Malaysia, Sabah and Sarawak. It has thick and cylindrical stems, and in the wild grows up to a height of 7 metres. Old trees produce branches with huge pinnate leaves of 1–2 metres, with as many as 50 pairs of leaflets on either side of the rachis or main leaf stem. The leaflets are long and thin and measure about 25 centimetres, as do the cylindrical and ovoid male cones. Young and developing leaves are tightly coiled, very much like those of ferns. Introduced *C. rumphii* have also been brought into Malaysia and are grown as ornamentals.

### C. macrocarpa

In Peninsular Malaysia, this species is found in the lowland dipterocarp forests of Perak, Kelantan and Pahang, and especially in Malaysia's National Park, Taman Negara. *C. macrocarpa*, or *paku gajah*, is often confused with *C. rumphii*, except that the former has a thicker trunk that is sometimes devoid of persistent leaf bases. Its trunk is also darker in colour and seldom grows up to 7 metres. Its pinnate leaves are about 1 metre long, and 40 pairs of leaflets line both sides of the rachis. These leaflets are almost linear and are 20 centimetres in length.

### C. pectinata

The third Malaysian species is native to the limestone hills of the Langkawi Islands and Perlis. It has white, bulbous true stems, which are partly underground, and thus the tree often looks like a small, stemless rosette palm. However, in the Langkawi Islands the grey and curved stems of *C. pectinata* are also seen jutting out from crevices in the limestone into the sea. The pinnate leaves are often less than a metre long. Male cones are oblong, whereas female cones are compact, globose structures with short, spiny, feather-like megasporophylls, each bearing two ovules which develop into deep yellow seeds when mature.

### C. revoluta

A native of south China and Japan, this species was introduced into Peninsular Malaysia and Singapore in the 19th century, and is now widely cultivated in gardens in both countries. It is a small, palm-like tree whose stems are thick and covered with conspicuous leaf bases. The pinnate leaves are about 70 centimetres long, with short, thin leaflets 9 centimetres long.

A female *Cycas rumphii* plant laden with young seeds. The male plant (above) has characteristic bright orange cones peeping through the foliage.

*Cycas revoluta* originates from China and Japan, but is now grown as an ornamental in Malaysia and Singapore. It is the only introduced species of cycads that is cultivated in Malaysia.

The young seeds of *Cycas macrocarpa*, a species found in the lowland dipterocarp forests of Perak, Pahang and Kelantan. It is often mistaken for *Cycas rumphii*, as the two look similar.

are already well formed. After the male cones and megasporophylls mature, pollination takes place. Wind carries the light pollen grains from the male cones onto the female cones, where a pollen tube begins to grow. This is followed by the development of the female sex cells, or archegonia, and the male sex cells, or spermatogenous cells. Fertilization takes place when the sperm is fully formed inside the male sex cells. After fertilization, the embryo starts to gradually develop and mature. At some point in the embryo's maturation, the seed falls to the ground where it is dispersed by birds or rodents attracted to the bright orange or red outer seed coat. *Cycas* seeds take a long time to germinate, even after the embryo is matured. This is thought to be because the embryo's ability to function is developed only after its structural maturation is complete. When eventually germination occurs, it takes several weeks before the first leaf appears on the new seedling.

## Food and medicine

Various parts of the cycad tree are used in traditional Malay food and medicine. The young and tender uncurled leaves, for example, are eaten as a vegetable. Starch from the seeds is also consumed by a local community in southern Johor, but is not widespread in Malaysia.

Sores, ulcers, wounds and other skin abrasions are healed with a preparation made from cycad seeds, while the stems are used as a medicine in childbirth by the Malays of Perak and Pahang. In Sabah and Sarawak, the bark is made into a poultice that can be applied to external inflammations.

Young cycad leaves which are eaten as a vegetable. They have a strong, bitter taste.

47

# Conifers

*Conifers, or cone-bearing plants, are the dominant group among gymnosperms, or plants with naked seeds. Worldwide, they comprise 60 genera and 600 species of trees and shrubs, distributed mainly in the mountains and flat plains of cold, temperate regions. In the tropics, they are confined to forests of high altitude. In Malaysia, conifers are represented by species of three native and four introduced families. A few species are an important source of timber for the country, while introduced species are used mainly as ornamentals.*

Agathis trees and cones (inset) in a natural *Agathis* forest on sandy peat soil.

*Dacrydium comosum* is an endemic conifer species that grows in the upper montane forests of Peninsular Malaysia.

## Native conifers

In Malaysia, the three families of native conifers are Araucariaceae, Phyllocladaceae and Podocarpaceae.

The family Araucariaceae consists of one native genus, *Agathis*, with six species which are distributed throughout the country. Most species are lofty trees reaching up to 55 metres, with the exception of *A. kinabaluensis*, which grows as a stunted shrub between the altitudes of 1500 and 2400 metres. *Agathis* species grow as scattered trees in lowland and lower montane forests up to an altitude of about 1600 metres. In Sabah and Sarawak, however, *A. borneensis* sometimes forms dense clumps in forests growing on sandy peat soil.

*Agathis* species can be distinguished from other Malaysian conifers by their mottled, dark grey to brown bark, which peels off into irregular, round flakes that are often splashed with sticky white copal or resin. The leaves are flat and broad. They have no midrib, but are furnished with many fine veins. Seeds are borne singly on the upper surface of woody, scale-like structures, and aggregated into roundish, egg-shaped cones.

Phyllocladaceae comprises a single genus, *Phyllocladus*, which has 4–5 species. Only one species, *P. hypophyllus*, is found in Malaysia, in the lower and upper montane forests of Sabah and Sarawak. It grows up to a height of 30 metres between an altitude of 1000 and 2500 metres, becoming a shrub of only a few metres near mountain summits above 3500 metres. *Phyllocladus* differs from other conifers in that its branches and leaves are fused into a highly complex structure, known as the phylloclade. This functions both as a leaf and an organ that bears ovules or pollen cones.

The podocarps of the family Podocarpaceae consist of 13–17 genera with about 170 species distributed in the tropical, subtropical and temperate regions of the southern hemisphere. Malaysia is home to six genera with 30 species. Of these, two are endemic to Peninsular Malaysia, four to Sabah and two to Sarawak. The podocarps have fissured or scaly, grey-brown bark, and either flat and narrow leaves with a midrib or needle-shaped leaves. Solitary seeds are enclosed by a fleshy envelope (epimatium), and become drupe-like as they mature.

## Introduced species

Members of the families Araucariaceae, Cupressaceae, Pinaceae and Taxodiaceae have all been introduced to Malaysia, where they are planted largely as ornamentals.

Among the *Araucaria* species of the family Araucariaceae are the hoop pine (*A. cunninghamii*), the Norfolk Island pine (*A. excelsa*) and the Klinky pine (*A. hunsteinii*). The Cupressaceae is a temperate family comprising 17 genera with about 110 species. They differ from other conifers by their scale-like, needle-shaped leaves and woody cone scales with two or more free seeds, which are organized into woody, rounded seed cones.

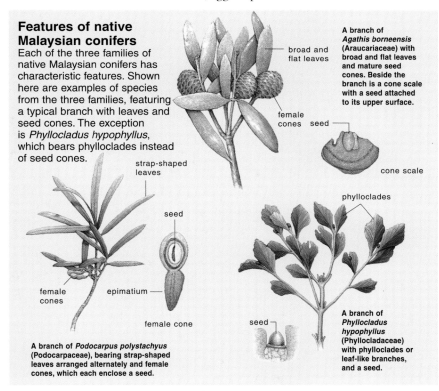

## Features of native Malaysian conifers

Each of the three families of native Malaysian conifers has characteristic features. Shown here are examples of species from the three families, featuring a typical branch with leaves and seed cones. The exception is *Phyllocladus hypophyllus*, which bears phylloclades instead of seed cones.

broad and flat leaves

female cones

seed

strap-shaped leaves

seed

female cones

epimatium

female cone

A branch of *Podocarpus polystachyus* (Podocarpaceae), bearing strap-shaped leaves arranged alternately and female cones, which each enclose a seed.

A branch of *Agathis borneensis* (Araucariaceae) with broad and flat leaves and mature seed cones. Beside the branch is a cone scale with a seed attached to its upper surface.

cone scale

phylloclades

seed

A branch of *Phyllocladus hypophyllus* (Phyllocladaceae) with phylloclades or leaf-like branches, and a seed.

Four species belonging to the Cupressaceae have been introduced: the Hinoki cypress (*Chamaecyparis obtusa*), the Monterey cypress (*Cupressus macrocarpa*), the Chinese juniper (*Juniperus chinensis*) and the Chinese arbor-vitae (*Thuja orientalis*).

The family Pinaceae has 9–12 genera with a total of 200 species, of which three are found in Malaysia. These pine trees, or *pokok pain*, are *Pinus caribea*, *P. kesiya* and *P. merkusii*. They are grown in plantations for their timber and oleoresin, besides being planted as ornamentals. Pine trees have long, needle-shaped 'leaves' which are grouped in bundles and spirally arranged on the branches. Each cone scale bears two winged seeds that are organized into woody, egg-shaped or conical seed cones.

In Malaysia, the family Taxodiaceae is known by a single introduced species, the Japanese cedar (*Cryptomeria japonica*). It is planted as an ornamental tree in hill stations, and can be distinguished from the closely related pine tree by its scale-like leaves and cone scales, each bearing 2–8 seeds.

## Conifer timber

Among the Malaysian conifers, the *Agathis* species are of significance as a source of valuable timber. The trade name for this timber is *damar minyak* or kauri pine, and it is classified as a lightweight softwood. The wood is excellent for joinery, boat building, panelling, moulding, packaging and foundry pattern making. It is also widely used for making matches, pencils, household utensils and furniture. Copal is another forest product that is harvested from damar minyak trees. This resin is obtained from the transluscent white exudate produced by the inner bark, and used as an important component in the manufacture of varnish and linoleum.

*Dacrycarpus imbricatus* (Podocarpaceae), known commercially as *cucur atap*, also reaches timber size. The timber is traded together with wood from three other podocarps—*Nageia*, *Podocarpus* and *Prumnopitys*—and is classified as lightweight to medium weight softwood. It is suitable for carving, panelling and light construction, and is used in the manufacture of furniture, tea chests, veneer and utensils.

The timber of *Dacrydium* species is traded as *sempilor* together with that of *Falcatifolium* and *Phyllocladus*, and is classified as a lightweight to medium weight softwood. Apart from its use in light construction, furniture making and joinery, it is made into mouldings, door and window frames, plywood and packing cases. Pulp and paper are also manufactured from sempilor.

## Introduced conifers

In Malaysia, there are 11 introduced species of conifers from 4 families. Planted mostly as ornamentals, they vary in shape and size from the short and round Chinese arbor-vitae to the tall and conical Chinese juniper. They originate from countries in Asia, with the exceptions of *Cupressus macrocarpa* and *Pinus caribea*.

Introduced conifers growing in a montane forest in Malaysia. The tree to the right is a pine and against the skyline is a species of *Araucaria*.

*Pinus caribea*, an introduced conifer species. Two brown young shoots are seen nestling amidst bunches of needle-shaped leaves.

| MALAYSIA'S INTRODUCED CONIFER SPECIES | | |
|---|---|---|
| SCIENTIFIC NAME | ENGLISH NAME | PLACE OF ORIGIN |
| *Araucaria cunninghamii* | Hoop pine | Papua New Guinea, Australia |
| *A. excelsa* | Norfolk Island pine | Papua New Guinea |
| *A. hunsteinii* | Klinky pine | Papua New Guinea |
| *Chamaecyparis obtusa* | Hinoki cypress | Japan, Taiwan |
| *Cupressus macrocarpa* | Monterey cypress | southern Mediterranean |
| *Juniperus chinensis* | Chinese juniper | China, Japan, Mongolia |
| *Thuja orientalis* | Chinese arbor-vitae | China |
| *Pinus caribea* | Caribbean pine | Central America, Cuba, the Bahamas |
| *P. kesiya* | Khasya pine | eastern India, Myanmar, Laos, the Philippines |
| *P. merkusii* | Merkus pine | eastern Myanmar, Indo-China, southern China, northern Thailand, the Philippines, and northern parts of Sumatra |
| *Cryptomeria japonica* | Japanese cedar | Japan |

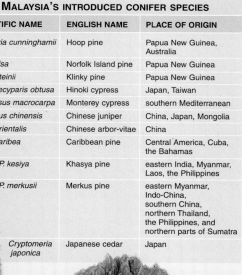

*Juniperus chinensis*, also known as the Chinese juniper, is a popular ornamental in Malaysia.

*Thuja orientalis*, or the Chinese arbor-vitae, is a commonly cultivated exotic conifer in Malaysia.

# Gnetum

*Gnetum is a tropical genus consisting mostly of woody climbers, with a few trees and shrubs. This genus is classified as a unique plant group and placed in its own family, the Gnetaceae, or gnetoid family. There are about 30 species in the tropical lowlands of the world, from northeastern South America, tropical West Africa, south China to Southeast Asia. In Malaysia, 15 species are found in rainforests below 1800 metres. The most well known is* belinjau *or* melinjau (G. gnemon *var.* gnemon), *which is the only tree species of this genus in the country.*

*Gnetum macrostachyum*, a common species in Malaysian forests. All but one species of *Gnetum* found in Malaysia are climbers, the exception being *G. gnemon*, a tree.

### The plant body

Most *Gnetum* species have stems that grow asymmetrically and which are covered by smooth bark. The asymmetry in stem growth is due to their unusual development. In most plants, growth in stem thickness occurs when a ring of cambial tissue divides to produce xylem inwards and phloem outwards. The division continues until a somewhat circular trunk is formed. In *Gnetum* species, however, vascular cambia occur one outside the other, and hence the xylem and phloem develop in alternating layers. Often the growth is lopsided, resulting in a flat or bent cross section. The alternating zones of the strong xylem tissue and the weak phloem tissue make the stem flexible. This is not a problem to *Gnetum* species because, as climbers, they do not need to stand erect. As for the tree *G. gnemon*, it does not grow to a great height.

The plants are unisexual, each bearing either male or female cones—the reproductive structures. The cones are borne in the axils of the leaves, and may be branched or otherwise. Along the stem, leaves develop in opposite pairs. The leaf blades are oval and

In Malaysia, *belinjau* trees are grown along the wayside and cultivated on a small scale in villages, especially in Terengganu.

### *Belinjau* trees: The most useful *Gnetum* species in Malaysia

*Belinjau* trees are cultivated in mixed-fruit gardens for their seeds. Cultivated trees are apomictic, that is, their ovules are able to produce seeds without first having to be fertilized. The seeds may be steamed, fried, roasted or eaten raw. Starch from the seeds is ground into flour that is used to make a dough cake, from which belinjau crisps are made. The dough is first cut into slivers before being laid out in the sun to dry. Once they are dried and hardened, the slices are deep fried into crisps. Malaysians eat the crisps as a snack, and also use crisps to garnish *gado gado*, which is a salad of boiled vegetables, potatoes and tofu with a peanut sauce.

Apart from being made into crisps, belinjau trees also have other food and medicinal uses. The leaves, young shoots and cones are eaten as vegetables and used in soups. Unfortunately, the presence of elongated, thick-walled cells in the raw leaves causes a slight itching in the mouth. Boiling the leaves is a way to avoid this. A paste made from the leaves is applied to snake bites. The root is used as a general antidote for poison.

Timber from belinjau trees is used for the construction of pillars for huts, mooring posts and outriggers of canoes. The wood is also collected for firewood. Split branches are used to repair containers, such as barrels and casks. Fibre from the bark can be made into fishing lines and nets, and used in paper manufacture. The inner bark of some *Gnetum* species is so fibrous that it can be used to make thread, string and cordage. Because of the attractive, cylindrical crown, belinjau trees are also planted as roadside trees.

1. *Belinjau* seeds, from which crisps are made, on sale in a market. The crisps are made from the starch extracted from the seeds.

2. The crisps are eaten on their own or with *gado gado*, a Malay salad.

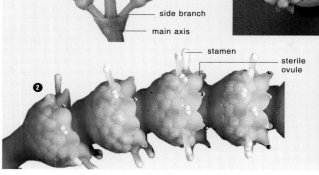

mature seed

collar

side branch

main axis

stamen

sterile ovule

### Parts of a *Gnetum* cone

1. A *Gnetum gnemon* male cone showing the main axis, side branches and collars.

2. A portion of a male cone of *Gnetum gnemon* with stamens and sterile ovules.

3. A female *Gnetum gnemon* cone bearing mature seeds and rings of ovules.

4. Seeds of *Gnetum gnemon* showing the cream-coloured starchy interior, and the dark brown and fleshy seed coat layers. This interior is the edible part.

5. Seeds on two cones of *Gnetum macrostachyum*. The seeds are a shiny pink, and embedded in a clump of thick hairs.

have net-like veins. They are characterized by bearded edges when torn, which are the result of elongated, thick-walled cells in the leaf tissue. *Gnetum* stems are also characterized by the swellings at the joints from which the leaves arise.

## Reproductive biology

Seed dispersal is by birds and monkeys, which are attracted to the brightly coloured outer fleshy rind of the seed. The fleshy rind is eaten, while the seed remains protected by a hard inner coat. Once dispersed and in a new location, the seed takes many months to germinate as the embryo slowly develops into a new plant.

Pyralid or geometrid moths visit *Gnetum* cones in the evening and night. Both male and female cones attract the moths by a strong odour secreted from the ovules and stamens. When the moths sip the nectar, they get covered with the pollen grains discharged by the stamens. The pollen grains are then transferred to the ovules when the same moths visit the female cones. During the night, the pollen grains float in the drop of nectar at the tip of the ovule. At sunrise, the fluid evaporates, shrinking the drop of nectar and pollen grains so they can move down the tiny canal inside the tip of the ovule.

Once inside the ovule, the pollen grains germinate. Each grain develops a tube which brings the male sex cells to the female sex cells. Fertilization takes place and, as a result, zygotes are produced. These in turn develop into embryos that are carried in the seeds. Only a few ovules per cone actually become fertilized and mature into seeds. The interior of the seeds is largely made up of a cream-coloured starchy tissue which provides nourishment for the growing embryo. Around the central starchy zone are a hard, dark brown inner seed coat and a fleshy, outermost rind.

## The missing link between gymnosperms and angiosperms

As a member of the gymnosperms, *Gnetum* possesses naked ovules and seeds arranged in cone-like structures. However, they share a number of characteristics with flowering plants (angiosperms), and were thought to be the link between the two plant groups. Although intensive studies have shown that the similarities are the result of convergent evolution, a process by which a similar characteristic evolves independently in unrelated plant groups, the 'missing link' theory was influential for a long time.

Certain features in the stems, leaves and cones of *Gnetum* resemble those of angiosperms. For example, present in the stems of *Gnetum* and most angiosperms are vessels, or pores, in the wood, which are not found in most other gymnosperms. Another angiosperm feature is the presence of phloem tissue which contains companion cells and cells specialized in transporting photosynthetic products from the leaves to other parts of the plant. The stem apex of *Gnetum* also has the same microscopic structure as that found in that of angiosperms. Like angiosperms, *Gnetum* leaves have a broad blade and a net-like pattern of veins, while most gymnosperm leaves are narrow with parallel veins.

The typical bearded edge of a torn *Gnetum* leaf blade is due to the numerous elongated and thick-walled cells in the leaf.

| *GNETUM* SPECIES AND VARIETIES FOUND IN MALAYSIA | | | |
|---|---|---|---|
| **SPECIES/VARIETY** | **HABIT** | **HABITAT** | **DISTRIBUTION** |
| G. acutum | large liana | lowland forest | Sarawak |
| G. cuspidatum | liana | lowland and montane forests up to 1600 metres | widespread throughout Malaysia |
| G. diminutum | liana | lowland and montane forests up to 1800 metres | Sarawak |
| G. globosum | liana | lowland forest | known only from type collected in Taman Negara |
| G. gnemon var. gnemon | tree of about 22 metres tall | rocky coasts and islands | east coast of Peninsular Malaysia |
| G. gnemonoides | liana | lowland forest | Peninsular Malaysia |
| G. klossii | liana | lowland and montane forests | Sabah |
| G. latifolium var. funiculare | large liana | lowland forest | Peninsular Malaysia |
| G. latifolium var. latifolium | large liana | hill forest | Pahang and Perak |
| G. leptostachyum | large liana | hill and montane forests up to 1500 metres | Sabah |
| G. macrostachyum | liana | lowland forest | Peninsular Malaysia |
| G. microcarpum | slender liana | lowland and hill forests | Peninsular Malaysia |
| G. neglectum | slender liana | lowland swamp forest | Sabah |
| G. raya | large liana | lowland forest below 500 metres | Sarawak |
| G. ridleyi | large liana | forest | endemic to Telom, Pahang |
| G. tenuifolium | slender liana | lowland forest | Peninsular Malaysia |

# Trees and shrubs

*Trees are plant species that have a thick, columnar woody stem, or trunk, from which branches grow. The presence of a trunk is what differentiates trees from shrubs, which are plants with no distinct trunk but with woody stems branching near the ground. In Malaysia's rainforests, trees make up most of the canopy and main storey layer, while shrubs dominate the shrub layer. The uses of trees are varied, from being wayside plants to a source of timber, food and medicine. Shrubs are popularly grown as ornamentals, especially those that flower abundantly and those with coloured leaves.*

## Tree crowns

The shape of a tree is determined by the shape of its crown. For example, a round and bushy crown is characteristic of this species of *Plumeria* (1), while a conical crown is a recognizable feature of the conifer *Araucaria cunninghamii* (2). The well-known *angsana* (*Pterocarpus indicus*) (3) has a weeping, drooping crown; an umbrella-shaped or flat-topped crown can be seen in the flame of the forest (*Delonix regia*) (4).

❶

❷

❸

❹

## Rulers of the rainforest

Of all the plant life forms found in a rainforest, trees are the most dominant. They make up the bulk of a forest's biomass and account for the highest number of species of flowering plants. The tallest species of tree in Malaysia is the *tualang* (*Koompassia excelsa*), which grows to a record 81 metres. On average, however, a forest tree grows to about 52 metres. In swamp forests, trees are smaller, standing at roughly 37 metres. Above the 1200-metre mark, trees are rarely more than 24 metres in height. Tall trees, that is, those above 60 metres, are scattered in lowland forests, mostly in sheltered valleys and long foothills.

Many forest trees have prominent buttresses—perpendicular flanges which develop over the main lateral roots and extend for some distance up the trunk. The presence, or absence, of buttresses and their shape, which may be steep or low and spreading, branched or unbranched, are characteristic features of tree species. Another feature that helps to identify a species of tree is the bark. Trees have bark that varies in colour from coal black to bright, reddish brown to greyish white. The bark surface may be smooth, scaly, fissured, scrolled or dippled. For a number of families, the bark may

The huge buttresses of this tree are twice the height of an adult human.

contain exudates. Latex, for example, is found in Apocynaceae and Sapotaceae, sap in Myristicaceae and resin in Burseraceae and Dipterocarpaceae.

In Malaysia, plants grow throughout the year, and the vegetation, on the whole, is evergreen. Trees may be ever-flowering or flower intermittently for short periods. Fruiting follows flowering, and the shape and structure of the fruits is a characteristic of most trees. For example, single-cavity pods with one row of seeds are characteristic of members of the tree family Leguminosae, whilst winged nuts are a feature of dipterocarp trees.

## Shrubs

Relatively small compared to trees, shrubs range in height from 50 centimetres to 5 metres and comprise several types of shrubs. Evergreen shrubs with large, broad leaves are known as hygromorphic shrubs, and are the shade plants of wet, tropical forests. Xeromorphic shrubs, on the other hand, produce short, linear leaves with margins that roll in, as in members of the heath, or rhododendron, family (Ericaceae). Species of the conifer *Dacrydium* are another example of xeromorphic shrubs, with leaves that are small, closely overlapping, short and needle-like.

Depending on their growth and flowering habit, shrubs are grown as ornamentals. Free-flowering shrubs, such as the Straits rhododendron, or *Melastoma malabathricum* (Melastomataceae), and *Calliandra emarginata* (Mimosaceae), are favourites. The former shrub grows up to 3 metres, produces large pink flowers and has stems that are covered with small, rough scales. *Melastoma*, which means 'black mouth', refers to the tiny, purplish black seeds found in the oval fruit that, if eaten, stain the tongue. *Calliandra emarginata* is originally from North America, but is now widely planted in Malaysia. The spherical flowers look like powder puffs, with their long, fine, red and bushy stamens.

## The trunk: The backbone of a tree

Comprising several concentric layers, a tree trunk is a tree's main support structure. The outer protective layer is the bark (1). It guards against changes in temperature and humidity and damage brought about by animals and man. The phloem (2) is a thin layer of tissue that transports sap from the leaves to other parts of the plant. Sandwiched between the phloem on the outside, and xylem on the inside, the one-cell thick cambium (3) is solely responsible for the growth in diameter of the tree trunk, continuously producing new cells to add to the tissue on either side. Encircled by the cambium is newly formed wood called sapwood (4), which comprises vessels that transport water and mineral nutrients from the roots to the leaves. Heartwood (5) is dead wood, and occurs nearest to the centre of the trunk. Apart from providing support, it is also a receptacle for the tree's waste products, such as deposits of resin, oil, starch and tannin. In the centre of the trunk is the pith (6). This part of the trunk is present only in the tree's first year of growth, shrinking or disappearing altogether as the tree matures.

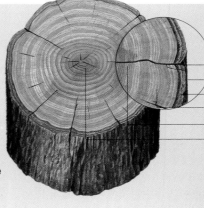

An area dense with trees in Kuak Forest Reserve in Perak. The total number of tree species in Peninsular Malaysia is 2,830, distributed among 532 genera in 106 families. Of all the tree species, 746 or 26.4 per cent are endemic and over 500 are endangered.

## Trees in Peninsular Malaysia

Peninsular Malaysia is abundant in tree species, which are found dominating habitats as varied as mangroves, peatswamps, lowland and hill dipterocarp forests and montane forests. Each of these habitats is home to trees that are characteristic of the vegetation. For example, species of *Sonneratia* and *Rhizophora* are distinctive in mangroves, while members of the oak and laurel families predominate in montane forests.

Besides growing in the wild, trees are also cultivated extensively in plantations, such as rubber and fruit trees, and in parks, gardens and along roadsides. Some places in Peninsular Malaysia are identified with certain trees. The Lake Gardens in Taiping, for example, is known for its grand avenue of rain trees that line the main road through the park;

and in the Residency Grounds of Penang stands the largest *angsana* tree in Malaysia.

Timber is the most important product obtained from trees (see 'Timber'). The Dipterocarpaceae and Leguminosae are the two most important timber-producing families in Malaysia, followed by the Myrtaceae, Meliaceae and Guttiferae. Other tree products and crops include fruits and nuts, spices, essential oils and medicines.

### DISTRIBUTION OF TREE SPECIES ENDEMIC TO EACH STATE IN PENINSULAR MALAYSIA

| | STATE | LAND AREA (km²) | NO. OF ENDEMIC SPECIES |
|---|---|---|---|
| 1. | Perlis | 695 | 2 |
| 2. | Kedah | 9425 | 13 |
| 3. | Pulau Pinang | 1033 | 13 |
| 4. | Perak | 21 005 | 103 |
| 5. | Kelantan | 14 921 | 9 |
| 6. | Terengganu | 12 955 | 18 |
| 7. | Pahang | 35 965 | 76 |
| 8. | Selangor | 8200 | 21 |
| 9. | Negeri Sembilan | 6643 | 0 |
| 10. | Melaka | 1650 | 7 |
| 11. | Johor | 18 985 | 39 |

Source: After Kiew (1991)

### THE TEN FAMILIES WITH THE MOST TREE SPECIES IN PENINSULAR MALAYSIA

| FAMILY | TREE SPECIES | TREE GENERA | ENDANGERED TREE SPECIES | EXAMPLES |
|---|---|---|---|---|
| Euphor-biaceae | 286 | 57 | 60 | *Baccaurea* and *Endospermum* spp. |
| Rubiaceae | 222 | 49 | 51 | *Morinda, Anthocephalus* and *Gardenia* spp. |
| Myrtaceae | 204 | 9 | 43 | *Eugenia, Melaleuca* and *Tristania* spp. |
| Lauraceae | 197 | 15 | 43 | *Cinnamomum* and *Litsea* spp. |
| Dipterocar-paceae | 155 | 9 | 9 | *Shorea, Hopea* and *Dipterocarpus* spp. |
| Guttiferae | 120 | 4 | 17 | *Garcinia, Calophyllum* and *Mesua* spp. |
| Annonaceae | 110 | 25 | 36 | *Polyalthia, Annona* and *Cananga* spp. |
| Leguminosae | 103 | 27 | 24 | *Koompassia, Pterocarpus* and *Sindora* spp. |
| Meliaceae | 89 | 14 | 1 | *Lansium, Azadirachta* and *Aglaia* spp. |
| Moraceae | 79 | 7 | 3 | *Artocarpus* and *Ficus* spp. |

Source: After Kiew (1991)

Perhaps the most widely grown shrub in Malaysia is the *Hibiscus*. Comprising numerous species and varieties, including *H. rosa-sinensis*, the National Flower, the plants can be grown either in pots or as a hedge. When planted in pots, however, shrub growth is restricted and plants reach a relatively small size. Flowers range in colour from a pristine white to bright yellow to deep red, and can grow up to 20–30 centimetres in diameter, although tiny flowers are found on certain species. While the flowers last for only a day, flowering is so abundant that there are almost always some blooms on a plant at any given time.

Another popular shrub in Malaysia is the *Ixora*. The species *I. javanica* is the most common, easily recognizable by its rich red-orange flowers. It is cultivated as a bush or as a hedge. Grown for its profuse, tiny flowers that come in clusters of white, orange and red, *Ixora* is seen along roadsides and in gardens across the country.

### Shrubs commonly grown as ornamentals

*Dillenia suffruticosa*, or *simpoh*, is a common shrub in damp and open places in the lowlands.

The red vibrant flowers of *Hibiscus rosa-sinensis*, the National Flower.

An *Ixora javanica* bush with its characteristic clusters of red flowers.

*Senna tora* or *gelenggang* is a common shrub in open and swampy places in the lowlands. The flowers are borne on candle-like clusters above the foliage.

# Palms

*Palms grow widely in Malaysia. Of the six palm subfamilies, four are represented. Malaysia's indigenous palm flora comprises 398 species in 33 genera, although the total number of species is probably in excess of 420. In comparison, the tropical Americas, with an area 12 and a half times the size of Malaysia, have about 550 species in 66 genera. Palms grow in a variety of habitats, but are most diverse in lowland forest. They are used traditionally as food, medicine and as weaving and building materials.*

Coconuts (*Cocos nucifera*) are a highly versatile palm fruit, and may be eaten fresh, cooked or desiccated. The juice, or 'milk', is a main ingredient in curry.

An inflorescence of *Areca tunku*, a recently described species, whose name honours the late Tunku Abdul Rahman for his major contribution to conservation in Malaysia.

## Diversity and distribution

Malaysia has a particularly diverse palm flora. Peninsular Malaysia has about 210 species of palms, while Sabah and Sarawak have 300. Of these, 96 species are endemic and restricted in distribution to Peninsular Malaysia, 14 to Sabah and 70 to Sarawak.

Many species of palms are distributed over and tolerant of a wide variety of habitats, while others have more specific requirements. However, certain habitats, such as valley bottoms, are especially rich in palms. The rattan *Calamus convallium*, in Sabah and Sarawak, for example, is only common in moist valleys and generally is absent on ridges. However, in some other instances, particularly in hill forests, some species of *Calamus*, *Daemonorops*, *Licuala* and *Pinanga* are noticeably more abundant on ridges and absent in valleys. Recent studies have shown that soil types strongly influence palm distribution patterns. In the relatively uniform topography of the Pasoh Forest Reserve, for example, *Licuala* species are strongly demarcated by the different soils found in the reserve.

Some palm species display a remarkable disjunct distribution, and it is impossible to understand the reason for such patterns. *Livistonia endauensis*, for example, is known from the Endau State Park in northern Johor and southern Pahang, where it grows very abundantly and gregariously on ridges and in the hill dipterocarp forest just behind the heath forest. It is now known that this species has another disjunct population on the coastal hills of Dungun in Terengganu, in very similar habitats. In between these two areas, *L. endauensis* is not found. Similarly, the rare *Borassodendron machadonis* is very common only on the west slope of Gunung Jerai in Kedah and absent elsewhere, but appears again in specific localities in Perak, Kelantan and parts of southern Thailand.

## Palm habits

A few of Malaysia's palms are tall trees, forming very distinctive elements of the forest canopy. In the lower montane forests of Peninsular Malaysia, as on the slopes and ridges of the Main Range, *Caryota maxima*, the giant fishtail palm, is prevalent. Other distinctive arborescent palms are found in the genera *Arenga*, *Borassodendron*, *Eugeissona*, *Livistona*, *Oncosperma*, *Orania* and *Pholidocarpus*.

In the forests, the understorey palms are the most diverse and two growth habits predominate. Stems are either erect and freestanding or flexible, as in climbing rattans (see 'Rattans'). In both instances, the stems can be either solitary or clustering. Freestanding palms often appear to be stemless. The stems are either very short and covered by overwrapping leaves, or are hidden underground. In rattans, climbing is affected by the production of backward–

### Mangrove swamp
1. and 2. A colony of *Nypa fruticans* and *Phoenix paludosa*. Communities of *P. paludosa* are sometimes found in the brackish inland margins of the mangrove forest, otherwise dominated by *N. fruticans*.

3. *Oncosperma tigillarium* commonly occurs on the landward side of coastal areas.

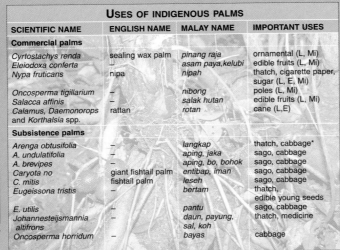

Palm leaves commonly used as thatch include nipa (*Nypa fruticans*) and *bertam* (*Eugeissona tristis*).

| USES OF INDIGENOUS PALMS | | | |
|---|---|---|---|
| **SCIENTIFIC NAME** | **ENGLISH NAME** | **MALAY NAME** | **IMPORTANT USES** |
| **Commercial palms** | | | |
| *Cyrtostachys renda* | sealing wax palm | pinang raja | ornamental (L, Mi) |
| *Eleiodoxa conferta* | – | asam paya, kelubi | edible fruits (L, Mi) |
| *Nypa fruticans* | nipa | nipah | thatch, cigarette paper, sugar (L, E, Mi) |
| *Oncosperma tigillarium* | – | nibong | poles (L, Mi) |
| *Salacca affinis* | – | salak hutan | edible fruits (L, Mi) |
| *Calamus*, *Daemonorops* and *Korthalsia* spp. | rattan | rotan | cane (L, E) |
| **Subsistence palms** | | | |
| *Arenga obtusifolia* | – | langkap | thatch, cabbage* |
| *A. undulatifolia* | – | aping, jaka | sago, cabbage |
| *A. brevipes* | – | aping, bo, bohok | sago, cabbage |
| *Caryota no* | giant fishtail palm | entibap, iman | sago, cabbage |
| *C. mitis* | fishtail palm | leseh | sago, cabbage |
| *Eugeissona tristis* | | bertam | thatch, edible young seeds |
| *E. utilis* | – | pantu | sago, cabbage |
| *Johannesteijsmannia altifrons* | – | daun, payung, sal, koh | thatch, medicine |
| *Oncosperma horridum* | – | bayas | cabbage |

Abbrev.: L—of local commercial importance   E—exported   Mi—of minor commercial importance
* Palm 'cabbage' refers to the young, apical shoot of the palm, also known as palm heart.

pointing spines. These spines are produced at the end of leaf fronds called cirri. In some rattan species, the climbing apparatus comprises sterile inflorescences, or flagella, produced from the stems. The cirri and flagella are like grapples which hook onto other plants. They hold the stem upright and allow it to grow into the forest canopy.

## The many roles of palms

Palms play important commercial and domestic roles in Malaysia. Although coconuts, rattans and the introduced African oil palm are the only palms of economic significance, native palms are common in the daily life of villagers.

Palms are a source of building materials, food and medicine, and are used for weaving and in cultural ceremonies. Traditionally, palm leaves have also been used for thatch. For example, nipa (*Nypa fruticans*) thatch, or *atap*, is made from the leaflets of mature leaves. *Nibong* (*Oncosperma tigillarium*) trunks, which are resistant to saltwater and marine borers, are used to build *kelong*—large, stake fish traps erected in estuaries. The cut stalk of the nipa inflorescence is tapped for its sap, which may be boiled to produce sugar, or fermented into either toddy or vinegar and distilled to produce alcohol. The heart of *bayas* (*Oncosperma horridum*), eaten by the Orang Asli, is also offered as a gift to important people by the Semai in Perak. Sago, obtained chiefly from *Eugeissona utilis*, is the staple food of the nomadic Penan people in Sarawak. Palms are also used by the Penan for making blowpipe darts, baskets, cordage, thatch and mats.

## Conservation

The most serious threat to the palm flora of Malaysia is the large-scale clearance of forest land for agriculture. Species with a very narrow distribution can become extinct once their habitat is destroyed. Although no palm species has yet been rated extinct in Malaysia, a recent exercise has classified 20 species as endangered in Peninsular Malaysia, 3 in

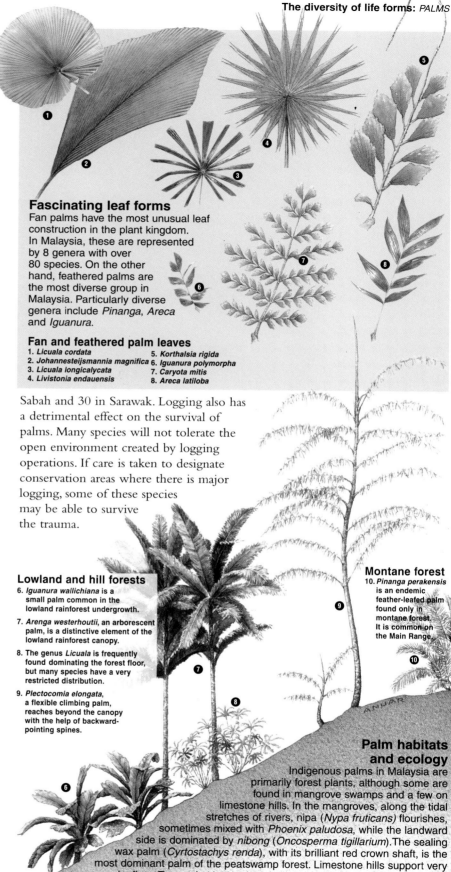

### Fascinating leaf forms

Fan palms have the most unusual leaf construction in the plant kingdom. In Malaysia, these are represented by 8 genera with over 80 species. On the other hand, feathered palms are the most diverse group in Malaysia. Particularly diverse genera include *Pinanga*, *Areca* and *Iguanura*.

#### Fan and feathered palm leaves
1. *Licuala cordata*
2. *Johannesteijsmannia magnifica*
3. *Licuala longicalycata*
4. *Livistonia endauensis*
5. *Korthalsia rigida*
6. *Iguanura polymorpha*
7. *Caryota mitis*
8. *Areca latiloba*

Sabah and 30 in Sarawak. Logging also has a detrimental effect on the survival of palms. Many species will not tolerate the open environment created by logging operations. If care is taken to designate conservation areas where there is major logging, some of these species may be able to survive the trauma.

### Lowland and hill forests
6. *Iguanura wallichiana* is a small palm common in the lowland rainforest undergrowth.

7. *Arenga westerhoutii*, an arborescent palm, is a distinctive element of the lowland rainforest canopy.

8. The genus *Licuala* is frequently found dominating the forest floor, but many species have a very restricted distribution.

9. *Plectocomia elongata*, a flexible climbing palm, reaches beyond the canopy with the help of backward-pointing spines.

### Montane forest
10. *Pinanga perakensis* is an endemic feather-leafed palm found only in montane forest. It is common on the Main Range.

### Peatswamp forest
4. *Cyrtostachys renda*, is the dominant palm of the undisturbed peatswamp forests of Perak, Selangor, Johor and Sarawak.

### Limestone hill
5. *Maxburretia rupicola*, a palm species that inhabits limestone hills. It is confined to Bukit Takun and the Batu Caves in Selangor.

### Palm habitats and ecology

Indigenous palms in Malaysia are primarily forest plants, although some are found in mangrove swamps and a few on limestone hills. In the mangroves, along the tidal stretches of rivers, nipa (*Nypa fruticans*) flourishes, sometimes mixed with *Phoenix paludosa*, while the landward side is dominated by *nibong* (*Oncosperma tigillarium*). The sealing wax palm (*Cyrtostachys renda*), with its brilliant red crown shaft, is the most dominant palm of the peatswamp forest. Limestone hills support very poor palm flora. Two endemic species predominate in this particular habitat— *Maxburretia rupicola* in Selangor and *M. gracilis* in Langkawi. Palm flora reaches its greatest diversity in the lowland and hill forests up to 1000 metres above sea level, where it dominates the understorey. For example, many rattan species, with their very noticeable spines, are a common feature of the lowland forests. At the 1000-metre mark, there is usually a conspicuous change in palm flora. A number of palm species begin to appear that are not seen in lowland forest, while the lowland species reach the limit of their range.

# Bamboos

*Bamboos form a distinct subfamily of the grasses and comprise an estimated 1,200–1,500 species worldwide. In Malaysia, 80 species, including native and introduced bamboos, are found. They are instantly recognizable and yet diverse in structure and behaviour. Used both as a raw material and an ornamental, bamboos are also important in the ecology of natural and modified landscapes. They have long been associated with a traditional and rural Malaysian lifestyle, but are gaining popularity in modern industries, such as furniture making.*

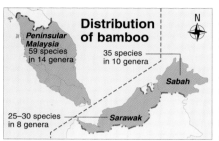

**Distribution of bamboo**

Peninsular Malaysia
59 species in 14 genera

35 species in 10 genera

Sabah

25–30 species in 8 genera

Sarawak

## Growth and flowering habit

Bamboos have interesting growth habits, ranging from the diminutive *Bambusa multiplex* var. *riviereorum*, just 30 centimetres high and cultivated in small pots, to towering, large-stemmed *Dendrocalamus giganteus* clumps that reach 30 metres in height. A number of species assume less erect growth habits through flexible culms, or stems, and branches that entangle with the surrounding vegetation, such as the *buluh akar* (*D. hirtellus*) and *buluh kapur* (*D. pendulus*) of Peninsular Malaysia, and the largely montane, small-stemmed *Racemobambos* species of Sabah and Sarawak. Species of the genus *Dinochloa* even twine around tree trunks and have been known to distort and smother young trees.

Vegetative growth in some species, such as *Dendrocalamus hirtellus*, *Gigantochloa scortechinii* and *Schizostachyum grande*, can be rapidly invasive, developing into

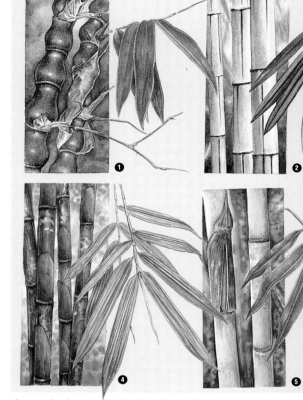

dense thickets in badly disturbed forest sites and open areas, which often prevent or retard the recovery of the original forest.

Flowering is mostly gregarious (involving most or all the clumps in a large area) and occurs at long intervals, after which the clumps die or regenerate from remaining rhizomes. Species such as *Dendrocalamus pendulus*, *Gigantochloa scortechinii* and *Schizostachyum zollingeri* display this flowering habit. These species, and others, can also flower in a diffuse and sporadic manner. Exceptions are species of *Schizostachyum*, which flower continuously once their clumps reach maturity.

### Bamboos and animal life

As they grow, bamboos harbour animals. Simple animal communities, comprising frogs, insects and spiders, utilize the internodal spaces and water that collects in the culms, where dissolved nutrients promote the growth of bacteria and protozoa that are food for larvae. Some of these insects have evolved interesting habits, such as the water strider (**1**) which defends its territory by wrestling intruding males underwater, and *Tetraponera* ants (**2**) that bail out water that has accumulated in the internodes by drinking their gasters (an enlarged part of the abdomen) full, and then egesting the water droplets from tiny holes in the culm.

In Peninsular Malaysia, flat-headed *Tylonycteris* bats (**3**) are small enough to move through slits just half a centimetre wide in segments in the culm where they roost. Most rodents associated with bamboo are known to gnaw their way into hollow culms. The large bamboo rat (*Rhizomys sumatrensis*) (**4**), however, prefers to burrow beneath the bamboo clumps for refuge, feeding on the roots.

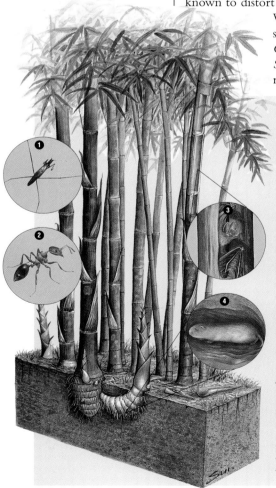

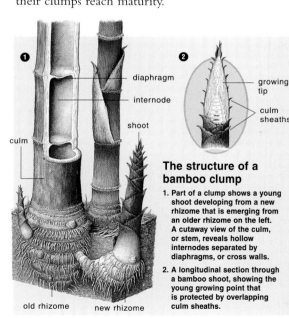

## The structure of a bamboo clump

diaphragm

internode

shoot

culm

growing tip

culm sheaths

1. Part of a clump shows a young shoot developing from a new rhizome that is emerging from an older rhizome on the left. A cutaway view of the culm, or stem, reveals hollow internodes separated by diaphragms, or cross walls.

2. A longitudinal section through a bamboo shoot, showing the young growing point that is protected by overlapping culm sheaths.

old rhizome    new rhizome

# Six bamboo species common in Malaysia

**1. *Bambusa vulgaris* cv. *wamin*** is also known as the Buddha's belly bamboo for its unusual bulging internodes. This popular garden ornamental grows up to 2 metres if potted, but can reach a height of 5–6 metres if planted in the ground.

**2. *Bambusa vulgaris*** is the most frequently cultivated species of bamboo in Southeast Asia. Although its origin is thought to be tropical Asia, in Malaysia it has never been seen growing wild in remote areas. The most common form of this species has green culms, but there is also a yellow variety (**B. vulgaris cv. vittata**) (see illustration). Reaching a height of 12–20 metres and a diameter of 4–10 centimetres, culms arch outwards as they mature, forming tall, bushy clumps.

**3. *Maclurochloa montana*** is endemic to Peninsular Malaysia, and has been recorded in Penang Hill, Gunung Jerai and Fraser's Hill. This clambering bamboo has long, very narrow and flexible culms that help the plant to reach upwards by entangling in surrounding vegetation. The culms can reach a length of 8–20 metres, but are only 1.5–2.5 centimetres in diameter. Characteristic of this bamboo species are its clambering habit and the band of white, matted hairs just below each node on the culm.

**4. *Gigantochloa scortechinii*** is found throughout Peninsular Malaysia, mostly in the foothills of the Main Range, in both forest fringes, such as along streams, and in disturbed areas. It also grows in peninsular Thailand. The culms grow up to 10–20 metres and are 6–12 centimetres wide. The bright orange young culm sheaths with green leaf-like blades that spread outwards, together with the copious white wax exudates from new culms, are identifiable features. The leaves are green, with pale, soft-hairy lower surfaces. An exception is a form which has pale, greenish white stripes on its leaves. This is Peninsular Malaysia's most useful bamboo.

A clump of mature bamboo in the Gombak Forest Reserve.

**5. *Schizostachyum brachycladum*,** the popular *lemang* bamboo, probably originates from Borneo and other eastern Indonesian islands, but is now widely cultivated in Peninsular Malaysia. The yellow form (see illustration) is a popular ornamental in Malaysia, Singapore and Java. The tall, elegant clumps have a stiffly erect habit and grow up to 6–8 metres, with internodes of 30–45 centimetres.

**6. *Schizostachyum gracile*** is common in southern Peninsular Malaysia and Singapore, and is also known from Terengganu, Pahang and Selangor. The medium green culms tend to arch strongly outwards, growing up to 4–5 metres long but only 1.5–2 centimetres wide. The culm sheaths are greenish orange-brown and are covered with short, pale brown hairs. Well-developed clumps are beautiful, but this species is only suitable for planting in very large gardens.

## Rare rainforest bamboos

In contrast to widespread and much-planted bamboo species, such as the tropical *Bambusa vulgaris*, a number of native species have a restricted distribution. *B. farinacea* and *Gigantochloa scortechinii* are reasonably common in the Malay Peninsula, but are not known elsewhere. The extremely rare genera, *Holttumochloa*, *Maclurochloa* and *Soejatmia*, are unique to Peninsular Malaysia and represent the distinct ever-wet rainforest forms that have evolved as bamboos spread from the north, where a more seasonal climate is experienced, to further south where the climate is more even. At the Malaysia–Thai border, classic Asiatic genera, such as *Bambusa*, *Dendrocalamus* and *Gigantochloa*, are well developed. The only two species of *Kinabaluchloa* known are found on mountains in Sabah and Sarawak and the Main Range in Peninsular Malaysia.

## Uses

Traditionally, bamboo is used as a supplementary material in house building, and for making bridges, rafts, water pipes, vegetable-growing stakes, traps, blowpipes, kites, musical instruments, household utensils and ornaments. In the first half of the 20th century, it was still common in some villages in Kelantan and Kedah to see bamboo poles being used to lift a wooden house off its supporting posts for removal to a different site.

*Gigantochloa scortechinii* shoots with young leaves. The shoots of some species are used in *sayur lemak*—vegetables cooked in coconut milk.

Various parts of the bamboo plant are used as food or in the preparation of food. Bamboo shoots, especially those of *Dendrocalamus asper*, *Gigantochloa levis* and *G. ligulata*, are relished as a local delicacy. Rice is cooked with coconut milk inside internodes of several species of *Schizostachyum* to produce *lemang*, and cut bamboo segments are used as moulds in which palm sugar, or *gula melaka*, is hardened. The broad leaves of *S. grande* and *Dinochloa trichogona* are used as wrappers for Chinese *bak chang* (glutinous rice dumplings).

In some minor industries in Malaysia, certain bamboo species are used in the manufacture of a variety of products. For example, *Gigantochloa scortechinii* and *G. wrayi* are used to make poultry cages, vegetable baskets and incense sticks. *Schizostachyum zollingeri* is woven into baskets for holding vegetables and fish. Many Malaysian states also have a thriving bamboo handicraft industry. Since the 1980s, there has also been an increasing use of bamboo in contemporary furniture design and fittings for offices and homes.

### Bamboo products

1. Incense sticks used by Buddhists for praying and making offerings are made in small-scale, family-run businesses in Malaysia. A number of such factories are found in the Ulu Langat district of Selangor.
2. A cutaway of a mould for setting palm sugar and a bowl made out of bamboo.
3. A vegetable basket made from finely split bamboo culms which are then woven together.
4. An *angklung*, a traditional Malay musical instrument made from hollow bamboo culms connected by bamboo rods. The player holds the rods and shakes the instrument gently. Each angklung is tuned to only one pitch, and therefore a small ensemble is needed to play a piece of music.
5. A poultry cage used in villages for keeping chickens. The cage is simply left on the ground and the chickens lowered in through the opening at the top.
6. A bamboo chair. Bamboo is less durable than wood, but is cheaper and more versatile. Treating bamboo with certain chemicals and keeping it dry will make it last longer.

# Herbaceous flowering plants

*Herbs are usually non-woody, small and soft-leaved plants, but there are exceptions to this which illustrate the wealth of variety of their shapes, forms and ways of life. Most monocotyledons, except the palms and bamboos, are herbs. Dicotyledons are also well represented. About 30 per cent of all species of flowering plants in Malaysia are herbs.*

Not drawn to scale

## Growth habits

Herbaceous flowering plants of Malaysia exhibit an extraordinary variation in size. They range from the tiny, moss-like, submerged *Malaccotristicha malayana* (Podostemonaceae) with its thread-like leaves just a few millimetres long to the gigantic wild *keladi* of Borneo, *Alocasia robusta*, with leaves up to 4 metres across and to the wild bananas with their false trunks growing to 9 metres tall and crown of leaves, each measuring up to 7 metres long.

Compared with trees, herbs produce an astonishing variety of leaf shapes, textures and colours. Shapes range from the strap-shaped leaves of grasses to the many times divided, umbrella-like leaves of *Amorphophallus* (Araceae). Textures vary from the thick, fleshy, smooth and shiny leaves of orchids, to the thin, soft and hairy toothed-leaves of *Didymocarpus platypus* (Gesneriaceae). The leaves of many herbs, such as the jewel orchids, are often strikingly coloured and patterned.

*Monophyllaea produces just one large leaf during its lifetime, which grows continuously from its base.*

**The three most species-rich herb genera in Peninsular Malaysia**
1. *Didymocarpus*, with trumpet-shaped flowers, numbers 85 species.
2. *Sonerila*, with 48 species, has dainty, three-petalled flowers.
3. *Argostemma*, with white, star-like flowers, has 42 species.

within a period of 11 weeks. The perennial rainforest herbs, such as *Argostemma* (Rubiaceae), *Didymocarpus* and *Sonerila* (Melastomataceae), live from a few months to a few years, and can carry out photosynthesis under a very low light density (as low as 1–3 per cent of full sunlight). The growth of these herbs is, however, extremely slow. For example, *Didymocarpus platypus*, a herb about 40 centimetres tall, lives for over 20 years but produces a new leaf only every 3 months and up to 8 flowers a year. The leaves of perennial herbs are also much longer lived (18–33 months) compared with leaves of trees that live for 6–12 months. The one-leafed plant *Monophyllaea* (Gesneriaceae), which throughout its life span produces a single leaf up to 1 metre across, shows an extreme condition. Many monocotyledons, including gingers, are potentially immortal. In these plants, as one stem dies, a new bud arising from its base appears and produces another stem, and so on forever.

A number of herbaceous plant species escape the gloom of the forest floor by growing in the tree canopy. The majority of orchids have adopted this

*The leaves of the giant Bornean keladi (Alocasia robusta) grow up to 4 metres across.*

## Life forms

The life forms of herbs range from the small, weedy annuals to the relatively large, perennial herbs that grow in the deep shade of the rainforest. Annual herbs, such as *Hedyotis dichotoma* (Rubiaceae), sprout quickly from seed, go on to flower, bear fruits and disperse their seeds all

*The herbaceous jewel orchid, with its elegant leaves, growing in the humid and shaded montane forest floor.*

### The beauty of leaves

The leaves of jewel orchids vary in colour from golden, deep purple to black with a fine contrasting tracery of silver, gold or red veins. Other herbs have deep velvety green leaves with purple undersides. Yet others are variegated and furnished with silver or white lines or blotches, or are iridescent blue or totally black. In most cases, the colour is due to the presence of pigments, usually purple or red, that mask the green chlorophyll. Blue leaves are, however, not blue because they are pigmented. Instead, their surface layer splits the incoming light into different wavelengths, so that on tilting the leaf of the peacock begonia, *Begonia pavonina*, it changes the colour from blue to green.

epiphytic way of life. Others, such as the non-photosynthesizing saprophytic and parasitic flowering plants, require the humid conditions of the rainforest undergrowth. Still others, such as the robust *bakung* or crinum lily (*Crinum asiaticum*), while not weeds, live in exposed but stable habitats, such as on seashores. Limestone hills also have their own assemblage of specially adapted herbaceous plants, such as paraboeas (*Paraboea* spp.) and balsams (*Impatiens* spp.).

Only a few species of indigenous herbs are able to thrive in the waterlogged conditions found on the margins of lakes or in swamps. These include sedges, like *Cyperus* and *Lepironia*, and bladderworts, such as *Utricularia*.

## Uses

Herbaceous flowering plants have many local uses, whether for food, particularly as ingredients of *ulam*, such as the *pegaga* (*Centella asiatica*); for medicines, especially the gingers, which are ingredients in almost all types of *jamu*; or for making baskets, such as strips of the *bemban* (*Donax grandis*) stem. The orchids hold the greatest commercial value for their ornamental attributes, while begonias and other decorative native species hold great potential in the horticultural trade. Several crops, such as rice and bananas, have evolved in the region, and their wild relatives are still growing in Malaysian forests and are an important gene pool for future breeding programmes.

## Conservation

There are economic reasons for conserving herbs besides their intrinsic and scientific value. However, over-collection of several commercially valuable species from their wild populations has endangered the long-term survival of the species.

But for the majority of herbs, habitat destruction or degradation is the prime threat. Many rare herbaceous species grow in very localized areas and are, therefore, extremely vulnerable to habitat disturbance. In addition, some of these species possess very small populations and are confined to a specialized habitat. A notable example is the primrose *Didymocarpus primulinus*, known from about 100 plants growing on a sheltered rock face measuring 10 metres by 4 metres on the Klang Gate Ridge near Kuala Lumpur.

Particularly vulnerable habitats for herbs include mountain tops, rocky streams and waterfalls in the forest, as well as limestone hills. The clearing of even a small area of the forest where these plants grow will drastically result in the decrease of their population size and critically endanger the long-term survival of the species.

### The eight major families of herbaceous flowering plants in Peninsular Malaysia

In Peninsular Malaysia, there are over 2,580 herbaceous flowering plant species in 554 genera and 94 families. Of these, eight families, each with more than a hundred species, account for more than half of the herbaceous flora. These are (1) the grasses (Graminae), (2) ginger family (Zingiberaceae), (3) sedges (Cyperaceae), (4) coffee family (Rubiaceae), (5) orchids (Orchidaceae), (6) African violets (Gesneriaceae), (7) acanthus family (Acanthaceae) and (8) aroids (Araceae).

The herbaceous flora of Sabah and Sarawak is still poorly known but probably shows a similar pattern, except that there are relatively fewer species of Acanthaceae and more species of begonias (Begoniaceae) and orchids.

# Orchids

*Orchids belong to the largest family of flowering plants in the plant kingdom, the Orchidaceae. Worldwide, there are about 25,000 species of orchids represented in 600 genera. Of these, some 850 species covering 120 genera are found in Peninsular Malaysia. In addition, Sabah and Sarawak are home to 2,500 species. Over-collecting and habitat destruction have endangered the continued existence of some orchid species. To protect these natural treasures, conservation centres have been set up across the country.*

## Orchid habitats

Moist, shaded rock is the habitat for *Paphiopedilum barbatum.*

Epiphytic orchids, such as this species of *Bulbophyllum*, grow on the branches of host trees.

A terrestrial orchid, such as *Calanthe pulchra*, makes its home on the forest floor.

In Malaysia, the orchid species with the biggest plants is *Grammatophyllum speciosum*. Because of its impressive size, it is an interesting and unique ornamental.

## Jewels of the forest

Wild orchids are the ornaments of the trees and jungle floor in the Malaysian rainforest. Certain areas are known for their orchid species diversity, such as Gunung Jerai, Cameron Highlands, Gunung Ledang, and Penang Hill in Peninsular Malaysia. In Sabah, Mount Kinabalu alone is home to 1,200 species of orchids, which make up about a quarter of all the flowering plants on the mountain.

Orchids generally do not grow under the dense forest canopy. They need a fair amount of sunlight, and hence prefer locations where a break in the forest occurs. Some perch on branches and tree trunks, whilst others find suitable homes on rocks, either on hills or by the coast. Yet others live in sheltered, moist places, such as along jungle streams, and in ravines and gullies. Most Malaysian orchid species are epiphytic. Some are terrestrial and a very small number are saprophytic (see 'Parasitic and saprophytic flowering plants').

## Growth habits

Malaysian orchids display a variety of forms and habits. The largest in Malaysia, the tiger orchid, or *Grammatophyllum speciosum*, grows in a sturdy cluster much like sugar cane. One of the smallest is a species of *Corybas*, which is an inconspicuous plant of only a few centimetres high.

A variety of leaf and inflorescence structures are found. The elephant ear orchid of Sabah, *Phalaenopsis gigantea*, has thick, succulent leaves that measure up to 60 centimetres long and 20 centimetres wide. In contrast, *Taeniophyllum obtusum* is leafless, with a stem that rarely reaches 2 centimetres. Unless this species is in flower, it is barely recognizable as an orchid. The jewel orchids, such as *Goodyera hispida* and *Ludisia discolor*, have beautiful, ornate leaves. *Corymborkis veratrifolia* and *Calanthe pulchra* have large, pleated leaves resembling those of palms, while species of *Dendrobium*, *Bulbophyllum* and *Vanda* have leathery, narrow leaves.

Some inflorescences are large, such as that of the tiger orchid, which grows up to 2–3 metres and bears many large flowers. Others are smaller, such as the inflorescence of *Renanthera elongata*, which is branched and

## Growth habits

1. Leaves of orchids come in a wide array of forms, such as the beautifully variegated leaves of a jewel orchid, *Ludisia discolor*.

2. Inflorescences may be large or small, single or branched. *Renanthera elongata*, for example, has small flowers on spreading inflorescences.

3. Orchid flowers have a characteristic shape, but vary in pattern, colour and size. Here is a single purple-white flower of *Rhynchostylis retusa.*

spreading, carrying a spray of tiny flowers. The fox-tailed orchid *Rhynchostylis retusa* has a pendulous inflorescence bearing a round cluster of delicate flowers, while that of *Geodorum densiflorum* is shaped like the shepherd's crook.

The most attractive part of an orchid is its flower. When in bloom, some flowers last for weeks, such as those of *Phalaenopsis*. Others live for barely a day. The flowers of *Bromheadia finlaysonianum*, for example, open at dawn and by noon are withered. Orchid flowers also emit different odours. While the blooms of *Vanilla pilifera* and *Vanda deari* are sweet-smelling, *Bulbophyllum maximum* flowers reek and are pollinated by blowflies.

## Orchid conservation

Of the 2,500 orchid species found in Sabah and Sarawak over 200 are listed as rare and endangered. This is largely due to the destruction of their habitats when forests are cleared for development and agriculture. In addition, the over-collecting of orchids also leads to a reduction in their wild

# Orchids of Peninsular Malaysia

The estimated 850 species of orchids found in Peninsular Malaysia are distributed over a wide range of habitats, from forest canopy to river banks, and altitudes, from sea level to mountain tops. Epiphytic orchids, which constitute the majority of Malaysian orchids, can be divided into those with short stems that creep along the stratum and those with long stems that climb. Among the former type of epiphytic orchids are members of the genera *Bulbophyllum*, *Coelogyne* and *Dendrobium*, while species of *Trichoglottis* and *Ventricularia* and *Papilionanthe hookeriana* belong to the latter. Terrestrial orchids are not as common as epiphytic orchids, and include species of *Paphiopedilum*, *Phaius*, *Arundina* and *Liparis*. Saprophytic orchids, the most poorly represented orchid group in Malaysian flora, number only 14 species found in 9 genera.

## Two epiphytic orchids

*Phalaenopsis violacea* bears 2–5 flowers on a short, stout and slightly zigzagged inflorescence. This plant is found growing in shady places on tree branches that overhang the rivers in Perak and Selangor. There are two forms of this species—the Malayan and the Bornean. The former has star-shaped flowers and elongated leaves, while the latter has bigger and rounder flowers, and rounder leaves. It is also more valued by collectors. Endemic to Sabah is *Phalaenopsis gigantea*, with huge, drooping succulent leaves and numerous flowers borne on an elegant, pendulous inflorescence.

*Papilionanthe hookeriana* is commonly known as the Kinta weed. It is a long-stemmed, climbing orchid that grows in the swampy areas of the Kinta Valley in Perak and some parts of Johor. Once found in abundance, this species is now rarely seen in the wild due to over-collecting and the destruction of its natural habitat.

The Malayan form of *Phalaenopsis violacea*. Its flowers measure about 5 centimetres and vary from pure white to deep purple.

The Kinta weed is actually the orchid *Papilionanthe hookeriana*. Swampy areas of the Kinta Valley in Perak are where it flourishes.

## Two terrestrial orchids

*Paphiopedilum barbatum* grows in high altitudes and is found on Penang Hill, Gunung Jerai and Gunung Ledang. It prefers rocks on the moist and shady forest floor. Another species of this genus, *P. rothschild-ianum*, grows at very high altitudes on Mount Kinabalu, whereas *P. niveum* flourishes at sea level on the limestone rocks of Pulau Langkawi.

*Bulbophyllum maximum* is an attractive terrestrial orchid species belonging to one of the largest genera in the Orchidaceae. Its flowers are arranged in ringed clusters, which when grouped together form a drooping inflorescence. The lip of the flower is rather prominent, swinging like a pendulum when it catches the breeze.

Apart from being native to Peninsular Malaysia, *Paphiopedilum barbatum* also occurs in Sumatra and Thailand.

The unusually shaped flowers of *Bulbophyllum maximum*.

### FLOWERING CHARACTERISTICS AND MAIN FLOWERING SEASONS OF SOME ORCHIDS FOUND IN PENINSULAR MALAYSIA

| ORCHID SPECIES | FLOWERING PERIOD | ORCHID SPECIES | FLOWERING PERIOD |
|---|---|---|---|
| Aerides multiflora<br>A. odoratum | April–May<br>May | Grammatophyllum speciosum | July, January |
| Arachnis flosaeris<br>A. flosaeris var. gracilis<br>A. hookeriana | May, November<br>June<br>Free flowering | Liparis viridiflora | Free flowering |
| | | Molaxis latifolia | Flowers frequently |
| Arundina graminifolia<br>A. miniatum | Seasonal<br>Free flowering | Phalaenopsis violacea | Free flowering |
| Bromheadia finlaysoniana | Gregarious flowering | Rhynchostylis coelestris | April–July |
| Bulbophyllum vaginatum | Gregarious flowering | Taeniophyllum obtusum | Gregarious flowering |
| Calanthe triplicata | May–June | | |
| Coelogyne foerstermannii | Gregarious flowering in June | Trichoglottis fasciata | April–May |
| | | Trixpermun calceolus | Gregarious flowering |
| Dendrobium crumenatum<br>D. farmeri | Gregarious flowering<br>March–April | Vanda hookeriana | Free flowering |
| Doritis pulcherrima | Free flowering,<br>peak in June–December | Vandopsis gigantea | Irregular |

### Main orchid localities

Pulau Langkawi · Gunung Jerai · Baling · Maxwell's Hill · Batu Gajah · Cameron Highlands · Taman Negara · Fraser's Hill · Gunung Benom · Genting Highlands · Strait of Melaka · Gunung Ledang · South China Sea · Gunung Belumut · N

Source: After Seidenfaden and Wood (1992)

population. Commercially valuable orchids are sought by collectors all over the world, with unique species, such as *Phalaenopsis violacea* and *Paphiopedilum rothschildianum*, fetching high prices. Hence, to protect the orchids and preserve their genetic material, the Malaysian Government and its related organizations have set up several centres of *ex situ* and *in situ* conservation.

Sabah has several *ex situ* orchid conservation centres, and Sarawak has one, run by the Forest Research Branch of the Forest Department. Established in the 1980s, it now houses many species of rare and endangered orchids, including those found in the lowlands. Mountain orchids are conserved in centres in Sabah, such as the Mountain Garden in Kinabalu Park and a centre on Mount Alab set up by the Tambunan District Council. The Forest Research Centre at Sepilok has a few hundred orchid species, of which a number are under threat in the wild. It was the first orchid collection in Sabah, started in 1977. At the Agricultural Research Station in Tenom, an orchid centre was opened in 1981 by the Department of Agriculture. In 1986, the Ministry of Environment, which funded the Tenom centre, opened another one at Poring, Ranau, headed by Sabah Parks.

A rare and beautiful native orchid, *Paphiopedilum lowii*, seen in the Kinabalu Park where orchid conservation is taking place.

# Gingers

*A diverse and fascinating group of perennial herbs, gingers, or the Zingiberaceae, are represented throughout the tropical and subtropical regions, but are mainly Asiatic in distribution. Of the 50 genera and 1,500 species known in the world, at least 20 genera and 288 species are found in Malaysia. Gingers are characterized by their aromatic parts, and are used as spices, made into condiments, essential oils and medicine, and grown as ornamentals.*

**Ginger plant sizes**

LEFT: *Etlingera elatior* easily grows up to 4 metres.

BELOW: A small ginger, *Camptandra parvula* grows to a maximun height of about 5–10 centimetres.

Several inflorescences of *Zingiber spectabile* in their natural habitat. This species of ginger is very common in the lowland and hill forests of Malaysia.

## Vegetative and floral habits

There are many sizes of ginger plants, ranging from small, rosette-like forms, as with species of *Kaempferia* and *Camptandra*, to tall clusters of fronds or leaf shoots more than 3 metres high, as seen in species of *Alpinia* and *Etlingera*.

A two-ranked, or distichous, arrangement of sheathing leaves is distinctive of most genera, but in *Curcuma*, *Elettariopsis* and *Scaphochlamys*, the leaves are more or less erect with petioles of variable length. The rhizomes, or modified underground stems, are sometimes fleshy, woody or runner-like, and branch by repeatedly dividing into two equal parts. Gingers are also closely related to the banana and heliconia families, and are thought to have evolved in parallel with the orchid family.

Flowers and inflorescences vary between genera. Some flowers are arranged in cincinnus inflorescences (where the lateral axes arise on alternate sides of the main axis) which break off into panicles, such as in the genus *Alpinia*. Other flowers grow out of the axils of conspicuous, specialized leaves, or bracts, which may be cup-shaped, such as in the genera *Curcuma*, *Camptandra* and *Zingiber*. These flowers or inflorescences are produced terminally on the leaf shoots or at the basal shoots, which are either partly embedded in the soil or borne on a stalk

**Gingers in different habitats in Malaysia**

1. *Hedychium muluense* growing on a tree trunk. This epiphytic ginger is native to Sabah and Sarawak.
2. The inflorescence of *Globba atrosanguinea*, a species of the dancing ladies found in the lowland forests of Sabah and Sarawak.
3. *Kaempferia pulchra* makes its home on limestone.
4. *Alpinia mutica* is one of the few species of ginger that can be found in swampy habitats.

above ground level. Except for *Alpinia havilandii*, *Plagiostachys* is the only genus which produces its inflorescence laterally through the leaf sheaths.

## Diversity and distribution

The Indo-Malayan region is the centre of diversity for the Zingiberaceae. More than 160 species are found in Peninsular Malaysia, and no fewer than 155 species in Sabah and Sarawak, with more waiting to be discovered and described. The majority of species grow in the wild and prefer shaded and moist habitats. Only slightly over 6 per cent have been cultivated. Gingers are most abundant in lowland forests between the altitudes of 200 and 500 metres, becoming less frequent higher up and scarce in very high altitudes. Very few species survive on islands which tend to be small, dry and isolated.

Although most ginger species are terrestrial, a few, such as *Hedychium longicornutum*, *H. muluense* and *Burbidgea stenantha*, are epiphytic. Often seen along riverine habitats, mountain paths and the edges of waterfalls are globbas, also known as dancing ladies because of their delicate, pretty flowers. Some *Zingiber* species are called shampoo gingers because of the foam-like, aromatic liquid contained in the bracts of the inflorescence. Several gingers, such as *Alpinia ligulata*, *A. mutica* and a few species of *Zingiber* are adapted to swampy areas. *Boesenbergia curtisii* and *Kaempferia pulchra* are endemic to limestone habitats, but have also been successfully cultivated in gardens. All known species of *Geostachys* are distributed in hill and mountain forests. Two genera—*Haplochorema* and *Burbidgea*—are confined to Sabah and Sarawak, and the endangered genus *Haniffia* is restricted to Peninsular Malaysia. Common gingers form huge or dense stands in secondary forests, along roadsides and in rubber plantations. Some examples of these are *Etlingera punicea*, *E. littoralis*, *Zingiber spectabile*, *Amomum uliginosum*, *A. biflorum* and *Alpinia mutica*.

## Uses of gingers in Malaysia

### Food

*Zingiber officinale*, from which commercial ginger is obtained, is the most well-known member of the ginger family (see 'Spices'). Ginger is consumed by all ethnic groups in Malaysia in a variety of fresh and processed foods, curries, beverages, pastries, cakes and sweets. Turmeric, or *Curcuma domestica*, is an essential ingredient in Malaysian curries. Rhizomes of turmeric and greater galangal, or *Alpinia galanga*, are used by the Malays as a spice and flavouring in traditional dishes. Other spices from the ginger family include cardamom, or *Elettaria cardamomum*, *Alpinia conchigera* and *Boesenbergia rotunda*. The bioactive substances in ginger include gingerols, shogaols and zingerone, while amongst the essential oils are zingiberene, camphene and linalool.

The young inflorescence of the torch ginger, or *kantan* (*Etlingera elatior*), is a prominent flavour in a popular local noodle dish called *laksa*.

A bowl of *laksa* garnished with *kantan*.

Leaves of *Kaempferia galanga* are used by villagers to flavour rice, and the young rhizomes of *Curcuma mangga*, *Boesenbergia rotunda* and *Zingiber zerumbet* and the young inflorescences of greater galangal and turmeric are eaten in salads with chilli sauce and rice. In Sabah, the young shoots of a few species of *Etlingera* are pickled and eaten with rice.

### Medicine

An estimated 7–8 per cent of all ginger species are medicinal, and of these, about 5 per cent are still in use. These species help to treat a variety of diseases and ailments, including high blood pressure, rheumatism and sinus allergies. Some are used as postpartum medicines in the form of tonics, decoctions, fresh rhizomes or poultices for external application. In rural areas, fresh turmeric was traditionally used as an antiseptic paste and applied to circumcision wounds and pierced ears. Certain cultivated species, such as *Zingiber zerumbet*, *Kaempferia galanga* and *Alpinia conchigera*, are known respectively for their anti-inflammatory, antifungal and antibacterial qualities.

*Jamu*, a traditional herbal mixture which originates from Indonesia, often contains turmeric and ginger. It is used as a medicine, as well as a health and beauty tonic. Other gingers, such as *Boesenbergia rotunda*, *Kaempferia galanga* and *Zingiber purpureum*, are also used in the preparation of various types of jamu.

| MEDICINAL GINGERS | | |
|---|---|---|
| **SCIENTIFIC NAME** | **MALAY NAME** | **USE** |
| *Alpinia conchigera* | lengkuas ranting | fungal skin infection |
| *Boesenbergia rotunda* | temu kunci | postpartum sickness |
| *Curcuma xanthorhiza* | temu lawak | stomach problems |
| *Kaempferia galanga* | cekur | inflammation, high blood pressure |
| *Zingiber officinale* | halia bara | postpartum sickness |
| *Z. purpureum* | bonglai | postpartum sickness |
| *Z. zerumbet* | lempoyang | inflammation, intestinal parasites high blood pressure |

*Cekur*, or *Kaempferia galanga*, is a traditional treatment for high blood pressure and inflammation.

| ORNAMENTAL GINGERS | | |
|---|---|---|
| **SCIENTIFIC NAME** | **ENGLISH NAME** | **USE** |
| *Alpinia purpurata* | red or pink ginger, plume ginger | garden plant, cut flower |
| *A. zerumbet* | shell ginger | garden plant |
| *Burbidgea stenantha* | – | garden plant |
| *Hedychium coronarium* | ginger lily | garden plant |
| *Kaempferia pulchra* | peacock ginger | potted and garden plant |
| *Zingiber spectabile* | earth ginger | garden plant, cut flower |

A small plant, the peacock ginger is suitable for growing in pots. It is also cultivated in rock gardens.

The unusually shaped inflorescence of the earth ginger make it a stunning ornamental plant.

### Ornamentals

Except for the mountain species, gingers are adaptable to indoor and conservatory cultivation. As ornaments, gingers exhibit attractive foliage, especially those with variegated leaves, exotic flowers and unique, cone-like inflorescences. Perhaps the most common ornamental ginger is the red ginger, or *Alpinia purpurata*, which is native to New Caledonia. A form of *A. purpurata* with pink inflorescence bracts has been introduced to Malaysia from Hawaii and Australia. Several native species of *Globba*, *Alpinia* and *Boesenbergia* have potential as ornamentals.

*RIGHT AND ABOVE*: The ornamental red ginger is an introduced species.

### Uses

Ginger is one of the oldest spices known to man. It is mentioned in the Qur'an, and was highly valued by the Greeks and Romans. In Malaysia, the people of traditional village communities sometimes wore a talisman made from small pieces of turmeric (*Curcuma domestica*) around the neck or wrist. Turmeric is also used by the Malays and Indians on ceremonial occasions, and is a source of yellow dye. Today, ginger is widely used as a spice and in medicine.

### Conservation

It is essential to conserve Malaysia's gingers not only because the Indo-Malayan region is home to many of the world's gingers, but also because this group of plants has a huge potential to be developed into a variety of commercial products. The loss of species and genetic resources that result from logging and other activities for economic development means that many wild species of gingers will become extinct before they can be recorded. Both *in situ* and *ex situ* conservation are needed, and this is best done in forest reserves, wildlife sanctuaries, national parks and botanic gardens.

The inflorescence of *Etlingera fimbriobracteata*. Huge, tall clumps of this species can be found growing at the edges of forests or in open areas in Sabah and Sarawak.

# Climbing flowering plants

*Climbers are plants that have abandoned the free-standing habit and instead crawl, grasp, twine and curl round other plants, mainly trees. The tropical rainforest abounds in climbers, an uncommon feature in temperate forests. Malaysia's forests are home to about 1,000 species, which make up 8 per cent of the country's flowering plant flora. There is an incredible variety of shapes and sizes, ranging from the delicate, thin-stemmed herbaceous creepers to the sturdy, woody perennial climbers. If growth is unrestricted, climbers choke up forest clearings and pull down trees. In Malaysia, however, climbers are a source of food, medicine and raw material for furniture and handicrafts.*

Passiflora foetida, or *timun dedang*, a tendril climber commonly found in secondary forests and other open habitats. It belongs to the Passifloraceae, a family that consists entirely of climbers.

## Common Malaysian twisting climbers

Bauhinia flammifera, or *akar katup katup*, is a common twister in lowland forests. When in full bloom, this woody climber brightens up the otherwise dull green forest canopy.

Tetracera indica, or *akar mempelas*, a common twisting woody climber in the secondary forests of the lowlands. The leaf with its rough surface is used by villagers as a substitute for sandpaper, while the pounded leaves and roots are applied to the skin to relieve itching.

### Malaysian climbers

A number of families in Malaysian flora, such as the Ancistrocladaceae, Connaraceae, Menispermaceae and Passifloraceae, consist entirely of climber species. Others, such as the Annonaceae, Leguminosae and Rubiaceae, comprise mainly trees and shrubs, with only some members being climbers. Species of *akar beluru* (*Entada*) and *akar tuba* (*Derris*), for example, belong to the Leguminosae, a family whose members are mostly free-standing trees or shrubs.

The composition of climber flora varies between the three major tropical forest regions in the world. In the tropical forests of Malaysia and its neighbouring countries, members of the Annonaceae and Connaraceae are the most dominant, while in the Central and South American tropics it is the Bignoniaceae, and in tropical Africa, the Apocynaceae. However, in the case of rattans—the climbing members of the palm family—although their centre of distribution is in the Southeast Asian tropics, many members occur in the tropical parts of Australia, Myanmar (Burma), India and Africa.

### Habit and habitat

Climbers act like pioneer species, preferring large openings in the forest to start their growth. Their seeds germinate readily, and the resulting seedlings quickly fill up gaps in the vegetation. Fallen stems can also take root and begin developing into new plants. Because of their rapid and aggressive growth, climbers are abundant in logged forests, at the edges of forests, along rivers and in forest clearings. These open spaces are often blanketed in an apparently impenetrable tangle of climbers.

In Malaysian forests, woody climbers are the most conspicuous, displaying a variety of growth forms, including the hoop-stemmed *belinjau* or *Gnetum*, the gnarl-stemmed *Bauhinia*, the hook-stemmed *akar gambir* or *Uncaria*, and the spiny climbing rattan. The big climbers festoon the forest, resting their foliage on the tops of tree crowns, with their flexible stems hanging free or clinging to tree trunks. A single climber can spread from crown to crown, sometimes over a considerable area of the forest canopy, interconnecting the crowns of up to 27 trees. In most cases, climbers reach the top of the forest canopy by climbing a series of successively taller trees. Exceptions are the uncommon root and tendril climbers.

## Climbing mechanisms

Climbers scale up trees in a variety of fascinating ways. They can be grouped into five categories which reflect the different climbing mechanisms they employ: twiners, hooks, thorns, tendrils and roots.

In **twiners (1)**, the active growing point of the main stem twines around the branches of trees. Upon touching a firm object, the part of the stem making contact stops growing, which stimulates its opposite side to grow. Common Malaysian twiners include species of *Aristolochia* and *Fibraurea*.

**Hook climbers (2)** exhibit a range of modifications. In some instances, specialized branches form hooks, as in species of *Artabotrys*, whereas in others, short, curved hooks are found in the axils of leaves, such as in species of *Uncaria*. Hooks are initially soft and flexible, but then thicken and stiffen when they catch hold of supports.

**Thorn climbers (3)** are not very common in Malaysian flora. They do, however, include the rattans, such as species of *Daemonorops* and *Korthalsia*. Stiff spines form a collar around the leaf sheath in certain rattans, while on the leaf stalks of others,

spines are arranged in whorls. Leaves sometimes have whip-like flagella (thin, supple shoots), bearing curved spines, extending from their midrib. With these thorns, the rattans affix themselves to standing vegetation.

**Tendrils (4)** are slender, clasping organs which twirl around their support. They originate from leaf tips, stalks or the midrib, as in *Gloriosa superba*, *Clematis triloba* and *Bauhinia* spp., respectively. In *Antigonon leptopus*, the tendrils grow from the inflorescence. If tendrils do not come into contact with a support, they fall off.

**Root climbers** use their roots to clasp the support. Well-known Malaysian root climbers include pandans, figs, aroids and peppers. In pandans and figs, the clasping roots arise from the nodes of the climbing stems, but in aroids, slender roots clasp the support, while thick, absorptive roots grow towards the ground.

A species of root-climbing pepper that has attractive and colourful leaves.

## Adaptive features

Although many understorey plants, such as herbs, shrubs and small trees, are adapted to low light conditions, climbers need full sunlight to grow well. To meet this requirement, climbers have developed several adaptations.

Not having to support their own weight, climbers channel extra energy into fast vegetative growth. It is not unusual for the stem to grow between 2 and 5 metres per year in length, reaching over 1 kilometre at maturity. Because of their rapid growth, the stems remain flexible and are able to twist and turn around the trunks and branches of other plants. Stem flexibility is also attributed to the presence of large areas of parenchyma (tissues comprising thin-walled, living cells) between isolated vascular bundles, and to the occurrence of anomalous secondary thickening in older stems.

Compared to trees, climbers have flat or round stems with a small diameter, although woody climbers with a stem as thick as 60 centimetres have been found. Considering the distance the stems cover, they are very efficient pipes which transport water and minerals from the roots to the foliage. The large vessels that fill the xylem, or woody tissue, of the stem facilitate this ability. In some climbers, such as *Bauhinia*, *Entada* and *Aristolochia*, these vessels can be seen with the naked eye, appearing as tiny pores scattered all over the cross section of the stem.

## Economic uses

Amongst the native species of climbers, rattans are an important raw material of the furniture and handicraft industries (see 'Rattans'). Young leaves and shoots

of *lakum* (*Cissus repens*), *akar melinjau* (*Gnetum tenuifolium*), *akar koyah* (*Millettia erantha*) and *sekentut* (*Paederia verticillata*) are used as vegetables, while the fruits of *akar mempisang* (*Anomianthus dulcis* and *Uvaria grandifolia*), *Gnetum latifolium*, a few rattan species and *Ziziphus calophylla* are edible. Vegetable dye is obtained from *akar kekunyit* (*Fibraurea chloroleuca*), and starch is prepared from the tubers of wild yam plants, such as *ubi gadung* (*Dioscorea hispida*), *ubi kipas* (*D. alata*) and *ubi torak* (*D. esculenta*). In traditional medicine, various preparations involve the use of the leaves, stems, bark and roots of *akar saga* (*Abrus praecatorius*), *akar beluru* (*Entada phaseoloides*), *akar gambir* (*Uncaria callophylla*), *akar kekunyit* (species of *Cyclaea*, *Fibraurea* and *Tinomiscum*), *putrawali* (*Tinospora crispa*) and many others. Only a few native species, such as those of *Bauhinia*, the pitcher plants (*Nepenthes* spp.) and wild peppers (*Piper* spp.) have been cultivated as ornamental plants.

In addition, many species of climbers have been introduced from other tropical countries into Malaysia and cultivated for food, such as various beans, cucumbers, gourds and melons. Others are grown as ornamentals, such as *Antigonon leptopus*, *Mucuna bennettii* and *Quisqualis indica*, and as commercial crops, such as black pepper (*Piper nigrum*) in Sarawak.

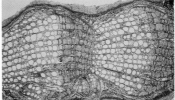

A cross section of an old flat stem of *Ampelocissus* showing the numerous vessels in the xylem and the broad parenchyma in between the vascular bundles. This anatomical configuration makes the liana flexible and enables it to efficiently transport water and mineral nutrients from the roots to the leaves.

*Akar kekunyit* (*Fibraurea chloroleuca*) is a member of the Menispermaceae, a family consisting entirely of climbers. Many members of this family are used in traditional medicine and as a source of vegetable dye.

## Tying the trees together

Woody climbers are common in Malaysian forests. They comprise almost 30 per cent of all woody plants. They are a vital part of the forest structure, literally tying the forest together. By draping themselves over the trees, they form canopy bridges for many aboreal animals. When forests are logged, these aerial walkways are broken and the animals driven out.

Although woody climbers help anchor trees and reduce wind damage, their overall effect on a forest can be detrimental. By growing on top of their host trees, woody climbers weigh the trees down and block out sunlight. In so doing, they reduce the rate of growth of the host tree and may cause the weaker trees to fall. When woody climbers become too big, as do some species of *Milletia*, whole trees may be uprooted. Because many trees are looped together by a single woody climber, the falling of one tree may have a domino effect, bringing others down with it. Hence, as a precautionary measure before logging operations, woody climbers are cut down first in order to prevent damaging the unlogged trees.

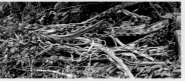

Stems of severed woody climbers in the Mata Ayer Forest Reserve, Perlis.

# Epiphytes

*Plants that grow on other plants for support are called epiphytes. By using other plants to perch high up above the ground, epiphytes attain favourable light conditions in the dense tropical rainforest. Unlike parasitic plants, which also grow on host plants, epiphytes do not steal water and nutrients from the hosts, absorbing them from rainwater instead. About 28,000 species in 84 families of all known vascular plants have taken to epiphytic life in the tropics. In addition, there are also many species of non-vascular epiphytes, such as algae, mosses and lichens, although in Malaysia they are outnumbered by species of ferns and orchids.*

1. The oak leaf fern (*Drynaria quercifolia*) is a common epiphyte species in the open habitats of the lowlands of Malaysia.

2. The stag's horn fern (*Platycerium coronarium*), growing on the main branch of a *kelat laut* (*Syzygium grandis*) tree at Port Dickson. The plant produces three kinds of leaves: photosynthetic leaves, basket leaves and hanging, spore-bearing leaves.

3. *Asplenium nidus*, or bird's nest fern or *paku langsuyar*, is frequently found in lowland, hill and submontane forests.

*Hymenophyllum*, a filmy fern commonly found in the montane forests of Malaysia. The delicate hanging leaves are finely dissected, one-cell thick and are able to withstand desiccation during dry spells by rolling and shrivelling. When the rains return, the leaves are able to revive without rupturing.

## Epiphytic flowering plants

1. *Hedychium longicornutum*, an epiphytic wild ginger growing on the stem of an understorey tree in the Pasoh Forest Reserve in Negeri Sembilan. Butterflies pollinate the brightly coloured flowers, while birds disperse the seeds, which are enclosed in a fleshy orange rind.

2. *Medinilla scortechinii*, a common epiphytic flowering plant of the *sendudok* family in the lower and upper montane forests of the Genting Highlands.

3. *Poikilospermum suaveolens*, an epiphytic flowering plant found in shaded and humid habitats along river banks in the lowland and hill forests.

### Habitat

Epiphytes are common in Malaysian montane and swamp forests as well as in the valleys of lowland and hill forests, where the air is always humid. Although epiphytes grow at all levels in a forest, most exist only in the canopy. Some live in exposed places, such as the crowns of tall forest trees, or on the trunks and branches of trees along roadsides and in forest clearings. Others grow in the cracks and crevices of bark, on the stems on lianas, and even on the leaves of larger plants. The filmy ferns *Hymenophyllum* and *Trichomanes* usually live in the deep shade of the forest undergrowth in the lowlands, and also flourish in the open in the montane forest environment.

Ferns and orchids constitute the majority of Malaysian epiphytic plant life forms. However, in addition, there are numerous species of algae, mosses, liverworts and lichens that grow as epiphytes. These small, non-vascular epiphytes are often found festooning the branches and trunks of trees in the upper montane forests, also called 'mossy forest', and are an important source of moisture and nutrients for other plants.

### Water, nutrients and epiphytes

Rainwater is the main source of moisture and nutrients for epiphytes, whose roots do not come into contact with the soil. At high altitudes, where there is plenty of condensation and precipitation, mist and rainfall are concentrated with nutrients, and thus make effective fertilizers.

Epiphytes either obtain moisture and nutrients directly from the rain, or indirectly from other plants. Mosses and liverworts, for example, absorb and regenerate nutrients, which are then washed off and passed onto other epiphytes. Nitrogenous nutrients, in particular, are circulated in this way. Water dripping from leaves and bark is another source of nutrients. It contains nutrients produced by nitrogen-fixing bacteria and blue-green algae, as well as nutrients from the remnants of decomposed leaves, bark and dead animals, and the excreta of beetles, caterpillars and birds.

### Epiphytic ferns

Of the 500 species of ferns that occur in Peninsular Malaysia, about half of them are epiphytes (see 'Ferns and fern allies'). To ensure an adequate supply of water and nutrients, several epiphytic ferns develop a unique humus-collecting mechanism. The older leaves form a nest- or basket-like device to intercept falling leaves from the host tree, which are used as a source of nutrients. Three such ferns are

## Three common epiphytic ferns in Malaysia

The **oak leaf fern (*Drynaria quercifolia*)** grows on the upper parts of trunks and major branches of roadside and forest trees in moderately exposed places in the lowlands. Its stout, creeping rhizome produces two kinds of leaves: nest and foliage leaves. Though less efficient than those of *Asplenium nidus* or *Platycerium coronarium*, the nest leaves trap and accumulate moisture, debris and humus, from which the roots can draw nutrients. The foliage leaves are longer than the nest leaves, much dissected and produce sporangia and spores.

The **stag's horn fern (*Platycerium coronarium*)** grows on trees in the lowlands and foothills, under full sunlight or partial shade. The short rhizome bears three different kinds of leaves: sterile, green upright leaves, basket leaves and fertile, pendulous dissected leaves. The basket leaves of a fully grown plant can completely encircle a large branch of the host tree, and form a dense crown which collects and retains a huge quantity of moisture, debris and humus. Other epiphytic plants may become established in the basket, and ants and other small animals may also make it their home.

The **bird's nest fern (*Asplenium nidus*)** is a common epiphyte found in both the lowlands and mountains. It grows frequently on roadsides trees, in plantations, and on forest trees. A nest-like rosette of leathery leaves is formed on top of the tough rhizome, beneath which is a large, spongy mass of roots and root hairs covered, in older plants, by the recurved dead leaves. Fallen leaves of the host tree and other airborne debris are trapped and accumulated in the nest, where they eventually decompose to become humus. The whole structure absorbs and stores a large quantity of water when it rains, and supplies moisture and nutrients to the bird's nest fern itself as well as to other species of ferns and bryophytes that are often found growing in the nest. Many small animals also make their home in the fern nest.

### CAM photosynthesis

Many epiphytes perform a special type of metabolism called Crassulacean Acid Metabolism (CAM). CAM is a process whereby carbon dioxide is absorbed by the leaf through open stomata at night, and then converted and stored in leaf tissues as malic and aspartic acids. During the day, the carbon dioxide is released and immediately assimilated by the plant for photosynthesis while the stomata remain closed. This allows photosynthesis to occur without the loss of water through transpiration. CAM is most common amongst epiphytic ferns and orchids, many of which live in habitats where water supply is frequently inadequate.

| open stomata through which carbon dioxide is absorbed | when the stomata are closed, carbon dioxide is released into the plant |
| --- | --- |

the common bird's nest fern (*Asplenium nidus*), stag's horn fern (*Platycerium coronarium*) and oak leaf fern (*Drynaria quercifolia*).

Filmy ferns grow well in habitats where humidity is always high, such as in valleys, by streams and waterfalls and in montane forests. Their fronds comprise small and delicate leaf blades which are one cell thick. The cells of the leaves are able to withstand desiccation during a brief dry spell, and revive without rupturing when the rains return.

## Epiphytic flowering plants

Species of epiphytic orchids are found at all altitudes, from sea level to mountain peaks. Many perch themselves on the branches and trunks of trees, whilst others nestle in sheltered, moist places along forest streams and near waterfalls.

Apart from orchids, there are several other species of flowering plants that live as epiphytes. Common Malaysian examples include *Fagraea* of the *tembusu* family, *Hedychium longicornutum* of the ginger family, *Medinilla scortechinii* of the *sendudok* family, *Poikilospermum suaveolens* (Cecropiaceae), a number of species of the rhododendron family, and species of *Schefflera* of the ivy family. To store water and to fasten themselves on the host plants, these epiphytes develop an extensive root system comprising fleshy or spongy roots. To reduce water loss through transpiration, the leaves are thick and fleshy, as in medinillas, or protected by a waxy cuticle, as in *Fagraea*, or covered with dense hairs or scales on the lower surface, as with certain species of rhododendrons.

## Dispersal

The microscopic fern spores, minute orchid seeds and small and winged fruits or seeds of other epiphytes are light enough to be carried by wind and deposited a distance away from the parent plant.

## Economic importance

A few species of epiphytic plants, such as the orchids *Dendrobium crumenatum* and *D. subulatum*, a wild ginger *Hedychium longicornutum*, and an ivy *Schefflera subulata* are reputed to have medicinal properties. A decoction of the orchid pseudobulbs, for example, is used to treat earache, while the roots of *Schefflera subulata* are used as a sedative and to relieve fevers and headaches.

Orchids are undoubtedly the most well-known epiphytic plants in Malaysian gardens. Examples of commonly cultivated species include *Bulbophyllum gracillimum*, *Cymbidium atropurpureun*, *Dendrobium anosmum*, *D. farmeri*, *Grammatophyllum speciosum*, the largest orchid in the world, and the moth orchids *Phalaenopsis amabilis* and *P. gigantea*.

In gardens all over Malaysia, epiphytic ferns, such as *Asplenium nidus*, *Davallia denticulata* and *Platycerium coronarium*, are a common sight. Easy to maintain, attractive and fast growing, these plants are favourites amongst home gardeners. The plants can reach a large size, and with their dense, long foliage, create a dramatic and impressive effect.

## Epiphytic orchids

Epiphytic orchids, such as many species of *Bulbophyllum* and *Dendrobium* and the tiger orchid *Grammatophyllum speciosum*, cope with the scarcity or periodic absence of moisture chiefly in two ways. First, they store excess water in the swollen stems, or pseudobulbs, and succulent leaves. To prevent excessive loss of moisture through transpiration, the leaves are protected by a waxy cuticle. In dry weather, the pseudo-bulbs shrivel as the plant uses up the water contained within. Secondly, orchids develop velamen in the roots, which comprise dead tissue that swells to retain excess water. Because the velamen surrounds the roots, it reduces excessive loss of moisture from the roots, and also protects them.

*Bulbophyllum uniflorum*, a common epiphytic orchid in lower montane forests. To conserve water, this species develops swollen psuedobulbs, thick, leathery and shiny leaves and an extensive root system.

# Ant-plants

*Ants are ubiquitous in Malaysia, and it is usual for them to be found crawling all over plants. However, the term 'ant-plant' is reserved for those constant associations between a particular species of plant and a particular species of ant. Out of the thousands of plant species in Malaysia only about a hundred can be considered ant-plants. These encompass a wide array of life forms, such as trees, shrubs, climbers and epiphytes, including ferns, and belong to many different families.*

Touching *Polyalthia insignis* causes aggressive stinging *Camponotus* ants to immediately swarm all over the plant surface.

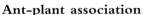

The rattan *Daemonorops verticillata* has ant nest tunnels between the concentric rings of long thorns.

### Ant-plant association

In most cases, the association between ants and plants is beneficial to both. The plant can benefit in one of two ways: by being protected against herbivores and plant competitors, or by obtaining an additional source of nutrients and sometimes also a suitable rooting medium. The ant gains a secure place to nest, which is beneficial for arboreal ants, as holes in dead wood in the tropics are in short supply due to rapid decay. In some associations, a source of food is also available to the ant.

### Protection against herbivores and plant competitors

The classic example of this association is the one between the *mahang* tree (*Macaranga triloba*) and the small, non-stinging ant *Crematogaster borneensis*.

In Malaysia, nine species of *Macaranga* (Euphorbiaceae), as well as the unrelated species *Zanthophyllum myriacanthum* (Rubiaceae), are associated with ants. The latter has extra-floral nectar glands which the ants can tap. In the shrubby *Clerodendron myrmecophilum* (Verbenaceae) and *Myrmeconauclea myrmecophilum* (Rubiaceae), the hollow stem develops spontaneously and is conspicuously swollen. These two species live in swampy areas or by rivers where terrestrial nesting places are absent or precarious. However, although the plant is always associated with ants, in the case of *Myrmeconauclea myrmecophilum*, the ant-associate is opportunistic; some nine ant species have been recorded as inhabiting its hollow stems, sometimes more than one species per plant.

Compared with *Crematogaster borneensis*, other species of ants, such as those of *Cladomyrma* and *Camponotus*, not only bite but also administer a painful sting. The aggressive behaviour of these ants can deter even the largest herbivore. For example, the palm heart (the large bud at the top of the stem and a favourite food of elephants) of the rattan *Daemonorops verticillata* is protected by the *Camponotus* ant. This ant builds its nest between the concentric rings of long thorns on the stem. The *Korthalsia* rattan provides a nesting place in a swollen extension of the leaf sheath (ocrea). This association is remarkable for the rustling noise caused by the synchronized drumming of the ants' heads against the dry ocrea—a warning to the herbivore to retreat or else be attacked.

Some relationships remain unclear. For example, the ant colonies that live in the base of the pitcher stalk of the fanged pitcher plant (*Nepenthes bicalcarata*) have been observed stealing the newly drowned prey from the pitcher.

### Epiphytes and ants

Three types of association can be recognized, and these are the classic epiphytic ant-plant that possesses special structures for the ants to nest; the ant gardens; and the ant trees. While the epiphytic way of life positions the plant in a well-lit habitat, it also poses a problem in obtaining sufficient nutrients for plant growth as the bark surface and rain provide very little. An association with ants enables the epiphyte to tap a supply of nutrients from the ant colony. Usually the small, black *Iridomyrmex* ant is the partner in these associations, but it is not a particularly aggressive ant compared with *Cladomyrma* and *Camponotus* which play a protective role.

The classic epiphytic ant-plant is the shrubby baboon's head (*Hydnophytum formicarium*) and *Myrmecodia tuberosa* of the family Rubiaceae. These plants have an enlarged stem base (hypocotyle) that is the special structure in which ants live. Its honeycombed interior is further specialized into rough-walled and smooth-walled cavities. Detritus and waste products of the ants are deposited in the rough-walled cavities, from which the plants absorb

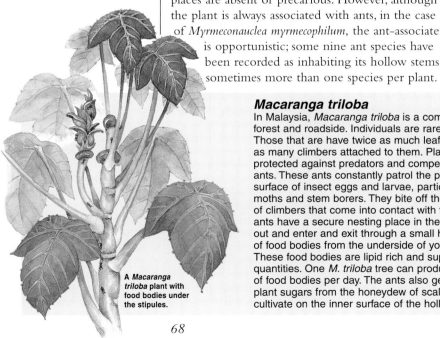

A *Macaranga triloba* plant with food bodies under the stipules.

#### *Macaranga triloba*

In Malaysia, *Macaranga triloba* is a common tree of secondary forest and roadside. Individuals are rarely found without ants. Those that are have twice as much leaf damage and 6–9 times as many climbers attached to them. Plants with ants are protected against predators and competition from climbers by the ants. These ants constantly patrol the plant and clear the leaf surface of insect eggs and larvae, particularly those of butterflies, moths and stem borers. They bite off the tendrils and shoot tips of climbers that come into contact with the tree. In return, the ants have a secure nesting place in the stem, which they hollow out and enter and exit through a small hole, and a regular supply of food bodies from the underside of young leaves and stipules. These food bodies are lipid rich and supplied in substantial quantities. One *M. triloba* tree can produce up to 250 milligrams of food bodies per day. The ants also get an additional supply of plant sugars from the honeydew of scale insects, which they cultivate on the inner surface of the hollowed stem.

The ant rears its brood in the hollow stem.

nutrients. The ant uses the smooth-walled cavities to raise its brood. This association is clearly beneficial to both partners as the ant has a secure home for its brood, and the epiphyte, which would otherwise have to depend on rainwater and the bark surface for nutrients, gains an additional supply.

Several other epiphytes have developed different structures that provide a place for ants to nest. In several species of the *Lecanopteris* fern, the old rhizome becomes hollow and provides a nesting place for ants. *Lecanopteris pumila* is remarkable as its old rhizome is black and shiny, as though made of plastic. In several *Dischidia* (Asclepiadaceae) species, such as *D. major*, the leaf blade grows to form a pot (ascidium) in which part of the ant brood is kept and which eventually becomes filled with detritus from the ant nest. When this happens, roots grow from the stem into the pot leaf, tapping the supply of nutrients.

### Ant trees

The ant tree association is more complicated than the ant garden one because a tree as well as epiphytes and ants are involved. One such tree is *gelam bukit* or *Leptospermum flavescens* (Myrtaceae). Here, the *Crematogaster* nests in cavities at the base of the tree and makes a system of tunnels through the trunk and branches. Exit holes are created high up in the crown, from where the ant emerges to scour the plant surface, removing all epiphytes, including mosses and lichens, except for ant garden species. For these species, the ant actively collects the seeds and drags them back into its nest.

Ant-plants continue to fascinate for the many variations on the theme of ant and plant associations, the disparate plant partners involved, and the bizarre structures that they can produce.

### Epiphytic ant-plants

LEFT: The pitcher or pot leaves of *Dischidia major*. INSET: An internal view of a pitcher leaf of *D. major*, showing the plant roots growing into the detritus accumulated by the ants.

RIGHT: A *Myrmecodia tuberosa* plant perching on the branch of a host tree, with its stem base sectioned to show the honeycombed interior where the ants live and raise their brood.

### Ant gardens

A regular assemblage of epiphytes also grow together in ant nests. Most have no specialized structures in which ants can nest. However, in all such epiphytes the ants seek out their seeds and actively bring them back to the nest or runways. In the runways, the carton (the nest structure made from soil and plant debris) and waste from the nest provide an ideal substrate for seed germination and root establishment. Besides the baboon's head, *Lecanopteris* species and *Dischidia major*, a variety of unrelated species are found in this ant-plant association. These include several hoyas, such as *Hoya lacunosa* (Asclepiadaceae); species of *Pachycentria* (Melastomataceae); most species of *Dischidia* and a few orchids, such as *Bulbophyllum*, *Dendrochilum* and *Acriopsis* species. These ant garden species are found in all permutations rooting in the ant nest or runways. It may be that their seeds emit a chemical that mimics the scent of prey, as most of these species do not have seeds with oil bodies or offer other sources of food for the ant. It is also not clear what benefit the ant gains from this association, though the roots may help bind the ant nest together.

### Plant species typical of an ant garden

1. *Lecanopteris* sp. is an epiphytic fern whose fleshy, hollow rhizomes are inhabited by ants.

2. *Pachycentria* sp., an epiphytic shrub commonly found on trees by the riverside.

3. A wild orchid, *Dendrochilum* sp. bears delicate yellow flowers less than a centimetre wide.

4. *Dischidia* sp., with its pitcher leaves growing along the host tree branch.

The hump-leafed *Dischidia astephana* grows in ant gardens. Here it is associated with an orchid.

# Insectivorous flowering plants

*In the flora of Malaysia, there are about 47 species which can be categorized as insectivorous flowering plants. These unique plants belong to three unrelated families: the Lentibulariaceae, or bladderwort family; the Droseraceae, or sundew family, and the Nepenthaceae, or pitcher plant family. Although they differ greatly in their morphology and habitat preference, all share common ecophysiological traits in being able to lure, trap and digest insects, and colonize and thrive well in nitrogen-deficient environments.*

A carpet of tightly clustered, flask-shaped basal pitchers of *Nepenthes ampullaria*, a species that grows in the lowlands, as in Endau State Park.

*Utricularia punctata* is an aquatic species found in still or slow-flowing waters in lakes, rivers and swamps in the lowlands of Malaysia.

### Examples of pitcher plants endemic to Malaysia

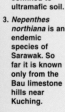

1. *Nepenthes sanguinea* is endemic to the mountains of Peninsular Malaysia. A young pitcher, as seen here, has a bright red rim with markings.
2. *Nepenthes rajah* is the largest pitcher plant in the world. It is endemic to Sabah and confined to ultramafic soil.
3. *Nepenthes northiana* is an endemic species of Sarawak. So far it is known only from the Bau limestone hills near Kuching.

## Bladderworts (*Utricularia*)

In Peninsular Malaysia, about 14 species of bladderworts have been described, of which four are free-floating, such as *Utricularia aurea* and *U. punctata*, and the remaining 10 are either terrestrial, such as *U. bifida* and *U. minutissima*, or semi-epiphytic, such as *U. striatula*. The free-floating species are found in ditches, ponds, lakes and streams containing stagnant or slow-flowing water. The plant is rootless. Its body comprises an elongated, slender, fragile and much-branched stem bearing numerous delicate, finely dissected leaves. Some leaves have small-sized, hollow, bladder-like traps. The terrestrial and epiphytic species possess roots and undissected leaves, and are found mainly in damp and shaded habitats ranging from lowlands to mountains.

## Sundews (*Drosera*)

The sundews, or *Drosera*, are represented by three species in Malaysian flora: *D. burmannii* and *D. indica* in Peninsular Malaysia and *D. spathulata* in Sabah and Sarawak. While *D. indica* is confined to habitats with a more seasonal climate, such as that in the northern parts of Peninsular Malaysia, *D. burmannii* and *D. spathulata* are restricted to localities under the influence of a constantly wet climate. However, all three species distinctly prefer sandy, acidic, nutrient-poor soils that are found in sandy beach, heath, peatswamp and montane forest habitats. The plant is a perennial, stemless (except in *D. indica*) herb, often with an underground tuber. The leaves are densely covered with glandular hairs, and in *D. burmanii* and *D. spathulata* these are spoon-shaped and arranged in rosettes pressed close to the ground; while in *D. indica* the leaves are linear with the lower ones often acting as stilt roots supporting the slender and flexible stem.

## Pitcher plants (*Nepenthes*)

*Nepenthes* or pitcher plants comprise about 60–70 species distributed mainly in the Old World tropics: Madagascar, the Seychelles,

The bright red tentacles of *Drosera burmanii* with their dewdrop-like secretion glistening in the sun.

Sri Lanka, Assam, south China, Indochina, Thailand, Malaysia, Indonesia, the Philippines, Papua New Guinea, northern Queensland and New Caledonia. However, most species occur in Southeast Asia, particularly in Borneo and Sumatra. In Malaysia, about 30 species and 7 natural hybrids are known. Of these, 3 species are endemic to Peninsular Malaysia, and 12 are endemic to Sabah and Sarawak. Most species are found in swampy or peaty habitats in the lowlands, on exposed ridges and on mountain summits. A few—*N. burbidgeae*, *N. rajah* and *N. villosa*—are confined to ultramafic soils, and *N. northiana* is known only from the Bau limestone hills in Sarawak. Both in lowland and mountain habitats, pitcher plants grow well in mineral-deficient soils. They are capable of supplementing their nourishment by trapping and digesting insect prey which is drowned in liquid accumulated in the pitchers. This liquid contains enzymes, including endopeptidase, aminopeptidase and chitinase, and also benzoic acid.

Pitchers produced by a young, rosetted plant and by the lower leaves of adult plants usually differ in size, shape and coloration from those developed by the leaves of the climbing stem. This great variation of the pitcher and the ability of several species to hybridize in nature have given rise to taxonomic confusion.

## Potential as ornamentals

In temperate countries, the appreciation of insectivorous plants, especially pitcher plants, which began in the 18th century has experienced a recent revival. However, in the tropics in general, and in Malaysia in particular, where insectivorous plants abound, their potential as ornamental plants is largely ignored and little appreciated.

# The insect traps

To capture their prey, insectivorous plants have developed three main types of trapping devices: an active trap, typified by the trapping device of the bladderworts; a semi-active trap, exemplified by the sundews; and a passive trap, shown by the pitcher plants. The active trap is equipped with an opening and closing trap door or valve that responds to the movement of prey. In semi-active traps, the trapping device is in the form of static leaves lined with mucilage glands or hairs. When touched, these glands secrete sticky liquid and bend forwards, entrapping the victim. In passive traps, the trapping apparatus is in the form of a pouch which exhibits no movement.

## The active bladderwort trap

The parts of the trap door or valve which initiate and activate movement are the hairs or bristles. These are sensitive to touch and are located at strategic points. The long, slender guide hairs help to deflect passing animals into the doorway of the trap, where they bump into small trigger hairs. Once touched, these spring the trap door open and suck the animal in; the door slams open and slams shut again almost immediately. The capture takes not more than 100th of a second and is one of the fastest reversible actions in the plant kingdom.

1. The structure of a typical free-floating species of *Utricularia*.
2. A bladder-like trap showing details of its various parts.

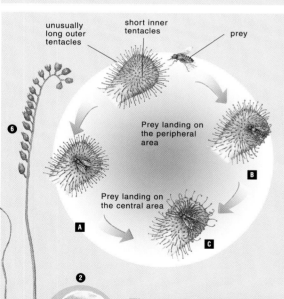

### How the bladderwort trap works

trap door **SET PHASE** trigger hairs

**DIGESTION PHASE**
secretion of enzyme is followed by digestion and absorption

**TRAP STIMULATED**
side walls concave

door is closed and prey is nearby

**RESETTING PHASE**
water is pumped out from the lumen

prey

prey is sucked in by outward movement of side walls

**AFTER FIRING**
side walls convex

**DOOR CLOSES**
prey within lumen

A. A vacuum is created when water is pumped out from the trap by special hairs on the bladder wall.

B. The trap door is triggered open by the movement of prey near the entrance. Both water and prey are sucked in.

C. The prey is trapped with the immediate closure of the trap door.

D. The plant then digests the prey with the help of secreted enzymes.

guide hairs
trap door
trigger hairs
two-armed glands
four-armed glands
globe-shaped glands

### How the sticky sundew works

A. The prey is held by sticky secretions of the glands concentrated in the central zone.

B. The marginal tentacles are capable of unusually fast movement, up to a complete course of 180 degrees in less than a minute. They will bend inwards, gradually conveying the creature to the central area where the glands are most numerous.

C. As the prey makes its last struggle, more neighbouring tentacles are activated that further immobilize the prey which is eventually digested by the gland secretion and assimilated into the sundew. The leaf reverts to its normal state and the cycle begins again with the next passing prey.

unusually long outer tentacles
short inner tentacles
prey

Prey landing on the peripheral area

Prey landing on the central area

## The semi-active sticky sundew trap

Sundew species found in Malaysia are mainly rosetted, that is, they are bulbous, rooted plants with flat rosettes of leaves as in the tropical sundew (*Drosera burmannii*). The touch-sensitive sticky leaves (1) are densely armed with two types of tentacles: the longer tentacles on the outer part of the leaf, which are involved in trapping the prey, such as the drosophilid fruit fly, and the shorter ones responsible for the secretion of digestive fluids. Each tentacle (2) comprises a lower stalk (3) and a head (4) covered with sticky slime (5). In the case of *D. burmannii*, the inflorescences are terminal and upright (6).

## The passive pitcher plant trap

An outstanding feature of the pitcher plant is the development of passive insect traps: the 'pitchers' produced at the tips of the tendril as an extension of the leaf.

lid evolved to shelter the pitcher from abundant tropical rain

The short, broad and rounded lower pitcher (1) forms a sharp contrast to the longer, funnel-shaped upper pitcher (2) of *Nepenthes rafflesiana*.

insect attracted by the sugary secretion

waxy rim which prevents the escape of fallen prey

a reserve of digestive fluids found at the base where both the digestion and absorption of prey take place

# Aquatic flowering plants

*Aquatic flowering plants are those that require the presence of permanent or semipermanent water bodies for their establishment, growth, reproduction and survival. In Malaysian flora, about 216 plant species in 30 families have adopted this way of life. These include both monocotyledonous plants, such as duckweed, jerangau, keladi bunting and sedges, as well as dicotyledonous plants like kangkong, lotus and water lilies. Although considered noxious weeds when they choke up water bodies, they are also used as food, medicine, fertilizer, ornamentals and are raw materials for various types of handicrafts.*

A natural inland lake, as in Tasik Bera in Pahang, is the habitat for many Malaysian aquatic plants.

## Habitat

In Malaysia, most species of aquatic flowering plants are inhabitants of freshwater bodies, such as ponds, ditches, lakes, dams, rivers, irrigation canals and wet paddy fields. Owing to their rapid vegetative growth and ability to regenerate by asexual and sexual means, as well as to their tolerance to a wide range of environmental conditions, most of them are considered weeds. Once they are established in a particular locality, their dense growth imposes a serious ecological problem. For example, a dense growth of duckweed (*Lemna perpusilla*) or water hyacinth, or *keladi bunting* (*Eichhornia crassipes*), on the water surface of a pond or lake will reduce the quantity and quality of sunlight penetrating the water body. This will, in turn, result in the drastic reduction of photosynthesis by suspended and submerged green plants, thus reducing the oxygen level in the water, eventually leading to the death of aquatic animal life. Dense growth of aquatic weeds on the surface of dams, lakes, rivers and irrigation canals gives rise to problems relating to the water supply, water transport and the maintenance of hydroelectric dams. A few native species, such as *Barclaya kunstleri* of the water lily family and *Cryptocoryne cordata* of the keladi family, thrive only in unpolluted water bodies like the edges of natural lakes and fast-flowing, shallow forest streams.

Sea grasses are found in the shallow, often rocky, coastal waters of Malaysia, and comprise 11 species from 6 genera and 2 families. They include species of *Enhalus*, *Halophila* and *Thalassia* (all Hydrocharitaceae) and *Cymodocea*, *Halodule* and *Syringodium* (all Potamogetonaceae). Ecologically, sea grasses play an important role in the coastal ecosystem by acting as stabilizers and providing shelter to many species of marine life, including commercially important species of fish and prawns, who also use these plants as feeding and breeding grounds.

## The three groups of aquatic flowering plants

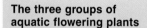

**FREE-FLOATING PLANTS**
Clumps of duckweed (*Lemna perpusilla*), one of the smallest and simplest free-floating plants in Malaysia.

**SUBMERGED PLANTS**
The completely submerged *Cymodocea rotumdata* is one of the 11 species of sea grasses found in the shallow coastal waters of Malaysia.

**EMERGENT PLANTS**
Bulrushes, or banat (*Typha angustifolia*), are an emergent species that grow well in the swampy and exposed habitats in the lowlands, hills and mountains up to 1700 metres.

*Barclaya kunstleri* is a rare and endangered species of submerged aquatic flowering plants. A member of the water lily family (Nymphaeaceae), this species is endemic to Peninsular Malaysia and confined to unpolluted, shallow forest streams.

## Adaptations and growth characteristics

Various methods of classifying hydrophytes have been suggested, but the most common one is to divide them into three major groups: free-floating, submerged and emergent.

Free-floating species have most of their parts exposed at or above the water surface, and only their roots, but occasionally the lower parts of the stems, submerged below the water surface. Common Malaysian examples include the duckweed, water hyacinth and water lettuce (*Pistia stratiotes*). These plants develop various adaptive structures. In duckweed, the plant body is extremely simple, comprising a tiny stem from which a flat and lens-shaped leaf measuring a few millimetres across and a feeble root system appear. The flowers are also minute, and the plant reproduces mainly through vegetative means. The upper leaf surface is coated with a waterproof layer of waxy material. In water lettuce, the stem is very short and fleshy. From this stem a rosette of stalkless leaves, a dense cluster of fibrous roots and tiny flowers arise. The leaf surface is densely covered with waterproof hairs and the internal tissues are filled with air spaces. The water hyacinth is a much larger and heavier plant than the duckweed or water lettuce. To float and maintain an upright position, the plant produces a dense, submerged fibrous root system and waterproof leaves supported by swollen, air-filled stalks, hence the Malay name *keladi bunting*, meaning literally 'pregnant yam'. The colourful flowers are borne in a cluster on long, upright stalks that are also filled with air spaces. A notorious aquatic weed introduced from Brazil to Malaysia in the early 20th century, the water hyacinth can regenerate through vegetative means as well as through seeds.

Submerged species have most of their parts located beneath the water surface, with only their flowers and the tips of their leaves occasionally

## The lotus: A symbol of purity and strength

For Hindus and Buddhists, the lotus (*Nelumbo nucifera*) reflects all that is pure. As the flower rises above the muddy waters in which it grows, it symbolizes the ability to remain clean despite its impure surroundings. The centre of its eight petals represents the core of the sun, or the navel of Vishnu, from which the universe originates. Another name for the goddess Lakshmi is *padma*, the Hindu term for lotus. The stance adopted by figures in meditation—the lotus position—symbolizes inner peace and a state of spiritual elevation.

Lotus flower buds are harvested by the Chinese and used as offerings to the Goddess of Mercy, Kwan Yin.

A luxuriant lotus garden. Apart from being a magnificent sight to behold, the lotus flower (inset) is sacred to Hindus and Buddhists, representing inner beauty and purity.

emerging or slightly above the water. The plants are rooted in the mud at the bottom of the water body. The stems are either short, upright and fleshy, such as in *Blyxa echinosperma*; or long, prostrate and tough, as in sea grasses; or long, slender and flexible, like those of *Hydrilla verticillata* and *Cyperus pilosus*. The leaves are a few cells thick and filled with air spaces. While the leaves of *Blyxa echinosperma* are strap-shaped, those of *Cyperus pilosus* are dissected into small, narrow leaflets, and those of *Hydrilla verticillata* are narrow and arranged in circles around the nodes. The flowers are unisexual and borne on long, slender and flexible stalks. Female flowers have feathery stigmas, while males ones are easily detached from the parent plant at maturity, releasing pollen in chains or clumps. All these features are adaptations to overcome the constant movement, low light intensity and low oxygen content of the water body. Vegetative reproduction is the primary means by which submerged species colonize water bodies. Water currents, animals and humans also carry tiny fragments of leafy nodes into uninfested areas, where the nodes multiply rapidly.

Emergent species can be subdivided into truly emergent and subemergent plants. In both cases, though, the plants are rooted in the muddy substrates of shallow water bodies, with only the lower parts of their stems or the whole leaf stalks submerged. The leaves or leaf blades only, as well as the flowers, emerge. With a few exceptions, the internal tissues of the submerged parts are filled with air spaces or reinforced with scattered but tough vascular bundles. Waterproof cuticles or a waxy substance protects the emergent plant parts. Reproduction is through vegetative means, such as stolons or rhizomes, or through seeds. In Malaysian flora, there are about 27 truly emergent and 140 subemergent species. Examples of the former include *Lepironia articulata*, genjir (*Limnocharis flava*) and *Monochoria hastata*; and subemergent species include the lotus (*Nelumbo nucifera*), kangkong (*Ipomoea aquatica*), the water lily (*Nymphaea*

*pubescens*) and the Indian gentian (*Nymphoides indica*). Emergent and subemergent species favour shallow water bodies, such as the edges of lakes and river banks. Their rate of growth is slower than that of free-floating species, but once an area is infested it is difficult for other potential invaders to get established.

### Uses

In Malaysia, more than 15 species are edible, including genjir, kangkong and the lotus. Of the latter species, all parts are edible. For example, unripe fruits and seeds are eaten raw, while ripe fruits and seeds are cooked eaten after removing the bitter part. The rhizomes are used by the Chinese for making a soup, but are also candied.

A number of species belonging to the grass and sedge families, as well as the water hyacinth, are harvested and used as animal fodder. Paddy farmers in Malaysia plough genjir, *Ludwigia hyssopifolia* and *Sagittaria guayanensis* into the wet paddy fields as green manure, which reputedly can increase crop yield by 50 per cent.

About 30 species from 16 families are claimed to have medicinal value. Among these, the sweet flag, or jerangau (*Acorus calamus*) is probably the most versatile. Other medicinal species include *Enhydra fluctuans* and *Neptunia oleracea*.

In fish tanks in homes and aquariums, certain species, such as *Blyxa echinosperma*, *Ceratophyllum demersum* and *Myriophyllum itermedium*, are planted both as ornamentals and a source of oxygen. Others, such as *Monochoria hastata*, *Nymphaea pubescens* and *Sagittaria sagittifolia*, are cultivated as ornamentals in ponds. Leaves and stems of *Lepironia articulata*, *Pandanus helicopus* and *Scirpus mucronatus* are used to make handicrafts.

## Aquatic flowering plants used in food, medicine and handicrafts

*Genjir* and *kangkong* growing in an abandoned drainage system. The latter is cooked with prawn paste for the dish, *sayur tumis kangkong.*

A whole *jerangau* plant, one of the most commonly used medicinal plants in Malaysia.

The dry stems of the sedge *Scirpus mucronatus* are used for making baskets, hats, mats and ropes.

### EDIBLE AQUATIC FLOWERING PLANTS

| SCIENTIFIC NAME | MALAY NAME | CULINARY USES |
|---|---|---|
| Alternanthera triandra | keremak | The young shoots are eaten. |
| Colocasia esculenta | keladi | The young shoots, leaves and corms are ingredients in *masak lemak* and *masak asam*. The rhizomes are eaten as a vegetable. |
| Eleocharis dulcis | Chinese water chestnut | The corm is used in *chop suey*, Chinese meat and fish dishes. It has a crisp, apple-like texture and tastes sweet. |
| Hygrophila quadrivalvis | chukal | The leaves are eaten. |
| Ipomoea aquatica | kangkong | The young shoots and leaves are eaten. This semi-aquatic form grows wild. |
| Limnocharis flava | genjir | The young shoots, leaves and flowers are eaten. |
| Nypa fruticans | nipah | The juice extracted from the inflorescence is converted to *gula melaka*, or *gula kabong*, and *air nira*, or toddy. The young shoots, or *umbut*, and fleshy nuts are eaten. |

### MEDICINAL AQUATIC FLOWERING PLANTS

| SCIENTIFIC NAME | MALAY NAME | MEDICINAL USES |
|---|---|---|
| Acanthus ebracteatus | jeruju | The seeds are used in cough mixtures. Pounded seeds are a poultice for boils. The decoction of roots treats shingles. |
| Acorus calamus | jerangau | Used to treat rheumatism and lumbago. The leaves are used for malaria and smallpox. The Chinese make a powder that is used for conjunctivitis. |
| Dysophylla auricularia | ekur kucing or awi tanah | Used to treat stomachaches in children. Other ailments it can help to relieve are sore throats, headaches and diarrhoea. |
| Enhydra fluctuans | chengkeru | Used as a general medicine by the Chinese. |
| Nelumbo nucifera | teratai or seroja | The rhizomes are used for diarrhoea and dysentry. Seeds are used for high fever and cholera. The petals are pounded and used to treat syphilis. |
| Neptunia oleracea | akar keman hantu | The root is used to treat syphilis. |

73

# Parasitic and saprophytic flowering plants

*During the course of evolution, a few species of flowering plants lost their green leaves and with it the ability to photosynthesize. To survive, some flowering plants (the holoparasites) rely totally on other living plants for their food, while others (the saprophytes) obtain organic nutrients from dead plant material. Still others (the hemiparasites) retain their green leaves but obtain their water and mineral nutrient source from a living plant. In Malaysia, it is notable that all holoparasites and hemiparasites are dicotyledons, while most saprophytes (with the exception of* **Epirixanthes**) *are monocotyledons.*

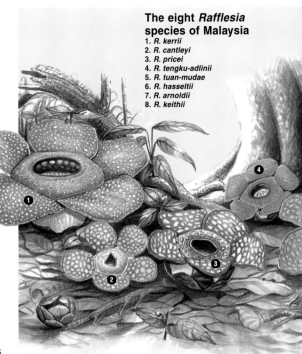

The eight *Rafflesia* species of Malaysia
1. *R. kerrii*
2. *R. cantleyi*
3. *R. pricei*
4. *R. tengku-adlinii*
5. *R. tuan-mudae*
6. *R. hasseltii*
7. *R. arnoldii*
8. *R. keithii*

A hemiparasite, *Striga asiatica* is a witchweed that parasitizes the roots of grasses.

The flowers (main picture) and haustoria (inset) of *Dendrophthoe pentandra*, a hemiparasitic mistletoe that attacks trees in the lowlands of Malaysia.

## Hemiparasites

On germination, the seedling root of the hemiparasite penetrates the branch of the host plant and forms a connection (called the haustorium) with the xylem. Through this connection, the hemiparasite siphons off water and mineral nutrients from the host. In some cases, this is done so efficiently that insufficient water is left for the host branch, which then dies back.

The hemiparasites include species of mistletoe, sandalwood and witchweed. All these plants have ordinary green leaves, except for *Viscum articulatum*, which is leafless. In *V. articulatum*, its green stem carries out photosynthesis. This species parasitizes other mistletoes, and so gets its water 'third hand'.

In Malaysia, *Scurrula ferruginea*, the common scurfy mistletoe, parasitizes a wide range of trees, including fruit trees. If it is not removed, it can cause serious damage to the tree crown, as well as act as a seed source, causing other trees in the orchard to quickly become infested.

The mistletoes have developed an effective seed dispersal mechanism which deposits the seeds directly onto the host tree branch. The seed has an extremely sticky inner layer, which when eaten by a bird is not removed as it passes through the digestive system. The bird has to actively rub its anus against a branch to be free of the sticky seed.

The witchweed genus *Striga* also has an efficient strategy to ensure that its seeds come into contact with its host. It usually parasitizes the roots of grasses. The seeds of this small herb, called *jarum emas* or *rumput siku siku*, will only germinate in response to the presence of chemicals that leach out of grass roots. This strategy enables the seed to contact the grass root and produce haustoria. Fortunately, the Malaysian species, *Striga asiatica*, is small and does not parasitize crop plants, but in Africa a much larger species devastates maize crops.

## Holoparasites

In Malaysia, all members of the Balanophoraceae and Rafflesiaceae, and a few species of the Convolvulaceae, Lauraceae and Scrophulariaceae belong to this category of parasitic flowering plant. The Balanophoraceae are root parasites of montane trees; the Rafflesiaceae are mostly parasitizing woody climbers of the *Tetrastigma* (Vitaceae), and the few members of the Scrophulariaceae are parasites of bamboo roots. They have no green leaves, but may nevertheless be colourful due to the presence of other pigments. Holoparasites have reduced vegetative parts. Leaves are absent, and roots are replaced by a haustorial system that taps not only the xylem but also the phloem of the host plants.

Species of *Balanophora* have a tuber-like vegetative body that produces inflorescences of many flowers. In contrast, *Rafflesia* produces a single enormous flower, and *Christisonia* and *Aeginetia* (both members of Scrophulariaceae) produce a few showy flowers. Although flower size in Malaysian holoparasites ranges from the largest in *Rafflesia* (up to 1 metre across) to the smallest in *Balanophora* (with female flowers less than 1 millimetre across), the seed size is uniformly minute. Dispersal of *Rafflesia* seeds may be effected by being carried on the paws of squirrels, and seeds of *Balanophora* might reach the host's roots by rain wash. The mode of dispersal of the other species remains unknown.

Two holoparasites, namely *Cassytha filiformis* and *Cucusta orientalis*, grow in disturbed and open habitats. These are the leafless dodders that produce thread-like stems which pierce the host stem by numerous tiny haustoria. The seeds of dodders germinate in the soil, then produce a fine twining stem which, on encountering a host stem, curls around it and on contact produces haustoria. Once the haustorial connection is established, its root system dies and the dodder is totally dependent on

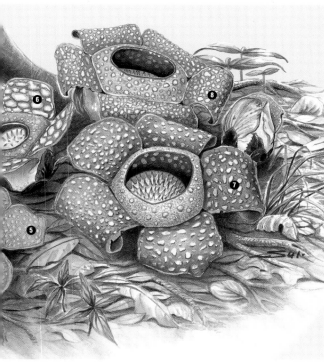

### *Rafflesia*: The largest flower in the world

The 15 species of *Rafflesia* are found only in Peninsular Malaysia, Sumatra, Java, Borneo and the Philippines. Eight of the 15 species occur in Malaysia—three in Peninsular Malaysia and five in Sabah and Sarawak. Flower size ranges from 15 centimetres across in *R. tengku-adlinii* to 97 centimetres in *R. arnoldii*, which weighs a massive 6.8 kilograms.

*Rafflesia* is also remarkable for the extreme reduction of its vegetative parts. It produces no roots, stems or leaves. Instead, microscopic strands spread throughout the host's stem tissues. From

*Rafflesia cantleyi* buds for sale at a roadside stall in Perak. Collecting of *Rafflesia* buds severely depletes their stock in the wild.

these threads buds develop and eventually break through the host's bark. After a further nine months, the mature bud is the size of a small cabbage, but the open flower lasts for only 2–5 days. These flowers produce a putrid smell which attracts clouds of bluebottle flies, the pollinators. These flies carry a sticky blob of pollen on their backs from the male to the female flower. In contrast to the large flowers, the seeds are tiny.

Conservation of *Rafflesia* is critical. They only parasitize a few species of the *Tetrastigma* vine, a member of the grape family. *Rafflesia* cannot be cultivated; it can only survive under natural conditions. While Sabah has set up a *Rafflesia* Sanctuary, in Peninsular Malaysia widespread collecting and sale of buds of *bunga pakma* (*R. cantleyi*) for medicinal purposes proceed unchecked. Its use as a medicine relies on the concept of 'doctrine of signatures' as the swollen bud suggests a womb, but there is no scientific or medical evidence to support this.

its host for nutrients. In Malaysia, dodders are a remarkable example of parallel evolution: their mode of parasitism and appearance is almost identical but the structure of the flowers is different. Thus, *Cassytha filiformis* belongs to the laurel family (Lauraceae), while *Cuscuta orientalis* is a member of the bindweed family (Convolvulaceae). The latter can be a troublesome weed in coffee estates, blanketing the coffee bush with a dense mat of thread-like stems. These two dodders produce small berries that are dispersed by birds.

### Saprophytes (Mycoheterotrophs)

No flowering plant is truely saprophytic and able to decompose dead plant material. The true saprophyte is the fungus that lives within its cells. This fungus produces enzymes that can break down organic matter in the leaf litter. The saprophytic flowering plant is, in fact, mycoheterotrophic, as it absorbs these simple decomposition products from the fungus. There is some doubt that the fungus–plant association is truly symbiotic, as it is not clear whether the fungus benefits from the association. This suggests that the mycoheterotrophic association may, in fact, be one of mild parasitism.

All Malaysian mycoheterotrophic flowering plants grow on the cool, damp forest floor where there is an accumulation of leaf litter, perhaps a habitat requirement of the fungal partner. Mycoheterotrophic flowering plants share several features in common. Their root system is short with knobbly, worm-like branches, which lack the root hairs that are the water-absorbing structure in normal plants. The shoot system is slender, has scale-like leaves and typically lacks stomata. Most are pallid and ghostly coloured, but in the case of a few orchid species and *Thismia* (Burmanniaceae) the flowers are colourful.

This mode of life has evolved independently many times in unrelated families. Although the majority of mycoheterotrophic flowering plants are orchids, several species of monocotyledonous families (Burmanniaceae, Melanthraceae and Triuridiaceae) and members of the dicotyledonous genus *Epirixanthes* (Polygalaceae) are mycoheterotrophs.

### Conservation

Species that require an association with another organism are particularly vulnerable to habitat changes which might eliminate one of the partners. This is particularly the case with mycoheterotrophic species and forest parasites that are nowhere common, and are dependent not only on the damp, shaded conditions of the forest to live, but on the web of interconnections with organisms that pollinate their flowers and disperse their seeds. In addition, many of these species are extremely rare. None have been successfully cultivated, either in the laboratory or in botanic gardens. Unless their forest habitat is protected in Malaysia and elsewhere, their long-term survival is not assured.

The thread-like stems of *Cuscuta orientalis*, a holoparasite, blanket its host plant.

A saprophytic orchid found growing on the forest floor in shaded and damp localities in the lowland and montane forests of Malaysia.

The strikingly coloured flowers of *Thismia aseroë*, a saprophytic flowering plant found in moist and sheltered localities in lowland mixed dipterocarp forests.

Some holoparasites, such as *Christisonia scortechinii* (left), live on the roots of bamboos, whilst others, like *Balanophora fungosa* (right), parasitize the roots of trees of lower and upper montane forests.

For tapping latex from a rubber tree, small sections of bark are removed until a large part of the trunk is stripped. Plantation workers, like this woman, collect the latex.

A tea picker gathering tea leaves in a plantation in the Cameron Highlands where most of Malaysia's tea is grown.

Rice seedlings being planted by hand in a wet paddy field.

❶

Most of the world's supply of palm oil comes from the oil palm plantations of Malaysia. In 1996, Malaysia exported over 11 million tonnes of palm oil to over 90 countries all over the globe, with the largest amount going to countries in Central and South America and Central and East Asia.

❷

❸

# PLANTS AND MAN

Plants have provided for human needs since man first appeared on earth. Prehistoric man gathered plant material from his surroundings for food, to make tools and to build shelter. As man became more socialized and his life more sedentary, he began, through trial and error, to select, introduce and cultivate various types of useful plants in and around his settlement areas. Today, man still cultivates plants to serve his needs, except that in addition to traditional farming methods, he also employs sophisticated technologies to harvest and exploit plant resources.

Rambutan trees are grown in fruit orchards and in kampong and urban gardens across Malaysia. When mature, the hairy skins turn a deep red or yellow.

Durians comprise Malaysia's largest native fruit crop and are exported to countries in Southeast Asia as well as consumed domestically.

In Malaysia, both native and introduced plants and their products are utilized for a variety of purposes. Different groups of aboriginal people, for example, gather many wild plant species and plant parts from the forest to meet their subsistence needs. Fruits, tubers, leaves and young shoots are consumed as food, while bamboo, rattan and timber serve as building materials and are used for making tools. Bamboo, as well as palm leaves, bark, wood and resins, is used for making household utensils. Villagers not only collect firewood but also convert the wood of some tree species into charcoal to supplement their fuel requirements. Certain forest products, such as timber and rattan, are also harvested in large quantities for industrial and commercial purposes. In traditional medicine, many species of native and introduced—but naturalized—plants are widely used in the preparation of decoctions, poultices, salves and tonics.

There are numerous exotic plant species that have been introduced to Malaysia specifically for the purpose of establishing large-scale agricultural, horticultural and industrial plantations. Malaysia's most prominent industrial crops are oil palm and rubber trees, introduced from tropical Africa and Brazil respectively. In the agricultural sector, plant species that produce commercially important fruits, vegetables and spices have been introduced and successfully cultivated in orchards and farms across the country. Other useful crops, such as rice, tapioca, tea, coffee and cocoa, have also been introduced. Introduced plants that have ornamental and horticultural value include begonias, bougainvilleas, heliconias, lilies and some orchids as well as temperate plants such as dahlias and roses that are grown mainly in the Cameron Highlands.

Both red and green chillies are an integral part of Malaysian cuisine, and are found in many dishes, sauces and condiments, including *sambal*, a widely used chilli paste.

Being an ethnically diverse country, Malaysia is rich in tradition, culture and religion. During important social occasions, such as the birth of a child, the marriage of a couple or the death of a member of the community, certain plants and plant parts are used ceremonially. In addition, the branches, stems, roots, flowers, leaves, fruits and seeds of certain plants are used to make a variety of handicraft products, such as baskets and mats.

**Plant uses and products**

1. The hardwood *chengal*, which comes from *Neobalanocarpus heimii*, is used to build boats, especially in Terengganu. Timber is Malaysia's most important forest product, and is sold in the form of sawn timber, processed timber, logs, plywood and veneer.

2. Woven from rattan and bamboo, this basket, called *karansang*, is made by the Kadazan (Dusun) people of Kota Belud in Sabah. The straps are made of bark cloth and are slung around the shoulders of the person carrying the basket. It is used for carrying agricultural produce.

3. An intricately patterned Kayan jacket made from tree bark. Many of Malaysia's indigenous ethnic groups use tree bark for this purpose. Some groups impose a distinct style or pattern on their tree bark garments.

# Timber trees

*In Malaysia's forests, there are 3,000–5,000 tree species that belong to about 500 genera in 100 families. These trees are distributed from lowland to montane forests, with the majority in lowland, hill and lower montane forests. About 700 species reach timber size, attaining a diameter of 40 centimetres or more. Of these, about 400 species are harvested for their valuable timbers which are classified into different timber groups. Members of the dipterocarp family constitute the most important timber resource in Malaysia.*

The Forestry Museum in Penang has on permanent display a typical timber tree which, together with related exhibits, helps to increase the public's awareness of Malaysia's rich timber resources.

## Diversity of timber trees

The term 'timber' refers to wood obtained from trees and processed for use in construction. In Malaysia, among the plant families with an abundance of timber trees are the Dipterocarpaceae (*keruing, meranti, selangan batu*), Leguminosae, (*kempas, merbau*), Burseraceae (*kedondong*), Anacardiaceae (mango), Sapotaceae (*nyatoh*), Lauraceae (*medang*), Fagaceae (*berangan* and *mempening*) and Myristicaceae (*penarahan*). Of these, the genera and species of the Dipterocarpaceae constitute the most important timber resource, and include timber groups such as the red meranti (*Shorea* spp.), keruing (*Dipterocarpus* spp.), *kapur* (*Dryobalanops* spp.) and *chengal* (*Neobalanocarpus heimii*). In the lowland mixed dipterocarp forests of Peninsular Malaysia, 50–60 per cent of the volume of growing stock over 30 centimetres in diameter are dipterocarp trees.

***Jelutong*: A well-known Malaysian timber tree**
The *jelutong* (*Dyera costulata*) is a huge, magnificent tree that reaches a height of up to 60 metres, with an enormous, unbuttressed columnar bole (1). In mature trees, an open, shallow, dome-shaped crown (2) with a big spread is observed. In unbuttressed timber trees, the diameter is taken at breast height, commonly known as d.b.h. (3), defined as 1.35 metres from the ground.

These form 75 per cent of the commercial timber volume. In Sabah and Sarawak, 67 per cent of the growing stock consists of species of *Shorea*. About 80 per cent of the commercial timber volume comes from the dipterocarp family.

## Distribution in the forests

The distribution and abundance of timber trees in Malaysia are closely linked to altitude, soil type, drainage and topography. There is great species diversity in the lowlands and hills, where species of *Shorea* and *Dipterocarpus* predominate up to an altitude of 1000 metres. Above this altitude, the composition changes drastically and trees which are found at lower altitudes seldom occur. Trees that occur at higher altitudes tend to be smaller and shorter. The dominant tree families above the 1000-metre elevation are members of the Fagaceae, Lauraceae, Myrtaceae (*kelat*) and conifers.

## Uses

Exploitation of forest timber is an important economic activity in Malaysia, and has a direct impact on the socioeconomic development of the country. Malaysia is one of the leading exporters of tropical timber. Although only processed timber and timber products are exported from Peninsular Malaysia, the bulk of exports from Sabah and Sarawak are in log form. The main importers

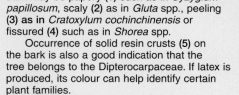

## General features of timber trees

Timber trees possess a wide variety of characteristics in different combinations, which help to distinguish one species from another.

First, the texture and colour of the bark's surface are clues to the tree's identity. The bark may be papery (1) such as in *Syzygium papillosum*, scaly (2) as in *Gluta* spp., peeling (3) as in *Cratoxylum cochinchinensis* or fissured (4) such as in *Shorea* spp.

Occurrence of solid resin crusts (5) on the bark is also a good indication that the tree belongs to the Dipterocarpaceae. If latex is produced, its colour can help identify certain plant families.

The base of the trunk may produce buttresses (6) in the form of large, protruding flanges. Characteristic of trees growing in swamp forests are stilt roots (7).

## DIPTEROCARPACEAE GENERA: THEIR TRADE NAMES, TIMBER GROUPS AND MAIN USES

| GENUS NAME | TRADE NAME OR OTHER COMMON NAMES | TOTAL NO. OF SPECIES IN MALAYSIA | TIMBER GROUP | MAIN USES |
|---|---|---|---|---|
| Anisoptera | mersawa | 6 | L–M | light construction |
| Cotylelobium | resak | 3 | H | heavy construction |
| Dipterocarpus | keruing | 38 | M–H | heavy and general building construction |
| Dryobalanops | kapur | 7 | M | light and heavy construction |
| Hopea | merawan or gagil, giam | 54 | L–H | light and medium construction |
| Neobalanocarpus | chengal | 1 | H | heavy construction |
| Parashorea | white seraya, gerutu, urat mata | 9 | L–M | light to medium construction |
| Shorea | balau or selangan batu | 38 | H | medium and heavy construction |
| | red meranti, dark red meranti, light red meranti or red seraya | 70 | L–M | a wide variety of general uses |
| | yellow meranti or yellow seraya | 31 | L | light construction |
| | white meranti or melapi | 22 | L | light to medium construction |
| Vatica | resak | 42 | M | heavy construction |
| Upuna | upun | 1 | H | heavy construction |

Abbrev.: L—light hardwood   M—medium hardwood   H—heavy hardwood

Source: After Ashton (1982); Wong (1982)

## MALAYSIA'S EXPORT OF MAJOR TIMBER PRODUCTS (1995)

PENINSULAR MALAYSIA   SABAH   7.744   SARAWAK

million m³

Logs · Sawn timber · Processed timber · Plywood · Veneer · Moulding

Source: Malaysian Timber Industry Board, Ministry of Primary Industries (1996)

of tropical timber are Japan, Taiwan and other countries of East Asia. Between them, they take the bulk of Malaysia's exported timber, totalling about 88 per cent.

Each type of timber is known by its trade name, which generally corresponds to botanical genera rather than to botanical species. In Peninsular Malaysia, there are 100 timber groups, which are classified as light, medium heavy, heavy and very heavy. Whether it is a major or minor commercial timber depends on the demand, abundance and availability of the group it belongs to. Timber products are exported in the form of planks,

plywood, veneer, moulding, blockboard, dowelings, wood chips and furniture. In Sabah and Sarawak, the timber groupings are similar to those in Peninsular Malaysia, with a few additional groups, such as *belian* (*Eusideroxylon zwageri*), *sempilor* (*Dacrydium* and *Phyllocladus* spp.) and *takalis* (*Pentace* spp.). *Ramin* (*Gonystylus* spp.) and *sempilor* are also important export products from Sarawak. With changing utilization patterns and the development of more sophisticated equipment, Malaysia's minor commercial timber trees will probably constitute an important timber resource in the future.

In addition to timber, the timber trees of Malaysia provide other products, including fruits, resins, fragrant wood or *gaharu*—wood from species of *Aetoxylon, Aquilaria* and *Gonystylus*—and tannins from mangrove bark. A recent finding shows that the latex of the *bintangor* tree may be able to help combat the AIDS virus (see 'Extinction is forever'). Certain timber trees are also planted as ornaments in parks, gardens and along roadsides.

### Conservation

With increased exploitation, the timber tree resources of Malaysia are likely to face depletion. Hence, adequate steps need to be taken to conserve different habitats and vegetation types so that the tree flora can continue to survive. For this purpose, the Malaysian Government has put aside about 14 million hectares of forest as Permanent Forest Estates designated for producing tropical timber on a sustainable basis, and about 1.56 million hectares as Totally Protected Areas in the form of national parks and wildlife and bird sanctuaries, where the country's rich biodiversity can be conserved.

## Classification of major timber groups

Timber groups are broadly classified into two categories:

1. Softwoods—timber produced from conifer trees or gymnosperms.

2. Hardwoods—timber produced from flower-bearing trees or angiosperms. Hardwoods are further classified into three main groups according to their density:

| HARDWOODS | Heavy | Medium | Light |
|---|---|---|---|
| DENSITY (kg/m³) | >800 | 500<800 | <500 |

### Timber processing

Selective felling of a mature, commercially valuable tree in the Malaysian rainforest is done by chain saw.

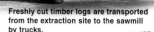

Freshly cut timber logs are transported from the extraction site to the sawmill by trucks.

The extracted logs are processed in the sawmill with the help of heavy machinery.

79

# Native ornamental plants

*There are over 10,000 species of native flowering plants in Malaysia, ranging from small shrubs to giant trees. Some have been transplanted from the forest to an urban setting, where they are grown as ornamentals, valued for the shade they provide and their beautifully coloured and scented flowers. These native ornamentals line the avenues of towns and cities, and decorate both public and private gardens. Previously overlooked in favour of introduced species, native species are gaining popularity as efforts are made to encourage their use.*

Fruits and flower of the *simpoh* shrub, and its characteristc oval, cabbage-like leaves. It has made a successful transition from its natural habitat of swamp forests to the roadsides of towns and cities.

A patch of *Ixora javanica* planted in a central reservation along a highway leading to Melaka. The large and round inflorescences (inset) each bear a small cluster of tiny red, four-petalled flowers. Out of the 20 species of *Ixora* found in Malaysia, this is the most popular as an ornamental.

## From the forest to the garden

Many attractive plants in Malaysia's forests have potential as ornamentals. These include over 800 species of native orchids, such as the elegant jewel orchid with its shimmering leaves, and pitcher plants (*Nepenthes* spp.) that hang beautifully on forest trees and look equally stunning in a garden.

Although most of Malaysia's garden or wayside plants are introduced species, the relatively smaller number of native ornamentals include well-known species such as *angsana* (*Pterocarpus indicus*) and *tembusu* (*Fagraea fragrans*). There has, however, been renewed interest in native plants species, as their intrinsic and aesthetic value is recognized. For example, Kuala Lumpur City Hall's Parks and Recreation Department is building a conservatory in Taman Tasik Perdana (the Lake Gardens) that will house a wide variety of native plants, including herbs and wild flowers, that have not been cultivated before.

## Trees

Perhaps the most frequently seen native ornamental plants are the trees which grow by the roadsides of towns and cities.

The angsana is a very large, deciduous tree, reaching up to a height of 40 metres. It grows rapidly from woodcuttings of 1.5–2 metres. A lush, dome-shaped crown gives useful shade. During the tree's flowering season, flushes of sweet-smelling yellow blossoms are produced. However, they are not long-lasting, and a carpet of petals is often seen littering the avenues along which these trees are planted.

Found throughout the tropics on seashores, the sea hibiscus, or *baru baru* (*Hibiscus tiliaceus*), is a small tree with a rounded crown and dark green foliage. It is propagated by seed. Bright yellow flowers are clustered on sparsely branched inflorescences. When the flowers are about to drop, their petals change colour and become orange-pink. Because of its compact size, it is a good tree for planting along paths or as a border.

A native to both Malaysia and Indonesia, tembusu is an evergreen tree. It is slow growing, but will eventually reach a height of 30 metres. The crown is usually thin, although that of very young trees is dense. Numerous groups of closely set leaves weigh the branches down and cause them to droop. If the trees are left unpruned, the branches will enlarge and bow down until they reach near the ground, and then turn upwards again. Because of the curious shapes brought about by this growth habit, the branches look very decorative when fully grown. The flowers are small, cream coloured and very fragrant, and will each develop into a small, orange berry. When flowering occurs, it is profuse and the pleasant scent wafts into the surrounding area. Tembusu is propagated by seed. This tree is suitable for planting in large, open spaces.

A native of Myanmar, Thailand and Peninsular Malaysia, *bungur* (*Lagerstroemia floribunda*) is a medium-sized evergreen tree with an oval crown. In the wild, it grows up to 18 metres, whereas cultivated individuals are much shorter. Amongst the dull, dark green leaves nestle pink and pale purple flowers that gradually turn white with age. Flowering occurs at regular intervals throughout the year. Propagation is easily done by seed. The tree remains at a manageable height of 4–6 metres, and is ideal for home gardens.

*Cempaka merah* (*Michelia champaca*) is native to both India and Malaysia. Its leaves are yellowish green, and the flowers orange. A favourite in gardens because of its small size and beautifully scented flowers, this species is propagated by seed and marcotting.

The ironwood tree, or *penaga* (*Mesua ferrea*), is native to the Himalayas and Malaysia. This graceful evergreen tree reaches a height of 20 metres. When young, it grows very slowly and the leaves are a brilliant red. By maturity, the crown is cone shaped, becoming increasingly rounded as the tree ages.

## Garden settings

1. The Penang Botanic Gardens, where native plant species have been cultivated since the 19th century by European botanists and horticulturalists. It houses a fine collection of palms, flowering trees and bamboos.

2. Resorts and hotels, such as The Regent in Kuala Lumpur, find value in landscaping their grounds in a tropical garden style.

3. A private residence in Kuala Lumpur, with a neatly trimmed row of *Ixora* shrubs lining the driveway.

## Malaysian trees: The most widely cultivated native ornamental plants

Amongst the different plant groups, such as trees, shrubs and herbs, trees are the most popularly grown as ornamentals in Malaysia. In towns, parks and villages across Peninsular Malaysia, certain ornamental tree species are recognizable features. Wayside trees have become part of a town's identity, such as the grand *angsana* trees that have lined the streets of Port Dickson since 1924. Some parks and botanical gardens are known for the tree species that have flourished, a fine example being the rain trees in the Lake Gardens of Taiping. In villages, trees that are frequently cultivated have also become associated with the area in which they grow. *Belinjau* trees, for example, are characteristic of kampongs in Terengganu, but are not commonly grown elsewhere in Peninsular Malaysia.

| CITIES AND TOWNS IN MALAYSIA NAMED AFTER TREES | | |
|---|---|---|
| | PLACE NAME | TREE SPECIES |
| 1. | Alor Setar | *Bouea macrophylla* |
| 2. | Guar Cempedak | *Artocarpus integer* |
| 3. | Penaga | *Mesua* sp. |
| 4. | Kuala Kangsar | *Hibiscus floccosus* |
| 5. | Ipoh | *Antiaris toxicaris* |
| 6. | Chegar Perah | *Elateriospermum tapos* |
| 7. | Kuala Lipis | *Pavetta indica* |
| 8. | Kampung Jambu Bongkok | *Eugenia* spp. |
| 9. | Dungun | *Heritiera littoralis* |
| 10. | Kalumpang | *Sterculia* spp. |
| 11. | Petaling | *Ochanostachys amentacea* |
| 12. | Durian Tipus | *Durio* spp. |
| 13. | Pengkalan Kempas | *Koompassia malaccensis* |
| 14. | Belimbing | *Averrhoa bilimbi* |
| 15. | Johor | *Cassia siamea* |
| 16. | Desaru | *Casuarina equisetifolia* |

*Penaga* trees are the namesake of a small town in Pulau Pinang. They have a well-defined crown, making them popular wayside trees.

The fruits of *Heritiera littoralis*, a tree that grows naturally on sandy beaches. A coastal town in Terengganu is named after this tree.

*Casuarina* trees are found in the towns along the east coast of Pahang. Their Malay name, *rhu*, occurs in various forms in some place names, such as Desaru.

### Common native ornamental trees

A. *Belinjau* trees are characteristic of village gardens in Terengganu.

B. Towering *tembusu* trees are a feature of towns in Selangor and Pahang.

C. *Baru baru* growing in sandy open ground near a residential area. This tree naturally occurs in sandy beach habitats, but is now also grown in towns and cities.

D. *Angsana* trees are ubiquitous in Malaysia, but are most common in Pulau Pinang, Perak, Selangor, Negeri Sembilan and Melaka.

E. The leaves and pale yellow flowers of the *cempaka* tree. Because of its thin foliage and small size, it is suitable for planting in home gardens.

F. The purple petals of the flowers of the *bungur* tree. This species is a favourite ornamental because it flowers at regular intervals throughout the year.

## Shrubs

A tall shrub, the Javanese *ixora* (*Ixora javanica*) has large leaves and flower heads, and enjoys being in semi-shade. The red, pink or yellow flowers are propagated by marcots and cuttings. This species is ideal as a hedge.

*Simpoh* (*Dillenia suffruticosa*) is a big evergreen shrub from Peninsular Malaysia. It grows up to 7 metres and has large, cabbage-like leaves. Propagation is by seed. The yellow flowers have pale cream stamens. Seldom cultivated in gardens, it is more commonly seen as a roadside plant.

## Orchids

Native orchids have made their way into private gardens and public parks. The biggest epiphytic orchid species known, the tiger orchid (*Grammatophyllum speciosum*), for example, originates from the jungles of Malaysia, but is now planted as an ornamental. It is a large plant that produces a succession of thick, leafy shoots. From a host tree, the long shoots hang down, and the inflorescence, up to 2 metres in length, grows upwards. When cultivated, however, the shoots are erect and curve outwards. The flowers are big and either pale yellow, dull orange or striped brown. As it only flowers once or twice a year, it is not the most popular ornamental plant.

The pigeon orchid (*Dendrobium crumenatum*) is a native of Myanmar and south China, as well as Malaysia. An epiphyte that grows wild on trees and bushes in the forests, the pigeon orchid flowers after a sudden drop in temperature following a rain storm (see 'Growth and reproductive seasonality'). White with a yellow lip, the flowers are fragrant but last for only a day. The plant multiplies rapidly by its thick bulb-like stems or pseudobulbs, but can also be propagated by division (dividing plant parts and replanting segments capable of producing roots).

The pigeon orchid (*Dendrobium crumenatum*) with its profuse blooms, is a highly valued ornamental plant.

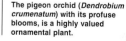

# Introduced ornamental plants

*Most ornamental flowering trees, shrubs and herbs are of tropical origin. Exceptions are plants such as roses and chrysanthemums. Some of the tropical flowering plants found in Malaysia, including the National Flower, originated in other regions of the world. A large number of temperate flowers were also introduced, and now flourish in Malaysia's highland resorts and nurseries. A great variety of ornamental flowering plants can be seen in gardens, towns and nurseries where they are grown and bred for the cut-flower industry.*

### Herbaceous highland species

*Top*: A commercial flower nursery in the Cameron Highlands where a wide range of chrysanthemum (*Chrysanthemum morifolum*) varieties and hybrids, originally from China, are grown.

*Middle*: The sunflower (*Helianthus annus*), introduced from North America, is grown both in the lowlands and highlands for its brilliant yellow flowers.

*Bottom*: The dahlia (*Dahlia pinnata*), a herbaceous annual native of Mexico, is grown on a commercial scale for the cut-flower trade in Malaysia's highlands because of its showy, brightly coloured flowers.

## Flowering trees and shrubs

Tropical countries such as Malaysia are well known for their evergreen forests. They do not have a spring season to exhibit their flowers as do temperate countries. In Malaysia, the flowering season of most plants coincides with the dry season. It is a spectacular sight to see trees in full bloom during or after a dry season, such as an avenue of flame of the forest trees without leaves but full of flowers. Introduced shrubs, such as *Bougainvillea* and *Mussaenda*, are also commonly seen by the roadside, in parks or as potted plants in home gardens.

## Herbaceous species

Many herbaceous ornamental flowering plants have been introduced to Malaysia from different parts of the world. A number are successfully grown in the lowlands, for example, species and cultivars of lilies and lily-alikes (*Crinum*, *Hippeastrum* and *Hymenocallis* spp.), lobster's claw (*Heliconia* spp.), and periwinkle (*Catharanthus roseus*). Other introduced ornamentals only do well if cultivated in the highlands, such as many members of the sunflower family (Compositae), including species of *Chrysanthemum*, *Gerbera*, *Helianthus* or sunflowers and *Tagetes* or marigolds.

In addition, many species of orchids and their hybrids have also been introduced to Malaysia for their attractive sprays of flowers. Among these are species and hybrids of *Aranda, Ascocentrum, Cattleya, Dendrobium, Oncidium, Phalaenopsis* and *Rhynchostylis*.

Many exotic species, varieties and hybrids of *Dendrobium* (above) and other orchid genera were introduced to Malaysia. These are grown on a commercial scale.

## The cultivation of temperate flowers

The only area in Malaysia where temperate flowers are grown on a commercial scale is the Cameron Highlands. There, nurseries are filled with chrysanthemums, roses, dahlias and other such temperate species, bred for the cut-flower and horticulture industries. The area around Kampung Kuala Terla, to the north of the Cameron Highlands, and the Bertam Valley, in the south, are the two most heavily cultivated.

### The *bunga raya*: Malaysia's National Flower

The hibiscus, an evergreen shrub believed to have originated in China and Indochina, is the national flower of two countries, Malaysia and Jamaica. It is also the state flower of Hawaii in the United States of America.

On 28 July 1960, the Government of Malaysia proclaimed the *bunga raya* (*Hibiscus rosa-sinensis*) the National Flower because it is popularly known and flourishes all over the country. The bright red colour of the flowers signifies bravery.

The bunga raya is aseasonal and flowers throughout the year. It also grows easily and vigorously, and requires very little maintenance. It is characterized by huge and beautiful petals and a brush-like, dangling stamen.

*Hibiscus schizopetalus* is one of the earliest *Hibiscus* species introduced to Malaysia.

The *bunga raya* is featured on the first-day cover issued by Pos Malaysia to commemorate Malaysia's 10th National Day, which was celebrated in 1973, on 31 August.

A stylized *bunga raya* is incorporated in the logo for the XVI Commonwealth Games held in Kuala Lumpur in 1998.

### Common ornamental plants grown in Malaysia

**TREES**

1. Spectacular scarlet flowers of the flame of the forest (*Delonix regia*), a deciduous tree native to Madagascar.

2. Lilac blue flowers cover the jacaranda (*Jacaranda ovalifolia*), a deciduous tree from South America. When in full bloom, the whole tree crown is covered with these flowers on bare branches.

3. The bottlebrush (*Callistemon lanceolatus*), a tree-like shrub introduced from New South Wales, Australia, has its flowers arranged in cylindrical spikes with brilliant crimson, brush-like stamens and dark yellow anthers.

4. The large, red, tulip-like flowers of the African tulip tree (*Spathodea campanulata*), which are borne on inflorescences at the top of the tree crown, have a distinct yellow border around the edge of their petals.

5. The large, fragrant, white flower of the greater frangipani (*Plumeria obtusa*) with its distinctive yellow centre. In Malaysia, this robust tree, native to tropical America, is also called the 'ghostly fingers tree' because it is frequently planted in graveyards.

**SHRUBS**

6. The bougainvillea is commonly grown as a decorative shrub in urban areas of Malaysia, such as outside Parliament House in Kuala Lumpur. This native shrub of Central and South America has been extensively hybridized since it was introduced to Malaysia.

7. The large, crimson, trumpet-shaped flowers of the desert rose (*Adenium coetenium*) are beautiful, but do not last long. This bushy shrub is a native of East Africa and Arabia.

8. The yellow allamanda (*Allamanda obesum*) produces its large, bright flowers throughout the year. Originally from Brazil, this sprawling shrub now grows widely in Malaysia, where a dwarf variety has also been cultivated. It is often planted in gardens and as a roadside shrub.

9. The prominent pink and velvety bracts of the mussaenda (*Mussaenda philippica*) might be mistaken for petals. The function of the bracts is to attract pollinators to the flowers, which are inconspicuous tubular structures found among the bracts. Introduced from the Philippines, it flowers all year round and is a popular garden shrub and pot plant.

**HERBS**

10. Of tropical origin, the bloody lily (*Haemanthus multiflorum*) is popularly cultivated as a potted plant in home gardens.

11. The striped-leafed lily (*Hippeastrum reticulatum*) was introduced from Brazil and is commonly planted in parks and gardens in cities.

12. Summer torch (*Billbergia pyramidalis*), a native of Brazil, is frequently found in Malaysian gardens. The flowers last for only a few days before falling.

# Native fruits

*Malaysia is rich in tropical fruits. It is home to 370 species of native fruits, among which are the* durian, rambutan, cempedak, langsat *and* salak. *These are cultivated in gardens, orchards and large estates across the country. In most cases, fruiting takes place twice annually, with the exception of salak, which fruits once a year. While mostly eaten fresh, these fruits are also cooked in a variety of ways and made into other types of food products.*

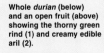

Malaysia's native fruits are commemorated in these colourful stamps, which show *rambutan* and *mangosteen*.

### Malaysia's fruits

The most important commercial native fruits in Malaysia are the *durian, mangosteen, rambutan, duku* and *langsat*. Less commercially important are the *cempedak, nangka* and *salak*. In addition, there are many under exploited wild fruits that are occasionally seen in local markets. These include *tampoi, sentul, mata kucing* and *pulasan*. Most native fruit species are seasonal, with the main fruiting seasons occurring from November to January and from June to August.

Governmental agencies, such as the Federal Agricultural Marketing Authority (FAMA) and the Malaysian Agricultural Research and Development Institute (MARDI), have been encouraging the cultivation and consumption of native fruits. As a result, Malaysia's fruits have become more popular amongst consumers and more economically significant for the country.

### *Durian*: The king of tropical fruits

The *durian* is perhaps the most fascinating fruit of Malaysia. It is famous for its thorny shell, strong odour and sweet, creamy taste. The commercially cultivated durian tree, *Durio zibethinus*, is grown in gardens, orchards and on large estates. In Sabah and Sarawak, *D. lowianus, D. oxleyanus* and *D. graveolens* are also cultivated and their fruits sold in markets.

Durian trees are tall, and grow up to a height of 40 metres. The fruits are woody, round or ellipsoid capsules, while the rind is covered with coarse spines, which are green or brown. Each locule, or segment, of the fruit holds one or more seeds that are enveloped in cream, yellow or orange flesh or arils. The aril tastes sweet and creamy, but is occasionally bitter.

There are many good durian clones and the most popular is D24. The nutritious aril is high in carbohydrates, protein, fat, calcium and vitamins A and C.

Durian is largely eaten fresh, as it does not keep for more than a few days at room temperature. Traditional Malay delicacies, such as *lempuk* and *dodol*, are made from durian. *Tempoyak* is fermented durian cooked with fish and eaten with rice and *sambal*. Modern food products that contain durian include candies, jam and flavourings.

Whole *durian* (below) and an open fruit (above) showing the thorny green rind (1) and creamy edible aril (2).

Clusters of flowers open in the evenings, produce a musky smell, and are pollinated by nectar-feeding bats and insects.

## Cultivation and trade of native fruits

Native fruit trees are grown on a small scale in orchards and plantations across Peninsular Malaysia. The most widespread is the *durian*, which is cultivated in every state. The fruit crops are sold domestically and exported to other countries in Southeast Asia, especially to Singapore, making a significant contribution to Malaysia's economy.

A market stall selling *rambutan, langsat* and *mangosteen*.

### Native fruits cultivated in each state on the Peninsula

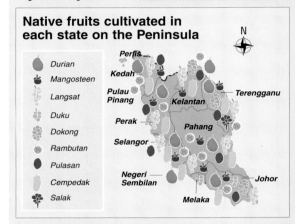

- Durian
- Mangosteen
- Langsat
- Duku
- Dokong
- Rambutan
- Pulasan
- Cempedak
- Salak

### AREA UNDER NATIVE FRUITS IN PENINSULAR MALAYSIA AND EXPORT WEIGHT AND VALUE (1996)

| | AREA (ha) | WEIGHT (t) | VALUE (RM '000) | COUNTRIES EXPORTED TO |
|---|---|---|---|---|
| Durian | 110 079 | 20 910 | 15 156 | Singapore, Hong Kong, Brunei |
| Mangosteen | 7916 | 3096 | 3077 | Singapore, Hong Kong, Japan |
| Langsat | 2617 | 910 | 0.78 | n.a |
| Duku | 16 466 | 910 | 0.78 | Thailand, Singapore, Brunei |
| Dokong | 15 127 | 910 | 0.78 | Thailand, Singapore, Brunei |
| Rambutan | 18 353 | 3231 | 1965 | Singapore, Brunei |
| Pulasan | 239 | n.a | n.a | n.a |
| Cempedak | 8496 | 3905 | 3355 | Singapore, Thailand, Hong Kong, Brunei |
| Salak | 667 | n.a | n.a | n.a |

Source: Malaysian Agricultural Research and Development Institute (1996)
n.a.—not available

### ANNUAL FRUITING SEASONS OF NATIVE MALAYSIAN FRUITS

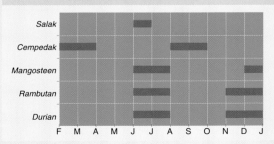

Salak
Cempedak
Mangosteen
Rambutan
Durian

F M A M J J A S O N D J

# Eight common native fruits

## *Rambutan* and *pulasan*: Two relatives

The *rambutan* tree (*Nephelium lappaceum*) is native to Malaysia and Indonesia. Its name is derived from the Malay word *rambut*, which means 'hair'. The tree is medium-sized, reaching a height of 25 metres when fully grown. Inflorescences occur in spikes, bearing either male or hermaphrodite flowers on different trees, although sometimes both male and hermaphrodite flowers are found on the same inflorescence. Small, yellow-green flowers emit a pleasant fragrance. The shape of the fruit ranges from round to ovoid to oblong, and the fruit turns yellow or red when ripe. Soft yet firm, the juicy, translucent flesh tastes sweet. It peels off easily from the seed, and the seed coat may come off with it. The fruits are moderately high in vitamin C, and are best eaten fresh. The flesh can be canned or made into jam.

A sectioned *rambutan* showing (1) the skin, (2) the fleshy, edible aril, (3) the testa and (4) the seed.

Pulasan (*Nephelium ramboutan-ake*) is a close relative of the rambutan. Wild trees are found in the forests, but crops are mainly cultivated in gardens and orchards. The oblong pulasan fruits differ from the rambutan in that their skin is thicker and the spines shorter and a darker red. In the fruits of some trees, the soft flesh peels off cleanly from the seed. Pulasan trees used to be grown from seed, but now they are propagated by grafting.

Whole and halved *pulasan* revealing (1) the skin, (2) the fleshy, edible aril and (3) the seed.

## Cempedak

Belonging to the family Moraceae, the *cempedak* (*Artocarpus integer*) is indigenous to Peninsular Malaysia. A strictly tropical fruit, it requires fertile, well-drained sandy to loamy soil. It is grown in home gardens and orchards, mostly in Kedah, Perak, Pahang and Terengganu.

The cempedak tree is evergreen, reaching a height of 20 metres at maturity. Budded trees, however, are usually shorter than 5 metres. Seedlings take about 4–6 years to bear fruit, whilst vegetatively propogated plants take 2–3 years. Male and female flowers are borne on separate inflorescences. The fruits are yellowish green to brown, covered with closely set, firm and obtuse prickles. As the fruits mature, the spines flatten, the fruit changes colour and emits a characteristic smell. Inside are light yellow to golden orange flesh balls, which are attached to the fruit core.

The carbohydrate and protein-rich flesh is eaten raw or covered with rice flour and deep fried. The seeds can also be eaten after boiling or roasting.

A whole *cempedak* fruit (left) and an opened one (right) showing its numerous flesh balls.

## Salak

In Malaysia, salak (*Salacca glabrescens*) is grown mainly in Terengganu. It is a short and rather dumpy palm that does not form a trunk, but sprouts its leaves from ground level. Individual plants are unisexual. The round or ovoid fruits are arranged in a compact bunch at the base of the palm frond. The dark brown fruit skin is covered with overlapping scales; the white, firm flesh surrounding each seed is sweet and fragrant.

Salak enjoys Malaysia's tropical climate and grows up to an altitude of 300 metres. It thrives in well-drained soil that contains a high percentage of organic matter. Previously propagated by seed, cultivators have found that this method does not guarantee the quality or sex of the offspring. Salak is now vegetatively propagated using its suckers.

A section of a bunch of mature *salak*, revealing (1) the scaly rind, (2) the white flesh and (3) the hard, round seed.

## Mangosteen

The *mangosteen* (*Garcinia mangostana*) is believed to have originated in Peninsular Malaysia. Of the 400 species of the genus *Garcinia*, about 50 are found in Malaysia. The mangosteen tree flourishes in the wet, tropical climate and prefers clay or sandy loam with a high level of organic matter. Most mangosteen trees are found in mixed orchards, or *dusun*, in Kuala Kangsar in Perak, Muar and Segamat in Johor, Ulu Langat in Selangor and parts of Negeri Sembilan and Pahang.

An opened *mangosteen* with its (1) soft and thin purple skin and (2) 5–7 fleshy, edible segments.

Because it has a weak root system, the tree is a slow-growing plant. It reaches a height of 10–25 metres. Only female flowers exist on cultivated trees, and male flowers are very rarely found. Interestingly, there is no need for fertilization before the fruit is formed. Single or clustered, the bright red female flowers are found at the tips of young branches. The fruits have a smooth skin that is thick and pale green when young, turning purple when ripe. When mature, the flesh is white, very sweet and soft and has a pleasant aroma. Larger fruit segments might contain a seed. Mangosteens are usually consumed fresh, but are also made into jam and juice. They are sold both in Malaysia and exported to countries such as Singapore and Japan.

## Langsat, duku and dokong

Langsat, *duku* and *dokong* belong to the same species, *Lansium domesticum*. They are native to Malaysia, as well as Indonesia, the Philippines and Thailand. The langsat tree is 10–20 metres tall, and is slender with a straggly crown. Small, spirally arranged flowers occur in spikes. The skin of the fruit is thin and yellow and contains a milky sap. The flesh has a slightly sour taste.

A peeled *duku* showing (1) the thick, brown skin and (2) the firm, translucent flesh.

Duku trees are large, growing up to 40 metres. A brownish yellow skin covers the fruit. The translucent, sweet-sour flesh is sometimes tinged pink. Dokong trees are even bigger, reaching up to 50 metres. They are mainly cultivated in Kelantan, Terengganu and Johor. Medium and small fruits do not have a seed. The flesh is acidic and sweet.

*Langsat* occur in bunches of about 20 fruits. Langsat trees are grown across Peninsular Malaysia, but mainly in the northern states.

These bunches of *dokong* on the tree are ready to be harvested.

# Introduced fruits

*Although many of Malaysia's fruits are indigenous, there are some which have been introduced from other tropical regions of the world. These include the papaya, pineapple, ciku, guava, star fruit and watermelon. They are cultivated widely and have become a part of Malaysia's economy and culture. Introduced temperate fruits are planted in the highlands, but they do not grow as well as and are of less economic importance than introduced tropical fruits.*

**Watermelons**

Watermelons nestling amongst the weak, creeping stems and tendrils of the watermelon plant.

Ripe watermelons being loaded onto a truck by plantation workers. The fruits are then transported to the market.

Thirst-quenching watermelon slices for sale in a market.

These young plants of star fruit trees, which have been produced from bud graftings, are ready to be planted in a field.

## Origin and diversity

Malaysia is well known for the great diversity of fruits found in its local markets and supermarkets. About 100 species of fruit plants grow in Malaysia, of which roughly half were introduced. Fruit plants of both tropical and temperate origins were introduced into the country during the colonial days when traders from as far away as South America, Africa, Europe, India and other parts of Asia brought fruits with them to Malaysia. Fruit plants that originated in temperate regions, such as orange, persimmon and strawberry, thrive in the cool highlands of Malaysia.

## Successful naturalization

Certain fruits from South America, Africa and India, including pineapples, papayas, watermelons, jackfruits and star fruits, flourished in the humid tropics. These fruit plants have adapted well to the local climate, and have become so popular among Malaysians that they are now regarded as local fruits. These fruits are tasty, suit the local palate and are easy to cultivate. They also grow very fast, either from seed or by means of vegetative propagation, such as bud grafting and marcotting. Fruits are produced in months or a year or two, unlike some indigenous fruits, such as durian and mangosteen, which may take 10–15 years to bear fruit.

## Economic and social significance

The fruit industry is the third most important agricultural industry in Malaysia after rubber and palm oil. However, its importance is growing with government plans to increase the area under fruit cultivation from 244 000 hectares in 1997 to 345 126 hectares, and production is expected to rise to 3.3 million tonnes by the year 2000. Smallholders used to dominate the industry, but with commercialization they are gradually being overtaken by the large estates.

Besides being eaten, fruits play a role in religion and culture. For example, pineapples and oranges are used as offerings by Buddhists in ceremonies performed during certain periods, such as the seventh lunar month when the Hungry Ghost Festival takes place. Oranges are also a traditional Chinese New Year gift. On the fifteenth day of the New Year, it is a Penang Straits Chinese custom for young, unmarried girls to throw oranges into the sea and wish for good husbands.

## Pineapple or *nanas* (*Ananas comosus*)

The home of the pineapple is the eastern part of South America. The Malay name *nanas* and the scientific name *Ananas* are both derived from the Tupi Indian name *nana*. In Malaysia, pineapple plantations cover about 15 600 hectares, and yield about 180 000 tonnes of fresh fruit per annum.

Good varieties of pineapples seldom produce seeds, and hence are propagated vegetatively. Such means of reproduction ensures that the fruits within a variety have uniform characteristics.

There are many cultivated varieties of pineapples. The most important commercial varieties in Malaysia fall into two groups—those for canning (*nanas merah* and *nanas hijau*) and those for eating raw (*nanas* Sarawak and *nanas* Morris). Pineapple is a main ingredient in a local salad called *rojak*. It also makes excellent jam and tarts.

Basic features of the pineapple plant are the crown (1), fruit (2) and side shoots (3).

A view of the majestic, star-shaped crowns in a pineapple plantation in Pekan Nenas, Johor.

The two most popular varieties of pineapples for fresh consumption are *nanas* Sarawak (1), a medium-sized fruit with pale yellow flesh and a thick, central, woody core; and *nanas* Morris (2), a small-sized fruit with bright yellow flesh and a thin, central, woody core. It is very sweet and is best for desserts.

### Pineapple-growing areas in Malaysia

* Pineapples for fresh consumption
○ Pineapples for canning

| TOTAL PINEAPPLE PRODUCTION IN MALAYSIA (1993–1995) (t) | | |
|---|---|---|
| YEAR | CANNED PINEAPPLE | FRESH PINEAPPLE |
| 1993 | 161 100 | 285 867 |
| 1994 | 156 200 | 273 523 |
| 1995 | 160 000 | 275 000 |

Source: Malaysian Pineapple Industry Board (1995)

# Eight common introduced fruits

## 1. Watermelon or *tembikai* (*Citrullus lanatus*)

The watermelon is a native of tropical and subtropical Africa, and has been cultivated for centuries. In Malaysia, plantations covering a total of 6000 hectares are concentrated in Perlis, Kedah, Kelantan, Terengganu, Pahang, Melaka, Sabah and Sarawak. The average yield of a plantation is 22.5 tonnes per hectare. Four clones—flower dragon, sugar baby, new dragon and yellow baby—are the most suitable for large-scale planting.

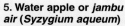
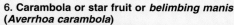

The watermelon is a favourite thirst quencher, and is usually eaten raw. The dried parched seeds, called *kuaci*, are also consumed.

## 2. Guava or *jambu batu* (*Psidium guajava*)

The guava is indigenous to tropical America, but has been naturalized in many tropical and subtropical countries. About 1500 hectares of guava plantations have been established in Peninsular Malaysia and Sarawak, and the average yield is 24–34 tonnes per hectare per annum. Several clones have been produced, including the Thai seedless guava.

In Malaysia, the ripe, juicy, sweet fruit is eaten fresh or made into juice. The two most common varieties are the yellow and pink-fleshed guavas.

## 3. Indian mango or *mangga* (*Mangifera indica*)

The Indian mango is the most common mango in Malaysia, and it has a number of varieties, such as the popular *mulgoa*. The tree can grow up to 27 metres and is cultivated on a small scale, mainly in the northern Malaysian states of Kedah and Perlis where the climate, with its pronounced dry seasons, is more favourable.

Apart from being eaten fresh, this fruit is also processed into a variety of other products, including juice, jam, jelly and ice cream.

## 4. Sapodilla or *ciku* (*Manilkara zapota*)

The *ciku* is an evergreen fruit tree native to Central America, Mexico and the West Indies. In Malaysia, it is grown in Penang, Selangor, Terengganu, Pahang, Negeri Sembilan, Melaka and Johor. In these states, the total area under ciku cultivation is about 1000 hectares, with the average rate of production at 15 tonnes per hectare per annum. The three main clones are *betawi*, *jantung* and *subang*. Ripe ciku are popular as a dessert, and are eaten fresh.

## 5. Water apple or *jambu air* (*Syzygium aqueum*)

The water apple is a native of India and has been cultivated for many centuries. Its name comes from its crisp and juicy pulp, which is also lightly scented, hence its other name, rose apple. The skin may be white to bright pink, and contains a high amount of vitamin A.

## 6. Carambola or star fruit or *belimbing manis* (*Averrhoa carambola*)

The star fruit is a native of the Orient. In Peninsular Malaysia, star fruit plantations cover a total area of only 550 hectares and are confined to small areas in Kedah, Perak, Selangor and Johor. The average yield for a 2–3 year-old plantation is 16–18 tonnes per hectare per annum, and for a 4–7 year-old plantation, it is 40–55 tonnes per hectare per annum. For plantations older than eight years, it is 60–70 tonnes per hectare per annum. No horticultural varieties have yet been named, but those cultivated around Sungai Besi and Serdang in Selangor are famous for being of a high quality. The star fruit has always been a common sight in kampongs, gardens and backyards, and recently it has also been grown in tin tailings.

The fruits, which are rich in vitamin C, are put to various uses. For example, the sweet varieties are made into desserts, and the sour ones into jelly, jam and juice.

## 7. Pomegranate or *delima* (*Punica granatum*)

The pomegranate originated in Persia, and was introduced to Malaysia a long time ago. However, it does not grow well and is not very widely cultivated. It is sometimes grown as an ornamental for its flowers, which are fairly large and attractive and bright orange in colour.

## 8. Passion fruit or *buah susu* (*Passiflora edulis*)

The passion fruit originates from South America. There are a few varieties, and the one most common in Malaysia is distinguished by its greenish yellow fruit. It is the same species as the purple variety found in the highlands.

In gardens, the tendrils of the passion fruit plant make it suitable for growing along fences or on lattices. The fruits can be eaten fresh or made into juice, and are used to flavour ice cream and cakes.

# Medicinal plants

*Plants have been used for thousands of years to treat man's illnesses and injuries. Despite the tremendous advances made by modern medical practices, traditional medicine is still the only form of health care for about 75 per cent of the world's population. In Malaysia, cures have been derived from roots, stems, leaves, fruits and bark for generations. Today, traditional medicine is used to complement modern medicine. The medicinal value of plants is recognized by the Malaysian Government, universities and research and conservation bodies, and steps are being taken to preserve this biological resource.*

I. H. Burkill's *A Dictionary of the Economic Products of the Malay Peninsula* (1935) is one of the earliest and most comprehensive records of the uses of plant species found in the Peninsula.

## Recent history

The use of plants in medicine, magic and religion in Malaysian culture dates back centuries. For various ethnic groups, many common plants are of medicinal value. As in other parts of the world, traditional medicine in Malaysia is practised by the native medicine men and women, known variously as *bomoh*, *pawang* and *bidan*, who with their special knowledge and skills are able to recognize and utilize the therapeutic qualities of different plants.

Much of the existing documentation on Malaysia's medicinal plants was compiled by European naturalists and medical officers during the colonial period, although the earliest record found is in a book translated in 1886 by Munshi Ismail. This translation was later edited by J. D. Gimlette and I. H. Burkill and published in 1930 as *The Medical Book of Malayan Medicine*. In 1935, Burkill while Director of the Singapore Botanic Gardens went on to draw up an index of the economic products of the Malay Peninsula. He was probably influenced by Sir George Watt, whose *Dictionary of the Economic Products of India* was also collated around that time. Many scientists today still accept that Burkill's monumental work contains a huge amount of information on medicinal plants, poisonous plants and the economic uses of plants.

Scepticism arose regarding traditional remedies because the medicinal properties of plants could not be scientifically proven. The unreliability of botanical identification, the lack of detailed knowledge of phytochemistry and the absence of scientifically sound clinical studies led many Malaysians to choose modern medicine over locally prepared herbal cures. However, from the 1980s, there has been a resurgence of interest by Malaysian scientists in the study of traditional medicine. For example, scientists working at the Forest Research Institute Malaysia (FRIM) and a number of Malaysian universities have investigated and recorded the medicinal properties of many plant species. The Institute of Chinese Medicine in Kuala Lumpur offers both formal academic tuition and practical training. Government regulation has also been introduced, including the setting up of a register of traditional medicines by the Health Ministry's Drug Control Division.

The long, skinny root of *tongkat ali*, seen on the left, is dried and sold as medicine.

## Potions, poultices and decoctions

There are over a thousand species of plants in Malaysia reported to have medicinal properties. These encompass species of ferns and fern allies, gymnosperms and flowering plants. Among the flowering plants, members of the legume (Leguminosae), coffee (Rubiaceae), rubber (Euphorbiaceae) and laurel (Lauraceae) families are the best known for their medicinal qualities.

A number of Malaysia's medicinal plants are also herbaceous species. *Jerangau* or *Acorus calamus* (Araceae), for example, is commonly used by the Malays to treat stomachaches. The tonic made from this plant also helps to stop convulsions and spasms. Fresh or dried leaves of *hempedu bumi* or *Andrographis paniculata* (Acanthaceae) are boiled to make a decoction which is drunk as a remedy for diarrhoea, fever and diabetes.

Parts of trees, such as the bark, roots and leaves, are used for medicinal purposes. The bark of *Alstonia scholaris* or *pulai* (Apocynaceae), for instance, is a traditional remedy for dysentry, worms and other intestinal problems. Many chemical compounds, including alkaloids, terpenoids and essential oils have been isolated from the bark. The treelet or shrub *Eurycoma longifolia* or *tongkat ali* (Simaroubaceae) has numerous uses in traditional medicine. A decoction made from the leaves and roots is taken for malaria, tuberculosis and fever, and functions as an antihistamine. Also contained in the plant are essential oils, such as saponins and sterols.

## Natural medicinal resources and synthetic drugs

With the advent of biotechnology, Malaysia's medicinal plants have become a sought-after resource and raw material for the world's pharmaceutical industry. This can bring economic benefits to the country if the right legal and business terms and conditions are set. To this end, Malaysia has given its support to the Biotrade Initiative launched by the United Nations Conference on Trade and Development (UNCTAD). This initiative aims to help countries who want to sell their biological resources get a fair deal in the international business arena. It proposes to conduct market research, offer model contracts and provide training in the technical and legal aspects of acquiring biological resources. Through the Biotrade Initiative, Malaysia can profit from its natural heritage without losing it.

| SOME TROPICAL PLANT SPECIES USED IN CLINICAL DRUGS | | | |
|---|---|---|---|
| **SCIENTIFIC NAME** | **MALAY NAME** | **DRUG** | **FUNCTION** |
| *Ananas comosus* | nanas | bromelain | reduces inflammation |
| *Andrographis paniculata* | hempedu bumi | andrographolide | acts on bacillary dysentry |
| *Areca catechu* | pokok pinang | arecoline | destroys or expels intestinal worms |
| *Carica papaya* | betik | chymopapain | aids digestion |
| *Catharanthus roseus* | kemunting cina | vinblastine, vincristine | treats tumours |
| *Centella asiatica* | pegaga | asiaticoside | heals wounds |
| *Curcuma longa* | kunyit | curcumin | treats cholera |
| *Datura meteloides* | kecubung | scopolamine | acts as a sedative |
| *Dioscorea triphylla* | ubi gadung | diosgenin | acts as a contraceptive |

Woody climbers play a role in traditional medicine too. The bitter seeds of the shrub *Brucea javanica* or *lada pahit* (Simaroubaceae), for instance, can treat diarrhoea, dysentry and hemorrhoids. Two or three seeds are taken orally every four hours. *Gelenggang besar* or *Senna alata* (Leguminosae) is a popular home remedy for ringworm. The leaves are either used fresh or pounded and mixed with lime and applied to the infected area of skin. *Tinospora crispa* (Menispermaceae) is used to cure microbial infections, including malaria and smallpox, and bacteria–infected abscesses, such as syphilitic sores. Extracts from this climber have been shown to kill bacteria such as *Staphylococcus aureus* and *S. faecalis*, and inhibit the growth of *Escherichia coli*, *Salmonella typhimurium* and the fungus *Candida utilis*.

### Selling traditional medicine

A Malay medicine man selling traditional remedies in Balik Pulau, Penang.

A Chinese medicine man measuring out a portion of herbs in his shop in Petaling Street, Kuala Lumpur.

## Plant species used in traditional medicine

There are at least 1,158 species of higher plants in Malaysia reported to have medicinal value. Of these, 1,075 are flowering plants, 76 are ferns and fern-allies and 7 are gymnosperms. Apart from treating common ailments such as headaches, coughs and colds, certain species are also used for tropical illnesses like malaria and cholera. The greatest number of plant-based medicines are used to treat fevers and skin wounds, followed by postnatal conditions, ringworm and dysentry.

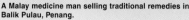

### Common medicinal plant species

1. *Eurycoma longifolia*, or *tongkat ali*, is Malaysia's most well-known medicinal plant. The root is the part that is valued. Besides being able to treat several illnesses, it is also thought to increase the male libido.

2. Although *Acorus calamus*, or *jerangau*, is a commonly known treatment for stomachaches and spasms, it is now only used in the rural areas of Malaysia.

3. The tree *Alstonia scholaris*, or *pulai*, contains active biological substances that work against malaria and hypoglycaemia (abnormally low blood sugar levels).

4. Thriving in damp, exposed habitats, *Senna alata*, or *gelenggang besar*, is known most for its antiparasitic qualities. Its roots and leaves are also a purgative.

5. Growing in damp, shady areas, *Andrographis paniculata*, or *hempudu bumi*, is particularly useful in the treatment of hypotension (low blood pressure) and bacterial infections.

6. *Tinospora crispa*, or *putrawali*, is most effective in treating bacterial infections.

7. *Brucea javanica*, or *lada pahit*, contains many important glycosides, such as brucein, that are active medicinal substances.

89

# Oil- and resin-producing plants

*Besides producing timber, trees are also a source of minor forest products such as oils and resins. The dipterocarp and conifer trees are the most commonly tapped. In Malaysia, people have been collecting these forest resources for centuries and using them for household items and for food. A small resin industry developed in the first few decades of the 20th century, with both the British and the Chinese exporting resin to countries in Southeast Asia as well as to Europe. Today, resins are employed in the manufacture of varnish and lacquer, whilst oils are used in the manufacture of cosmetics, soap and food flavouring.*

A species of *Agathis*, from which the resin *damar minyak* is obtained and used as a varnish. It is the only varnish used on traditional Malay houses.

## Oils from plants

Many different parts of plants, including the nuts, buds, stems, leaves and bark, contain oils that can be extracted. The dipterocarp trees of Malaysia, for example, are a well-known source. The illipe nuts of *Shorea* species, such as *engkabang jantung* (*S. macrophylla*), *engkabang terendak* (*S. seminis*) and *engkabang asu* (*S. palembanica*), produce a yellow or green tallow-like substance consisting largely of the glyceride of stearic acid and palmitic and oleic acid. *Shorea* trees flower between September and October, and the nuts are harvested between January and February. Another dipterocarp species that is tapped for oils is *Dipterocarpus kerrii*, which is used especially by the Semelai of Tasik Bera, Pahang.

Spices such as cloves, cinnamon, nutmeg and mace (see 'Spices') are used for their fragrant oils as well as for flavouring. The bark of *kayu manis* (*Cinnamomum zeylanicum*), for example, produces aromatic oil, whilst in nutmeg (*Myristica fragrans*) it is the fruit. Cloves (*Syzygium caryophyllus*) produce eugenol, a colourless or pale yellow fragrant oil. This oil is obtained by distillation, as are most plant oils. On average, cloves takes 8–24 hours to distil, depending on the quality of the cloves and the condition of the still. Flower buds, leaves and stems are all used for their oil, with clove flower bud oil being the most commercially important.

### Oil-producing nuts
1. Illipe nuts collected in Julau, Sarawak. The oil extracted from them is used mainly in the manufacture of chocolate.
2. Whole and halved nutmegs, showing the seeds from which nutmeg oil is extracted.
3. Bottles of nutmeg oil that are sold in shops. Nutmeg oil aids digestion and is a very effective treatment for diarrhoea.

## Plant resins

In Malaysia, trees belonging to the Dipterocarpaceae are the most important source of resin after species of *Agathis* (Araucariaceae). The latter trees produce clear, white resin called *damar minyak*, which hardens on exposure, turning an opaque white or yellow or dark brown, eventually becoming a fragile mass. The resin is a complex, alcohol-soluble mixture of the unsaturated hydrocarbons monoterpene, diterpene and sesquiterpene, with a melting point between 115 and 135 °C.

Among the dipterocarps, *Neobalanocarpus heimii* produces a high-grade resin known as *damar penak*, which in the first half of the 20th century was also known by its trade name, M. D. P. (Malayan damar penak). Although this resin is hard, it does not keep well, and will deteriorate if left for over a year. The acid content increases and causes discoloration, which decreases the value of the resin. *Hopea* species are also known for the high-grade, clear, pale resin they produce, known as *damar luis*. Oleoresins—a combination of resins and essential oils—come from *keruing* (*Dipterocarpus* spp.) and *resak* (*Vatica* spp.) trees. A variety of non-fragrant resins are also produced by dipterocarp trees.

## Traditional and commercial uses

Resins have traditionally been used in Sabah and Sarawak to make torches. Powdered resin is mixed with rotting wood, and pieces of bark and oil extracted from wood. Dark damar is best. Large, tapered palm leaves, about 60 centimetres in length,

## Bornean camphor

*Dryobanalops aromatica*, a native of the northwest coast of Sumatra, Sabah and Sarawak, supplies the oil known as Bornean camphor. The oil occurs in a crystalline form in cavities made by insect larvae boring into the tree trunk. The presence of borneol (a white, solid, terpene alcohol) makes this oil akin to true camphor obtained from *Cinnamomum camphora*.

As not every *D. aromatica* tree produces camphor, collectors first make a small incision in the bark to test for the oil. If no odour of camphor is traceable, the tree is not tapped. The strength of the odour repels insects, such as termites, making the timber from *D. aromatica*, called *kapur*, valued for construction. A lightweight timber, it is used in the manufacture of furniture, such as camphor chests which are used for storing clothes. The presence of the camphor in the wood acts as a natural insect repellent. The Malays and the Chinese also use Bornean camphor for embalming. They are willing to pay high prices for the pure camphor, despite the fact that there are cheaper synthetic forms available in the market.

*Dryobanalops aromatica* trees from which Bornean camphor is tapped.

## The resin industry

Malaysia was a small-scale resin producer and exporter in the first half of the 20th century. Although the resin industry was overshadowed by rubber and tin, it nonetheless made a valuable contribution to the country's economy, and was systematically organized.

Resin was processed and sold under government-run schemes, which meant that activities were centralized in official sorting and grading houses. Collectors would bring the resin to purchasing stations where impure or unhardened chunks of resin were discarded and the rest taken to the sorting and grading stations. Once there, the resin was divided into several grades according to colour, opacity and firmness. For example, the top grade of the resin *damar penak* was 'fine dust' followed by 'seed', the next grade down. What was left after these finest grades had been picked was then sorted by size and colour. The different sized lumps were graded into 'pale', 'yellow' and 'amber'. Resin that contained impurities, but was not so contaminated that it had to be discarded, was graded as 'coarse'. Finally, floor sweepings were sold as 'fine dust 2nd grade'. All grades of resin were exported to countries such as Singapore, Germany, the Netherlands, Italy and the United Kingdom.

When the Great Depression of the 1930s hit the world's resin markets, Malaysia's resin industry suffered badly and did not recover, partly because better sources of revenue, such as rubber and tin, emerged. Today, Malaysia still produces a small volume of resin, but is more important as an entrepôt centre in the world resin trade.

### Collecting and storing resin

1. The traditional way of collecting resin is by cutting notches in the stems and larger branches to allow the resin to exude.

2. After the resin has hardened, it is scraped off and the notches reopened to promote a fresh flow.

3. In the forest, resin is found in clumps at the base of trees, where it naturally settles as it is secreted from the tree trunk. These clumps are simply broken off and collected.

4. Bamboo tubes are used to store resin, such as *minyak engkabang*, that is to be sold local markets.

### Resins produced in Malaysia

| MALAY NAME | PLANT SOURCE | CHARACTERISTICS |
|---|---|---|
| Damar batu | Shorea smithiana | light brown |
| Damar chengal pasir | Hopea sp. | translucent, white |
| Damar hitam | Shorea faguetiana, | black |
| Damar kawang | Shorea mecistopteryx | dark brown |
| Damar kedondong | Canarium spp. | soft, fragrant |
| Damar kepong | Shorea rigida, S. sericea | soft, opaque, yellow with streaks |
| Damar mata kuching | Hopea spp. | translucent, white |
| Damar minyak | Agathis borneensis | opaque white, yellow or dark brown |
| Damar penak | Neobalanocarpus heimii | hard, yellow |
| Damar sengai | Canarium sp. | very dark brown |
| Damar seraya | Shorea curtisii | hard, reddish brown, glass-like fractures |
| Damar temak | Shorea hypoleuca | pale |

**PRODUCTION OF *DAMAR* IN PENINSULAR MALAYSIA (1970–1991) (RM)**

95,974

100,000
20,000
15,000
10,000
5,000
0

'70 '71 '72 '73 '74 '75 '76 '77 '78 '79 '80 '81 '82 '83 '84 '85 '86 '87 '88 '89 '90 '91

*Source: Forestry Department, Peninsular Malaysia (1992)*

are wrapped round the mixture, and held in place by split rattan canes. Copious amounts of smoke are produced when the torches are burnt, blackening the walls of the dwellings in which they are used. Because of this, they quickly fell into disuse with the advent of kerosene lamps and electric lights. Today, resin torches are reserved for outdoor activities such as night fishing.

Malay houses are often built with the hardwood *chengal*, which is resilient to insect pests, except termites. To prevent termites from damaging the wood, damar minyak is applied. Not only does it serve as an effective termite repellent, it also gives the wood a deep brown glow, and brings out the details of the grain. Most of the wooden parts of a Malay house, especially the structural elements, are treated with damar minyak. Another use of this resin is as a filler for cracks and crevices in boats, as it is an effective waterproofing agent.

Commercially, resins are used in the production of lacquer. Incorporating resins into lacquer improves both the lustre of the finish and its ability to stick. A quality resin, such as turpentine, which is

colourless, has a high melting point and mixes with the solvent naptha, is selected for this purpose. The chosen resin must also be compatible with other solutions used in lacquer, such as ketones, which are used for making cellulose nitrate (a compound found in plastics, lacquer and explosives).

Traditionally, plant oils are used as food and in medicine. In Sarawak, for example, where most of Malaysia's *Shorea* trees are found, the fat from illipe nuts is a local delicacy, eaten with piping hot rice. Clove oil is valued for its stimulative and antispasmodic properties.

Some very common household products contain plant oils. Candles and soap, for example, are made with the oil from illipe nuts, which is also used in the manufacture of cosmetics and chocolate. Nutmeg and pepper (*Piper nigrum*) oil are common ingredients in perfumes. In the food industry, clove oil is used for vanilla flavouring and, in the pharmaceutical field, to make dental products such as mouthwash.

### Products made with plant oil
*CLOCKWISE:* Plant oil is used to manufacture certain household products, such as candles, mouthwash, food flavouring, cosmetics, chocolate and perfume.

# Plants as a source of energy

*Wood has been a principal source of plant fuel for man for millions of years. Today, it accounts for almost 20 per cent of the world's annual commercial fuel consumption. In Malaysia, rubber wood is the main source of firewood, and is important in the rubber, brick, tobacco and charcoal-making industries. New technologies have been devised to turn wood left over or residue from manufacturing processes into other forms of solid fuel, thus reducing industrial wastage. Plant liquid fuel in the form of alcohol is also used on a small scale for domestic tasks.*

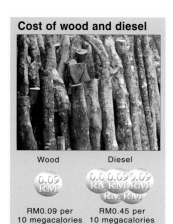

### Cost of wood and diesel

| Wood | Diesel |
| --- | --- |
| 0.09 RM | 0.0 0.09 0.09 RM RM RM 0.09 RM RM |
| RM0.09 per 10 megacalories | RM0.45 per 10 megacalories |

For most Malaysian wood species, the gross calorific value of oven-dried wood is about 18 megajoules per kilogram. However, high levels of lignin and resin, as found in certain dense wood species, increase the calorific value, whereas moisture decreases it. In air-dried wood, which has a higher moisture content than oven-dried wood, the calorific value is 16 megajoules per kilogram.

## Smoking rubber and firing bricks

The main form of wood fuel used in industries in Malaysia is firewood. In the rubber industry, the smoking of rubber sheets to produce Ribbed Smoked Sheets (RSS) is wholly wood fuelled; and the brick-making industry uses firewood for the firing of clay bricks.

Sheet rubber is produced from latex that has been dried in a smokehouse by exposure to flue gas generated from the burning of wood. A typical smokehouse found in the rural areas of Malaysia is capable of drying about 25 tonnes of rubber sheets at a time. The walls of the smokehouse are built of bricks and wood, and are about 6 metres high. A simple, brick-lined stove is the furnace. As the rubber wood is burnt and the flue gas is produced, the gas rises and passes through the wet rubber sheets, which are hung on rattan rods. Moisture from the sheets is absorbed by the gas. The wet gas then leaves the smokehouse through vents between the roof and

the walls. Drying time is 4–10 days. It takes about 1.5–2 kilograms of rubber wood to produce 1 kilogram of smoked sheets. The fuel cost represents a mere 5 per cent of the total value of the final product.

The most commonly used method of firing bricks in Malaysia is the updraught kiln method. A kiln comprises sturdy outer walls, base and fire tunnels, all made of bricks, and has no permanent top. The walls are also buttressed and their corners heavily reinforced. Access into the kiln is through a doorway at either end, which during firing is filled with closely laid bricks.

The process of firing begins with loading wet, green bricks into the kiln. Small spaces are left in between the bricks to allow hot gases produced by the fire at the base to rise. Rubber wood is placed in the

A beehive kiln that is used for converting mangrove wood into charcoal. The logs stacked against the kiln are waiting to be fired.

The Orang Asli of Peninsular Malaysia and the indigenous peoples of Sabah and Sarawak gather firewood for their domestic fuel needs, a practice unchanged for years.

### Cost and efficiency of cooking technologies using biomass

| TYPE OF FUEL | EFFICIENCY(%) | COST OF STOVE (RM)* |
| --- | --- | --- |
| Agricultural residue | 13–17 | 0.00 |
| Wood | 15–19 | 0.00 |
| Improved wood | 40–44 | 23.00 |
| Charcoal | 19–23 | 6.90 |
| Improved charcoal | 29–34 | 18.40 |
| Alcohol | 40–45 | 46.00 |

Source: United Nations report (1995)
*Converted from US$ as given in the United Nations report.

## Plant energy sources: Rubber wood and oil palm residue

Energy from a plant is derived from its biomass, which is the renewable organic matter produced by photosynthesis. In Malaysia, the two types of biomass that are used as a source of energy are rubber and oil palm.

Rubber wood residue is the wood that cannot be marketed at a profit from a manufacturing operation with the available technology and the given economic situation. This residue is generated at three stages of rubber wood processing: replanting, primary manufacturing and secondary manufacturing. It is essential in the smoking and drying of rubber sheets to produce Ribbed Smoked Sheets (RRS). All RSS rubber produced in Malaysia uses rubber wood residue as fuel.

By burning palm fruit fibres and empty fruit bunches to generate electricity, palm oil mills provide for their own energy needs. A kilogram of fruit fibre and empty fruit bunches will give about 9.6 megajoules of calorific energy. Assuming that a mill burns all the palm fruit fibre produced on site, the weight ratio of Crude Palm Oil (CPO) to fibre production is 1:0.8, almost double.

In palm oil factories, used oil palm bunches are burnt to fuel the production process, thereby reducing industrial wastage and lowering costs.

Processing rubber wood leaves behind trimmings that are reused as fuel.

### THREE TYPES OF RUBBER WOOD RESIDUE
1. **Replanting residue** comprises bark, stumps, tops and branches of trees, broken logs, defective logs and injured trees.
2. **Primary manufacturing residue** is generated in primary rubber wood-based industries, and includes slabs, edgings, trimmings and sawdust.
3. **Secondary manufacturing residue** is generated by moulding plants, flooring mills and furniture factories. It comes in the form of sawdust, planer shavings, small pieces of timber trimmings, edgings and wood fragments.

firing tunnel and set alight. Only 0.3–0.4 kilograms of wood are needed to manufacture 1 kilogram of bricks. At this initial stage, the flames are kept low to dry the bricks and gradually heat the kiln to the right temperature. When the kiln is hot enough, a characteristic red glow is seen from the top. The firing period is 4–10 days. Marks on the side wall, showing the shrinkage of the bricks, are an indication that the process is complete.

## Tobacco curing and charcoal making

Freshly harvested tobacco leaves contain about 70 per cent moisture, and in order to produce good tobacco, need to be dried immediately in a curing barn. The process of drying takes 4–6 days. In Malaysia, a curing barn is likely to have asbestos walls and a furnace in the form of a simple chamber at the base of the barn. Rubber wood is fired through the furnace door, producing hot flue gas, which then passes through the barn via a series of heat exchanger pipes that eventually lead to the chimney. Heat from these pipes is transferred to the air inside the barn, drying the tobacco leaves laid out there.

In certain parts of Malaysia, the high cost of transporting wood over long distances cancels out the low cost of wood as fuel. However, the economic value of wood can be increased by converting it into charcoal, which has about twice the calorific value of wood but a fifth of its volume. This enables charcoal to remain economically viable when transported over longer distances. Furthermore, because it is a cleaner fuel compared to wood, it commands almost 10 times the price in the major towns.

Charcoal production has been practised in Malaysia for centuries. The methods vary from the basic sawdust pit method to the efficient beehive kiln

## Plants as a source of liquid fuel

Liquid plant fuel is normally in the form of alcohol. For over 150 years, alcohol derived from plants, such as the nipa palm, has been used in Malaysia, although more as a beverage than as a fuel. From around 1900, alcohol became a popular fuel for lighting and cooking, surpassing solidified whale oil, commonly used up till then. Alcohol was preferred for the high temperature of its vapour, the low temperature at which it burned, its cleaner burning and the ease with which it could be transported and stored. In the 1950s, however, alcohol fuel was replaced by kerosene, a cheaper source.

Up to the 1970s, almost all alcohol produced from nipa stock was done by yeast fermentation, drawing on the plant's naturally available sugars. This remains the most common traditional method of fermenting nipa stock to obtain alcohol. Yeast is added to nipa that has already been sitting in 100-litre urns for 4–7 days, depending on the maturity of the stock. The nipa is then allowed to ferment at 30–35 °C for another 4–7 days, after which a 10 per cent alcohol solution is formed. A process of distillation concentrates and purifies the alcohol further, so it can be sold or stored. During fermentation, large quantities of carbon dioxide saturated with water vapour are emitted together with effluents and spillage. These are potential pollutants and have to be treated properly.

The traditional way of extracting juice from the inflorescence of the nipa palm.

method. The latter method is the most popular, and is used to produce both domestic mangrove charcoal and industrial rubber wood charcoal. Beehive kilns are therefore located in coastal areas near mangrove forests or in rubber tree-growing areas. About 5 tonnes of green wood are required to make 1 tonne of charcoal. Annual consumption stands at about 60 000 tonnes, which is used mainly in the steel and chemical industries. Only about 20 per cent of charcoal produced in Malaysia is used for domestic purposes such as cooking and grilling.

## Wood as solid, briquetted fuel

As a source of fuel, wood is cheap, clean burning, low in ash and emits very little sulphur. To capitalize on this, there has in recent years been substantial development in different forms of wood-based solid fuel. One of the most successful and popular forms is the wood briquette.

Wood briquetting is the process of converting loose wood waste into a dense, compact unit through the application of high temperature and pressure. No binding agent is required because, at 163 °C and under high pressure, the granular material in the wood becomes self-binding. The most commonly used briquetting press in Malaysia is the screw extrusion type. Each extruder requires two workers to operate, and produces about 120 kilograms of briquettes per hour. The briquettes are hexagonal, measure about 30 centimetres across and have a hole in the centre to assist combustion. Although their exterior is a dark glossy brown, the interior is the colour of sawdust. Easy to break and absorbent, if soaked in water they crumble within a few minutes. Sometimes charcoal bits are added to the sawdust to enable the briquettes to be more resistant to moisture content variation.

### Uses of rubber wood as fuel

A smokehouse where Ribbed Smoked Sheets are produced. Gas from burnt rubber wood smokes the rubber sheets.

A firing tunnel in a brick-firing kiln. Rubber wood is laid out among the bricks and burnt, thus baking the bricks solid.

| RUBBER WOOD REQUIREMENTS PER KILOGRAM PRODUCTION | |
|---|---|
| **PRODUCT** | **SPECIFIC FUEL WOOD CONSUMPTION (kg)** |
| Smoked rubber | 1.5–2.0 |
| Dried tobacco leaves | 8.0–10.0 |
| Bricks | 0.3–0.4 |
| Charcoal | 5.0–6.0 |

# Rubber

*From the late 19th century, when it was introduced by the British, rubber has been a major crop in Malaysia. It has been cultivated on extensive plantations and smallholdings across the country. From the extraction of raw latex to the production of consumer products, a huge industry has been established, and rubber wood is now also an important timber source. Today, Malaysia is the third largest producer of natural rubber in the world.*

A typical rubber estate in which trees are planted in rows, with about 270 trees per hectare.

### Wickham and Ridley

The story of Malaysia's multimillion dollar rubber industry began in the 1870s, initiated by British administrators in India. A certain Henry Wickham collected 70,000 rubber seeds from the Amazonian rainforest in Brazil, from where they were taken to Kew Gardens in London and germinated. Seedlings were then sent out to British colonial posts, and in 1876 nine were planted in Kuala Kangsar in Perak. The trees that descended from the original Wickham stock were then used to establish the first plantation, which is credited to H. N. Ridley, then Director of the Singapore Botanic Gardens. The area under cultivation rose rapidly. The 'rubber revolution' of the early 20th century saw virtually all other cash crops being brushed aside to make way for rubber plantations, and by the 1930s Malaysia's rubber industry dwarfed that of Brazil's. The growing demand for natural rubber worldwide,

Henry Wickham in Brazil where he collected rubber seeds that were later planted in Malaysia.

notably for the making of pneumatic tyres for the newly invented motorcar, gave the industry room to expand and achieve high profits.

### Rubber plants

Rubber trees, or *Hevea brasiliensis* (Euphorbiaceae), grow vigorously in well-drained, clayey soils to an average height of 25 metres. The trunk is straight and covered with smooth, light grey bark, and the

## Latex extraction

The traditional method of latex extraction begins with pricking or making an incision in the tree bark. A deep, V-shaped cut is then made at a 30 degree angle to the trunk to ensure that the maximum number of latex vessels are tapped. Latex flows most freely in the early morning and runs down the channel made in the bark into a glass or earthenware cup at a distance below its base. Trees are first tapped when they are 4–7 years old. The initial cut is tapped repeatedly at daily, or slightly longer, intervals. At each tapping, a slice of bark about 1 millimetre thick is removed from the incision's lower edge, until eventually a wound of up to 2 metres is made on one side of the tree. Tapping techniques have been designed to ensure a steady supply of latex, with sufficient time given for the wound to heal before the same part of the tree is retapped.

An alternative form of extraction is by puncturing, such as the RRIMFLOW and REACTORRIM systems. These two techniques were introduced to overcome labour shortages and to speed up the tapping process. Puncturing considerably reduces damage to the cambium layer, ensuring the high quality of the wood is maintained for timber. Future developments may include the use of mechanized tapping knives and the collection of latex by pipe systems.

### Methods of extraction

1. Traditional tapping methods are labour intensive.
2. The RRIMFLOW system employs a recurrent gas stimulant to tap the latex.
3. REACTORRIM works by releasing a gas stimulant slowly from a canister. Both RRIMFLOW and REACTORRIM require significantly less manpower than the traditional method.

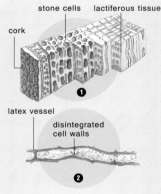

### Bark and latex vessel

1. A section of bark showing the cork layer, stone cells and lactiferous tissue.
2. This latex vessel shows the dissolution of its cell walls to form part of the lactiferous system. Latex vessels are derived from the cambium, and exist in a series of cylinders which alternate with cylinders of phloem tissue.

### Forms of latex

Extracted latex (A) is 60 per cent water and can be processed by coagulation to produce Ribbed Rubber Sheets (RRS) (B); and Standard Malaysian Rubber (SMR) (C), which has a longer and more complex production method.

| AREA UNDER RUBBER CULTIVATION ('000 ha) | | | | | | |
|---|---|---|---|---|---|---|
| YEAR | PENINSULAR MALAYSIA | | SABAH | | SARAWAK | |
| | ESTATE | SMALL-HOLDING | ESTATE | SMALL-HOLDING | ESTATE | SMALL-HOLDING |
| 1991 | 327 | 1174 | 6 | 78 | 1 | 211 |
| 1992 | 314 | 1008 | 4 | 73 | 1 | 211 |
| 1993e | 299 | 954 | 4 | 73 | 1 | 211 |
| 1994e | 284 | 918 | 3 | 73 | 1 | 211 |

Source: Malaysian Rubber Research and Development Board (MRRDB); Department of Statistics, Malaysia; RRIM; Sabah Rubber Fund Board; Sarawak Department of Agriculture
Abbrev.: e—estimates

slender branches open up to a leafy crown. The young leaves are bronze red in colour and, as they mature, turn into thin, dark green, elliptical leaflets. Pollination is facilitated by insects, mostly small midges and thrips. The fruit is a large, three-lobed capsule containing three big, mottled brown seeds. The seeds are oily and poisonous because they contain a cyanogenic glucoside, though this can be removed by boiling.

The stocks for large-scale planting are mainly obtained by budding the shoots from selected high-yielding trees onto vigorous root stocks to establish high-yielding clones. Besides giving a high yield, other important factors, such as resistance to crippling leaf blights, the absence of undesirable low branching, the efficiency of replacing wounded bark, and resistance to wind damage, are all notable characteristics of a good rubber tree.

## Cultivation

The ultimate yield of any rubber plantation or holding depends on factors such as the genetic potential of the cloned plant, the quality of planting materials, the soil and microclimatic conditions and human control of the plants. In plantations, trees are grown close together, and land terracing is necessary in hilly areas to achieve optimum planting density. It is usual for a mixture of leguminous cover crops to be grown in rubber plantations to prevent soil erosion, smother weeds, maintain soil moisture and supply beneficial nitrogen to the ground. Edible groundnuts, rattans and other short-term crops are interplanted among the rubber plants for the same reasons, and also to supply smallholder cultivators

## Rubber wood

With the decline of rainforest timber resources, rubber plantations are being looked to as a valuable new supply of wood. Rubber trees have a 25–30 year regeneration span, in contrast to the 100–300 year period required before rainforest trees can be felled for their wood. Rubber wood has long been a source of cheap fuel for domestic use and for drying and curing bricks, tobacco and rubber sheets (see 'Plants as a source of energy'). It is also made into charcoal which is used by the steel industry.

The production of sawn rubber timber only started in 1979. Since then, chipboard, fire board, plywood and veneer have been produced at an increasing rate. Initially, all the timber was for export, but after government encouragement, home-grown processing was established. To ensure that rubber trees are not over exploited, strict codes have been introduced since 1990 to limit the amount of raw timber that is exported.

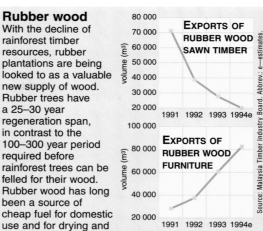

EXPORTS OF RUBBER WOOD SAWN TIMBER
(volume m³)

EXPORTS OF RUBBER WOOD FURNITURE
(volume m³)

Source: Malaysia Timber Industry Board. Abbrev.: e—estimates.

Rubber wood being sawn into planks.

Treatment of rubber wood to prevent insect and fungal attack.

Rubber wood takes an average of 60 days to air dry, and the percentage of shrinkage is low.

### Rubber wood furniture
Rubber wood is now Malaysia's most popular furniture timber. It has a light colour and is a convincing substitute for *nyatoh* and *ramin* (rainforest timbers), or may be stained to give the appearance of oak.

with an additional source of income during the seasons when the rubber trees are not mature enough to be tapped.

## Future productivity

The Rubber Research Institute of Malaysia (RRIM) is the sole department responsible for rubber production development. It has successfully established a number of important clones which have significantly contributed to the rapid development of natural rubber production and industries in Malaysia. The new clones of the RRIM 2000 series are able to produce trees with high-quality latex, vigorous growth and straight trunks which are resistant to wind and disease. Timber can be harvested after 10–12 years, and in the meantime tapping can be carried out. With an anticipated reduction in log production from natural forest, high-quality rubber wood is an important supplementary source of Malaysian timber.

With the new approach, Malaysia is able to sustain the country's yearly rubber production of 1.2 million tonnes, and maintain its position as the third largest producer of natural rubber in the world.

### RUBBER PRODUCTS EXPORTED FROM MALAYSIA (1994)

latex goods 64%
tyres 14%
footwear 3%
industrial 6%
general rubber goods 13%

Source: RRIM

### Rubber and rubber-derived products

Rubber products include (1) cables, (2) gloves, (3) flippers, (4) boots, (5) seismic bearings and (6) car tyres. The manufacture of this wide selection of product types is made possible by improved processing techniques and the production of rubbers that have uniform processing characteristics. Rubber-derived products, such as high-value proteins and quebrachitol, also have high commercial worth in the biochemical, pharmaceutical and medical fields.

# Tea, coffee and cocoa

*From the late 19th century, tea plantations were developed in the highlands of Malaysia and coffee was grown commercially. The cocoa industry, however, did not begin until the mid-20th century in Peninsular Malaysia. Today, tea, coffee and cocoa are three important minor crops that are produced for domestic use as well as for export. Not only are they of economic significance, but they are also an important part of Malaysian life and culture.*

'Pokok chempedak' is a Malaysian brand of tea. This tea has been flavoured with *wangi ros*, or essence of rose.

## Tea

Tea (*Camellia sinensis*) belongs to the family Theaceae. It has long been grown in China, but its place of origin is near the source of the Irrawaddy River in Myanmar (Burma). From there it spread to southeastern China, Indochina and Assam, and with the establishment of Dutch and British trade routes in the 17th century, it arrived in Europe.

The earliest use of tea was probably medicinal, although tea leaves have for the last 2,000–3,000 years been used to make a beverage. In the 19th century, tea cultivation developed into an important plantation industry in Asia, in countries such as India, Sri Lanka (Ceylon) and China. In Malaysia, tea was, and still is, grown mainly on the mountain slopes of the Cameron Highlands, where the equable temperatures, moderate to high rainfall and high humidity are conducive. A few botanical varieties have emerged, among which are *C. sinensis* var. *sinensis*, *C. sinensis* var. *assamica* and *C. sinensis* var. *macrophylla*.

The best soil for tea is deep, permeable, well-drained and acidic, conditions which are often found in tropical red earth. Wild tea grows into a small tree, but under cultivation it is pruned into a low, spreading bush. It has a strong tap root and lateral roots which give rise to a surface mat of

In the Cameron Highlands, where most of Malaysia's tea is grown, lie the gently rolling slopes of the Blue Valley tea plantation. *INSET*: The young shoots of the plant are the most desired by tea manufacturers.

*LEFT*: A tea plant in a plantation in the Cameron Highlands. *MIDDLE*: Workers bagging freshly picked tea leaves to take to the factory for processing. *RIGHT*: Dried tea leaves sitting in the machine after being processed.

feeding roots. The fragrant white or pink flowers are either solitary or clustered, and the fruit is a thick-walled capsule. It takes 3–4 years before the tree can be harvested. The young shoots and leaves make the best tea and so are sought after.

Most of the tea consumed in the world is black tea. It is manufactured by a highly technical process carried out in factories on tea plantations. The leaves are heated by a hot air current, which liberates the caffeine and develops the flavour and colour of the tea. Another type of tea, green tea, is

Coffee berries grow in clumps at regular intervals along the stems and branches of the coffee plant.

Drying coffee fruits takes about 10–12 days.

## Aromatic coffee

Mature coffee fruits are processed by either dry or wet methods. In Malaysia, the dry method is more widely practised because it is simpler and cheaper.

Fruits are spread out to dry in the sun before being hulled. The beans are then collected and roasted, during which much of the water is lost and the sugars partially caramelized. This process develops and seals the aroma and flavour, which are later released into the drink when the beans are ground and brewed with hot water.

Roasting plays an important part in determining the final flavour of the coffee, as do other conditions, such as the variety of the plant, the conditions under which it is grown and the location of the plantation.

These coffee beans from a plantation in Sabah are ready to be roasted.

### NUTRITIONAL COMPOSITION OF COFFEE BEANS

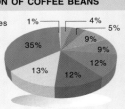

- Cellulose and related substances
- Protein
- Water
- Fat
- Sugar
- Caffeic acid
- Water soluble substances
- Ash
- Caffeine

1% — 4%
5%
9%
35%
9%
12%
13%
12%

made by steaming, rolling and drying the leaves. The dried tea is graded and sorted by colour and fineness, and the different grades are then blended to create varieties to suit the tastes and preferences of tea drinkers. Today, Malaysia produces tea both for export and home consumption.

## Coffee

The coffee plant is a member of the family Rubiaceae, which has species distributed in Africa, Madagascar, Mauritius and Southeast Asia. All species are woody, but they range from slender, sprawling plants and lianas to shrubs of all sizes to robust trees. The most economically important species are *Coffea arabica*, *C. canephora* and *C. liberica*. The latter two species have been grown commercially in Malaysia since the 19th century, and now occupy a total of about 25 000 hectares.

*Coffea liberica* was introduced to Malaysia from tropical West Africa. If not pruned, the plant can grow to a height of 8 metres. Its leaves are thick and large, and the berries do not soften or drop when ripe, but remain hard and fibrous. The best and most consistent crop comes from plants grown on peaty soil in the lowlands and in direct sunlight. The crop takes about 10 months to reach maturity. Seeds from only fully ripened berries are harvested. Harvesting takes place twice a year, once in May or June and again in December or January.

*Coffea canephora* grows more rapidly than *C. liberica*. Its branches are longer, its leaves thinner, larger and paler, and the berries much smaller. However, the beans of both species are practically the same size. *C. canephora* thrives on a loose clay-loam soil and in direct sunlight for the first two years, after which it requires shade.

## Cocoa

The cocoa tree (*Theobroma cacao*) is a member of the Sterculiaceae, a family to which the cola nut tree also belongs. The name *Theobroma*, meaning 'food of the gods', was given by the Indians in Central America who cultivated cocoa and believed it to be of divine origin. It was brought to Southeast Asia by the Spanish and the Dutch around 1670, but it was only in the early 1950s that cocoa was planted commercially—at Jerangau in Terengganu. By the mid-1950s, it had also been introduced to Sabah. In Peninsular Malaysia, cocoa plantations are found in Perak, Selangor, Johor and Pahang, and in Sabah in Tawau, Sandakan and Kudat.

In 1989, the Malaysian Cocoa Board was established. Its aims are to increase bean production by improving the productivity of crops and methods of harvesting as well as to strengthen Malaysia's existing cocoa markets and to penetrate new ones.

Other organizations involved in the development of the cocoa industry are the Malaysian Agricultural Research and Development Institute and the Sabah Agicultural Department.

Cocoa is strictly a tropical crop. It grows best in well-drained soil with plenty of water and nutrients. Inflorescences are produced on the older, leafless part of the main stems and branches. The pod is indehiscent (it does not split open and release its seeds spontaneously) and is white, green or red when young, turning a green, yellow or purple as it matures. Fresh seeds are surrounded by a mucilaginous, whitish, sugary and acidic pulp, which is removed during processing.

Cocoa pods are produced throughout the year. When ripe, they stay suitable for harvesting for 2–3 weeks. Beans from unripe pods do not process well, and overripe beans may have already germinated in the pod. After harvesting, the beans are cleaned, graded and dried before they are sent to chocolate factories where the critical roasting process takes place. Roasting the beans at 140 °C melts them into a chocolate-like substance, which is then mixed with milk and sugar. Malaysia is the seventh largest supplier of chocolate in the world, the two main producers being Ghana and Brazil.

*LEFT: A Chinese wedding tea ceremony. The bride is offering tea, using a ceremonial tea set, to her father-in-law.*

*RIGHT: A delicate Chinese wedding tea pot used in the tea ceremony.*

*BELOW: This finely crafted pewter tea set is designed and produced by Royal Selangor, Malaysia's leading house of pewter.*

## Tea: Culture and tradition

When the British came to Malaya in the 19th century, there was already a well-established tea drinking culture amongst the Chinese. The two cultures appreciate their tea in very different ways. While the British take their tea with milk and sugar, the Chinese always drink their *cha* black. A traditional Chinese tea drinker also warms his tea cup by spilling boiling water over it before pouring the tea. In the first pot, the leaves are rinsed and the water discarded, and the second pot is drunk.

The Chinese also use tea in ceremonies. During a Chinese wedding, tea is offered by the couple to their new in-laws and relatives, who in return give *angpow*, or red packets with money. The oldest members of the families are served first, followed by the younger ones. The couple do not, however, pour tea for relatives younger than themselves, but are served by them instead. This tradition is still practised today by the Chinese in Malaysia.

Cocoa is a major ingredient in chocolate and Milo, Malaysia's leading cocoa product. These are the two main products that Malaysia manufactures from cocoa.

## The cocoa trade in Malaysia

Malaysia exports most of its cocoa, either in the form of raw cocoa beans or cocoa products, such as chocolate, cocoa powder, butter and paste. Singapore is the major importer of cocoa beans, full-fat cocoa paste and chocolate, whilst for low-fat cocoa paste and cocoa butter it is the United States of America.

Mature cocoa pods on the tree just before harvesting.

Husking cocoa pods after collecting.

Before processing, cocoa beans are covered in a white, sticky pulp.

Dried cocoa beans waiting to be sent to the chocolate factory.

### INCREASE IN AREA UNDER COCOA CULTIVATION (1965–1992) (ha)

136 000

119 500

57 200

2187

761

1965

1992

Peninsular Malaysia    Sabah    Sarawak*

*Cocoa cultivation did not start in Sarawak until 1974, and only on a very small scale.

# Tuber crops

*There has been a steady decline in the cultivation of tuber crops in Malaysia in favour of more economically successful crops such as rubber and oil palm. Although tuber crops only play a minor role as a staple food, they are widely used in their raw form in the production of snacks. Starch extracted from the tubers is useful in a host of other manufacturing industries too. Cassava is the most important tuber crop for starch processing, and continues to be grown both in large plantations and at subsistence level.*

In Malaysia, carrots (*Daucus carota*) are harvested 70–85 days after sowing. A carrot has reached maturity when it is orange from the inside to its blunt tip.

Vine-turning at a sweetpotato farm. It is a traditional method for the prevention of small tuber formation. (Inset) Newly unearthed sweetpotato (*Ipomoea batatas*) tubers.

Harvesting sweetpotatoes at a farm in Kedah. This land was formerly a paddy field.

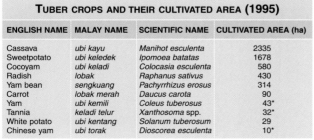

Sweetpotatoes on sale at an open-air market in Tawau, Sabah.

## Types of tuber crops

Each plant in a tuber crop develops one or more swollen organs, or tubers, which store starch and are located underground. The tuber may be either a modified stem, as in the white potato or cocoyam when it is known as a corm, or a modified root such as the sweetpotato or cassava. In Malaysia, tuber crops are either indigenous or introduced types brought from far afield during the colonial days. Indigenous species are seldom cultivated, and are found growing wild in secondary jungle. Of the introduced species, cassava, cocoyams, sweetpotatoes, tannia, various yams and yam beans are tropical in origin, whereas white potatoes, carrots and radishes come from temperate regions.

Tuber crops in Malaysia differ greatly in size, shape and appearance, and belong to a broad range of plant families. Cassava, of the Euphorbiaceae family, is related to the rubber and castor-oil plant. The white potato belongs to the nightshade family (Solanaceae), which it shares with the chilli and tomato, and the yam bean is actually a legume, or bean, as its name suggests. The largest group of tuber crops are the aroids (Araceae). A common feature among the aroids is their distinctive inflorescence, which in many species emits an odour resembling rotting meat. This odour attracts flies to visit and pollinate the flowers.

## Uses for different crops

Tuber crops play a varied role in the Malaysian diet. However, in times of staple shortages they have proved useful food supplements. For example, cassava and sweetpotatoes were important during World War II when rice was in short supply.

Temperate tuber crops are grown mainly as vegetables in the highlands of Malaysia, where milder conditions are more conducive for their growth. Tropical tuber crops are widely used as an ingredient in traditional and new local snacks. Some popular preparations are cassava or sweetpotato fritters and crisps. These two types of tubers and cocoyams, are used in the production of snacks made from reconstituted food. The sweetpotato is used in *cakar ayam*, a biscuit comprising caramel-coated fried strips, and is also turned into dried, sweetened slices.

Some tuber crops even have medicinal applications. The acrid juice of *Alocasia macrorrhiza* has been used in traditional medicine to relieve nettle stings, while its chopped up roots and leaves can be applied to aching joints. The mashed tubers of the sweetpotato and some climbing yams are used as a poultice to alleviate soreness and inflammation.

A cocoyam plant (*Colocasia esculenta*). The underground tuber grows until it reaches the surface. If more soil is added, it will grow until it protrudes through the soil.

## How safe are they to eat?

Some tuber crops can be toxic if not properly prepared before eating. The shoots, young leaves and root rind of all cassava varieties contain cyanide (see 'Plant defences against herbivores'), and even the safe-to-eat root pith or flesh of edible varieties has a low cyanide content. However, cyanide is highly water soluble and volatile, and with proper processing the poisonous parts can be rendered safe for humans.

Sweetpotatoes, cocoyams, giant swamp taros and especially giant taros can inhibit growth, as the anti-trypsin properties they possess interfere with normal protein metabolism. Fortunately, trypsin inhibitors are destroyed by heat, and can be easily deactivated by cooking. Certain tubers produce poisonous alkaloids. Some climbing yams, such as *Dioscorea hispida*, produce the alkaloids dioscorine and dioscoricine which have to be washed out before the tubers can be eaten. Even the white potato can be dangerous. If its tubers are exposed to sunlight, they turn green and the poisonous solanin is allowed to form.

### TUBER CROPS AND THEIR CULTIVATED AREA (1995)

| ENGLISH NAME | MALAY NAME | SCIENTIFIC NAME | CULTIVATED AREA (ha) |
|---|---|---|---|
| Cassava | ubi kayu | Manihot esculenta | 2335 |
| Sweetpotato | ubi keledek | Ipomoea batatas | 1678 |
| Cocoyam | ubi keladi | Colocasia esculenta | 580 |
| Radish | lobak | Raphanus sativus | 430 |
| Yam bean | sengkuang | Pachyrrhizus erosus | 314 |
| Carrot | lobak merah | Daucus carota | 90 |
| Yam | ubi kemili | Coleus tuberosus | 43* |
| Tannia | keladi telur | Xanthosoma spp. | 32* |
| White potato | ubi kentang | Solanum tuberosum | 29 |
| Chinese yam | ubi torak | Dioscorea esculenta | 10* |

+ Peninsular Malaysia only. In Sabah and Sarawak, tuber crops are cultivated mostly on smallholdings. Figures are for 1995 except those marked * which are for 1993.

# Cassava: Commercial versus subsistence use

**AREA UNDER CASSAVA CULTIVATION IN PENINSULAR MALAYSIA, (1967–1995)**

Area ('000 ha)

25
20
15
10
5
0

1967   1972   1977   1982   1987   1992  1995

Cassava (*Manihot esculenta*), or tapioca as it is known in its processed form, plays a dual role in Malaysia's agriculture. It is a commercial crop of some importance, providing raw material for the starch extraction industry. On a smaller scale, it is cultivated in gardens as a subsistence crop, and grown by farmers for sale at local markets.

The varieties grown for their starch tend to be the 'poisonous' ones with a high cyanide content. Their toxicity effectively deters them from mammalian pests, such as rats and pigs.

Perak has long been the centre for cassava starch production, where large centrifugal separators (rotating drums) extract the starch from the tubers. However, the cultivated area in Peninsular Malaysia has declined from a peak of 20 900 hectares in 1976 to a mere 2335 hectares in 1995. Locally, starch is used to manufacture monosodium glutamate (MSG), a flavour enhancer used in processed foods. It is also used to make glucose and a range of fermented products, including vinegar and industrial alcohol. Starch is commonly used in baking products as a partial substitute for wheat flour, and in the manufacture of paper and textiles.

Edible cassava is grown for sale at local markets and for home consumption. There are local cakes or *kuih*, whose main ingredient is cassava, such as *bingka*, which is a baked mixture of grated cassava precooked with coconut and sugar. In the dessert *tapai ubi*, slices of cassava are parboiled and left to ferment for 3–4 days. *Kerepek*, or fried crisps, is a popular cassava snack as is *kerupuk*, crackers made from cassava starch and flavoured with fish, shrimp or chopped up vegetables.

## Cassava processing

1. A field of cassava at a farm in Perak.
2. Farm workers preparing cassava cuttings for planting.
3. Cassava is the only tuber crop of significance in the starch-processing industry.
4. Starch, which is processed from cassava, can be found in flour and pearl form.
5. A small backyard crop of edible cassava.
6. Cassava on sale at an open-air market in Ranau, Sabah.
7. Slicing cassava roots for making crisps.
8., 9. and 10. Because of its ability to expand when deep fried, cassava is the base ingredient in fish, prawn and vegetable-flavoured crackers.

# Vegetables

*A plant counts as a vegetable if its parts are eaten as an accompaniment to the staple food, which in Malaysia is rice. Over 100 species of plants in Malaysia are vegetables, cultivated either in farms or garden plots. Some native species can be found in the jungle, growing wild. Traditional vegetables, or ulam, are usually eaten raw, and have high nutritional as well as medicinal value. Tropical vegetables are grown by smallholders in the lowlands of Malaysia, while temperate species, such as cabbages and cauliflowers, are found in highland farms. Wild vegetables are collected for home consumption and sold in small, rural markets.*

Terraced vegetable farms in the Cameron Highlands, where the majority of temperate vegetables are grown in Malaysia.

A cabbage, or *kubis* (*Brassica* spp.), farm plot. Kubis is the most widely grown vegetable crop in the highland farms of Malaysia.

## Vegetables and agriculture

Vegetable production makes up a significant portion of the agricultural industry in Malaysia, ranking alongside other important cash crops such as fruits and nuts. The Malaysian Agricultural Research and Development Institute (MARDI) has, since 1970, been making efforts to improve and broaden the quality and variety of vegetables cultivated in Malaysia. Over 2,000 varieties and species of vegetables from more than 10 countries, including Thailand, India, Japan, the United Kingdom, Australia and the United States of America, have been brought in by MARDI for testing under different agro-ecological conditions. These tests revealed the more high-yielding, resilient and pest-resistant varieties which were then selected for cultivation. While the tropical vegetables have no shortage of farm space in the lowlands, to expand

## Vegetables commonly used in Malaysia

A variety of native and introduced, tropical and temperate vegetables are used in Malaysia. Certain introduced vegetables, such as the aubergine or *terong*, are so widely used that they have become naturalized, and are considered Malaysian. Temperate vegetables are cultivated mainly in the highlands of Malaysia, where crops such as cauliflower, carrot and lettuce are found on terraced vegetables farms.

### 1. Cauliflower, *kubis bunga* (*Brassica oleracea* var. *botrytis*)
The cauliflower originates from the Mediterranean, but is now cultivated in many Asian countries, such as India, the Philippines and Malaysia. A variety of cabbage, it has a similar short stem with long, elliptical leaves. The stump-like flowers and the thick branches on which they grow together form the edible part of the plant. It is cultivated above an altitude of 1000 metres, but there are also lowland varieties that can be grown at lower altitudes.

### 2. Lady's fingers, *kacang bendi* (*Abelmoschus esculentus*)
The exact origin of lady's fingers is uncertain, but it is cultivated in tropical and subtropical regions, and is especially popular in the West Indies, West Africa and India. It is also common in Malaysia, Thailand, Vietnam and the Philippines. An annual herb that grows up to 2 metres, the plant bears spirally arranged leaves with yellow, solitary flowers. Young, immature fruits are eaten raw, fried or cooked in curries and sauces. A significant amount of protein and vegetable oil is contained in the seeds.

### 3. Bitter gourd, *peria* (*Momordica charantia*)
The bitter gourd belongs to a genus that originates from the Old World. On slave trade routes, it was brought from Africa to Brazil, from where it was distributed to the rest of South America. In Asia, bitter gourds were first cultivated in eastern India and southern China, but are now grown in some parts of Southeast Asia, including Malaysia. The immature fruits are the vegetable product, and may be fried, pickled or dried. Soaking the fruits in salted water before cooking helps to reduce the bitterness. In traditional medicine, bitter gourds are used to treat diabetes. The juice is applied externally for skin disorders, and ingested for the treatment of arthritis, rheumatism and asthma.

### 4. Aubergine, *terong* (*Solanum melongena*)
Originally from India, this egg-shaped fruit is white, dark purple or black in colour. It is a short-lived, perennial herb that grows to 0.5–1.5 metres, with hairy stems, simple leaves and single flowers. When mature, it bears fruits which can be harvested over a two-month period. Both unripe and ripe fruits are eaten. They are fried or made into curries.

### 5. Carrot, *lobak merah* (*Daucus carota*)
Originally from Europe, the carrot has spread to Asia and Africa. Although it is a biennial in its natural state, it is often cultivated as an annual. The tap root is the edible part, varying in length from 5 centimetres in baby carrots to 25–40 centimetres in larger varieties. It swells and thickens as it grows, turning an orange or reddish colour. Firm leaves occur alternately on a stem, while white flowers are found in clusters. Rich in carotene and vitamin A, carrots are made into juice as well as eaten as a vegetable. In Malaysia, carrots are grown in the highlands, where the temperature range of 16–24 °C is conducive.

### 6. Shallot, *bawang merah* (*Allium cepa* var. *aggregatum*)
The shallot has its origin in central or west Asia, although it is most widely cultivated in India. It is an annual plant. A single parent bulb produces a few new bulbs, from which long, slender leaves grow.

The huge indoor market in Kota Bharu, on the east coast of Peninsular Malaysia, has on sale commonly available vegetables, as well as local produce used only in the food dishes of that area.

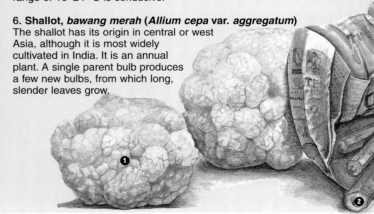

the area under temperate vegetables, a rain shelter system is used. This allows temperate vegetables to be grown at low altitudes in Malaysia, and is suitable for crops like tomatoes and cabbages.

With the aim of achieving the optimum yield from a vegetable crop, MARDI has undertaken research into specific nutrient requirements and the management of pests and diseases. Important crops, such as *kangkong*, *pak choi* and cauliflower have had their nutrient uptake monitored, and the results combined with those from fertilizer trials. The amalgamated result has been used in the drawing up of a fertilizer programme tailored to meet the needs of each of these crops. Published diagnostic guides on nutrient deficiencies have also armed farmers with the knowledge they require to identify and treat ailing crops.

The major pests and diseases affecting vegetable crops are leaf-devouring insects, shoot and fruit borers, leaf spots, mildew and viral infections. To control these, insecticides and fungicides are used alongside non-chemical methods, such as the use of plastic mulches.

## AREA UNDER VEGETABLE CULTIVATION IN MALAYSIA (1970–2000)

Source: Department of Agriculture (1997)

## THE OCCURRENCE AND IMPORTANCE OF MAJOR VEGETABLES IN MALAYSIA

| SCIENTIFIC NAME | MALAY NAME | OCCURRENCE | IMPORTANCE (urban markets) |
| --- | --- | --- | --- |
| Abelmoschus esculentus | kacang bendi | common | medium quantity |
| Allium cepa var. aggregatum | bawang merah | very frequent | large quantity |
| Brassica oleracea | kobis bunga | common | medium quantity |
| B. campestris var. chinensis | sawi putih | frequent | large quantity |
| Cucumis sativus | timun | very frequent | large quantity |
| Daucus carota | lobak merah | frequent | large quantity |
| Glycine max | kacang soya | common | medium quantity |
| Ipomoea aquatica | kangkong | very frequent | large quantity |
| Lactuca sativa | daun salad | frequent | large quantity |
| Momordica spp. | peria | frequent | large quantity |
| Parkia speciosa | petai | common | medium quantity |
| Phaseolus vulgaris | kacang buncis | frequent | large quantity |
| Solanum melongena | terong | very frequent | large quantity |
| Several species of bamboo | rebung | very frequent | large quantity |

Source: Plant Resources of Southeast Asia (PROSEA) (1994)

The edible bulbs vary in size and colour, and are covered with thin, reddish, membranous scaly leaves. Greenish white flowers are formed in clusters at the end of leafless stalks. Upon reaching maturity, the leaves dry up and the bulbs are harvested. Shallots can be pickled, eaten raw or cooked in curries and stir-fried dishes.

### 7. Chinese cabbage, *sawi putih* (*Brassica campestris* var. *chinensis*)
The cultivation of Chinese cabbage goes as far back as the 5th century CE in China. In the 15th century, it was introduced to Melaka, and spread to other parts of Southeast Asia. It is now widely cultivated in Malaysia and the Philippines, and to a smaller extent in Indonesia and Thailand. All exposed parts of the plant are edible, but the young, immature leaves and juicy petioles are preferred. It is a major ingredient in Chinese cuisine, and is often used in stir-fried dishes and soups.

### 8. Lettuce, *daun salad* (*Latuca sativa*)
Lettuce originated from the Middle East, and later spread to Europe, China and the tropics. It is grown in both temperate and tropical regions. An annual plant, it is cultivated from seed. Long, narrow leaves form a loose, upright and cylindrical head. Although lettuce is often overlooked as a main ingredient and used instead as a garnish, it is actually an excellent source of vitamin A which, if lacking in a person's diet, causes blindness. This is especially important in countries such as Malaysia, where polished rice is the staple food.

### 9. String bean, *kacang buncis* (*Phaseolus vulgaris*)
A plant that comes from southern Mexico, the string bean is either a bush or a climber. As a bush, it grows up to only 1 metre, but as a climber it can reach a length of 3 metres with the help of supports such as poles. The leaves alternate along the stem, each leaf having three leaflets. Long, narrow pods contain 4–8 seeds. The flowers are white, pink or mauve. String beans can be fried with *sambal* (a chilli sauce) and used in curries and salads.

### 10. *Petai* (*Parkia speciosa*)
A native to Malaysia, Indonesia and peninsular Thailand, *petai* is rarely cultivated outside these areas. It grows on a tree, which can reach up to 30 metres in height. The tree bears pear-shaped inflorescences with numerous, small, brownish yellow flowers. Edible seeds are contained inside long, green pods. Despite their strong smell, the seeds are eaten raw. If not consumed fresh, they are dried in the sun, then peeled and soaked for a day before frying or roasting.

# Oil palm

*Malaysia is the world's largest producer and exporter of palm oil. First introduced as an ornamental plant in the 1870s, it only began to be commercially exploited in the early 20th century. Successful harnessing of technology in planting the crop and strict quality control during processing, storage and transportation, have contributed to the development of the oil palm industry into the multibillion ringgit success that it is today. Maintaining such productivity is crucially important for the hundreds of thousands of Malaysians who work on the oil palm estates or in associated industries.*

| AREA UNDER OIL PALM CULTIVATION AND WEIGHT OF PALM OIL PRODUCTION (1995–1996) | | | | |
| --- | --- | --- | --- | --- |
| AREA ('000 ha) | 1995 | % CHANGE FROM 1994 | 1996e | % CHANGE FROM 1995 |
| Total planted area | 2507 | 4.0 | 2567 | 2.4 |
| Mature plantations | 2235 | 6.5 | 2326 | 4.1 |
| Crop yield (kg/ha) | 3490 | 1.4 | 3730 | 6.9 |
| PRODUCTION ('000 t) | | | | |
| Crude palm oil | 7810 | 8.2 | 8040 | 2.9 |
| Palm kernel oil | 1036 | 7.9 | 1130 | 9.1 |

Source: Ministry of Primary Industries (1997). Abbrev.: e—estimate

A typical plantation with a cover crop growing in between the rows of oil palms. The cover crop is planted at the same time as the oil palms, so that soil erosion is kept under control from the start.

An individual oil palm tree produces up to 30 fruit bunches per annum. A tree takes 3–4 years to mature, after which it is productive for about another 25 years.

## Origin

The oil palm *Elaeis guineensis* originated in the rainforests of West Africa where it grew along river banks and in coastal areas. In 1848, the Dutch brought seeds from Africa to the Bogor Botanical Gardens in West Java, thereby introducing the oil palm to Southeast Asia. Seeds from these plants were gradually planted throughout the region. By 1909, oil palm was seen growing in the public gardens of Kuala Lumpur and at an experimental plantation in Batu Tiga. Economic exploitation of the oil palm in Malaysia began with the first commercial plantation in 1917 in Kuala Selangor.

## Cultivation

The oil palm is a single-stemmed tree that reaches a height of 12 metres in its mature form, and is topped with 35–60 pinnate leaves or fronds. It is grown from seed. The seedlings are maintained in a nursery for 12–18 months before being planted in the fields. Approximately 140 palms are planted per hectare. Oil palm flourishes in alluvial, marine clay and volcanic soils, though it is

## The world's largest producer and exporter of palm oil

Malaysia is the world's leading processor, refiner and exporter of palm oil. In 1995, 94 million tonnes of oils and fats were produced worldwide, of which just over 18 per cent was palm oil. More than one-third of this, or 6.5 million tonnes, was provided by Malaysia. Analysts predict that by the year 2020, the world's production of vegetable oils will increase to 141.7 million tonnes, with palm oil constituting nearly 26 per cent.

There are 274 palm oil mills in Malaysia to handle freshly harvested fruits. Johor, Pahang and Sabah are the major centres of production. There are also 41 refineries, the largest capacity in the world, where the crude oil has its unwanted ingredients removed. Refined oil can be used in a greater variety of products and is thus more economically significant than the crude form. Some countries export their crude oil to Malaysia for refining, after which it is exported back to them for use.

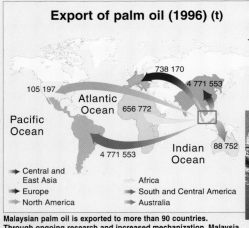

### Export of palm oil (1996) (t)

N

738 170
4 771 553
105 197
Atlantic Ocean 656 772
Pacific Ocean
4 771 553
Indian Ocean 88 752

- Central and East Asia
- Europe
- North America
- Africa
- South and Central America
- Australia

Malaysian palm oil is exported to more than 90 countries. Through ongoing research and increased mechanization, Malaysia maintains its strong global market position.

The most common way of exporting processed palm oil is by tanker.

A mature oil palm tree bearing fruits ready for harvest, which is done every 10–12 days.

reasonably adaptable to less favourable soils provided it receives adequate water and sunlight. During planting, a leguminous cover crop is introduced to prevent soil erosion, provide humus, supply nitrogen and control weeds. It takes about six months from pollination for the fruits to be ready for harvesting. The fruit bunches, each consisting of 1,000–3,000 tightly packed fruits, are still gathered by hand. The first harvest takes place three years after field planting.

## The oil palm industry: A major employer

In 1960, the total area in Malaysia under oil palm cultivation was 55 000 hectares. The cultivation of oil palm since then has increased rapidly through intensive planting by both the private sector and government agencies such as the Federal Land Development Authority (FELDA), Federal Land Consolidation and Rehabilitation Authority (FELCRA), Rubber Industry Smallholders' Development Authority (RISDA) and other state land schemes. Nearly half the area is owned by the private sector and the rest by government agencies and independent smallholders.

By the 1990s, the total planted area was more than 2.5 million hectares. Such an increase has been matched by an enhanced output. This is a result of mechanization of various operations which were once carried out manually, for example, weed control, fertilizer application, and transportation of fruit bunches from field to mill.

### Edible and inedible oils

Two types of palm oil are produced. Crude palm oil (CPO) is derived from the fruit flesh or mesocarp, and palm kernel oil (PKO) is obtained from the endosperm or kernel. Both forms of palm oil are very versatile and are used for manufacturing edible and non-edible products, although nearly 90 per cent of it is used in foods. Non-edible palm oil can be used in its pure form as an ingredient in soap or as a diesel substitute, and is also refined through oleochemical processing to produce fatty acids, fatty alcohols, fatty nitrogens and glycerol. Malaysia is concentrating its efforts on refined oils because of the financial rewards they yield. There are 13 oleochemical plants in Malaysia, each with a production capacity of 800 000 tonnes per year. It is projected that by the year 2000 Malaysia will supply 20 per cent of the world's total production of non-edible oleochemicals.

A longtitudinal section of an oil palm fruit. The palm kernel is surrounded by a layer of hard shell, and the yellow oil-bearing mesocarp by a thin but tough shiny rind.

Some products made from crude palm oil (CPO) include olein and stearin.

Vitamin E is extracted from palm oil and put into capsules for easy consumption.

Palm kernel oil (PKO) is largely used in the manufacture of soap, detergent and cosmetics.

Palm oil is now one of the world's most widely consumed edible oils. It is used for frying and in salad dressings, margarine and confectioneries.

Nearly 200,000 families derive a livelihood from the oil palm industry, either by running independent smallholdings or through government land schemes. There are also about 10,000 workers employed in the private estates and supporting industries, such as trading, milling, processing and manufacturing. A number of these workers, however, have come from other countries, and are needed to supplement local labour. To keep the workforce at the strength required to maintain the country's production at a profitable level, the government provides incentives to the estate workers in the form of improved housing and free education and health services.

*Ganoderma*, a basal stem-rot fungus, is the major cause of oil palm disease in Malaysia.

### From the plantation to the mill

1. Harvesting fresh fruit bunches from a dwarf palm with the help of lightweight aluminium poles.

2. Within the plantation, the harvest is carried by wheelbarrow.

3. Lorries are used to transport fruit bunches from the plantation to the oil palm mill, like this one in Perak.

4. Fruit bunches sit in sterilizer cages before actual processing begins.

# Spices

*Spices, derived from the Latin word* species, *meaning 'an article of special value', were traded as luxury goods in ancient and medieval times, and are the taste of the Orient. Many of the major spices originated in the East, but some later became established in other regions. Spices have little or no nutritional value, but their exotic aromas, distinct flavours, enhancing colours and healing properties have been extensively exploited for culinary, medicinal and other purposes throughout Malaysia.*

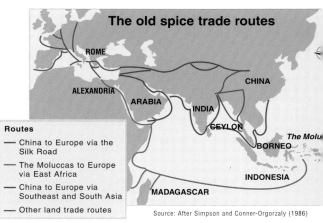

**The old spice trade routes**

Routes
— China to Europe via the Silk Road
— The Moluccas to Europe via East Africa
— China to Europe via Southeast and South Asia
— Other land trade routes

Source: After Simpson and Conner-Orgorzaly (1986)

Bird peppers, or *cili padi*, a ferociously hot variety of *Capsicum frutescens* which is eaten fresh.

## The spice trade

Spices have been known to the local populations in the Far East for thousands of years, but from the 11th century they were increasingly appreciated by a wider world. Explorers from the West, in search of new lands and trade routes, valued these 'new' commodities as highly as gold and jewellery. Arab traders were the first to transport these aromatic and pungent vegetables from the East, via land and sea, to Arabia and Egypt and from there to Europe. Spices were also taken from China to the West, along what was known as the Silk Road. Venice was the major European centre for the spice trade during the Crusades (1096–1291 CE), and Portugal was important from the 1300s to 1500s.

The Dutch monopolized trade for the following 200 years until the 18th century when control was shared with the British. As spices and other artificial flavourings became more readily available in the West, the importance of spice trading decreased and hence the significance of the Far East as a spice centre gradually diminished.

## Chillies

Chillies, also called capsicum peppers or chilli peppers, are traditionally the hot spice of choice for Malaysians and other Southeast Asians. The burning sensation is caused by the compound capsaicin, a powerful irritant and pungent source.

Chillie plants are perennial subshrubs native to tropical America, but are now cultivated throughout the tropics and warm temperate regions of the Old World. In some areas, they have become naturalized and many new varieties have been produced. For example, *Capsicum annuum* produces several varieties, including paprika and bell peppers, that can be obtained in different shapes, sizes, colours and degrees of hotness. *C. frutescens* produces bird peppers which are much smaller and more fiery.

### Pepper: Malaysia's most significant spice

Pepper is the most significant Malaysian spice export, with a yearly value of RM12–14 million. Pepper comes from *Piper nigrum* (Piperaceae), a perennial, woody climber native to the Malabar Coast of southern India, but now widely cultivated in the tropics.

Malaysia was once the largest pepper producer in the world, but it has now been surpassed by Indonesia, India and Brazil. In Malaysia, pepper is grown chiefly in Sarawak, which accounts for almost 98 per cent of the total production. Sarawak pepper is said to be milder than the Indian and Indonesian varieties. In Peninsular Malaysia, pepper is grown in Johor, mainly for local domestic consumption.

Piperine is the major pungent component of pepper, and it is used as a seasoning in sauces, gravies, snacks and even in perfume. In ancient times, it was utilized in medicine as a stimulant and an aid to digestion.

Pepper fruits on the vine. Black pepper is obtained from the unripe dried fruit, while white pepper is produced from ripe, dried fruits.

A typical pepper plantation in Sarawak, where most of Malaysia's pepper is grown. Harvesting starts in April, reaches a peak in May and June, and continues through to September.

Threshing berries before drying them. This process separates the berries from the unwanted stalks.

Berries being laid out to dry on thin rattan mats. Green berries turn a dark brown as they dry, and are then sold as black pepper.

Pepper products manufactured in Malaysia include ground pepper and pepper sauce. The fruits, seen in front, can also be bought in packets.

A cinnamon tree (*Cinnamomum zeylanicum*), and quills made from its inner bark.

## Cinnamon and cassia

True cinnamon is the dried, inner bark of *Cinnamomum zeylanicum*, which is indigenous to Sri Lanka and India, the former being the world's largest producer. The bark and young leaves are reddish in colour and turn dark green when they mature.

Although a widely used spice, it is hardly cultivated in Malaysia.

Cassia is a spice that is obtained from two species of cinnamon trees: *C. loureirii* and *C. burmanii*. Small rolls of bark or quills are prepared using the whole thickness of the bark, and hence are fatter than cinnamon quills.

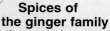

| MAJOR MALAYSIAN SPICES | | | |
|---|---|---|---|
| **ENGLISH NAME** | **MALAY NAME** | **SCIENTIFIC NAME** | **PARTS USED** |
| Chillies, capsicum, paprika, pepper | cili, cabai, lada hijau | Capsicum annuum | fruit |
| Bird pepper | cili apil padi, cabai burung | Capsicum frutescens | fruit |
| Carvies | jintan | Carum carvi | fruit |
| Cinnamon | kulit kayu manis | Cinnamomum zeylanicum | inner bark |
| Cassia | kulit kayu manis | Cinnamomum cassia | whole bark |
| Coriander | ketumbar | Coriandrum sativum | leaf and seed |
| Cumin | jintan putih | Cuminum cyminum | fruit |
| Turmeric | kunyit | Curcuma domestica | rhizome |
| Nutmeg | buah pala | Myristica fragrans | kernel |
| Mace | bunga pala | Myristica fragrans | aril |
| Cardamom | buah pelaga | Elettaria cardamomum | fruit and seed |
| Clove | bunga cengkih | Syzygium caryophyllus | flower bud |
| Star anise | bunga lawang | Illicium verum | fruit |
| Pepper (black/white) | lada hitam /putih | Piper nigrum | fruit |
| Ginger | halia | Zingiber officinale | rhizome |

Both cinnamon and cassia are utilized for a range of culinary purposes, such as flavourings in puddings, sauces and pickles, and ingredients in curry powder, beverages and confectionery. In Malaysia, they are essential spices in local dishes. Cinnamon oil is also used in dental and pharmaceutical preparations.

### Cloves

A clove tree (*Syzygium caryophyllus*), and the dried unopened flower buds that are used as spice.

Cloves are the dried, unopened flower buds of *Syzygium caryophyllus* that are harvested just before they bloom. The clove tree is believed to be indigenous to the Moluccas in Indonesia. In Peninsular Malaysia, cloves were formerly widely cultivated but are now grown mainly in Penang. In local cooking, they are used in some rice and meat dishes, and also in baking. Another major use of cloves is in the commercial manufacture of sauces and pickles.

### Nutmeg and mace

A nutmeg tree (*Myristica fragrans*) and its fruit. Nutmeg comes from the dried kernel, and mace from the fleshy aril around the seed.

Nutmeg and mace are two unique, dissimilarly flavoured spices which come from different parts of the fruit of *Myristica fragrans*. The plant is native to the Moluccas and was introduced to Penang in 1796 by the British, where it still grows. Both spices are used in the food industry. The mesocarp of the nutmeg, or *pala*, is also popular as a sweet pickle and shredded preserve. As a drug, nutmeg is said to have stimulative, carminative, astringent and aphrodisiac properties.

## Spices of the ginger family

The three most important Malaysian spices are cardamom, ginger and turmeric. They are all herbaceous, aromatic perennials which can be vegetatively propagated from rhizomes rather than from seed.

**Cardamom** comes from the dried fruits and seeds of *Elettaria cardamomum*, indigenous to southern India and Sri Lanka. In Malaysia, it is difficult to grow as it is basically a mountain plant. A cardamom substitute, *Amomum kepulaga*, is grown in many villages chiefly for home consumption, and is believed to have been introduced from Java. In combination with cinnamon, star anise and several seed spices, cardamom is an essential ingredient in Malaysian curries, spiced rice, meat dishes and some vegetable dishes.

**Ginger** (see 'Ginger') is obtained from the dried or fresh rhizomes of *Zingiber officinale*. It was one of the earliest Oriental spices known in Europe and is in high demand today. In Asia, it has been cultivated and used as a spice and medicine from ancient times.

Its country of origin is uncertain, although it may have come from either China or India. Commercially, ginger is available in ground form, and as a fresh or dried rhizome. It is one of the most widely used spices in Malaysian cooking, and is also used in pickles, baking products and health drinks.

*Curcuma domestica*, or *kunyit*, otherwise known as **turmeric**, is a fast-growing herb with striking yellow, fleshy rhizomes, each bearing 6–8 large, fragrant leaves. Along with ginger, turmeric was also one of the earliest Oriental spices traded in Europe. Turmeric has been extensively domesticated throughout Malaysia, and can be grown easily. Apart from its use as a principal spice in curry powder, there is an endless list of products in which turmeric is utilized, ranging from food preparations to dye for textiles and traditional cosmetics. It is also one of the main ingredients in a herbal medicine known as *jamu*, which is primarily manufactured in Java, but is sold in Malaysia.

fruit

flower

fruits

seeds

A cardamom plant (*Elettaria cardamomum*) (left) showing the rhizome, roots, stem, leaves, flowers, fruits and (above) seeds.

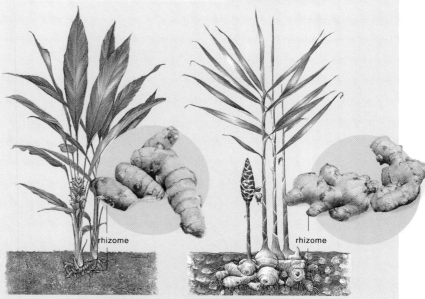

rhizome

rhizome

A turmeric plant (*Curcuma domestica*) and the rhizome which is the part that is used as a spice.

A ginger plant (*Zingiber officinale*) and the familiar ginger rhizome that is a household ingredient in Malaysia.

# Rattans

*Rattans and their relatives constitute a very diverse group of palms in Malaysia. Together with some common palms, such as sago and salak, they belong to the subfamily Calamoideae. A characteristic they all share are the overlapping scales on their fruits. Rattans are restricted to the tropics and subtropics of the Old World, and comprise a total of 600 species, of which 200 species in 10 genera are found in Malaysia. They are used traditionally for making cordage, basketry and fishtraps and as food and medicine.*

**Ant-nests in rattans**
Some species of ants make their nests in rattans. The leaf sheath of *Calamus javensis* (left) is home to ants, whereas in *Pogonotium ursinum* (right) the large, spiny auricles harbour ants.

The scaly fruits of *Calamus lobbianus*, a short-stemmed rattan.

A large rattan, *Calamus erinaceus* grows in thickets, as behind this mangrove forest in Kuala Rompin, Pahang.

Sturdy but light rattan rings form the corset, or *rawai*, around the torso of this Iban woman. This picture was taken by Charles Hose (1863–1929), who worked in the Sarawak Civil Service under Rajah Brooke.

## Structure

Most species of rattans are climbers. Under favourable conditions, some can grow to considerable lengths—the longest cane recorded was over 175 metres. Rattans climb using either cirri or flagella. A cirrus is an extension of the leaf rachis (the main stem of a compound leaf) that goes beyond the terminal leaflets, while a flagellum is a sterile inflorescence borne on the leaf sheath. Both are whip-like and bear groups of very rigid, short and grapnel-like spines. These make very effective climbing apparatus that support and take the rattan crown into the forest canopy. The species with which people are familiar are covered by overlapping leaf sheaths on the upper, younger parts of the stem, and are almost always armed with fierce spines. In the lower and older portions, the leaf sheaths may rot away, exposing the canes. The canes themselves are never spiny.

Some rattan species are single stemmed, while others are clustered. This has commercial significance, as single-stemmed rattans can only be harvested once, whereas it is possible to harvest clustered species repeatedly. For example, *rotan manau* (*Calamus manan*) is a solitary species, whose individual plants die after their cane is harvested. *Rotan sega* (*C. caesius*), on the other hand, can be harvested many times over without sacrificing the plant.

## Rattans and ants

One intriguing phenomenon seen in some rattan species is their symbiotic relationship with ants (see 'Ant-plants'). Some ant species build their nests only on rattans, and will fiercely attack any intruder, thereby protecting the plant against being eaten by herbivores or attacked by parasitic insects. The rattan, in turn, provides the ants with shelter and refuge from predators, who are deterred by the rattan's spiny stem. The ants also raise aphids and scale insects on the rattan, from which they gain an additional source of food.

A specific ant–rattan relationship involves ants dwelling in specially adapted leaflets and inflorescences in the rattan. In *C. laevigatus* and some forms of *C. javensis*, for example, the leaf is sessile (possessing no stalk, growing directly from the stem) with the lowermost leaflets curved across the stem and enclosing the leaf sheath, which is frequently used by ants as a nesting site. In some species of *Daemonorops*, ants move into the inflorescences after the bracts have split. *Pogonotium ursinum* has curious auricles (ear-like extensions from the leaf sheath) which enclose narrow tunnels that ants inhabit. The swollen and hollow ocrea (tongue-like extension from the leaf sheath) in some species of *Korthalsia* forms a spiny chamber, and is home to ants.

## The rattan ware of Sarawak

Woven rattan crafts from Sarawak, such as hats, baskets and mats, are renowned for their fine and intricate styles and patterns. Different ethnic groups make specific, recognizable designs. For example, *ingan* baskets are woven by the Kayan, *tambok* by the Bidayuh and *iban* by the Iban. Hats called *terindak* are made by the Melanau, and those called *sa'ong* by the Kayan and Kenyah. Although weaving styles in Sabah and Peninsular Malaysia are also distinctive and attractive, they are not as varied.

The women of the Kanowit, Iban and other indigenous peoples of Sarawak wear the traditional *rawai* or *sabit* for festive occasions. The rawai is a bodice made from hoops of rattan held together by interlocking brass rings to form a delicate mail design. This full bodice then rests on the woman's hips and may also cover her chest.

An Iban rice basket used in hill paddy cultivation. Woven from rattan, it is used to carry rice seeds during sowing.

Penan women weaving long, thin strands of rattan, some of which are dyed, into mats for sleeping on. A Penan rattan mat (inset) made from natural and dyed-black strands, features a bird motif, and was woven by a woman from Long Abang, Sungei Akah, Baram.

*K. jala*, for instance, has a net-like, expanded and funnel-shaped ocrea which is occupied by a species of large, fierce ants. A few species of *Daemonorops* and *Calamus* have interlocking whorls of spines that form tunnels in which ants nest.

## Rattans and indigenous peoples

Rattans are a versatile material and are used for a wide range of traditional purposes by people in Malaysia. For example, because of their strength and flexibility, rattans are ideal for binding. Their smooth outer surface also makes them suitable for matting and basketware.

The weaving traditions of many of Malaysia's indigenous peoples are rooted in their agricultural and food gathering needs, especially amongst those who practise shifting cultivation. Not only are their farms a fair distance from their homes, but they also spend significant periods of time in the forest hunting and gathering. Therefore, rattan baskets are designed so that they can hold crops and produce, and be carried for long periods over long distances. Mats and hats are also made to suit these agricultural practices. For example, a personal mat, or *tikar burit*, worn around the waist provides a seat in the forest, and a mat for sleeping on is sometimes carried too.

## Trade

Rattans are the most important minor forest product of Malaysia. About 20 species of rattans are traded commercially. The large canes of *C. manan* are among the best for making furniture. Smaller sized canes are used for binding and weaving. As prime canes become more scarce, other species are used as substitutes, or are proving to be excellent in their own right. *C. subinermis*, for example, a species endemic to Sabah, has cane that rivals the quality of *C. manan*. Almost all commercial rattans are collected from wild plants. It is estimated that about 15,000 people, mainly Orang Asli, are involved in rattan collecting in Peninsular Malaysia.

As a result of collecting and deforestation, rattans have come under increasing pressure as a natural resource. As it becomes more difficult for collectors to obtain enough material, they go deeper into the forest to find the desired species.

The increasing demand and shortage of rattan worldwide has resulted in an overall rise in prices. In response, a number of countries in Southeast Asia, including Thailand, the Philippines, Indonesia and Malaysia, have imposed a ban on the export of raw or partially processed rattan. The rationale behind this is that commercial value is added at each stage of processing. Thus, a tonne of rattan furniture is worth ten times the equivalent weight of partially processed rattan. In Malaysia, to deal with rattan shortages and to protect the interests of large rattan furniture export companies, the Government first, in 1987, substantially increased the tax on raw and partially processed rattan, and then implemented a total restriction in 1989.

## Harvesting and processing rattan

Rattan is harvested from the wild. Small groups of Orang Asli set out into the forests, often for some distance, to collect rattan. This task is labour intensive and difficult, and collectors face the danger of dead tree branches falling as the rattan is pulled and tugged at. If the uppermost part of the rattan cannot be freed from the forest canopy, it is left behind and goes to waste. As the stem is brought to the ground, it is dragged against a tree trunk so that the spiny leaf sheaths come off. The immature parts of the stem are discarded, and the remainder cut into manageable lengths, tied up in bundles and transported to the processing site.

Rattan canes must be treated before they can be used to prevent deterioration of the cane. Freshly harvested cane that is still wet from the forest must be treated within 15 days of collection.

Big canes contain large quantities of gums and resins which, along with the water, must be removed. Large canes are cut into 3-metre long sticks that are boiled in diesel or palm oil. They are then cleaned with rags or sand, and stacked upright in the sun to dry.

The smaller canes are coiled into rolls before processing. They are either laid out on racks to dry immediately after collecting, or if this is delayed, stored under water for about a week. These thin rattans can be used whole or split. Sometimes the skin is also used, but in most instances only the core is taken.

1. *Calamus manan* is Malaysia's most commercially important rattan, and is used to make furniture. It is seen growing along the Pahang Road to Kuala Juram in Taman Negara.
2. Rattan canes are harvested from the forest.
3. The canes are then sorted out for processing.
4. After processing, the canes are stacked and left out in the sun to dry.
5. Rattan products, such as furniture, baskets and mats, are a common sight in Malaysian homes, much of which is made locally, as in this shop in Kota Kinabalu.

RM (million)

**MALAYSIA'S EXPORT OF RATTAN FURNITURE (1980–1995) (RM)**

| Year | RM (million) |
|---|---|
| 1980 | 2.8 |
| 1985 | 6.5 |
| 1995 | 91 |

## Commercial planting

In the long term, the depletion of natural rattan resources, coupled with increasing demand, can only be met by rattan cultivation on a commercial scale. However, rattan planting is still a recent development. Rattans are almost always propagated from seed. Trials using mass propagation methods have not been successful on a commercial scale. Some of the more important species under plantation trials are *C. manan* and *C. subinermis*, valued for their large diameter canes. Two small diameter canes—*C. trachycoleus* and *C. caesius*—have gone through extensive trials, and are showing promising growth rates under cultivation. Canes from these species have been successfully harvested from plantations in Sabah and Peninsular Malaysia.

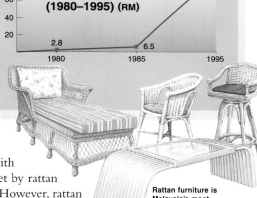

Rattan furniture is Malaysia's most important rattan product, whose export value has increased dramatically since 1985.

A range of Iban basketry on sale in a shop in Miri, Sarawak.

107

# Hybrid orchids

*Orchids are unique in that hybrids can be produced by crossing different species within the same genus or between different but related genera. Hybrids are bred to produce flowers that are more beautiful and longer lasting than the parental studs. In this quest for perfection, about 1,000 new hybrids are created each year. At present, there are no fewer than 75,000 hybrid orchids in existence. Malaysia has been hybridizing orchids since the early decades of the 20th century, but it was only from the 1960s that this became a thriving industry.*

Orchids displaying their vibrant colours at a flower show held in Shah Alam.

Professor R. E. Holttum, Director of the Singapore Botanic Gardens in the early 20th century. He was instrumental in developing and promoting orchid hybridization.

## Orchid hybridizing and seed germination

A pollen grain is removed from one parent orchid using a toothpick, needle or matchstick (1), and placed on the stigma of another. Upon successful pollination, a seed pod develops (2). When mature, the seed pod is harvested, washed and dried over a flame (3). The young seeds are then scooped out and placed on a germination medium in a flask (4). Within 6–8 weeks, numerous plantlets start to appear (5). After 3–4 months, the seedlings are large enough to be transferred to pots (6).

### The development of hybridization

Although orchid hybridization is carried out mainly in Asia and the Pacific, it began in England in 1856, when gardeners there produced the first orchid hybrid, *Calanthe dominni*. Some 50 years later, around 1900–10, orchid hybridization was introduced to Singapore by Professor R. E. Holttum, then Director of the Singapore Botanic Gardens. He initiated and developed a successful orchid hybridization programme, and was able to greatly increase the number of orchid hybrids.

Up until the 1920s, orchid seeds were germinated on decayed organic matter mixed with a fungus. Scientists in Europe and the United States of America discovered then how to germinate orchids using an artificial medium, which allowed numerous seedlings to be produced from a single seed pod. In the 1950s, a French scientist called Morel discovered the tissue culture technique, enabling selected orchids to be mass-produced and cloned. This achievement is the greatest contribution to the cut flower industry. When commercial tissue culturing services became available in France, Malaysian growers sent some plants for cloning. Around this time, Hawaii was also producing high-quality hybrids of *Vanda*, *Oncidium* and *Dendrobium*, many of which were imported by Malaysia.

Malaysia produced its own hybrids of vandaceous orchids in 1960. *Aranda*, a cross between the genera *Arachnis* and *Vanda*, was created. The well-known *Aranda Wendy Scott* and *A. Christine* were propagated by a Mr L. F. Wong in Penang, and sold nationwide. In the 1970s, commercial orchid growing, as well as hybrid production, seed sowing and tissue culturing services, were established in Thailand. The 1980s saw a booming interest in commercial orchid growing in Malaysia, with areas in Selangor and Johor coming under orchid cultivation.

### A popular hobby

Up until the 1950s in Malaysia, the cultivation of orchids was a hobby for the rich élite, as only they could afford to buy quality seedlings. But by the 1970s, orchid seedlings were produced abundantly and cheaply with the use of modern methods of in-vitro culture. Growing orchids became a popular activity.

Orchid breeders generally prefer hybrids over native species because the attractive flowers stay on the plant for weeks or even months. Amongst orchid enthusiasts, trends and fads are set and followed according to their tastes, priorities and preferences. They are constantly on the look-out for good stud plants from which to produce new hybrids. Qualities that mark a good hybrid are roundness, fullness and flatness of the petals, brightly

### The orchid cut flower industry
In Malaysia, orchids are a major product of the cut flower industry and can be found in commercial gardens and nurseries across the country.

An orchid farm in Malaysia, where orchids are harvested to be sold as cut flowers (inset). They are exported to countries all over the world.

| ORCHID HYBRIDS CULTIVATED FOR CUT FLOWER PRODUCTION | | |
|---|---|---|
| **HYBRID** | **ORIGIN** | **COLOUR OF FLOWERS** |
| *Arachnis Maggie Oei* | Singapore | yellow with brown stripes |
| *Aranda Christine* | Malaysia | purple with dots |
| *A. Wan Chak Kuan* | Malaysia | deep blue flowers |
| *A. Wendy Scott* | Singapore | purple flowers |
| *Aranthera James Storie* | Singapore | dark red or maroon |
| *Dendrobium Ekapol* | Thailand | purple and white |
| *D. Sharifah Fatimah* | Singapore | yellow |
| *D. Sonia* | Thailand | purple |
| *Mokara Chak Kuan* | Malaysia | purple with dots |
| *M. Khaw Phaik Suan* | Malaysia | yellow |
| *M. Mak Chin On* | Singapore | dark purple |

# Malaysian orchid hybrids

Since the first orchid hybrid was created in Malaysia, a number of orchids have emerged and are being constantly upgraded in orchid-growing circles. These hybrids, including *Vanda*, *Aranda*, *Phalaenopsis*, *Cattleya*, *Renanthera*, *Oncidium* and *Dendrobium*, were created in Malaysia in the 1960s when there was a surge in orchid hybridizing. They have been used by orchid growers everywhere, gaining for Malaysia an international reputation as a centre for orchid hybridization.

## Oncidium

Oncidium, or dancing lady, hybrid flowers.

Flowers of *Oncidium* hybrids have a characteristic large lip, evoking the swirling skirt of a 'dancing lady', hence their common name. Borne on inflorescences, the flowers either occur singly or in showers of dozens, ranging from pure yellow to rosy pink to chocolate.

## Aranda

An *Aranda* is a cross between a *Vanda* and an *Arachnis*. The first *Aranda* was created in 1938 by Professor Eric Holttum, who crossed *Arachnis hookeriana* with *Vanda lamellata* to produce *Aranda Deborah*. Since then, numerous *Aranda* hybrids have been derived, including *A. Wendy Scott* and *A. Christine*. They are popular hybrids, and have been used to create other hybrids of *Aranda*.

Aranda Christine (*Arachnis hookeriana* x *Vanda Hilo Blue*).

## Cattleya

Flowers of a *Cattleya* hybrid.

This hybrid has large, showy, colourful flowers. Purple is the usual colour, but hybrids have produced blooms of white, yellow, green and brown. As with *Vanda*, intergeneric hybrids have been created, such as *Laeliocattleya* (*Cattleya* x *Laelia*) and *Brassocattleya* (*Cattleya* x *Brassavola*).

## Vanda

*Vanda* is known for its voluptuous round flowers that come in a spectrum of colours, and which grow in large, impressive clusters. In Malaysia, *Vanda* hybrids are very common and include intergeneric hybrids such as *Aeridovanda* (*Vanda* x *Aerides*), *Vandaenopsis* (*Vanda* x *Phalaenopsis*) and *Vascostylis* (*Vanda* x *Arachnopsis*).

Vanda Miss Joaquim (*V. hookeriana* x *V. teres*), probably the most well-known *Vanda* hybrid.

## Phalaenopsis

Commonly known as the moon or moth orchid, *Phalaenopsis* flowers are round and carried on curved inflorescences. The colour of the flowers ranges from pure white to pink; some are striped while others are dotted. Although the orchid is well suited to a tropical climate, it is not an easy hybrid to grow as it is prone to crown rot and its leaves cannot withstand direct sunlight. It thrives best in a shady spot that receives bright, but not direct, sun.

Phalaenopsis, or the moth orchid, so-called because of the shape of its flowers.

## Dendrobium

Some of the first hybrids were created by crossing *Dendrobium* species. *Dendrobium* hybrids are known for making good cut flowers because of their durability. The flowers, borne on graceful, arching inflorescences can last for months. Millions of *Dendrobium* sprays are exported each year from Malaysia.

Sprays of *Dendrobium* flowers.

## Renanthera

*Renanthera* hybrids are known for their glowing red flowers which grow in large numbers on branched, spreading, horizontal inflorescences. The species *R. storei*, or the fire orchid, is popularly used for hybridizing. Some intergeneric *Renanthera* hybrids include *Renaglottis* (*Renanthera* x *Trichoglottis*), *Renantanda* (*Renanthera* x *Vanda*) and *Holttumara* (*Renanthera* x *Aranda*).

A hybrid of *Renanthera*.

coloured and well-defined flowers and firm stems and leaves. The size of the hybrid flower should be equal or greater than that of the parent, and it is preferable that the blooms at the lower end of the inflorescence do not fade prematurely. Free-flowering plants are also considered superior to those that flower seasonally.

## A lucrative business

Orchid growing is a lucrative business. There are numerous orchid nurseries in Malaysia where seedlings are raised for sale. A nursery may also create its own line of hybrids, distributing the seedlings to other nurseries. Another facet of the orchid-growing business is the cut flower industry, where selected hybrids are grown on a large scale, especially for their flowers. The chosen orchids must flower heavily, be attractive and be easy to grow. Due to the nature of this trade, the flowers also need to have a long shelf life and be able to withstand packing and handling. Apart from being sold locally, cut orchids are exported from Malaysia to Europe, East Asia and Australia, where they are marketed as exotic blooms.

Manufacturers sometimes turn orchids into ornaments and jewellery by encasing the flowers in plastic or gold plate. These are sold as tourist souvenirs and gifts. Fresh flowers are used in different types of floral arrangements, such as bouquets, corsages and wreaths.

Cattleya is a stunning ornamental because of its conspicuous and brightly coloured flowers.

# Rice

*Rice or Oryza sativa is indigenous to the region between the Himalayan foothills across to the northern parts of Thailand, Myanmar (Burma) and Laos. It has long been a staple in the Malaysian diet. The varieties of rice are numerous, as are the planting methods and uses. With modernization, means of production have changed, brought about by the breeding of new strains, more sophisticated irrigation facilities and machinery. Rice is cooked in a variety of different ways by the peoples of Malaysia, and plays an integral role in cultural and religious ceremonies.*

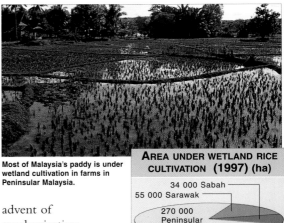

Most of Malaysia's paddy is under wetland cultivation in farms in Peninsular Malaysia.

**AREA UNDER WETLAND RICE CULTIVATION (1997) (ha)**

34 000 Sabah
55 000 Sarawak
270 000 Peninsular Malaysia

Dryland, or hill paddy, is planted mostly in Sabah and Sarawak. Less than 1 per cent of Malaysia's total area under hill paddy is in Peninsular Malaysia.

## Rice in Malaysia

Rice has a long history in Malaysia. Spreading widely from its centre of origin in the Himalayan foothills across to northern Myanmar and northern Laos, it is thought to have established itself in Southeast Asia around 4000–5000 BCE. Since then, it has been treated as more than a food crop, and has become an integral part of Malaysian culture and beliefs. A *semangat*, or spirit, is said to inhabit rice, which must be appeased at all times. Many rites and ceremonies are devoted to this aim, and to warding off evil spirits from crops.

Intially a dryland crop, rice then evolved into a wetland one. Wetland planting began in Malaysia around the 1st century CE. This practice did not change for centuries. It was only in the 1960s that rice production made a quantum leap with the advent of mechanization, modern irrigation and the breeding of new high-yield varieties (HYV). These improvements allowed rice to be cultivated from seed, a technique which Malaysian farmers started to employ in the early 1980s. Highly mechanized methods of planting helped to both increase the country's rice production and offset the labour shortage.

## Morphology and varieties

Indigenous varieties of rice are characterized by their tall stems, long and droopy leaves and long maturation period. Modern varieties tend to have shorter stems, smaller, more compact panicles and a shorter maturation period. In general, the husk varies from very light yellow to reddish brown and even to black. The mature spikelet, together with the husk, is called paddy.

The growth of the rice plant can be divided into two phases—vegetative and reproductive. For most of its life, the rice plant is in its vegetative state, and the reproductive phase occurs only during the last 60 days or so when the plant is mature. Maturation takes 100–200 days, depending on the strain of rice. Indigenous varieties, for example, flower during the time of the year when the day shortens. The Malaysian Agricultural Research and Development Institute (MARDI) and the International Rice Research Institute (IRRI) have produced varieties that do not depend on daylight length to initiate flowering and can flower all year round. These varieties also give a high yield and display uniform traits. The most popular variety is MR84, which is planted in about 75 per cent of the rice areas in Peninsular Malaysia. Other varieties planted over significant areas include MR77, MR106, MR167 and IR42.

## Dryland and wetland cultivation

While most of the rice grown in Malaysia is wetland paddy, a small proportion is cultivated in dry fields. Also called hill rice, dryland rice is cultivated on dry, flat uplands and hill sides. About 80 per cent of Malaysia's dryland rice is grown in Sarawak and 20 per cent in Sabah. In Peninsular Malaysia, it is planted only in Hulu Terengganu, and

## Modern methods of planting, harvesting and processing rice

To prepare the paddy field, tractors are used to level the land and dig up weeds. Once the field is drained, it is ready for sowing. The rice seeds are first germinated by soaking in water for 1–2 days, followed by airing for another 1–2 days. Seeds are then sown with the help of a motorized blower **(1)**, which disperses the seeds evenly at about 60–80 kilograms per hectare. The aim is to establish 100–150 seedlings per square metre. When the crop matures, it is harvested with a combine rice harvester **(2)**, loaded onto a lorry and transported directly to the mill **(3)**. In the rice mill, the husk and the outer layer **(inset, left)** of the rice grains are removed, leaving behind the polished rice **(inset, right)**. The processed rice is then packed and sent to the suppliers, who in turn sell the rice to supermarkets and grocery shops **(4)**.

by the Orang Asli in Pahang, Perak and Kelantan. Planting takes place prior to the wet season. The vegetation is first cleared by slashing and burning, and then the rice seeds are sowed manually. Only after the heavy downpours will the seeds germinate, therefore making it vital that the sowing is done just before the onset of the rains.

Wetland rice is planted in flooded fields, such as on coastal flood plains, near river banks and in inland valleys. These fields may either be naturally inundated with rainwater, in which case the rice crop is called rain-fed rice, or they may be irrigated, in which case the crop is known as irrigated rice. In more than 80 per cent of Malaysia's wetland rice areas, direct seeding is practised. It requires a steady and plentiful water supply, as in irrigated fields. Before direct seeding was introduced, the most common method used was transplanting. This involved raising seedlings in a nursery before transplanting them in the fields. A corner of the field served as the nursery, where seedlings were kept for about 21 days. Methods of planting which are suited to periodic rainfall are used in a few rain-fed areas in Sabah and Sarawak.

## Methods of rice production

Mechanization has taken over rice production in Malaysia's rice basin, the Kedah area, but traditional methods of planting, harvesting and processing are still practised in parts of Peninsular Malaysia and in Sabah and Sarawak.

The modern method of planting is known as direct seeding. After the ground has been prepared, seeds are evenly sown either manually or by a motorized blower. Of the traditional method of transplanting, a unique example is found in Krian Laut, in north Perak, where seedlings are grown in a floating nursery made of organic material. The seedlings are then transferred to a second nursery where they remain in standing water for a few more weeks before being moved to the fields. When the

paddy matures, it is harvested, threshed, dried and taken to the mill. There, the husk of the rice grains is removed, leaving behind brown rice. To get polished, or white, rice, the outer layer (consisting of the pericarp, seed coat, nucleus and aleurone layer) is removed together with the husk.

## Food and other uses

There are some uniquely Malaysian ways of preparing rice. *Ringgi* is made from very young, waxy grains that are pounded and then roasted till they are soft and sweet. It is the first product of the harvest. Slightly underripe rice is made into *emping*, or rice flakes, which are eaten with coconut milk or roasted and turned into snacks. In Peninsular Malaysia, a dessert called *bubur pulut hitam* is made from a special black glutinous rice, and *ketupat*—rice steamed in woven coconut leaves—is made from polished rice and eaten with meat and vegetable dishes. Rice flour is used to make noodles and cookies, while fermented rice, or *tapai*, is turned into alcohol and vinegar. A non-edible product that is made from rice is a powder called *bedak sejuk*, which women mix with water and rub on their faces to keep cool.

Rice by-products have a number of uses. The husk is used in building materials and as fuel and mulch. Burnt husk is used to make a type of cement, and is also a cleaning and abrasive agent. Oil extracted from the bran is used as high-quality cooking oil, while the bran itself is mixed into animal food. Rice straw is used in making paper.

### Types of rice used in Malaysia
*LEFT TO RIGHT:* **Pulut hitam**, which is black glutinous rice; **beras nasi dagang**, or red unpolished rice, eaten mainly in Kelantan; and **beras pulut**, or glutinous rice.

### Rice food products
1. Packets woven from coconut leaves are filled with rice, which is steamed until it becomes a cake, called *ketupat*. It is eaten with *satay*, or skewered barbecued meat on festive occasions.
2. *Nasi kunyit*, a Malay glutinous rice dish. Turmeric is added to the rice to give it a yellow colour.
3. *Tepung*, or rice flour, is used for making Malay cakes, such as *dodol* and *karas*.

## Traditional methods of planting, harvesting and processing rice

The field is ploughed either by a manually operated tractor or water buffalo-drawn plough (1). Seedlings, which have been cultivated in nurseries, are planted in the field in bunches of 2–3, spaced about 25 centimetres apart, and the roots pushed into 5 centimetres of soil either by hand (2) or with the aid of a forked stick (*kuku kambing*). It is preferable that the seedlings are planted when young, as older ones generally tend to yield a lower crop. When the paddy is mature (3), it

is harvested manually with the aid of a sickle (4). The plants are grasped in bunches and cut near the base so as to reap the stems, leaves and panicles. All the harvested paddy is then brought to a corner of the field to be threshed. Using a threshing tub, or *tong* (5), the grains are separated from the straw. The threshed rice is brought back from the field to the longhouse, where it is laid out on mats to dry (6). After drying, the rice grains are put through a winnower (7) to remove the husks and outer layer. The end-product is polished rice.

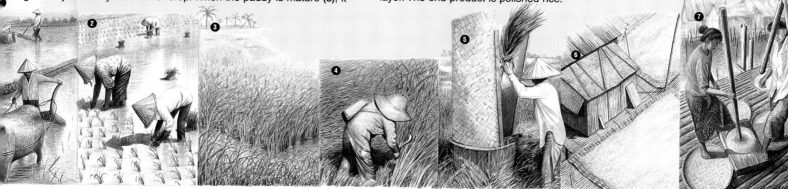

# Plants and culture

*Tradition, religion and taboo are behind the cultural uses of plants. In Malaysia, the relationship between plants and culture is steeped in history, existing in different forms among the country's various ethnic groups. Flowers, spices and fruits make generous offerings and beautiful, scented decorations during important religious and cultural ceremonies. Each culture places its own significance on the plants it uses, which come from shape, smell and colour. Traditional festivals are still very much a part of Malaysian life, despite the many changes that have taken place in the country over the years.*

## Food receptacles made from plants

LEFT: *Lemang* is a traditional Malay rice dish cooked in bamboo stems, and eaten on festive occasions.

TOP RIGHT: Banana leaves act as a plate on which rice, curry and dhal (lentil curry), a favourite Indian meal, is served.

RIGHT: *Bak chang* or glutinous rice dumplings are wrapped in palm leaves and steamed. They are eaten by the Chinese every year during the Duan Wu festival. Legend has it that when the good official Duan Wu drowned himself in a river rather than face unjust persecution, his loyal supporters threw bak chang into the water so that the fish would eat the dumplings and leave his body alone.

## Flower motifs on Peranakan ceramic tiles

A stylized flower dominates this tile in a house in Jalan Tun Tan Cheng Lok, formerly Heeren Straat, in Melaka, where wealthy Peranakan families lived.

Occupying nearly the whole tile is a lily-like flower. The tips of the leaves are on the adjoining tiles, a pattern which requires precision craftsmanship.

A cluster of rosettes and leaves form the pattern on this tile.

## Plants used as ceremonial offerings

1. Traditionally, boiled eggs attached to artificial flowers are placed on the wedding dais of a Malay bridal couple and distributed to guests as a symbol of fertility.

2. Heaps of fruits, such as watermelons, apples and mandarin oranges are arranged in front of a Chinese altar.

3. Thick and fragrant garlands of yellow chrysanthemums and strings of jasmine are placed around the necks of an Indian bridal couple.

## Malaysian culture

Malaysia is a country of many peoples, with the major ethnic groups being the Malays, Chinese and Indians. Plants are used as offerings and food and employed as symbols and motifs by these three communities, as well as by the Orang Asli and the indigenous peoples of Sabah and Sarawak. Some customs are unique to Malaysia, whilst others are also practised elsewhere in Asia where populations of the same groups reside.

Plants are associated with religion, magic and healing. They are also a part of birth celebrations, marriage festivals, funerals and harvest rites. Parts of plants, such as flowers, leaves and fruits, are offered to gods and deities, used to decorate places of worship and homes and to adorn people. The plant–culture relationship is at its most evident during festive seasons, when many types of brightly coloured fruits, flowers and vegetables are on sale and display. During a Malay festival, for example, shops and stalls are stocked with young coconut leaves, *palas* leaves, bamboo stems and palm sugar.

## The Malays

Plants are woven into many aspects of the Malay culture, and are seen in works of literature and art, in patterns used in crafts and religious ceremonies.

The *bunga raya*, Malaysia's National Flower, forms the principal motif for this Muzium Negara sign.

In poems and songs, for instance, the names of plants are sometimes cited. They are part of the language, as when they rhyme with other words, and are also used symbolically.

Cultural beliefs surround certain plants and affect how people use them. Evil spirits are believed to be warded off by *setawar* (*Bryophyllum pinnatum*), *aruda* (*Ruta graveolens*) and plants with thorns. Other plants, such as *cempaka putih* (*Michelia alba*) and *cempaka merah* (*M. champaca*), are said to attract unwanted spirits by the aromas they emit in the night, and are therefore not to be grown near homes. Tall and strong forest trees, like the towering *tualang* (*Koompassia excelsa*), are also thought to be the haunts of spirits and best approached carefully or left alone. Honey collectors who have to climb these trees first offer prayers and perform rituals to appease the spirits.

Food is an essential part of any Malay festival. During Hari Raya Puasa, the festival that celebrates the end of the fasting month, glutinous rice is the

main ingredient for the essential dishes. For a dish called *lemang*, glutinous rice is first washed and poured into bamboo stems, then mixed with coconut milk and cooked over an open fire. The hollow interior of the stems which acts as a vessel, is first lined with banana leaves. *Ketupat* is made from either ordinary rice or glutinous rice. If the latter is used, it is wrapped in *palas* leaves (*Licuala palas*) in pyramidal shapes and boiled until it is cooked. Glutinous rice flour is also used to make a fragrant, dark brown sweet—*dodol*. After adding coconut milk and sugar to the flour, the mixture is cooked slowly in a *kuali* or wok for many hours until the mixture thickens.

## The Chinese

The altars in Chinese homes and temples are laden with fruit offerings. Both the colour and the Chinese names of the fruit are important when choosing which offering to make. Yellow, for example, is an auspicious colour, and bright yellow oranges (*Citrus reticulata* and *C. sinensis*) and bananas (*Musa sapientum*) are common offerings. Red is also favoured, but black and white are taboo. Thus, during festive seasons, red and not black melon seeds are served. Black seaweed, however, is not taboo because its name—*fatt choy*—means 'good fortune'. Lettuce, or *sang choy*, means 'to grow and multiply', and the name for pineapple sounds like the words for luck and prosperity. The pomegranate, with its numerous seeds, is a symbol of fertility and is placed on the altars of married couples.

Flowers are given as both gifts and offerings. Yellow and red flowers are appropriate for happy occasions, while purple or white flowers are not. An exception is the white tuberose (*Polyanthes tuberosa*) or *yok chum*, although even this is sometimes dyed in subtle shades of colour.

In Chinese paintings, certain plants are depicted because of the qualities they represent. A smooth pine, for example, represents a youth with endurance, power and strength, whereas a rugged pine symbolizes a vigorous man with wisdom and benevolence. An old pine represents longevity and strength of character. Bamboos reflect resilience and endurance. The shoots are a symbol of filial piety, and the straight stems a sign of sincerity and constancy. Plum blossoms embody femininity, beauty and courage, while dignity and steadfastness are associated with chrysanthemums.

## The Indians

Jasmine flowers, bananas, coconuts and limes feature prominently during Indian festivals and ceremonies. During Deepavali, for example, these fruits and flowers and turmeric powder are used generously. During a Hindu wedding, a pair of small, fruiting banana plants are placed at the entrance of the temple and marital home as a symbol of fertility. Floral bouquets are used in the wedding ceremonies of many communities for a similar reason.

# Plant motifs in Malaysian crafts

Flowers, shoots, tendrils, fruits and seeds are plant motifs peppered across Malaysian crafts. Some motifs, such as the bamboo shoot and clove flower, date back hundreds of years and are associated with magic and healing; whilst more Western motifs, like the rose and sunflower, are more recently introduced.

A leaf and floral pattern is set in gold in this 18th-century tobacco box, whose shape also represents a lotus flower.

The bamboo shoot motif, seen here woven in gold, is ubiquitous in embroidery, weaving and batik.

An exquisite wood carving displays an intricate design of leaves, flowers and seed pods.

## Traditional Iban leaf designs
The leaf motif is a basic component of Iban design. From a palette of motifs, the designer can create different arrangements and combinations to produce an overall pattern to be used in carvings and paintings.

### Putting together a leaf design
1. Before implementing the pattern, the trunk or base design must be drawn to act as a guideline. A floral and leaf pattern is shown here.
2. The pattern is executed one layer at a time.
3. Two layers are sometimes placed back to back to form a reverse design.

Jackets made from tree bark are sometimes worn by the Kelabit people of Sarawak.

## Uses of plants by smaller ethnic groups
The indigenous people of Malaysia, such as the Orang Asli, Iban and Dusun, use various plant sources of latex and dye to make face and body paint. They obtain their materials mostly from jungle fruits. Red, black and white are the most common colours. Lines, dots, curves, geometrical shapes and even sketches are drawn on the face, chest and back.

Traditional clothing is made from the bark of some trees, such as *terap* (*Artocarpus kunsleri*), *upas* (*Antiaris toxicaria*) and *karas* (*Aquilaria malaccensis*).

Food taboos are still observed among the Orang Asli. So is the practice of tree ownership. Sometimes a tree is also used as a final resting place. The corpse is placed on a platform built high up a tree in the belief that the spirit of the deceased will find it easier to reach heaven.

Bold tattoos cover the back of this elderly Iban man.

**Plants and animals in a forest ecosystem**

1. Rhinoceros hornbill (*Buceros rhinoceros*)
2. Silvered leaf monkey (*Presbytis cristata*)
3. Orchid (*Dendrobium* sp.)
4. Orang utan (*Pongo pygmaeus*)
5. Orchid (*Paphiopedilum* sp.)
6. Sambar deer (*Cervus unicolor*)
7. Wild ginger (*Zingiber spectabile*)
8. Fungus (*Ganoderma* sp.)
9. Fungus (*Hygrophorus* sp.)
10. Dragonfly (*Neurothemis terminata*)
11. Caterpillar (*Othreis* sp.)
12. Scarab beetle (*Chalcosoma* sp.)
13. Rajah Brooke's birdwing (*Trogonoptera brookiana*)
14. Malayan tapir (*Tapirus indicus*)
15. Fern (*Dipteris conjugata*)
16. Banded palm civet (*Hemigalus derbyanus*)
17. Aroid (*Amorphophallus* sp.)
18. Atlas moth (*Attacus atlas*)
19. Pitcher plant (*Nepenthes burbidgeae*)
20. Seladang (*Bos gaurus*)
21. *Rafflesia pricei*
22. Asian elephant (*Elephas maximus*)
23. Banana (*Musa borneensis*)
24. Long-tongued nectar bat (*Macroglossus minimus*)

# INTERACTIONS

The giant honeybee
(*Apis dorsata*) collects
nectar and pollen from a
cosmos flower (Compositae).

Intricate but harmonious interactions between plants, animals and their environment exist in the complex and species-rich tropical forest ecosystem of Malaysia. In food chains and energy flows, for example, autotrophic or photosynthesizing plants are the primary producers, while animals and other heterotrophic or non-photosynthesizing plants are the consumers. Green plants possessing chlorophyll perform photosynthesis. During this process, inorganic carbon dioxide from the atmosphere and water absorbed by the roots are converted, with the help of sunlight, into organic compounds in the form of carbohydrates, proteins and vitamins. These photosynthetic products are then transferred to and stored in various plant tissues, such as roots, stems and branches, leaves, flowers, fruits and seeds. Through various means, animals and other heterotrophic organisms utilize photosynthetic products as food. When plants and animals die, organisms like bacteria and fungi begin to decompose the dead organic matter, returning its inorganic nutrients to the ecosystem.

Plant communities in the forest also provide homes for animals in which to breed and raise their offspring. In return, certain animals, including insects, birds, bats, squirrels, primates, civets, elephants and tapirs, act as pollinators of flowers or dispersers of fruits and seeds. For successful seed germination and seedling establishment of many plant species, the assistance of a fungus or bacteria is sometimes needed. To avoid being damaged by the animals, the plants protect themselves by developing hard tissue or by producing chemicals that are poisonous or unpalatable. In ant-plants, the harmonious interaction is mutually beneficial. Plants, such as *Macaranga triloba*, provide the ants with food and a place to live and breed, while the ants protect the plant from being attacked by herbivores. Ants that live in *Myrmecodia tuberosa* also collect and accumulate organic and inorganic debris which is tapped by the plants' roots.

Interactions between plants and the environment are seen in photosynthesis, respiration and evapotranspiration. Through these processes, plants and forests play important roles in maintaining the environmental quality and the ecological balance of their surrounding areas. Particularly important is the function of forests and other vegetation types in the hydrological and nutrient cycles and in maintaining heat balance and regulating the oxygen and carbon dioxide content of the atmosphere. The presence of dense vegetation in water catchment areas also helps in reducing soil erosion and siltation of rivers and streams, thereby ensuring a supply of clean water. In cities and other urban areas, plants are grown in gardens, along roadsides, and in parks and other open spaces to mitigate and alleviate the impact of air, heat, noise and water pollution, as well as to create a more pleasant living environment.

Plants grown in built-up areas,
such as these bougainvilleas
outside Parliament House in Kuala
Lumpur, improve both the urban
setting and the environment.

# Plants and cities

*Rapid urban and industrial development in Malaysia has brought various environmental problems in its wake. But as forests and agricultural plantations are cleared to make way for concrete jungles, a new complement of plants adapted to city conditions—some wild, others introduced by man—are springing up. Wayside trees and shrubs are being planted, and parks and gardens developed to create a more aesthetic urban landscape.*

This aerial view of Kuala Lumpur shows how pockets of greenery can brighten up an urban setting.

An *angsana* tree in full bloom. Its flowers last for only a day before they fall. A carpet of yellow petals will be seen littering the ground below the trees.

## Wayside trees

To break up the monotonous urban landscape of houses and factories, city planners have always advocated the introduction of greenery in built-up areas. Trees are not only important as shade for pedestrians and other road users, but they also add a pleasing visual aspect to thoroughfares.

During the 18th century, in the British colonies of Melaka and Penang, the native *angsana* tree (*Pterocarpus indicus*) was planted extensively. This magnificent tree, with its large, rounded crown and slender, hanging branches, provided shade along major promenades. Although a fungal epidemic subsequently killed most of the trees, enough survived for this species to become a popular roadside tree today.

The cassias (*Cassia siamea* and *C. spectabilis*), yellow flame (*Peltophorum pterocarpum*) and flame of the forest (*Delonix regia*) are well adapted to the Malaysian city environment, and provide cheerful colour when they flower. The popular South American rain tree (*Samanea saman*) has been in Malaysia since the 19th century, and older settlements like Taiping and Kuala Lumpur have a number of these majestic trees, overgrown with a rich mix of epiphytic ferns and orchids. Palms are also impressive in appearance, and are planted along avenues, on traffic islands and in central reservations. The native sealing wax palm (*Cyrtostachys renda*) is a favourite of the Chinese for whom the bright, scarlet leaf sheaths are auspicious.

## Weed flora

A weed is defined as a plant out of place, especially one that grows among cultivated plants and competes with them for space and food. Weeds proliferate on buildings, along walkways, on the sides of concrete drains, as well as along roads and in private gardens and housing compounds. The facades of the older buildings in Kuala Lumpur, Taiping, Melaka and Johor Bahru are overgrown with strangling figs and ferns. Ornamental plants such as the periwinkle (*Catharanthus roseus*), and fruit trees such as the pomegranate (*Punica granatum*) and papaya (*Carica papaya*), may escape from private gardens and grow on ledges and roofs. On the walls of newer buildings, the alga *Trentepohlia odorata* is common. If allowed to go unchecked, it leads to the more serious growth of blue-green algae which turns the walls an unsightly black. Herbaceous plants, such as *Euphorbia hirta*, *E. thymifolia* and *Pilea microphylla*, infiltrate pavements as they sprout up between concrete slabs or on the sides of drains.

Many weeds that predominate in private gardens originate from other Asian countries, tropical Africa and India. Some were introduced to Malaysia as ornamental plants, while others were brought in as food or medicine. Yet others were inadvertently transported in packaging material or soil carried on imported produce, and have subsequently taken root.

In open waste ground, exotic woody weeds predominate, such as the African tulip (*Spathodea campanulata*) and acacias. On lawns, weedy grasses are found, including plush grass (*Chloris barbata*), goose grass (*Eleusine indica*) and love grass (*Chrysopogon aciculatus*). Small creepers, such as the lesser clover-leafed desmodium (*Desmodium*

### A garden nation by the year 2000

A nationwide campaign to promote greenery in urban areas was launched in 1997 by Malaysia's Prime Minister, Dato' Seri Dr Mahathir Mohamad. The programme aims to turn Malaysia into a 'Garden Nation' by planting 3 million trees in built-up areas across all 13 states and the Federal Territory by the year 2000. A further 17 million trees are planned for 2020, bringing the total number to 20 million.

The Prime Minister of Malaysia, Dato' Seri Dr Mahathir Mohamad, leading a tree-planting ceremony to mark the start of Malaysia's greening campaign.

As part of this campaign, local authorities have been encouraged to make landscaping an essential part of all development projects, and to allocate roadside areas for trees. Businesses and residents owning vacant plots of land are urged to use it to grow plants. The government is also taking steps to stop indiscriminate felling by reinforcing a 1976 Town and Country Planning Act that says trees are to be relocated, not cut down, when the land they are on is needed for other purposes.

The Forest Research Institute Malaysia (FRIM) has identified 10 species of trees for urban landscaping. The selected trees are sturdy, fast-growing local species with deep, penetrative roots and the ability to withstand stormy weather, such as *sentang* (*Melia excelsa*), *kelumpang* (*Sterculia foetida*) and *janda merana* (*Salix babylonica*). The Malaysian Government is setting up six nurseries, with the cooperation of FRIM and the Forestry Department, for the cultivation of these trees. Peninsular Malaysia will have four nurseries and Sabah and Sarawak one each. After the campaign objective has been achieved, the nurseries will be converted into public parks.

116

## Epiphytes on rain trees

The rain tree, or *Samanea saman*, was brought to Southeast Asia from South America in the 1870s. It was widely planted as a shade-providing tree in towns and villages throughout Malaysia.

Old rain trees are always heavily laden with epiphytes, the more prominent being the stag's horn ferns (*Platycerium coronarium*), whose large nests are filled with the decaying leaves collected from the host tree. This mass of organic matter soaks up rainwater and acts as a reservoir of moisture for the fern during periods when there is no rain. It is also a source of nutrients for the fern as well as for a host of other plants, like the rabbit's foot fern (*Davallia denticulata*), shoestring fern (*Vittaria ensiformis*) and pigeon orchid (*Dendrobium crumenatum*).

The strangling figs (*Ficus benjamina*, *F. microcarpa* and *F. religiosa*) are common on these trees, their thin aerial roots spiralling down the trunk and branches. As the roots touch the ground they increase in girth, and with time form a mesh of coalescing roots round the trunk. Eventually covering the entire surface of the trunk, they slowly strangle the host tree to death.

A group of rain trees grandly line a road in the beautiful Lake Gardens in Taiping, Perak.

**A typical community of epiphytes on a rain tree**
1. Stag's horn fern (*Platycerium coronarium*)
2. Strangling fig (*Ficus* sp.)
3. Bird's nest fern (*Asplenium nidus*)
4. Shoestring fern (*Vittaria ensiformis*)
5. Pigeon orchid (*Dendrobium crumenatum*)
6. Dragon's scales fern (*Pyrrosia piloselloides*)

*triflorum*), yellow sorrel (*Oxalis corniculata*) and Malayan eyebright (*Torenia polygonoides*), blend inconspicuously with the grasses. In waterlogged grounds, sedges are the main invaders.

## A greener city

In urban areas in Malaysia, trees and other green plants play a vital role in moderating the environmental damage caused by development and pollution.

By intercepting rainfall, plants are able to minimize surface runoff, soil erosion and the siltation of drainage systems which cause frequent flooding. The effects of acid rain are also easily detected on plants, often before they have

manifested themselves elsewhere. Soil and plant tissues capture moisture and gradually release it back into the environment. This process, called evapotranspiration, helps to both lower the ambient temperature and raise the relative humidity of the atmosphere.

Photosynthesis purifies the air by absorbing carbon dioxide gas and releasing oxygen. Air pollution is also reduced because plants intercept airborne pollutants. Moreover, sound pollution is ameliorated when sound waves are deflected or absorbed. If there are enough plants growing together, they provide habitats for small wildlife, thus allowing mini-ecosystems to develop in the midst of an urban setting.

The sealing wax plant is often seen in the gardens of Chinese homes.

## Weeds that grow on buildings

A variety of plants—periwinkle, pomegranate and papaya—growing on the facade of a shophouse. This is a frequent sight on the older buildings in towns and cities in Malaysia.

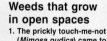

**Weeds that grow in open spaces**
1. The prickly touch-me-not (*Mimosa pudica*) came to Malaysia as an introduced ornamental, but is now a weed that grows in grassy areas, such as lawns and fields.
2. The lesser clover-leaved desmodium (*Desmodium triflorum*) is a weed among the native grass *Zoysia matrella*.
3. The native *sendudok* (*Melastoma malabathricum*) is a weed of open spaces, spread by birds eating the succulent berries and passing out the numerous small seeds.

117

# Plants and water

*Although the earth has an abundance of water, most of it does not occur in a form that is readily usable by plants. Sea water, for example, is useless for the majority of plants. A phenomenon known as the hydrological cycle converts water into more accessible states, and determines the kind of vegetation in a given area and its relative abundance. It also plays a major role in habitat formation. In Malaysia, different hydrological conditions have given rise to habitats as varied as mangroves, peatswamps, montane forests and limestone hills.*

Plants are made up mostly of water. The functions water performs are vital to the plant's survival, and include exerting the pressure that keeps the plant from collapsing.

## A life-giving force

The largest component of almost all living matter is water. Most organisms, especially plants, comprise 85–95 per cent water. Exceptions are some plant organs, such as seeds and spores, which contain as little as 5 per cent water. While it is possible for plants to survive longer without food, death is imminent once water becomes scarce.

Basic biological mechanisms in plants control and balance the input and output of water. For example, living cells take up water via the physical processes of capillary action and osmosis (the movement of water from a less concentrated solution to a more concentrated solution). In plants, roots draw water up via osmosis, and stems 'pull' water up via capillary action, which allows water to travel against the force of gravity. By these means, water moves up the xylem tissue to different parts of the plant. Specialized tissue structures ensure that each part of the plant receives the amount of water it requires. Water also helps plants maintain turgidity, and is a medium for the biochemical reactions that take place in cells. Salt and minerals are absorbed and transported while dissolved in water, as are other nutrients, such as amino acids and sugars.

**The uptake, transport and release of water in plants**

**TRANSPIRATION** is the process whereby water vapour is lost from the surface of plant organs, especially the leaves.

**CAPILLARY ACTION** is the pressure exerted between the side of a narrow tube and the water in it, resulting in a force that moves the water along the tube.

**OSMOSIS** in plants is the process by which roots absorb water from the soil.

The process of transpiration is a precise regulator of water content and keeps the plant surface cool. The rate of vapour loss through leaves is controlled by specially adapted cells, known as guard cells, which open up the pores (stomata) in the leaves during the day, and shut them at night. This process also has an impact on the level of water vapour in the atmosphere, thus affecting the formation and distribution of rainfall. Water vapour is also lost from plants through evaporation, although it is indistinguishable from that lost by transpiration. Hence, the term 'evapotranspiration' is used to refer collectively to water vapour from these two processes.

## Rainfall and plant habitats

The greater part of Malaysia receives a high annual rainfall, ranging from 200 to 400 centimetres. In such localities, rainforest formations of various types are well developed. Because of the heavy rainfall, the soil is waterlogged and the forest floor is always moist. Soil runoff is high and, as a result, the soil is poor in nutrients. While the rainforest supports an extremely diverse flora, it becomes very vulnerable if the water content drops below a certain level.

In the northern parts of Peninsular Malaysia along the Thai–Malaysian border, however, a short but rather pronounced dry season is experienced every year. Here, the semi-evergreen rainforest develops. During the dry season, there is a moderate shortage of water in the soil, causing a number of tree species, such as *Bombax valetonii*, *Celtis rigescens* and *Tetrameles nudiflora*, to shed their leaves. Deciduous trees constitute up to 30 per cent of the taller trees, but do not all become leafless at the same time. Although the semi-evergreen rainforest is less luxuriant than the evergreen rainforest, it is just as species rich and is home to a high number of endemics.

## Soil moisture and plant habitats

The quality and quantity of moisture in the soil exerts a pronounced effect on the development and distribution of forest formations. In Malaysia, these can be divided into the drylands, which have a low water table, and the wetlands, with a high water

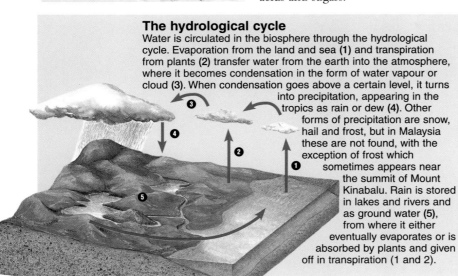

**The hydrological cycle**

Water is circulated in the biosphere through the hydrological cycle. Evaporation from the land and sea (1) and transpiration from plants (2) transfer water from the earth into the atmosphere, where it becomes condensation in the form of water vapour or cloud (3). When condensation goes above a certain level, it turns into precipitation, appearing in the tropics as rain or dew (4). Other forms of precipitation are snow, hail and frost, but in Malaysia these are not found, with the exception of frost which sometimes appears near the summit of Mount Kinabalu. Rain is stored in lakes and rivers and as ground water (5), from where it either eventually evaporates or is absorbed by plants and given off in transpiration (1 and 2).

## Wetland forest formations

In Malaysia, the wetland forest formations—mangroves, freshwater swamps and peatswamps—cover an area of approximately 2.72 million hectares, of which 0.57 million are in Peninsular Malaysia, 0.51 million in Sabah and 1.64 million in Sarawak.

1. Mangrove forest develops on marine alluvial soil composed of silt, sand and partly decomposed organic matter. This soil type is saline, anaerobic and acidic. It also contains a high concentration of sulphate ions and is waterlogged. These conditions do not make mangrove soil conducive to plant growth. Therefore, most plant species that live in mangrove forests display special adaptive features.

2. Freshwater forest develops on alluvium recently deposited by rivers and lakes. The physical and chemical properties of alluvial soil vary from place to place, depending on the topography and geological formations in the area.

3. Peatswamp forest occurs on peat soil that contains a high percentage of semi-decomposed organic matter. With a pH of less than 4, the soil is acidic and extremely deficient in mineral nutrients. Water that drains from peatswamps is also highly acidic and has a characteristic tea colour.

### WATER AND SOIL CONDITIONS IN WETLAND FOREST FORMATIONS IN MALAYSIA

| FOREST FORMATION | CLIMATE | SOIL WATER | LOCALITY | SOIL TYPE |
|---|---|---|---|---|
| Mangrove forest | ever wet | salt water | coastal | silt, sand and organic material |
| Brackish water forest | ever wet | brackish water | coastal | silt and clay |
| Peatswamp forest | ever wet | fresh water | inland | nutrient-deficient peat |
| Freshwater swamp | ever wet | fresh water | inland | nutrient-rich forest soil |
| Seasonal freshwater | ever wet | fresh water | inland | nutrient-rich forest soil |

table. Drylands include sandy beach and rocky shore vegetation, lowland and hill mixed dipterocarp forests, lower and upper montane forests, *kerangas* forests and forests over limestone and ultramafic soil. Included under wetlands are mangrove forests, peatswamps and freshwater swamps. Peatswamps, for instance, have a constantly high level of nutrients in the soil due to the presence of organic matter. States in Peninsular Malaysia where significant areas of peatswamps are found are Selangor and Pahang. In Johor, peatswamps have been converted to land for agriculture, in particular for the growing of pineapples. When wetlands are designated for conversion to land for other uses, the soil has to be drained and reinforced, sometimes resulting in the loss of plant species.

Certain habitats contain water with an exceptionally high or low level of a particular chemical. Water found on limestone, for example, has a high pH and calcium content, while mangrove forests are inundated with sea water. Plants that grow in these habitats have developed adaptive features to deal with these unique conditions. Plants growing in salt water, for instance, have a higher osmotic pressure in their roots than that of the surrounding water to help prevent water loss. However, despite their adaptive features, mangrove plants thrive best in areas where tidal waters meet the mouth of a river bringing fresh water.

The rainforest—Malaysia's most extensive dryland forest. Although water is present in generous amounts in the soil, it is often poor in nutrients due to the lack of organic matter.

### WATER AND SOIL CONDITIONS IN DRYLAND FOREST FORMATIONS IN MALAYSIA

| FOREST FORMATION | CLIMATE | SOIL WATER TABLE | LOCALITY | SOIL TYPE |
|---|---|---|---|---|
| Lowland and hill mixed dipterocarp forests | ever wet | low | inland | zonal soil |
| Lower and upper montane forests | ever wet | low | inland | zonal soil |
| Subalpine forest | ever wet | low | inland | zonal soil |
| *Kerangas* forest | ever wet | low | inland | podolized sand |
| Forest over limestone | ever wet | low | inland | limestone |
| Forest over ultramafic rock | ever wet | low | inland | ultramafic soil |
| Sandy beach and rocky shore vegetation | ever wet | low | coastal | sand and coral |
| Semi-evergreen forest | seasonally dry | moderate annual shortage | inland | zonal soil |

### Classification of plants according to the water conditions in which they grow

1. Mesophytes are plants that are found in places where water is abundant, such as in tropical rainforests.

2. Xerophytes are plants that are adapted to conditions where there is a lack of fresh water, such as plants that grow in mangrove forests.

3. Hydrophytes are plants that grow in water. Their roots are always submerged, although other plant parts may be above the water surface.

# Pollination strategies

*Plants have a sex life too. In the Malaysian rainforest, plant sex life is unrivalled in its variety, the partners involved and the strategies it adopts. It is generally acknowledged that sexual reproduction maintains variation, which is necessary to the long-term survival of species. This genetic variation increases the chances of at least some individuals being able to adapt to changing conditions, whether climatic or attack from pests and diseases. Thus, different types of pollination strategies ensure that sexual reproduction occurs between individuals, rather than between flowers on the same plant, as the latter does not maximize genetic variation.*

### Sexual reproduction in plants

Unlike animals, plants cannot move around and seek out a partner for sex. Instead, they have evolved a myriad of ways of transporting the sperm inside a pollen grain to the egg inside an ovule.

In flowering plants, the pollen grains are produced in the anthers of the stamens and the eggs in the ovules. Flowering plants are unique in that the ovules are produced within the ovary, and to gain entry into the ovary, the pollen must germinate and grow through the stigmatic surface. The stigmatic surface plays a crucial role in the chemical recognition of pollen. It facilitates germination and pollen tube growth of pollen from other individuals of the same species. On the other hand, it can prevent the germination of foreign pollen (pollen from different species), and slow down the germination of pollen and pollen tube growth of pollen of the same individuals. This strategy encourages sex between different individuals of the same species and results in greater genetic variation of the offspring.

### Pollination syndromes

Flowering plants have evolved to develop flowers that ensure successful pollination. To attract the right types of insects and other animal pollinators, the petals, for instance, must have the appropriate colour, shape, size and scent. Similarly, to induce regular visitation by the pollinators, the flowers must produce the right types of rewards in the form of high-energy nectar, protein-rich pollen or, in the case of insect pollinators, provide a place for the insect to lay its eggs. Indeed, the tremendous species diversity of flowering plants in the Malaysian rainforest is attributed to the coevolution between an enormous spectrum of insects and other animal pollinators and flowers specially adapted to them.

Because of this coevolution, flowers with the same pollinator tend to have a similar combination of characteristics, or pollination syndromes. Thus, in Malaysia, there are the so-called bat flowers (for example, durian, *pedada* and *petai* flowers), bee flowers (such as star fruit and *angsana* flowers), bird flowers (like *dedap* and *Firmiana malayana* flowers) and so on. Flowers pollinated by wind and water currents have evolved from the animal-pollinated ones. Notable Malaysian examples are flowers of grasses and *rhu laut* (*Casuarina equisetifolia*) for wind pollination, and flowers of sea grasses and *Hydrilla verticillata* for water current pollination.

### Cross-pollination

Flowers exhibit different strategies to ensure that the egg is fertilized by a sperm from a different individual of the same species. One of the totally effective strategies is the unisexual plant that produces single-sex flowers, that is, one plant produces flowers with stamens and another develops female flowers with ovaries only, such as in *rhu laut* trees. Pollination is then possible only between different individuals of the same species. In some species, the stigmas are much longer than the stamens and are positioned in such a way that self-pollination is prevented.

Another strategy to prevent self-pollination is shown by plants which possess bisexual flowers that

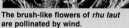

The brush-like flowers of *rhu laut* are pollinated by wind.

Birds are the pollinators of *dedap* flowers.

The pollen of *Hydrilla verticillata* is transported by water currents.

| POLLINATION SYNDROMES | | |
|---|---|---|
| **POLLINATOR** | **GENERAL CHARACTERISTICS EXHIBITED BY FLOWERS** | **EXAMPLE** |
| Bats | Foetid or sour odour; white or cream; open at night; borne on leafless branches or located outside the foliage on a long, strong, upright or dangling stalk; produce copious pollen or dilute nectar. | Durian, *kapok*, *kekabu*, *pedada*, *petai*, midnight horror (*Oroxylon indicum*) |
| Bees | Unscented; white, yellow, purple or red, frequently with nectar guides; open during the day; exposed or if hidden within foliage borne in dense clusters; corolla open or with a shallow, cup-shaped tube with a landing stage; nectar gland located at the base of the corolla tube; produce concentrated nectar and/or copious, sticky pollen. | *Angsana*, star fruit, sunflower |
| Beetles | Strong odour, usually fruity or foetid; off-white or purple; open at night or during the day; structure open with many floral parts; produce copious pollen; fleshy floral parts as rewards or used for laying eggs. | Aroids, *cempaka*, *sendudok* (*Melastoma malabathricum*) |
| Birds | Unscented; bright red to scarlet; open during the day; borne in clusters on strong stalks; relatively broad, deep corolla tube with a landing stage; nectar gland located at the base of the corolla tube; produce copious, dilute nectar. | Dedap (*Erythrina* spp.), *Firmiana malayana*, African tulip tree |
| Butterflies | Unscented; yellow, orange or red; exposed outside foliage and borne in dense clusters; nectar gland hidden at the base of the long, narrow corolla tube; produce concentrated nectar. | *Jejarum* (*Ixora* spp.), *Mussaenda frondosa* |
| Flies | Musty or foetid odour; dirty white, purple or red-brown; small to large flowers, often with a trap device; open during the day; fleshy parts for laying eggs. | *Rafflesia*, aroids, Dutch pipe climbers (*Aristolochia* spp.) |
| Moths | Open and emit a strong fragrance at dusk; white or pale yellow; exposed outside foliage; nectar gland hidden at the base of a deep, narrow corolla tube; produce concentrated nectar as a reward. | Tembusu (*Fagraea fragrans*), lady of the night (*Cestrum nocturnum*), *Wrightia religiosa* |
| Water currents | Colourless and scentless; sepals and petals reduced in size or absent; at maturity, stamens or the whole male flower easily detached; stigmas feathery, submerged or exposed at the surface of water; pollen often produced in clumps or in long chains. | Sea grasses and other submerged aquatic flowering plants, such as species of *Hydrilla* and *Najas*. |
| Wind | Scentless; exposed outside foliage; sepals and petals rudimentary to expose long-stalked anthers and large, feathery or hairy stigmas or flowers arranged in dangling catkin-like inflorescence; pollen produced in large quantity. | Grasses, *mempening* (*Quercua* spp.), *rhu laut* (*Casuarina equisetifolia*) |

A nectarivorous bat, *Macroglossus minimus*, approaching (1) the flowers of *Sonneratia alba*. After feeding and pollinating (2) the flowers, it sets off (3) and flies away into the night (4).

## Bat pollination

In Peninsular Malaysia, three species of bats depend on nectar and pollen as their main food source. One species lives in mangroves and pollinates *pedada* or *Sonneratia* flowers, the second lives mostly on wild bananas, while the third, the cave bat, is famous as the pollinator of economically important plants like durian, *petai* and *kapok*. These bats thrust their head deep into the flower to sip the nectar with their long, brush-like tongue. At the same time, their body and head are dusted with pollen from the many long-stalked stamens, and in this way pollen is carried to the next flower they visit.

A *Macroglossus minimus* bat showing its long tongue that helps in licking and sipping nectar from flowers.

Pollen grains of *Sonneratia* species recovered from bat's guano or faeces.

are equipped with a stigmatic barrier (with the stamen and stigma maturing at different times). In the star fruit (*Averrhoa carambola*), flowers of different trees have styles of one or two lengths, so pollen only reaches the stigma of a tree which produces flowers with a different style length. The farmer knows this, and so, to get a heavier fruit crop, he grafts a branch with long-styled flowers onto his star fruit tree that has short-styled flowers, and vice versa.

Specificity of pollinator is also an isolating mechanism to prevent self-pollination. It is, therefore, not surprising that several of the largest groups of flowering plants have one-to-one pollinators, meaning that one species of insect pollinates only flowers of one species of plant. In Malaysia, this pollination strategy is shown by many species of orchids and figs.

## Self-pollination

A few plant species have adopted self-pollination, which is more reliable in that it does not depend on a pollinating agent. Many members of the sunflower family (Compositae) have long stigmas, which if pollen has not already been deposited from another flower of the same plant, will roll back to pick up pollen released from the anthers below. Flowers of a few species of orchids never open, and the pollen just falls onto the stigma within the closed petals.

## Hybridization

Under natural conditions it is rare for pollen that is transferred from one species to result in the fertilization of another, because most species not only operate isolating mechanisms at the pollinator stage but also at the fertilization and embryo development stages. However, should this occur, then a hybrid is produced. In Malaysia, two plant groups where hybridization regularly occurs in the wild are the rhododendrons and pitcher plants. Some groups are effectively isolated by the

pollinator and have no internal isolating mechanisms, such as the orchids. This is the reason why it is possible to create hybrids by hand-pollination between species of different orchid genera. A notable example in Malaysia is *Holttumara*, which is a hybrid between species of three orchid genera: *Arachnis*, *Renanthera* and *Vanda*.

## Conservation

Because so few flowering plants in Malaysia are self-pollinated or are pollinated by wind or water currents, it is vital to consider the conservation of the pollinator at all the stages of its life cycle in order to ensure the long-term survival of the plant species. And yet, this is a field so neglected that only in the last 10 years was it conclusively shown that blowflies pollinate *Rafflesia* flowers and that tiny thrips are the pollinators of some dipterocarps. Indeed, the depth of our ignorance of pollinators and the sexual behaviour of flowers is only matched by the incredible variety of shape, size, colour and odour of the flowers themselves.

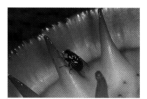

Flies are attracted to the foetid *Rafflesia* flowers.

A butterfly (*Paphilio* sp.) drawing nectar from *jejarum* flowers (*Ixora javanica*).

## Long- and short-styled flowers of the star fruit (*Averrhoa carambola*)

A star fruit plant bears flowers of all the same style length, but different plants have flowers with either long or short styles. This unique feature prevents self-pollination. The long styles droop over the anthers, while the short styles crouch under the anthers, making self-pollination impossible in both cases. A pollinator, such as the carpenter bee, is needed to transport pollen from the flowers of one plant to those of another, thus ensuring cross-pollination.

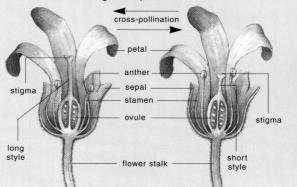

cross-pollination

petal
anther
sepal
stamen
ovule
stigma
long style
short style
flower stalk
stigma

A carpenter bee approaching the flowers of a star fruit tree.

# Fruit and seed dispersal

*The tropical rainforests of Malaysia are home to a large number of plant species, each possessing a distinct mode of reproduction and propagation. Alongside this high species diversity, varied means of fruit and seed dispersal have evolved. Animals, including humans, and non-living agents, such as wind and water currents, are involved in the dispersal of fruits and seeds.*

These fruits and seeds (inset), all adapted for dispersal by water currents, were found washed ashore on Langkawi Island (above).

Fruits of the *pong-pong* tree (*Cerbera odollam*) have a water-impermeable outer rind and a fibrous middle rind that contains air sacs.

### The role of dispersal

The removal of fruits and seeds from the immediate vicinity of the parent plants, through various dispersing agents, is a way for parents and seedlings to avoid competition for space, sunlight, water and nutrients. Most fruits and seeds end up in unsuitable places, but some will find their way to localities conducive to germination and growth. Dispersal also prevents overcrowding and inbreeding, thus helping to maintain genetic variability in the population.

### Dispersal by wind

In Malaysia, the fruits and seeds of a few species of plants that live in open habitats, such as sandy beaches, the edges of forests and mountain summits, are well suited for wind dispersal.

Wind-borne fruits or seeds are characteristically small and light, or have other surface modifications that facilitate buoyancy and decelerate falling. In *lalang* (*Imperata cylindrica*), for example, the fruits are equipped with a plume of fine hairs at one end, whereas in *kekabu* (*Bombax valetonii*) the seeds are surrounded by woolly hairs. *Kempas* (*Koompassia malaccensis*) fruits are flat and wing-like, while the fruit wall of *kembang semangkok* (*Scaphium linearicarpum*) is thin and boat-shaped. The fruits of *kapur* trees (*Dryobalanops aromatica*) have wing-like extensions derived from the sepals, and those of *rengas* (*Gluta wallichii*) fruits have similar extensions, but which are derived from the petals.

In a tropical forest, wind movement is negligible. Consequently, most plant species of the Malaysian rainforest have developed fruits and seeds that are better adapted to dispersal by water currents and animals.

### Dispersal by water currents

Plants that grow near or in water bodies, such as coastal areas, river banks and lakes, have fruits and seeds that are

## Malaysian animals that disperse fruits

Most tropical plants have fruits and seeds that are adapted for dispersal by animals. In Malaysia, five groups of animals—fruit-eating bats, birds, primates, rodents and ground herbivores—are important dispersing agents. Less important and understood are the roles of reptiles, fishes and invertebrates.

Birds that frequent forest edges and gaps, such as bulbuls and green pigeons, often eat the ripe fruits of *Hedychium longicornutum*, an epiphytic ginger plant. At maturity, the fruits split open to expose the seeds that are coated with a fleshy red aril, making them attractive to birds.

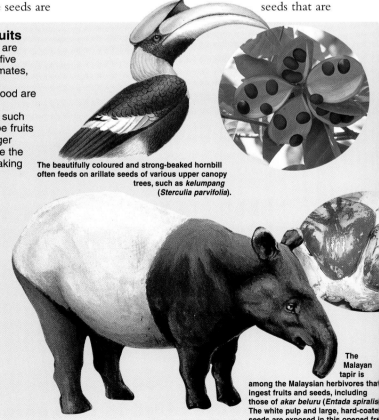

The beautifully coloured and strong-beaked hornbill often feeds on arillate seeds of various upper canopy trees, such as *kelumpang* (*Sterculia parvifolia*).

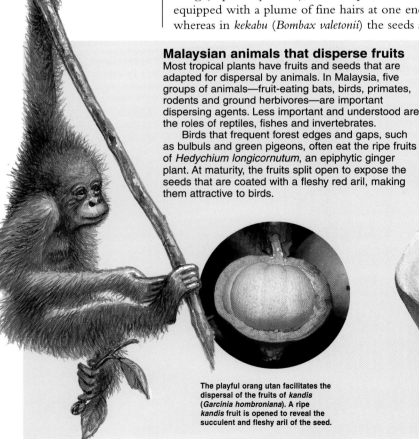

The playful orang utan facilitates the dispersal of the fruits of *kandis* (*Garcinia hombroniana*). A ripe *kandis* fruit is opened to reveal the succulent and fleshy aril of the seed.

The Malayan tapir is among the Malaysian herbivores that ingest fruits and seeds, including those of *akar beluru* (*Entada spiralis*). The white pulp and large, hard-coated seeds are exposed in this opened fr[...]

dispersed by water currents. In the coconut, nipa palm, *pong-pong* (*Cerbera odollam*) and *putat laut* (*Barringtonia asiatica*), for example, the outermost layer of the fruit wall is tough and water-impermeable. The middle layer is fibrous, spongy and contains air sacs, while the innermost wall is thick and hard. Ample food reserves are kept in the seeds in the form of either solid or liquid endosperm. When ripe, the fruits are easily detached from the parent trees and are carried by water currents, sometimes for long distances, to their new destination where the seeds germinate.

The fruits and seeds of aquatic flowering plants, such as *Hydrilla* and *Limnanthemum*, are entirely dependent on dispersal by water currents.

## Dispersal by bats and birds

There are at least 15 species of fruit-eating bats, including the grey fruit bat, short-nosed bat, dusky fruit bat and flying foxes. These bats are colour-blind and nocturnal, flying for long distances to feed. During the day, except for flying foxes, they roost in dark and damp places, such as the roofs of dark limestone caves. When feeding, the bats do not ingest the fruits, but simply chew and suck the juice and flesh, discarding the seeds. Bats do, however, ingest small-seeded fruits, such as figs and peppers, and later regurgitate or excrete the seeds while flying or roosting.

Fruits that are specially adapted for dispersal by bats normally remain attached to the parent trees for a long duration, and are held out by long stalks so they protrude from the foliage. They are drab and musty, and have fleshy edible parts and hard-coated

This bat is feeding on a ripe, bright orange fig of the *ara* (*Ficus* sp.) tree.

The giant squirrel finds the mature pink fruits of the *pinang* palm attractive and will unwittingly help to disperse the seeds.

seeds, such as the fruits of *ketapang* (*Terminalia catappa*) and *jambu batu* (*Psidium guajava*).

Some, but not all, fruits and seeds that are dispersed by birds have special adaptations. Those that do are either eaten or get attached to the bird's body. Among the fruit-eating birds in Malaysia are bulbuls, hornbills and pigeons. Fruits and seeds that these birds ingest, such as those of the *ara* (*Ficus* sp.) and *kelumpang* (*Sterculia* sp.) trees, have ways of protecting themselves against being eaten prematurely, but when ripe possess attractive edible parts, an appetizing colour and no odour. The fruits stay on the parent trees for a long time and tend not to have hard rinds, or if they do, the fruit wall splits open at maturity to expose the seeds.

Fruits and seeds that are dispersed by being carried on a bird's body are equipped with attachment apparatus, such as sticky surfaces, spines and hooks. For example, the fruits of *Pisonia umbellifera* are sticky, whereas those of *pepulut* (*Urena lobata*) have sticky hooks.

## Dispersal by primates and squirrels

In Malaysia, there are at least five species of primates that are fruit eaters: the long-tailed macaque or *kera*, white-handed gibbon, *siamang*, orang utan and proboscis monkey. The fruits they prefer are *rambutan pacat* (*Xerospermum naronhianum*), *kelat* (*Syzygium* spp.), *pelong* (*Pentaspadon velutinum*) and *sengkuang* (*Dracontomelum mangiferum*). To prevent premature feeding, unripe fruits have a dull colour, bitter or astringent taste and irritating sap. Nevertheless, the primates' vigorous biting and chewing may harm the seeds. However, hard-coated seeds survive and are discarded some distance away from the parent trees.

A number of aboreal rodents inhabiting the Malaysian forest are fruit eaters, such as the giant, plaintain, provost and slender squirrels. They eat the fruits of *ara*, *berangan* and *kedondong* trees. While foraging, the squirrels move swiftly from one tree to another, and on finding a tree they prefer, feed on the spot or pluck the fruits to take back to their nesting site. Along the way, some fruits and seeds may accidentally drop and land on the ground, by then a distance away from the parent trees.

## Dispersal by herbivores

Large herbivores, such as elephants, seladang and tapirs, ingest large fruits and later defecate the seeds at a distance from the parent trees. These fruits have a pulpy or fibrous outer rind and hard-coated seeds, and include those of many palms, wild mangoes and *akar beluru* (*Entada spiralis*). A number of trees, like the durian, *medang* (*Litsea* sp.) and *mendong* (*Elaeocarpus* sp.), produce fruits with a high protein and vegetable fat content that are consumed by civets, tigers and other large carnivores.

### Tiny wind-borne fruits

The plumed fruits of *lalang* grass (*Imperata cylindrica*).

Minute seeds of the orchid *Spathaglottis plicata*.

### Winged fruits that are dispersed by wind

Fruits of the *kapur* tree (*Dryobalanops aromatica*) on the ground and germinating.

The wings of the fruits of *Engelhardia spicata* are derived from the bracts of the flowers.

The winged fruits of *Dipterocarpus* still attached to the parent tree.

# Plant defences against herbivores

*There are many animals, ranging from tiny insects to elephants, eager to eat the nutritious parts of plants, particularly the relatively protein- and mineral-rich leaves. Malaysia's luxuriant plant growth is maintained through different plants having evolved specific physical and chemical defences against their potential herbivore attackers, and in turn, some animals have evolved their own counter defences.*

The leaves of the oak tree *Lithocarpus conocarpus* (inset) are covered with a combination of fine hairs and wax plates (main picture). The wax toughens the leaf surface, and makes chewing through the leaf surface laborious, thereby minimizing attacks from insects such as beetles.

## Types of defences

Plants defend themselves in ways most appropriate to the form of animal attack that they are likely to experience. Defences can either be physical or chemical, and will either deter an animal from approaching or even lead to death if certain plant parts are ingested. There are some plants that seem much less well defended than others. These are usually fast-growing species which rely on being able to rapidly replace the tissues lost to herbivores in preference to incurring the cost of energy expended in making defences.

These small but voracious caterpillars cause serious leaf damage to the plants they feed on.

The Asian elephant (*Elephas maximus*) enjoys a diet of grass, palm shoots, stems of banana plants and wild ginger. An adult elephant needs to consume 150 kilograms of forage every day to meet its nutritional requirements.

## Physical defence

Nearly all plant species employ at least one, if not more, methods of defence. In the Malaysian rainforest, spiny or prickly plants are rarely far away. Spines, both external and internal, can be large or small to deter large mammals or insects. Perhaps the most notorious are palms, particularly the rattans, with their multitude of long, sharp spines on the stems, and often also on the leaf stalk and midrib.

Palms are uniquely susceptible to herbivores, because they cannot recover if their shoot

The ferociously spiny stem of a rattan deters animals like rats, squirrels and porcupines from eating it.

apex is damaged. The young shoot at the top of the palm tree or rattan stem is good to eat, and is much relished by elephants, but the abundant spines help deter attack. However, large spines are not going to put off small insects, which in large numbers can be just as dangerous to the plants as big mammals. The hairs, or smaller spines, which cover the leaves of many plants discourage insects by blocking their access to the succulent tissues below. Some may even entangle the feet of caterpillars or beetles, trapping them before they do too much damage.

### Cellulose: The secret weapon

Part of the secret of success for higher plants is the use of cellulose as a form of physical defence. Present in most plants, it is of major importance in making it difficult for animals to get at the nutritious goodies inside the plant cells, which the cells need for their own survival.

Cellulose is a complex chemical made up of many linked sugar molecules. While nearly all animals possess the ability to digest the sugar molecules (glucose monomers), very few can break down the fibre-rich cellulose in the first place. Plants use cellulose to make walls around each cell in the plant body, and thus a high proportion of a plant is made up of indigestible cellulose. Most herbivores have to be very selective, searching for tender young leaves in which the cellulose fibre content is low and the more digestible protein relatively high. Some big mammals, like seladang and elephants, are less fussy because they have millions of microorganisms in their huge stomachs to help break down the cellulose. In fact, these immense beasts can probably be thought of as microbe farms, swallowing plant material to feed their microorganism colonies, and then feeding off the excess microbes.

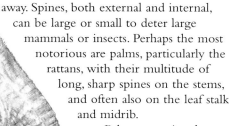

glucose monomer — cell walls — fibril — microfibril — cellulose chains

Cellulose in plant cell walls is made up of glucose monomers, the most basic units, which are linked to form a cellulose chain. The chains are grouped together, and about 80 of them make a microfibril. The microfibrils in turn intertwine to create a fibril, which is tough and fibrous.

Certain plants have spines inside them, usually in the form of sharp, pointed crystals, generally of calcium oxalate, as in *Rhaphidophora* spp. (Araceae). These crystals, or raphides as they are called, can pierce the soft tissues of animals touching or eating the plant. Many aroids have raphide-bearing cells, and some even have the ability to shoot out the needle-sharp crystals when the plant is damaged.

Plants can also have rounded crystals in their cells. A herbivore may have the unpleasant experience when it bites into a succulent leaf and its teeth hit the hard crystal. Grasses and sedges often accumulate silica in their cell walls, which is resistant to the biting and chewing of herbivores. Another way of keeping off biting animals may be to gum them up. Many plants produce sticky sap from cut parts. A big mouthful of caustic latex may deter all but the hardiest of attackers.

## Chemical defence: Poisons

Some of the most deadly poisons are found in plants. These include alkaloids, such as strychnine, nicotine and caffeine, which the plant produces, and other poisons, such as cyanide, which exist within the plant. These poisons or toxins are generally small chemical molecules which may enter an animal's blood, respiratory or nervous system and cause death. If these substances are dangerous, what then prevents the plants from poisoning themselves? The poisons are stored in a less toxic form and only become active when the plant is attacked. In the *ipoh* or *upas* tree (*Antiaris toxicaria*), commonly found in the forests of Malaysia, the poison antiarin consists of an extremely toxic molecule joined to a sugar. Only when an animal attempts to eat the leaves does the tree produce an enzyme that separates the molecules, releasing the poison into the animal's system.

The cells of this leaf that contain tannin have been stained black.

### Chemical defence: Tannins

Other plant chemicals are less toxic, but still highly deterring. An important group is tannins. These are large molecules that get their name from man's traditional use of them for tanning leather. Tannins possess the ability to attach themselves to protein molecules, often linking several molecules together,

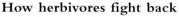

### Cyanide: An example of chemical defence

A large number of plants, including *Passiflora* spp. and the common cassava or tapioca plant (*Manihot esculenta*), release hydrogen cyanide (prussic acid) when damaged. This extremely noxious chemical is attached to a larger molecule, usually a type of sugar, making it safe to keep inside the plant cells. When a herbivore bites into the leaf, either the plant releases enzymes to free the cyanide from the sugar, or the digestive enzymes of the herbivore do the same thing, both resulting in the herbivore receiving a dose of potentially deadly cyanide.

Cassava is toxic because the complex chemical linamarin contained in the plant is split by linamarase, an enzyme, into glucose and poisonous cyanohydrin. The poison is a combination of prussic acid and acetone.

and give the plant a bitter or astringent taste.

They also interfere with the digestion and uptake of protein by herbivores by binding to the scarce protein in the plant material and the animal's digestive enzymes. Leaves and twigs of the *gambir* (*Uncaria gambir*) and the bark of the *bakau* tree (*Rhizophora* spp.) contain tannins.

The leaves and seeds of the castor oil plant (*Ricinus communis*) contain the toxic protein ricin.

## How herbivores fight back

Animals may evolve ways to overcome the defences that plants have built up. Many herbivores possess detoxification mechanisms that prevent them from being harmed by the poisons in the plants they eat. Sometimes the poisons may be reused to protect the herbivores from their own enemies. There is an ongoing evolutionary battle between plants and animals, as in turn they evolve new defences and new ways of overcoming them. One important implication this has for man is that there is a huge chemical diversity on offer, some of which may have value as medicines, spices or flavourings.

The seeds of *akar saga* (*Abrus precatorius*) are extremely poisonous.

## Plant poisons used by man

The ipoh tree is not as dangerous as it is reputed, but it makes a very effective poison used in arrows by many forest-inhabiting people in Southeast Asia.

The beautiful red and black seeds of *akar saga* (*Abrus precatorius*) contain abrin, a poison so potent that one seed contains enough to kill a man. Its hard, shiny coat keeps the poison locked away, making the seeds safe to handle, provided the seed coat is not ruptured. Saga seeds have traditionally been used as fine measures of weight in South and Southeast Asia.

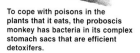

To cope with poisons in the plants that it eats, the proboscis monkey has bacteria in its complex stomach sacs that are efficient detoxifers.

ABOVE: The canopy walk at the Forest Research Institute Malaysia (FRIM) is an excellent way for visitors to enjoy the forest without disturbing the vegetation or animals. Such facilities are set up to promote ecotourism, thereby allowing Malaysia to preserve its natural habitats while reaping the economic benefits from the tourist industry.

LEFT: The slipper orchid, such as *Paphiopedilum barbatum*, is valued as an ornamental, which has led to a strain on its population in the wild.

BELOW: Pitcher plants, such as *Nepenthes rajah*, are best represented on Mount Kinabalu although they are found in other parts of Malaysia too. Only in Sarawak are pitcher plants accorded protected status. This means that collecting is prohibited except for the purpose of scientific research.

## Land use in Malaysia

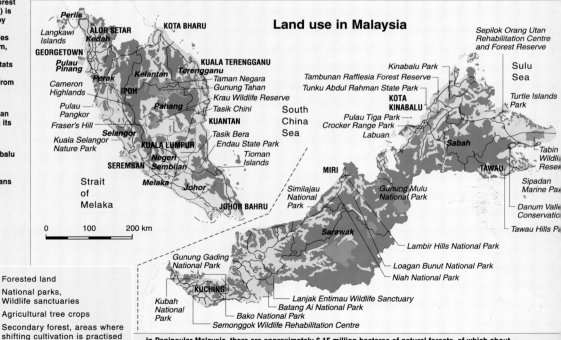

Perlis
Langkawi Islands
ALOR SETAR
Kedah
KOTA BHARU
GEORGETOWN
Pulau Pinang
Perak
Kelantan
KUALA TERENGGANU
Terengganu
Cameron Highlands
IPOH
Taman Negara
Gunung Tahan
Krau Wildlife Reserve
Pahang
Tasik Chini
Pulau Pangkor
KUANTAN
Fraser's Hill
Selangor
Tasik Bera
Kuala Selangor Nature Park
KUALA LUMPUR
Endau State Park
Tioman Islands
SEREMBAN
Negeri Sembilan
Melaka
Johor
Strait of Melaka
JOHOR BAHRU

South China Sea

Sepilok Orang Utan Rehabilitation Centre and Forest Reserve
Kinabalu Park
Sulu Sea
Tambunan Rafflesia Forest Reserve
Tunku Abdul Rahman State Park
KOTA KINABALU
Turtle Islands Park
Pulau Tiga Park
Crocker Range Park
Labuan
Sabah
TAWAU
Tabin Wildlife Reserve
Sipadan Marine Park
Danum Valley Conservation
Tawau Hills Park

MIRI
Similajau National Park
Gunung Mulu National Park
Sarawak
Lambir Hills National Park
Gunung Gading National Park
Loagan Bunut National Park
Niah National Park
KUCHING
Kubah National Park
Lanjak Entimau Wildlife Sanctuary
Batang Ai National Park
Bako National Park
Semonggok Wildlife Rehabilitation Centre

0    100    200 km

- Forested land
- National parks, Wildlife sanctuaries
- Agricultural tree crops
- Secondary forest, areas where shifting cultivation is practised
- Urban areas and other land use

In Peninsular Malaysia, there are approximately 6.15 million hectares of natural forests, of which about 0.76 million are Totally Protected Areas (TPAs). These include national parks and wildlife sanctuaries. In Sabah, TPAs occupy about 0.66 million hectares and in Sarawak they cover about 0.29 million hectares.

# SYNTHESIS

Because of its vast size, varied climate and soil composition, Taman Negara supports a rich diversity of plants, including many endemic trees, palms and herbs. It is Malaysia's oldest and biggest national park.

Mount Kinabalu, one of the world's greatest centres of plant diversity, is a Totally Protected Area. It is home to at least 180 families and 950 genera of plants, with well over 4,500 species of vascular plants.

The Endau State Park is unusual because it harbours species which occur in Borneo and the southern part of Peninsular Malaysia, but not elsewhere in the Peninsula. Examples include trees such as *Chionanthus lucens*, rattans like *Daemonorops scapigera* and ferns such as *Lindsaea borneensis*.

The Malaysian Tourism Promotion Board or Tourism Malaysia does much to attract visitors to the country's national parks, which offer accommodation and a variety of ecofriendly activities.

Malaysia, with its varied geological history, topography and stable environment, is richly endowed with plant life forms and habitats, making it one of most biodiverse countries in the world. Its lowland and hill dipterocarp and montane forests, for example, are home to a wide range of plant life forms such as trees, shrubs, herbs, climbers, stranglers, epiphytes, myrmecophytes, parasites and saprophytes. Also abundant are ferns, lichens, bryophytes and fungi. There are at least 15 different recognized forest types, each with its own characteristic structural complexity and species composition. The natural vegetation of Malaysia is also extremely rich in plant species. An amazing 12,500 or more species of flowering plants are found in the different forest types. Of these, 1,000 are orchids, representing about 12 per cent of all known orchid species in the world.

This great biodiversity is under constant threat because of habitat destruction by human activities, such as burning and clearing forests for other land use. This loss of habitats and the plant species that dwell in them will result not only in the elimination of plant genetic material, but also in the depletion of some of the country's natural resources, such as timber. Already an estimated 170 species of flowering plants have become extinct in Malaysia since 1948 as a direct consequence of habitat destruction. Others have become rare and endangered, partly because of the loss of habitats, but also in the case of commercially valuable plant species, because of over collecting.

To curb habitat destruction, prevent species extinction or endangerment and preserve Malaysia's biodiversity, the government has designated conservation areas whose status and management revolve around two strategies: *in situ* and *ex situ*. The best strategy is *in situ* conservation, whereby plants are protected in their natural habitat. *In situ* conservation is carried out in the form of Totally Protected Areas (TPAs), comprising national and state parks, wildlife sanctuaries and marine parks, and Permanent Forest Estates (PFEs), which include forest reserves. In a TPA, neither agricultural and other developmental activities nor the collecting or harvesting of plants or plant parts are allowed. Scientific research projects and certain ecofriendly tourist activites are, however, encouraged. PFEs, on the other hand, are set aside for the purpose of harvesting and managing timber resources on a sustainable basis. *Ex situ* conservation is undertaken by universities, government agencies, research institutions and botanical gardens, whose arboreta and greenhouses accommodate many groups of plants. Although these steps are being taken to protect Malaysia's biodiversity, they are being outpaced by development. In order to safeguard the future of Malaysia's biodiversity, more areas, especially vulnerable habitats, need to be set aside for conservation. Tighter legislation regarding the protection of plant species and their habitats is also needed, as well as enhanced public awareness of the importance of biodiversity conservation. To this end, a National Policy on Biological Diversity has been endorsed by the government.

# Extinction is forever

*The extinction of plant species is a silent process that usually occurs without notice or concern. And yet, from an ethical point of view, every extinction is an irreversible loss of a unique life form. It is mankind's responsibility to see that every species has a safe niche in which to survive in perpetuity. Extinction of plants in Malaysia is mainly the result of habitat loss. The highest extinction rates occur in habitats that are species rich and harbour unique species with narrow geographical distribution.*

The beautiful Rajah's begonia, first collected in 1892 in Terengganu, was rediscovered after it was thought to be extinct for over a hundred years.

## Destruction of habitats

**BURNING**
When forests are burnt to clear the land for agriculture, many species of plants are eliminated.

**LOGGING**
Vegetation is razed when loggers cut through forest.

**DROWNING**
For massive hydroelectricity projects, such as the building of dams, large areas of forest are flooded.

**DRAINING**
Swamps are drained to make way for land reclamation or resort development, as with this mangrove swamp in Pulau Langkawi.

## Species extinction in Malaysia

The first recorded extinction in Malaysia was the loss of the very rare primitive herb *Echinodorus ridleyi* (formerly known as *Ranalisma rostrata*), which was discovered and described in 1900 based on two specimens collected from a patch of black mud in dense forest at Batu Caves. This species has not been seen since the turn of the century and indeed no forest survives in the vicinity of Batu Caves. In Malaysia, there are at least three plant habitats that are known to have suffered high extinction rates.

The first is the forest that grew on the tin-rich soil in the Kinta region of Perak, which has been stripped away for opencast tin mining. Along with the forest, 66 tree species that only grew there have also become extinct and have not been seen since the 1940s.

The second is the species-rich limestone flora, which in the last 20 years has proved to be very vulnerable to extermination when the surrounding forest is cleared, leaving the hills exposed to burning. The limestone flora is not only very rich in species, but many of its component species are confined to a single hill, thus making them particularly vulnerable to extinction through habitat disturbance. In the Kinta area, botanical exploration on limestone hills started in the 1880s when the area was still untouched by man's activities. Today, 16 of the plant species recorded from those early days have not been seen for over 50 years. As their habitats are now destroyed or degraded, they too are added to the list of extinct species.

The third species-rich habitat that has suffered high rates of extinction is the montane forest. Each mountain peak is home to a considerable number of endemic species. One example, which has been studied in detail, is Fraser's Hill. Since the area was opened up as a hill resort in the 1920s, 13 plant species have probably become extinct due to habitat disturbance by resort development.

## Assessing extinction

The problem in assessing extinction is that it is difficult to prove that a species indeed no longer exists as not every square inch of Malaysia can be searched. However, a species is considered extinct if it has not been seen for many years in the places from which it was known to grow, nor has it been found in similar habitats elsewhere.

The woolly stalked begonia (*Begonia eiromischa*), which was only ever known from one rocky place in Penang, and was in 1894 already recorded as being very rare, has not been seen in the wild since then. Search of the area where it was known to occur shows that its natural habitat has long since been lost to agriculture. This species is therefore presumed to be extinct. The beautiful Rajah's begonia (*Begonia rajah*) was first collected in 1892 in Terengganu. Because of its attractive foliage, it was brought into cultivation and prized as a pot plant. However, it was not refound for more than a hundred years and was believed to be extinct in the wild. Search of the appropriate habitat, such as the rocky banks of waterfalls, led to its rediscovery. However, its existence is still highly endangered as the forest where it grows is not protected and plants that grow near waterfalls are particularly vulnerable to logging, which opens up the canopy and causes siltation that covers the rocky banks with mud.

Another flaw in ascertaining extinction is whether the so-called very rare species ever existed as a distinct entity in the first place. In the early days when there were few collections of specimens available for study, unusual or aberrant individuals were often described as new species. As information accumulated and the natural variation of the species became better understood, these unusual 'species' were reclassified within their correct category. An example of this is the small rosette *Didymocarpus perdita*, thought to be extinct, but has been shown to belong to a more widespread species, *D. puncticulata*.

## Vulnerable and endangered species

The excitement of rediscovering extinct species must be balanced by the alarm at the number of plants which, while not yet

*Echinodorus ridleyi* has not been seen in the wild since 1900, and is therefore presumed to be extinct.

## On the road to extinction

The rate of extinction of the flora of Peninsular Malaysia is about 2 per cent, or about 170 of the estimated 8,500 species of flowering plants. The majority of these have become extinct in the last 50 years, although extinctions began about a hundred years ago. The extinction rate of 2 per cent is low compared with theoretical figures given for the world's tropical rainforest. The latter are based on the current rates of forest clearance, which range from 1 to 11 per cent per decade from the 1970s, and predict that by the turn of the 20th century, 90 per cent of the world's rainforest will have disappeared. Along with it about half of its species will become extinct. This translates into a loss of 4,250 species for Peninsular Malaysia.

The percentage of endangered species is much higher. For example, although none of the 195 species of palms in Peninsular Malaysia are extinct, nearly 20 per cent of them are endangered, as are just over 15 per cent of trees.

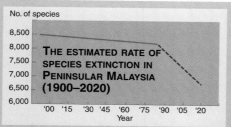

No. of species

**THE ESTIMATED RATE OF SPECIES EXTINCTION IN PENINSULAR MALAYSIA (1900–2020)**

8,500 — 8,000 — 7,500 — 7,000 — 6,500 — 6,000

'00 '15 '30 '45 '60 '75 '90 '05 '20
Year

At 2 per cent, the rate of species extinction of Peninsular Malaysia is low, but changes in land use since the 1970s have possibly raised the rate to 20 per cent from about 1985.

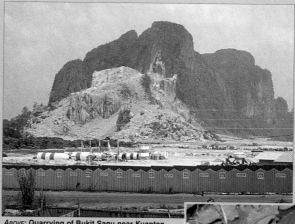

*ABOVE:* Quarrying of Bukit Sagu near Kuantan for cement will have consumed the entire hill by the year 2000. *Paraboea bakeri* (inset), which grows only on Bukit Sagu, faces certain extinction by the year 2000.

*LEFT:* The Kinta region in Perak, where tin mining has led to the loss of 66 plant species.

extinct, are nevertheless threatened with extinction. The comparatively low figure of 2 per cent extinction rate for Peninsular Malaysia is no cause for complacency as the percentage of endangered species, that is, those on the brink of extinction, is very much higher.

Standing at around 15–20 per cent, this translates into between 1,275 and 1,700 species of flowering plants that are currently on the brink of extinction. These endangered species are those endemic species with a small population size or those that are restricted to a small area, and which are threatened by habitat destruction or disturbance. Examples of man's activities threatening the survival of such plant species include the destruction of lowland and hill dipterocarp forests, the quarrying of limestone hills, the burning of vegetation on limestone, quartzite or ultramafic soils, the development of resorts on islands and in the highlands, and the draining and clearing of swamp forests. In addition, the commercial collecting of wild plants is endangering the survival of some species, in particular orchids and pitcher plants.

### Loss of valuable genetic material

Why should we care about extinction when habitat destruction has resulted in economic gains from tin mining, agriculture or resort development? The answer is not only the ethical one that man should not destroy what he cannot create, but also because, together with the loss of a species goes the loss of genes that may prove to be valuable in the future. An outstanding example is the outbreak of the HIV virus. Unheard of a decade or two ago, AIDS is now a major problem throughout the world, for which there is no cure. Pharmaceutical companies have screened many thousands of plants and three appear to hold potential. One of these is a wild *bintangor* tree (*Calophyllum lanigerum* var. *austrocoriaceum*). It grows wild in Malaysian forests,

## Endangerment by commercial collecting

Commercial collecting of wild plants is endangering the survival of some species, in particular orchids and pitcher plants. For both these groups, trade of plants collected from wild populations is banned under international law (Convention on International Trade in Endangered Species). In Sarawak, they are also totally protected. However, in some cases this has come too late.

**PERCENTAGE OF EXTINCTION AND ENDANGERMENT IN SOME FLOWERING PLANTS OF PENINSULAR MALAYSIA**

| PLANT GROUP | EXTINCT | ENDANGERED |
|---|---|---|
| Palms | 0 | 19.5 |
| Trees | 2.3 | 15.7 |
| Flora of Fraser's Hill | 1.6 | 19.3 |

*LEFT:* The black form of *Nepenthes gracillima*, the rarest endemic species in Peninsular Malaysia, only grows at Genting Highlands, and is endangered not only by habitat destruction but also by indiscriminate commercial collecting.

*RIGHT:* In Malaysia, the beautiful Philippine slipper orchid (*Paphiopedilum philippinense*) is now extinct on Pulau Balambangan, Sabah, where the entire population has been stripped by commercial plant collectors.

and previously was not known to have any use. This illustrates the importance of conserving the biodiversity of Malaysia's rainforests as we cannot predict what mankind's needs will be in the future.

Besides their pharmaceutical attributes, many wild species have potential commercial value as ornamental plants, as minor forest products, or for producing bioactive chemicals, like pesticides. They also form a gene pool necessary for future improvement of their domesticated relatives, such as breeding for resistance to new pests and diseases.

It is a pity that the extinction of plant species is unintentional and due to man's ignorance, and in most cases could have been avoided if the conservation of biodiversity had been taken into account. If conservation of biodiversity is not taken seriously, both for habitat protection and the control of collecting of commercially valuable species, Malaysia can expect to see extinction rates rising rapidly within the next decade from the 2 per cent at present to at least 20 per cent.

### The price of progress

*ABOVE:* New roads, like the Karak Highway, make difficult-to-reach places accessible, but destroy habitats and, along with them, plant species.

*BELOW:* Irreversible destruction by resort development, road building and forest clearance seriously endangers the montane flora.

# Totally Protected Areas and Permanent Forest Estates

*Malaysia is rich in life forms that occur in a variety of forest habitats, all of which are represented in Totally Protected Areas and Permanent Forest Estates. Forest reserves encompassing productive, protective and amenity forests come under Permanent Forest Estates. On the other hand, Totally Protected Areas consist of national and state parks, wildlife reserves and sanctuaries, virgin jungles and marine parks. The entire network plays a crucial role in conserving plant diversity, stabilizing the ecosystem, and maintaining a high standard of ecological services.*

The long-tailed macaque (*Macaca fascicularis*) is a protected animal in Malaysia. Licences are issued by the Government to control the number of individuals poached for sale as exotic pets.

### Forest reserves with recreational facilities

Chalets at Sungai Chongkak in Selangor provide overnight accommodation for guests.

The Forest Reserve at Kanching is well-known in Malaysia for its series of small waterfalls in which visitors can swim and paddle.

## Totally Protected Areas: Wildlife sanctuaries and reserves

The Lanjak-Entimau Wildlife Sanctuary in Sarawak and the Krau Wildlife Reserve in Pahang have both been accorded the status of Totally Protected Areas.

Spanning the border between Sarawak and Indonesian Kalimantan, the Lanjak-Entimau Wildlife Sanctuary comprises principally hill and montane habitats between the altitudes of 600 and 1200 metres. Adjoining the sanctuary is Bentuang-Karimun National Park in Kalimantan. Because it falls under two countries' jurisdictions, the sanctuary's biological diversity is uniquely managed. The sanctuary is located in an area of rich plant diversity and endemism, with an estimated 1,800 species of trees and 177 species of herbs, palms and climbers. This sanctuary is thus an important plant gene bank for both Malaysia and Indonesia.

The Krau Wildlife Reserve consists of the inland forest habitats of Peninsular Malaysia, such as lowland, hill, and lower and upper montane forests. Both the lowland and hill forests are dominated by tree species belonging to the Dipterocarpaceae, Euphorbiaceae and Leguminosae. In the hill forests, *seraya* (*Shorea curtisii*) is found, easily recognizable by its bluish grey crown. Oaks and laurels dominate the lower montane vegetation, while upper montane forests are home to luxuriant mosses, epiphytic orchids, bryophytes and ferns and fern allies.

## Permanent Forest Estates: Forest reserves

Under the Permanent Forest Estates, forest reserves are listed as productive forests, which means that they can be licensed for timber harvesting. However, unless they are degazetted, they cannot be converted to land for other uses. Within the boundaries of productive forests often lie protection forests and virgin jungle reserves. Protection forests are set aside for the purpose of maintaining the quality of the water and environment, while virgin jungle reserves are used solely for scientific research.

Although forest reserves are less effective in conservation than Totally Protected Areas because of the way the former are managed, the web of forest reserves comprises all the habitats found in Malaysia,

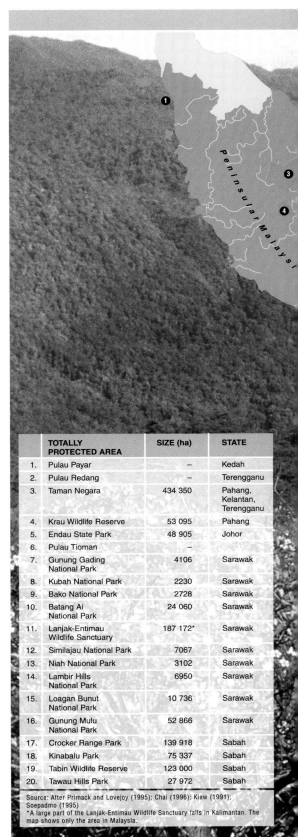

| | TOTALLY PROTECTED AREA | SIZE (ha) | STATE |
|---|---|---|---|
| 1. | Pulau Payar | – | Kedah |
| 2. | Pulau Redang | – | Terengganu |
| 3. | Taman Negara | 434 350 | Pahang, Kelantan, Terengganu |
| 4. | Krau Wildlife Reserve | 53 095 | Pahang |
| 5. | Endau State Park | 48 905 | Johor |
| 6. | Pulau Tioman | – | |
| 7. | Gunung Gading National Park | 4106 | Sarawak |
| 8. | Kubah National Park | 2230 | Sarawak |
| 9. | Bako National Park | 2728 | Sarawak |
| 10. | Batang Ai National Park | 24 060 | Sarawak |
| 11. | Lanjak-Entimau Wildlife Sanctuary | 187 172* | Sarawak |
| 12. | Similajau National Park | 7067 | Sarawak |
| 13. | Niah National Park | 3102 | Sarawak |
| 14. | Lambir Hills National Park | 6950 | Sarawak |
| 15. | Loagan Bunut National Park | 10 736 | Sarawak |
| 16. | Gunung Mulu National Park | 52 866 | Sarawak |
| 17. | Crocker Range Park | 139 918 | Sabah |
| 18. | Kinabalu Park | 75 337 | Sabah |
| 19. | Tabin Wildlife Reserve | 123 000 | Sabah |
| 20. | Tawau Hills Park | 27 972 | Sabah |

Source: After Primack and Lovejoy (1995); Chai (1996); Kiew (1991); Soepadmo (1995)
*A large part of the Lanjak-Entimau Wildlife Sanctuary falls in Kalimantan. The map shows only the area in Malaysia.

from coastal to mangrove to subalpine forests. Each habitat boasts a unique array of plants and a high degree of endemism. Many herbaceous plants, such as orchids and pitcher plants, for example, exhibit a very restricted pattern of distribution. These circumstances heighten the already urgent need for more rigorous conservation efforts in Malaysia.

## Some Totally Protected Areas in Malaysia

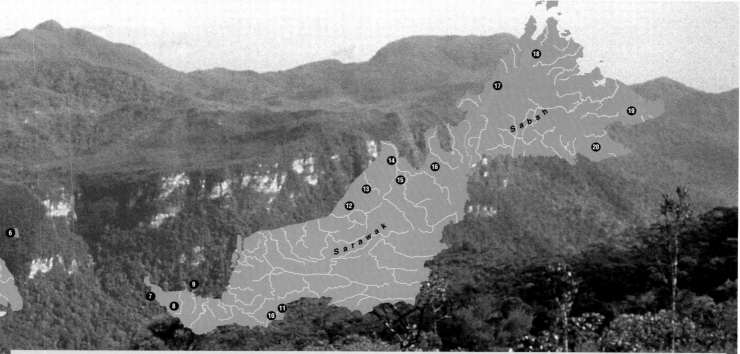

## National parks

There are 14 national and state parks in Malaysia, 9 of which are in Sarawak, 3 in Sabah and 2 in Peninsular Malaysia. Taman Negara, the National Park, is also the country's largest. Other big parks include Gunung Mulu National Park, Kinabalu Park and Endau-Rompin State Park.

Taman Negara occupies an area of 434 350 hectares, of which 57 per cent lies in Pahang, and 24 and 19 per cent in Kelantan and Terengganu, respectively.

*BACKGROUND*: The Teku Gorge near Gunung Tahan in Taman Negara.

### Taman Negara

Taman Negara, formerly known as King George V National Park, is Malaysia's oldest national park. It is the most extensive protected tract of pristine, lowland, tropical evergreen rainforest in Malaysia, and is unique in harbouring a myriad of forest habitats, with the exception of coastal and swamp forests. Distributed between the altitudes of 75 and 2187 metres are lowland dipterocarp and mixed dipterocarp forests, riverine vegetation, limestone forests and forests on quartzite outcrops, hill forests, montane forests and, in Padang, on the summit plateau of Gunung Tahan, scrub vegetation.

Because of its vast size and varied soil and climate composition, Taman Negara supports a rich diversity of plants. More than 3,000 species of vascular plants are estimated to be in the park, although this figure is probably too low. Many endemic plant species occur here, including trees, palms and herbs, such as *Polyosma robusta*, *Livistona tahanensis* and *Argostemma albociliatum*, respectively. The park is also home to several distinct variations of plant species, such as the mountain form of *Agathis borneensis* and the white form of *Nepenthes gracillima*. Spectacular *neram* trees (*Dipterocarpus oblongifolius*) overhang rivers where a diverse assemblage of rheophytes (plants that prefer to live near flowing water) flourish. Because of this remarkable diversity, Taman Negara is a valuable gene pool for commercially important timber species, fruit trees, rattans and ornamental plants.

### Gunung Mulu National Park

This park contains all the major inland forest vegetation types occurring in Sarawak, including a very extensive and impressive cave system. A wide range of habitats are found, from lowland dipterocarp forests to limestone forests, montane forests on sandstone and shale, riverine forests, heath forests and peatswamp forests. Endemism is high, mainly because of specific soil types in many areas. The Melinau area, for example, is covered with luxuriant limestone vegetation capped by formidable, precipitous mountains with razor-edged pinnacles. Many gesneriads (Gesneriaceae) and orchids are restricted to this location and are not found elsewhere in the world.

The Mulu Caves are a grand attraction for visitors to Gunung Mulu National Park.

### Kinabalu Park

Encompassing altitudes from 150 to 4101 metres, Kinabalu Park is one of the world's most remarkable and fascinating centres of plant diversity. It supports at least 18 vegetation types, consisting of montane forests, with some lowland rainforests, ultramafic forests (see 'Limestone, quartzite and ultramafic vegetation'), subalpine and alpine forests (see 'Montane forest') and scrub vegetation. Lowland and hill forests cover over a third of the park, and are dominated by the families of timber (Dipterocarpaceae), rambutan (Sapindaceae), *petai* (Leguminosae) and mango (Anacardiaceae).

Perhaps the most intriguing of all the species of vascular plants in Kinabalu Park are the unrivalled pitcher plants, such as *Nepenthes rajah* and *N. lowii*; the world's largest flowers, *Rafflesia pricei* and *R. keithii*; and the rare slipper orchid *Paphiopedilum rothschildianum*. Many endemic taxa have an extremely restricted distribution on the mountain, with as much as 40 per cent of the park's flora known from just a single location. The rarest species are often restricted to areas with specific soil types, such as ultramafic outcrops.

The park trail leading up to the summit of Mount Kinabalu.

# Plant diversity and conservation

*Malaysia is one of the world's richest centres of plant diversity. Peninsular Malaysia is home to an estimated 12,500 species of flowering plants, while Borneo (Sabah, Sarawak and Indonesian Kalimantan) harbours between 10,000 and 12,000, including a huge number of endemics. To preserve this invaluable natural resource, Malaysia practises several forms of conservation. Sarawak has, in addition, drawn up stringent legislation. International conventions also play a major part. Despite these efforts, conservation remains an uphill task in the face of rapid development.*

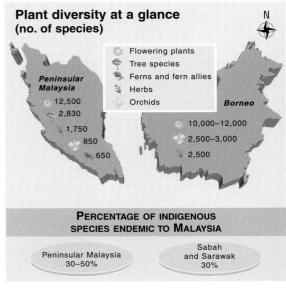

**Plant diversity at a glance (no. of species)**

Flowering plants
Tree species
Ferns and fern allies
Herbs
Orchids

Peninsular Malaysia
12,500
2,830
1,750
850
650

Borneo
10,000–12,000
2,500–3,000
2,500

**PERCENTAGE OF INDIGENOUS SPECIES ENDEMIC TO MALAYSIA**

Peninsular Malaysia
30–50%

Sabah and Sarawak
30%

---

## Some protected plant species in Sarawak

**MANGROVE SPECIES**
*Sonneratia alba, S. caseolaris, Avicennia alba* (above), *A. marina* and *A. lanata.*

**TIMBER SPECIES**
*Shorea splendida, S. macrophylla, Koompassia excelsa* (above) and *K. malaccensis.*

**ORCHID SPECIES**
*Paphiopedilum* spp.

**MEDICINAL PLANTS**
*Eurycoma longifolia* (above), *Goniothalamus velutinus* and *Antiaris toxicaria.*

**PITCHER PLANTS**
*Nepenthes* spp.

---

## Why is plant diversity important?

Apart from its intrinsic value, Malaysia's plant megadiversity has significant economic, social and technological implications. Edible crops such as paddy, vegetables and fruits fulfil the nation's daily food requirements, while timber species and industrial crops provide primary raw materials for export. The traditional use of plants in medicine in Malaysia is being actively researched by academic institutions and pharmaceutical industries.

## Conservation: Two approaches

Malaysia has adopted both *in situ* and *ex situ* approaches towards conservation. *In situ* conservation involves the maintenance of natural habitats where plants flourish, such as primary forests. This approach is crucial, as plants are not mobile and cannot respond adaptively to disruptive changes in their environment. Destruction of habitats only hastens both the loss of populations and genetic diversity. *Ex situ* conservation, on the other hand, maintains species outside their original habitats, in facilities such as botanical gardens and seed banks. This approach is also a rescue measure that is used when the clearing of forests is unavoidable, and the threat of extinction to plant populations inevitable. Although the two approaches complement each other, *in situ* conservation is by far the more effective in managing plant diversity.

Several *in situ* conservation measures have been adopted by the Malaysian Government. They include the creation of a network of Totally Protected Areas (TPAs), which include national and state parks, wildlife sanctuaries and virgin jungle reserves. A few TPAs, such as the Endau State Park, have management guidelines to ensure that economic activities related to ecotourism do not, in any way, destroy the forest habitats. Almost all the forest types found in Malaysia are represented in the TPA network, although no single TPA encompasses them all. In spite of this, many forest habitats, such as limestone and ultramafic habitats are still inadequately protected in terms of size. Another forest management system is the forest reserve, where, for example, timber harvesting is limited to specifically designated areas.

All species of *Rafflesia* are given totally protected status in Sarawak but not elsewhere in Malaysia.

Malaysia's main centres of *ex situ* conservation comprise arboreta of research institutions, universities and government agencies, and botanic gardens. The universities include Universiti Malaya, Universiti Putra Malaysia and Universiti Kebangsaan Malaysia; while the government-funded research centres include those in Semenggok in Sarawak and Sepilok and Poring in Sabah. The Botanic Gardens in Penang is an important conservation site. Of the research institutions, the Palm Oil Research Institute Malaysia, Rubber Research Institute Malaysia, Forest Research Institute Malaysia and Malaysian Agricultural Research and Development Institute have arboreta where various groups of plants are grown. The limitation of *ex situ* conservation is that some groups of plants are better represented than others. While tree, fruit tree and orchid species and industrial crops can be found in research institutions across the country, the herbaceous and non-vascular plants, such as fungi, algae and mosses, are poorly represented.

## Legislation and international commitments

The Sarawak Government has placed some of its indigenous plant species under legal protection. Species that are totally protected cannot be collected, harvested or traded, while those that are designated protected may be collected solely for scientific research, with prior consent from the Sarawak Government. Totally protected species include the magnificent *Rafflesia* spp. and *Dipterocarpus oblongifolius*. The list of protected species is much longer, comprising mangrove species, timber species, pitcher plants, orchids, palms and medicinal plants. There is no similar system for the protection of plant species in Sabah and Peninsular Malaysia, nor is there comprehensive legislation in Malaysia which covers plant diversity conservation and management as a whole.

International legislation on trade and conservation offers a form of protection to endangered plant species not covered under Malaysia's legislation. The Convention on International Trade in Endangered Species of Wild Fauna and Flora (CITES), for example, issues a list of plant species, including rare and endangered ones, that may only be traded if they are cultivated. Adherence to the rules of this Convention is closely monitored by member countries, of which Malaysia is one. The level of protection accorded to a species depends on its status in the natural habitat. Those that are critically endangered are given a higher degree of protection than those that are less vulnerable. Some Malaysian plants that CITES protects are the orchids (Orchidaceae) and pitcher plants (Nepenthaceae). Another international convention which relates to plant diversity and of which Malaysia is a signatory is the Convention on Biological Diversity. Under its guidelines, Malaysia is now obliged to fulfil certain terms with regards to the conservation of biological diversity.

## A dilemma

Since the 1970s, plant diversity conservation in Malaysia has been under increasing pressure from the rising demand for land. Large areas of natural forests, particularly those in the lowlands, have been razed to make way for agriculture and development projects, leaving behind fragments of forest which are often too small to support viable breeding plant populations. More recent threats to natural habitats include forest fires and large-scale infrastructure projects, such as the building of dams. Forest fires, proliferating as a result of changes in global weather patterns, have affected large areas. Peatswamp forests are particularly vulnerable, and harbour a unique

### The Forest Research Institute Malaysia (FRIM): An example of *ex situ* conservation

FRIM, formerly known as the Forest Research Institute, was set up in 1929 and has since become Malaysia's leading institute for forestry research and development. Its principal roles are to undertake research on forest management, conservation and resource utilization, to coordinate these projects nationwide and liaise with organizations outside Malaysia and to be a source of official information.

1. Canopy walkway
2. Dipterocarp arboretum
3. Non-dipterocarp arboretum
4. Campsite
5. Fruit tree arboretum
6. Monocotyledon arboretum
7. Coniferatum
8. Main building and museum

The main building of FRIM, which also houses the museum. Displayed in the museum are traditional timber and non-timber products and information on FRIM's current research projects.

In the coniferatum, a research plot of *Pinus caribea* is grown.

The dipterocarp arboretum was established in 1929 and boasts 150 species.

| ARBORETA AT FRIM | | | |
|---|---|---|---|
| ARBORETA | YEAR ESTABLISHED | AREA (ha) | NO. OF SPECIES |
| Dipterocarp | 1929 | 6.5 | 150 |
| Non-dipterocarp | 1929 | 14 | 275 |
| Gymnosperm | 1949 | 2.5 | 17 |
| Fruit tree | 1979 | 0.6 | 34 |
| Monocotyledon | 1981 | 1.5 | 35 |

array of species not found in other forest types. Important examples include *Shorea teysmanniana*, *S. uliginosa* (both Dipterocarpaceae), *Gonystylus bacanus* (Thymelaeaceae) and *Santiria rubiginosa* var. *nana* (Burseraceae). The destruction of natural habitats invariably leads to the extermination of plant populations and species, and consequently, the natural wealth of the country.

## Ecotourism

In 1983, Hector Ceballos-Lascurian coined the term *ecotourism*, meaning 'tourism which involves travel to undisturbed natural areas with the aim of studying, admiring and enjoying the scenery, plants and wildlife, as well as any cultural elements that exist'. This has become the basis on which ecotourism is interpreted, understood and applied by conservation organizations, governments and the tourism industry. In Malaysia, this has been translated into a conscious effort to keep certain tourist facilities and activities ecofriendly. In amenity forests and state and national parks, tourists are provided with facilities such as canopy bridges, forest trails and camp sites. These enable visitors to view and learn about the natural world in a natural setting without causing extensive harm to the habitats.

For ecotourism to work, it has to be sustainable, that is, it has to meet the needs of the present generation without depleting resources so much that future generations are prevented from meeting their own needs. To achieve this, the golden rules are that:

- Development does not exhaust or degrade the resource on which it depends;
- Cultural, economic and ecological diversity is maintained;
- The characteristics that give an area its identity are enhanced and preserved;
- The cultural and natural resources are used for the economic growth of the local community;
- Local manpower is used.

### Ecofriendly tourist activities

1. Birdwatching allows tourists to appreciate the beauty of birds without disrupting their natural behaviour or habitat.
2. On a forest canopy walkway, as in the Forest Research Institute Malaysia (FRIM) and Taman Negara, visitors are greeted with a stunning view of the surrounding vegetation. Walkways like this make the forest accessible to humans whilst protecting it from harm.
3. Tourists travelling up Sungai Tembeling with a guide in Taman Negara. This mode of travel does not modify the natural landscape or cause excessive pollution.

# Glossary

## A

**Aerobic**: Containing oxygen or taking place in the presence of oxygen.

**Alga**: Simple plant, containing chlorophyll, which is not differentiated into stems, roots or leaves. Also absent is a vascular system.

**Anaerobic**: Devoid of or occurring in the absence of oxygen.

**Angiosperms**: Flowering seed plants whose ovules are enclosed fully in the ovaries.

**Anther**: Terminal part of the stamen of a flowering plant, on which pollen-bearing sacs occur.

**Axil**: Upper angle where a leaf stalk joins the stem. or where a small stem joins a larger one.

## B

**Bark**: Outer layer of a tree trunk, composed of phloem tissue. Its texture varies from being smooth, scaly to fissured.

**Bract**: Reduced or modified leaf which protects a flower or inflorescence in its axil.

**Bryophyte**: Plant division that comprises hornworts, liverworts and mosses.

## C

**Calyx**: Collective term for the sepals of a flower.

**Cambium**: Layer of cells lying between the xylem and phloem in the roots and stems of vascular plants. Throughout the plant's lifetime these cells divide, thereby increasing the girth of the stem.

**Carpel**: Female reproductive organ of a flowering plant, comprising an ovary and a terminal style tipped by a stigma.

**Centre of diversity**: Geographical location or region where a particular family, genus or species displays a greater genetic diversity than it does anywhere else. Areas in the tropics are the centre of diversity for many taxa.

**Centre of origin**: Geographical location or region, often in the tropics, where a group of organisms originated, frequently a centre of diversity.

**Chlorophyll**: Green pigment in plants that absorbs radiant energy from the sun for use in photosynthesis.

**Cotyledon**: Seed leaf borne on a plant embryo.

## D

**Deciduous**: Used to describe trees that shed their leaves seasonally.

**Dicotyledon**: One of the two divisions of flowering plants in which the embryo has at least two cotyledons or seed leaves.

**Dipterocarp**: Trees belonging to the family Dipterocarpaceae, which is the main source of Malaysian hardwood timber.

**Dipterocarpaceae**: Family of lofty, resinous trees very common in the lowland rainforests of western Malesia, with characteristic simple alternate leaves, twisted sepals and petals. The nuts are embedded in a calyx that has wing-like sepals.

**Durian**: Famous Southeast Asian fruit with woody, spiny skin, known for its pungent smell but delicious taste. The species *Durio zibethinus* is the most commonly cultivated in Malaysia.

## E

**Ecosystem**: Interdependence of species in the living world with one another and their environment. Ecosystems encompass communities of all sizes, from a small pond to the entire planet.

**Endemism**: Situation where a species is confined to a particular geographical region due to factors such as isolation or response to climatic or soil conditions.

**Endosperm**: Structure found in seeds of flowering plants, that stores food substances which are utilized by the developing embryo and broken down during seed germination.

**Epiphyte**: Plant that uses another plant, often a tree, for support but without drawing nutrients from it.

**Evapotranspiration**: Water lost by evaporation and transpiration.

**Evergreen**: Used to describe a tree or shrub that never sheds its leaves completely and so whose crown is never bare.

## F

**Fertilization**: Union of a male and female gamete, during sexual reproduction, that produces a zygote.

**Food chain**: Transfer of energy from primary producers, or green plants, through a number of organisms who are both predators and prey. When food chains interlink they form a food web.

**Fungus**: Non-photosynthetic organism that obtains its nutrients by absorbing organic compounds from its surroundings.

## G

**Gamete**: Sex cell which fuses with another of the opposite sex during fertilization.

**Germination**: Start of growth of a seed, spore or pollen grain, usually followed by a dormant period.

**Gymnosperms**: Seed plants whose ovules or seeds are carried naked on the cone scales. Hence, also known as naked-seed plants.

## H

**Habitat**: Living place of any organism or community of organisms, defined by its physical characteristics or its living components.

**Haustorium**: Specialized absorptive organ of a parasitic flowering plant, or in fungi an outgrowth of hyphae, that penetrates host cells to draw nutrients.

*Hibiscus*: Genus of trees and shrubs of the family Malvaceae, whose flowers have a characteristically prominent stamen tube.

**Hypha**: Thread-like filament found in fungi.

**Hypocotyl**: Part of the seedling located below the cotyledon and above the roots.

## I

**Inflorescence**: Reproductive structure of flowering plants that comprises more than one flower.

## J

*Jambu*: Malay term for trees belonging to the genus *Syzygium*.

*Jamu*: Traditional Malay herbal medicine made from ingredients such as ginger, tamarind, acacia and eucalyptus oil. Up to 150 plants may be used for different types of jamu. Sold in both liquid and dried form, it is mixed with a raw egg and drunk. It is used as a beauty tonic, for maintaining one's energy levels and to increase the male libido.

## K

*Kerangas*: Heath forest found in Southeast Asia, the Amazon Basin, Guyana and on the coast of Gabon in central Africa. It grows on podzolic soil that is rich in silica, and obtains most of its water from rainfall.

## L

**Lamina**: Blade of a leaf.

**Liana**: Woody, free-climbing plant. It is a characteristic component of lowland and hill tropical rainforests.

**Lichen**: Composite organism comprising a fungus and an alga in a symbiotic relationship.

**Life form**: Structure, form, habit and history of an organism. In plants, associated with different habitats.

**Limestone forest**: Forest that grows over limestone hills, a distinctive forest type found in Southeast Asia and the Caribbean.

**Litter**: Dead plant remains on the soil surface.

# M

**Malesia**: Floristic region that covers the landmasses on and between the Sahul and Sunda Shelves, which include Malaysia, Singapore, Brunei, Papua New Guinea, Indonesia and the Philippines. It is one of the richest floristic regions in the world.

**Mangrove forest**: Swamp forest that develops in brackish or saline water, on tropical tidal mud flats in estuaries.

**Megasporophyll**: Modified leaf that bears the megaspores which are the reproductive structures where the female sex cells are located.

**Mesocarp**: Middle layer of the fruit wall or pericarp.

**Microsporophyll**: Modified leaf that bears microspores which are the reproductive structures where the male sex cells are located.

**Midrib**: Central, thick and linear structure that runs along the length of a leaf blade or lamina.

**Monocotyledon**: One of the two great divisions of flowering plants in which the embryo has one cotyledon or seed leaf.

# N

**Neotropics**: Floristic region that corresponds with Central and South America, except for the southernmost tip which is part of the Antarctic floristic zone.

**Nipa**: Palm *Nypa fruticans* that inhabits mangrove swamps from Bangladesh to the Solomon and Mariana Islands. Fermented sap extracted from the stalks of its inflorescence is used to make toddy, an alcoholic drink.

**Nitrogen fixation**: Reduction of gaseous nitrogen and its reconfiguration into nitrogenous compounds.

# O

**Old World Tropics**: Tropical region of the Eastern hemisphere which comprises Africa, Asia, Papua New Guinea and parts of Australia.

**Ovary**: Structure in a flower that encloses the ovules.

**Ovule**: Structure in angiosperms and gymnosperms that develops into a seed when fertilized.

# P

**Paddy**: Unhusked rice grains. *Oryza sativa* is the most commonly cultivated species of rice, grown mainly in Asia.

**Panicle**: Compound raceme, an inflorescence whose main axis grows continuously, producing flowers laterally so that the youngest ones are at the centre. This structure is often found in grains, such as paddy, wheat and oats.

**Parasite**: Plant that lives on or in another plant, the host plant, obtaining from it water, nutrients and shelter.

**Peatswamp forest**: Swamp forest that occurs on a thick layer of acidic, nutrient-deficient peat soil.

*Petai*: Malay term for seeds of trees of the genus *Parkia*, which are commonly eaten as a vegetable.

**Petiole**: Stalk by which a leaf is attached to the stem.

**pH**: Value on a scale of 0–14 that measures the acidity (0–6) or alkalinity (8–14) of a substance. A pH of 7 indicates that the substance is neutral.

**Phloem**: Tissue found in vascular plants, that transports dissolved organic and inorganic substances from the leaves to other parts of the plant.

**Photosynthesis**: In green plants, a series of metabolic reactions in which energy absorbed from sunlight by chlorophyll is used for the conversion of carbon dioxide into organic compounds which the plants uses as food. The process may be expressed in the equation:

$$CO_2 + 2H_2O \xrightarrow{\text{chlorophyll}} CH_2O + H_2O + O_2\uparrow$$

**Phytogeography**: Study of the distribution of plant taxon in terms of historical, geological continental make-up and plant migration routes.

**Pinnate**: Compound leaves with leaflets arising on either side of a central stalk or rachis.

**Pitcher plants**: Carnivorous tropical herbs and shrubs belonging to the family Nepenthaceae that comprises only one genus, *Nepenthes*. There are over 30 species in Malaysia.

**Pith**: Plant tissue that is composed of parenchyma or basic cells that lie in the central part of the stem.

**Protoplasm**: Translucent, colourless subtance in a cell, differentiated in plants and animals into the nucleoplasm, which is protoplasm in the nucleus, and cytoplasm, which is protoplasm in the rest of the cell.

# R

**Rachis**: Axis that bears the flower, or in plants with compound leaves, the leaflets.

*Rafflesia*: Genus belonging to the family Rafflesiaceae, that are wholly parasitic on vines of the family Vitaceae.

**Rambutan**: Fruit of the species *Nephelium lappaceum*. The edible aril envelops a seed and is covered by a leathery, spiny pericarp.

# S

**Saprophyte**: Plant that absorbs organic nutrients from inanimate sources such as dead wood or dung. Fungi are the most common form of saprophytes.

**Seed**: Body from which a new plant develops in the sexual reproduction of seed-bearing plants. It comprises an outer layer or testa which encloses an embryo and food storage tissues.

**Sepal**: One of the greenish outer floral leaves that are borne in a tight spiral.

*Shorea*: Genus of the Dipterocarpaceae, that comprises many species of huge trees with winged fruits. These trees yield commercially valuable timber and resins. In Malaysia, *Shorea* trees and their timber are known as *meranti* and *seraya*, and the resin is called *damar*.

**Stamen**: Male organ of a flower comprising a stalk or filament and the anther.

**Stele**: Cylinder of vascular tissue found inside stems and roots, consisting in part of xylem and phloem.

**Stigma**: Part of the female reproductive organs of a plant where pollen germinates.

**Stipule**: Leafy appendage found, often in pairs, at or near the base of the petiole of a leaf.

**Stomata**: Small openings in the epidermal layer of plants, especially that of leaves, which allow for the absorption of carbon dioxide and release of oxygen and water vapour.

**Strangling fig**: Fig tree that germinates in the crown of the host tree, sending roots to the ground which link up and envelop the host tree, eventually killing it.

**Style**: Extension of the carpel, on which the stigma is borne.

**Symbiosis**: Mutually beneficial relationship between dissimilar organisms, such as that between certain plants and ants, or fungi and trees.

# T

**Taxon**: Group of organisms belonging to a taxanomic rank, such as species, genus or family.

**Transpiration**: Loss of water vapour from the plant to the atmosphere through the stomata of leaves.

**Turgor pressure**: Pressure exerted by water in cells on the cell walls, contributing to the rigidity of the plant.

# V

**Vascular bundle**: Longtitudinal strand consisting of xylem and phloem. Vascular bundles transport water and soluble nutrients, and contribute towards the support of the plant.

# X

**Xylem**: Tissue found in vascular plants, that transports water and dissolved inorganic nutrients from the roots to the leaves.

# Z

**Zygote**: Fertilized ovule that is formed by the fusion of male and female gametes. It develops into a new individual.

# Bibliography

Abdul Latiff (1982), 'Notes on the Vegetation and Flora of Pulau Pemanggil', *Malayan Nature Journal*, 35: 217–23.

Ahmad Nawawi (1978), 'Lichens', *Nature Malaysiana*, 3 (2): 30–5.

Ainsworth, G. C. et al. (1995), *Ainsworth and Bisby's Dictionary of the Fungi*, 8th edn, Kew: Commonwealth Mycological Institute.

Aishah Salleh (1993), 'Notes on Marine Red Algae (Rhodophyta) from Peninsular Malaysia', *Jurnal Sains*, 1 (1): 13–23.

Aishah Salleh and Kamsari, S. (1994), 'Studies on *Cephaleuros virescens* Kunze, a Parasitic Alga from Malaysia', in S. M. Phang et al. (eds.), *Algal Biotechnology in the Asia–Pacific Region*, Kuala Lumpur: Universiti Malaya.

Appanah, S. (1981), 'Pollination in Malaysian Primary Forest', *Malaysian Forester*, 44: 37–42.

_____ (1982), 'Pollination of Androdioecious *Xerospermum intermedium* Radlk. (Sapindaceae) in Rain Forest', *Botanical Journal of the Linnean Society*, 18: 11–34.

Appanah, S. and Chan, H. T. (1981), 'Thrips: The Pollinators of Some Dipterocarps', *Malaysian Forester*, 44: 234–52.

Ashton, P. S. (1982), 'Dipterocarpaceae', *Flora Malaysiana*, 1, 9 (2): 237–552.

Brierly, J. H. (1994), *Spices*, Kuala Lumpur: Oxford University Press.

Burkill, I. H. (1935), *A Dictionary of the Economic Products of the Malay Peninsula*, London: Crown Agents.

Chai, Paul P. K. (1996), 'A Floral Inventory of Lanjak-Entimau Wildlife Sanctuary', in *Proceedings of the Seminar on the Development and Management of the Lanjak-Entimau Biodiversity Conservation Area*, Sarawak: Sarawak Forest Department and International Tropical Timber Organization.

Chan, C. L. et al. (1994), *Orchids of Borneo 1*, Kota Kinabalu: Sabah Society and Kew: Royal Botanic Gardens.

Chan, K. L. et al. (eds.) (1993), *Trends in Traditional Medicine Research*, Penang: Universiti Sains Malaysia.

Chan, H. T. and Appanah, S. (1980), 'Reproductive Biology of Some Malaysian Dipterocarps. I. Flowering Biology', *Malaysian Forester*, 43: 132–43.

Chin, H. F. (1989), *Malaysian Flowers in Colour*, Kuala Lumpur: Tropical Press.

Corner, E. J. H. (1952), *Wayside Trees of Malaya*, Vol. 1, Singapore: Government Printing Office.

_____ (1988), *Wayside Trees of Malaya*, Vols. 1 & 2, 3rd edn, Kuala Lumpur: Malayan Nature Society.

Davis, S. D.; Heywood, V. H. and Hamilton, A. C. (eds.) (1995), *Centres of Plant Diversity: A Guide and Strategy for Their Conservation, Vol. 2: Asia, Australasia and the Pacific*, World Wide Fund for Nature and World Conservation Union.

Dransfield, J. (1979), 'A Manual of the Rattans of the Malay Peninsula', *Malayan Forest Records*, No. 29, Kuala Lumpur: Peninsular Malaysia Forest Department.

_____ (1984), 'The Rattans of Sabah', *Sabah Forest Record*, No. 13, Kota Kinabalu: Sabah Forest Department.

_____ (1990), 'The Palms of Taman Negara', *Journal of Wildlife and Parks*, 10: 38–45.

_____ (1992), *The Rattans of Sarawak*, Kuching: Sarawak Forest Department and Kew: Royal Botanic Gardens.

Gimlette, J. D. and Burkill, I. H. (1930), 'The Medical Book of Malayan Medicine', *Gardens' Bulletin of the Straits Settlements*, 6: 333–499.

Holttum, R. E. (1969), *Plant Life in Malaya*, Kuala Lumpur: Longman.

_____ (1986), *Revised Flora of Malaya: Ferns of Malaya*, Vol. 2, 2nd edn, Singapore: Government Printing Office.

Holttum, R. E. and Enoch, I. (1991), *Gardening in the Tropics*, Singapore: Times Editions.

Ibrahim, H. (1990a), 'Gingers of Sabah: Conservation, Research and Exploitation of Species with Economic Potential', in Ghazally Ismail et al. (eds.), *Proceedings of the International Conference on Forest Biology and Conservation in Borneo*, pp. 32–40.

_____ (1990b), 'The Ornamental Potential and Conservation of Underexploited Zingiberaceae Species', in H. Nair (ed.), *Proceedings of the International Conference and Exhibition on Orchids and Ornamental Plants*, pp. 84–8.

_____ (1995), 'Peninsular Malaysia Gingers: Their Traditional Uses', *Bulletin Heliconia Society International*, 7 (3): 1–4.

Jermy, A. C. (ed.) (1984), *Studies on the Flora of Gunung Mulu National Park, Sarawak*, Kuching: Sarawak Forest Department.

Keng, Hsuan (1978), *Orders and Families of Malayan Seed Plants: Coniferales*, Singapore: University of Malaya Press.

Khozirah, S. et al. (eds.) (1992), *Medicinal Products from Tropical Rain Forests*, Kepong: Forest Research Institute Malaysia.

Kiew, R. (1978), 'The Genus *Balanophora* in Peninsular Malaysia', *Malayan Nature Journal*, 30: 539–49.

_____ (1982), 'The Klang Gates Ridge', *Malayan Nature Journal*, 36 (1): 22–8.

_____ (1984), 'Towards a Flora in Borneo', in S. Ismail et al. (eds.), *Research Priorities in Malaysian Biology*, Bangi: Universiti Kebangsaan Malaysia.

_____ (1986), 'Phenological Studies of Some Rain Forest Herbs in Peninsular Malaysia', *Kew Bulletin*, 41: 733–46.

_____ (1987), 'The Herbaceous Flora of Ulu Endau, Johore–Pahang, Malaysia Including Taxonomic Notes and Descriptions of New Species', *Malayan Nature Journal*, 41: 201–34.

_____ (1989a), 'Conservation Status of Malaysian Palms: Peninsular Malaysia', *Malayan Naturalist*, 43: 3–15.

_____ (1989b), 'Lost and Found: *Begonia eiromischa* and *B. rajah*', *Malayan Naturalist*, 14: 64–7.

_____ (1990a), 'Conservation of Plants in Malaysia', in P. Baas, K. Kalkman and R. Geesink (eds.), *The Plant Diversity of Malesia*, Dordrecht: Kluwer Academic Publishers.

_____ (1990b), 'Pitcher Plants of Taman Negara', *Journal of Wildlife and Parks*, 10: 34–7.

Kiew, R. (ed.) (1991), *The State of Nature Conservation in Malaysia*, Kuala Lumpur: Malayan Nature Society and the International Development and Research Centre of Canada.

Kiew, R. et al. (1987), 'The Ferns and Fern-allies of Ulu Endau, Johore, Malaysia', *Malayan Nature Journal*, 41: 191–200.

Kochummen, K. M.; La Frankie, J. V. and Manokaran, N. (1990), 'Floristic Composition of Pasoh Forest Reserve, a Lowland Rain Forest in Peninsular Malaysia', *Journal of Tropical Forest Science*, 3 (1): 1–13.

Luping, M.; Chin, W. and Dingley, E. R. (eds.) (1978), *Kinabalu: Summit of Borneo*, Kota Kinabalu: Sabah Society.

Ng, F. S. P. (ed.) (1978), 'Tree Flora of Malaya, Vol. 3', *Malayan Forest Records*, No. 26, Kuala Lumpur: Longman.

_____ (1979), 'Tree Flora of Malaya, Vol. 4', *Malayan Forest Records*, No. 26, Kuala Lumpur: Longman.

Parris, B. S.; Beaman, R. S. and Beaman, J. H. (1992), *The Plants of Mount Kinabalu I: Ferns and Fern Allies*, Kew: Royal Botanic Gardens.

Payne, J.; Francis, E. M. and Phillipps, K. (1985), *A Field Guide to the Mammals of Borneo*, Kota Kinabalu: Sabah Society and World Wide Fund for Nature.

Phillipps, A. and Lamb, A. (1996), *Pitcher-plants of Borneo*, Kota Kinabalu: Natural History Publications.

Polunin, I. (1992), *Plants and Flowers of Malaysia*, Singapore: Times Editions.

Primack, R. B. and Lovejoy, T. E. (eds.), *Ecology, Conservation and Management of Southeast Asian Rainforest*, New Haven: Yale University Press

PROSEA (1994), 'Timber Trees: Major Commercial Timbers', *Plant Resources of South East Asia*, 5 (1) and (2), Bogor: Prosea Foundation.

Ratnam, L. (1995), *Windows on the Forest*, Kepong: Forest Research Institute Malaysia.

Ridley, H. N. (1930), *The Dispersal of Plants throughout the World*, Ashford: Reeve and Co.

Rubeli, K. (1986), *Tropical Rain Forest in South East Asia: A Pictorial Journey*, Kuala Lumpur: Tropical Press.

Salleh Mohamad Nor; Wong, Y. K. and Ng, F. S. P. (1990), *The Tropical Garden City: Its Creation and Maintenance*, Kepong: Forest Research Institute Malaysia.

Saw, L. G. (1993), '*Tacca*: Flowering and Fruiting Behaviour', *Nature Malaysiana*, 18 (1): 3–7.

Seidenfaden, G. and Wood, J. J. (1992), *The Orchids of Peninsular Malaysia and Singapore*, Fredenborg: Olsen and Olsen.

Sharnoff, S. D. (1997), 'Lichens: More than Meets the Eye', *National Geographic*, 191 (2): 58–71.

Simpson, B. B. and Conner-Orgorzaly, M. (1986), *Economic Botany: Plants in Our World*, New York: McGraw Hill.

Siti Hasidah Naim. and Khatijah, Idris (1994), 'Food Uses of Tuber Crops', in S. L. Tan et al. (eds.), *Proceedings of the National Seminar on Tuber Crop Production and Utilization*, Kuantan: Malaysian Agricultural Research and Development Institute, Universiti Pertanian Malaysia and Malaysian Society for Horticultural Science, pp. 184–96.

Soepadmo, E. (1971), 'Plants and Vegetation along the Path from Kuala Tahan to Gunung Tahan', *Malayan Nature Journal*, 24: 118–24.

_____ (1972), 'Fagaceae', *Flora Malesiana*, 1 (7): 265–403.

_____ (1978a), 'Ant-plants', *Nature Malaysiana*, 3 (4): 12–19.

_____ (1978b), 'Parasitic Flowering Plants', *Nature Malaysiana*, 3 (1): 24–31.

_____ (1979), 'Plants of the Sandy Beach', *Nature Malaysiana*, 4 (2): 24–33.

_____ (1980), 'Mangroves', *Nature Malaysiana*, 5 (1): 14–23.

_____ (1984), 'The Role of Tree-planting in Urban Ecology', in Y. H. Yip and K. S. Low (eds.), *Urbanization and Ecodevelopment: With Special References to Kuala Lumpur*, Kuala Lumpur: Institute of Advanced Studies, Universiti Malaya.

_____ (1986a), 'Aquatic Flowering Plants', *Nature Malaysiana*, 11 (3): 16–25.

_____ (1986b), 'Climbers', *Nature Malaysiana*, 11 (4): 14–15.

_____ (1986c), 'The Impact of Man's Activities on the Unique Floras of Malaysian Mountains', in Yusuf Hadi et al. (eds.), *Impact of Man's Activities on Tropical Upland Forest Ecosystems*, Serdang: Universiti Pertanian Malaysia, Faculty of Forestry, pp. 7–23.

_____ (1989), 'Contribution of Reproductive Biological Studies towards the Conservation and Development of Malaysian Plant Genetic Resources', in A. H. Zakri (ed.), *Genetic Resources of Underutilized Plants in Malaysia*, Kuala Lumpur: Malaysian National Committee on Plant Genetic Resources, pp. 1–41.

Soepadmo, E. and Abdul Latiff (1988), 'The Roles of Plants in Mitigating Urban Stress', in Sham Sani and M. Ahmad Badri (eds.), *Environmental Monitoring and Assessment: Tropical Urban Application*, Bangi: Universiti Kebangsaan Malaysia, pp. 370–82.

Soepadmo, E. and Eow, B. K. (1976), 'The Reproductive Biology of *Durio zibethinus* Murr', *Gardens' Bulletin of Singapore*, 29: 25–33.

Soepadmo, E.; Rao, A. N. and Macintosh, D. J. (eds.) (1984), *Proceedings of the Asian Symposium on Mangrove Environment: Research and Development*, Kuala Lumpur: UNESCO and Universiti Malaya.

Soepadmo, E. et al. (eds.) (1989), *Proceedings of the Seminar on Malaysian Traditional Medicine*, Kuala Lumpur: Institute of Advanced Studies, Universiti Malaya and Malaysian Institute of Chemistry.

Stewart, L. (1994), *A Guide to Palms and Cycads of the World*, Sydney: Cassell Publishers.

Tan, S. L. (1995), 'Conservation of Tuber Crops', in Mohamad Osman, Wan Mohamad Othman and Norliah Nasir (eds.), *Proceedings of the National Seminar on "The Indigenous Food Crops Conservation in Malaysia"*, Kuala Lumpur: Malaysian Agricultural Research and Development Institute.

Tan, T. K., (1990), *A Guide to Tropical Fungi*, Singapore: Singapore Science Centre.

van Steenis, C. G. G. J. (1950), 'The Delimitation of Malaysia and Its Main Geographical Division', *Flora Malesiana*, 1 (1): 70–5.

_____ (1961), 'Discrimination of Tropical Shore Formations', *Proceedings of the Symposium on Humid Tropical Vegetation*, Bogor: UNESCO, pp. 215–18.

_____ (1964), 'Plant Geography of the Mountain Flora of Mt. Kinabalu', *Proceedings of the Royal Society of London*, Series B, 161: 7–38.

Wee, Y. C. (1984), *Common Ferns and Fern-allies of Singapore*, Singapore: Malayan Nature Society.

_____ (1992), *A Guide to the Ferns of Singapore*, 2nd edn, Singapore: Singapore Science Centre.

Wee, Y. C. and Corlett, R. (1986), *The City and the Forest: Plant Life in Urban Singapore*, Singapore: Singapore University Press.

Wee, Y. C. and Keng, H. (1990), *An Illustrated Dictionary of Chinese Medicinal Herbs*, Singapore: Times Editions.

Whitmore, T. C. (1973), *Palms of Malaya*, Kuala Lumpur: Oxford University Press.

_____ (1980), 'A Monograph of *Agathis*', *Plant Systematics and Evolution*, 135: 41–69.

_____ (1984), *Tropical Rain Forest of the Far East*, Oxford: Clarendon Press.

_____ (1987), *Biogeographical Evolution of the Malay Archipelago*, Oxford: Clarendon Press.

_____ (1990), *Tropical Rain Forests*, Oxford: Clarendon Press.

_____ (1993), *An Introduction to Tropical Rain Forests*, Oxford: Oxford University Press.

Whitmore, T. C. (ed.) (1972), 'Tree Flora of Malaya, Vol. 1', *Malayan Forest Records*, No. 26, Kuala Lumpur: Longman.

_____ (1973), 'Tree Flora of Malaya, Vol. 2', *Malayan Forest Records*, No. 26, Kuala Lumpur: Longman.

Whitmore, T. C. and Sayer, J. A. (eds.) (1992), *Tropical Deforestation and Species Extinction*, London: Chapman and Hall.

Wong, K. M. (1982), 'Malaysian Bamboos in Use', *Nature Malaysiana*, 7 (1): 34–9.

_____ (1987), 'The Bamboos of Ulu Endau Area, Johor, Malaysia', *Malayan Nature Journal*, 41: 249–56.

_____ (1995a), 'The Morphology, Anatomy, Biology and Classification of Peninsular Malaysian Bamboos', *University of Malaya Botanical Monographs*, No. 1, Kuala Lumpur: Universiti Malaya.

_____ (1995b), 'The Bamboos of Peninsular Malaysia', *Malayan Forest Records*, No. 41, Kepong: Forest Research Institute Malaysia.

Wong, K. M. and Chan, C. L. (1997), *Mount Kinabalu: Borneo's Magic Mountain*, Kota Kinabalu: Natural History Publications.

Wong, K. M. and Phillips, A. (eds.) (1996), *Kinabalu: Summit of Borneo*, Kota Kinabalu: Sabah Society and Sabah Parks.

Wong, K. M.; Saw, L. G. and Kochummen, K. (1987), 'A Survey of the Forests of the Endau–Rompin Area, Peninsular Malaysia: Principal Forest Types and Floristic Notes', *Malayan Nature Journal*, 41: 125–44.

Wong, T. M. (1982), 'A Dictionary of Malaysian Timbers', *Malayan Forest Records*, No. 30, Kepong: Forest Research Institute Malaysia.

Wood, J. J.; Beaman, B. S. and Beaman, J. H. (1993), *Plants of Mount Kinabalu II: Orchids*, Kew: Royal Botanic Gardens.

# Index

# Picture Credits

**Abdul Halim Mohd Noor**, p. 41, *songket*; p. 113, woodcarving. **Aishah Salleh**, p. 39, cyanobacteria, chlorophyta, close-up of *Spirogyra*, diatom, pyrrophyta. **Anuar bin Abdul Rahim**, p. 22, mangrove forest; p. 34, diversity of life forms; p. 38, algae in a freshwater ecosystem; p. 46, cycads; p. 48, conifers; p. 50, *belinjau* trees; pp. 54–5, palm habitats; p. 55 palm leaves; p. 64, climbers; p. 71, bladderwort trap, sticky sundew trap, pitcher plant; p. 79, close-up of man and tree; p. 83, ornamental plants; p. 91, products made with plant oils; pp. 92–3, charcoal kiln; p. 94, rubber tree, section of bark and latex vessel; p. 107, rattan furniture; p. 108, orchid hybridization; p. 109, *Aranda Christine*, *Renanthera*, *Vanda* Miss Joaquim; p. 112, tile (middle); p. 113, Iban leaf design series; p. 121, section of a star fruit flower; p. 122, tapir (detail of larger illustration); p. 123, bat; p. 125, proboscis monkey; p. 128, *Echinodorus ridleyi*. **Atang Fachruroji**, p. 5, *Hibiscus*; p. 109, *Phalaenopsis*; p. 122, hornbill. **Chan, Wendy**, p. 144, threshing rice. **Chang, Tommy**, p. 8, rhododendron; p. 45, collecting *paku*; p. 76, rattan carrier; p. 96, coffee plant, drying coffee beans; p. 97, husking cocoa pods, dried cocoa beans; p. 110, hill paddy. **Cheksum Supiah Tawan**, p. 73, *genjir* and *kangkong, Acorus*; p. 90, *Agathis*; p. 91, bamboo tubes; p. 93, extracting nipa juice. **Chia Boon Kiang**, p. 36, *Termitomyces*; p. 37, fungi and dipterocarps; p. 39, rhodophyta, phaeophyta; p. 124, elephant, cellulose structure. **Chin Hoong Fong**, p. 15, *jambu mawar*; p. 80, *simpoh*; p. 81, *penaga, cempaka, bungur*, pigeon orchid; p. 82, *Denbrobium* sp., sunflower, dahlia; p. 100, vegetable farm. **Choong Mei Fun**, p. 124, leaf of oak tree, microscopic view of leaf; p. 125, stained leaf cells. **Chu Min Foo**, p. 47, *Cycas rumphii*; p. 49, Chinese arbor-vitae, Chinese juniper; p. 52, cross section of tree trunk, p. 58, herbaceous plants; pp. 100–1, vegetables; p. 118, water in plants, hydrological cycle; p. 128, Rajah's begonia. **Chua Swee Lian, Lillian**, p. 130, chalets, Forest Reserve in Kanching; p. 132, pitcher plant. **Chung, R. C. K.**, p. 67, open stomata, closed stomata. **Compost, Alan**, p. 20,

*Barringtonia* seed; p. 97, raw cocoa beans; p. 121, fly. **Creative Sphere**, p. 50, *belinjau* crisps; p. 88, old book. **Davison, Julian**, p. 69, ant garden. **Design Dimension**, p. 8, bird of paradise, fungus; p. 14, orchid; p. 15, Pulau Siligan; p. 28, Taman Negara; p. 33, oil palm plantation; p. 76, planting rice seedlings; p. 80, highway, Regent Hotel, private garden; p. 87, baskets of fruit. **Falconer, John**, p. 106, Iban woman; p. 112, tile with flower (top). **Forestry Department of Peninsular Malaysia**, p. 49, plywood; p. 52, *Delonix regia*. **Forestry Department of Sarawak**, p. 70, *Nepenthes northiana*; p. 76, boat; p. 103, oil palm fruits on lorry. **Forestry Museum of Penang**, p. 78, timber tree display. **Granquist, Bruce**, p. 85, peeled mangosteen; pp. 85 and 134, sectioned rambutan. **Haleywood Industries**, p. 95, processing rubber wood series. **Halijah Ibrahim**, p. 62, *Zingiber, Hedychium, Globba, Kaempferia, Alpinia, Etlingera, Camptandra*; p. 63, *cekur*, red ginger (photo), *Etlingera*; p. 104, cinnamon tree, cinnamon quills; p. 105, clove tree, dried clove buds, nutmeg tree, nutmeg fruit, turmeric rhizome, ginger rhizome. **Hoi Why Kong**, p. 92, empty oil palm fruit bunches; p. 93, smoking rubber sheets. **Hon Photo**, p. 15, limestone hills; p. 18, alpine vegetation; p. 33 bamboo (background to table); p. 43, seedlings in nursery; p. 47, *Cycas revoluta*; p. 52, buttresses; p. 53, *Hibiscus*; p. 57, bamboo shoots; p. 79, softwood trees; p. 97, mature cocoa pods; p. 100, *kubis* farm; p. 107, stacks of rattan canes. **Ibrahim Ahmad**, p. 113, textile with bamboo shoot motif. **Isa Ipor**, p. 13, nipa fruit; p. 18, mangrove forest; p. 19, beach; p. 20, *Terminalia*; p. 22, *Sonneratia*; p. 53, *Hibiscus*; p. 81, *baru baru*; p. 92, mangrove wood. **Jansen, Jeffrey Mark**, p. 122, orang utan. **Kiew, Ruth**, p. 14, *Homalanthus*; p. 15, *Orchadocarpa, Klossia, Didissandra*; p. 16, cinnamon tree, flowering cinnamon tree; p. 17, *Ficus*; p. 26, Klang Gate Ridge; p. 27, Gunung Tempurung; p. 58, *keladi*, p. 59, sedge, acanthus; p. 68, *Polyalthia*, p. 69, ant garden (photo); p. 75, *Cuscuta, Balanophora*; p. 128, Rajah's begonia (photo); p. 129, Bukit

Sagu, *Paraboea*, resorts, pitcher plant, orchid. **Kochummen, K. M.**, p. 78, bark series, buttresses, stilt roots; p. 79, hardwood trees, processing timber series. **Komang Agus Bagiada**, p. 40, lichen structure. **Laily bin Din**, p. 40, *Teloschistes* sp.; p. 41, foliose lichen, fruticose lichen, crustose lichen. **Lau, Dennis**, p. 106, women weaving. **Lee Su See**, p. 36, stinkhorn fungus, *Termitomyces*; p. 37, *Phellinus, Scleroderma, Russula, Amanita*, tree roots, transverse section of roots. **Lim, Lawrence**, p. 97, Nonya teapot; p. 106, Iban rice basket, Penan rattan mat. **Loh Choi Ying**, p. 103, box and bottle of vitamin E, edible palm oil products, palm kernel oil products. **Lueras, Leonard**, p. 113, Iban man with tattoos. **Malaysian Timber Council:** Lim Kah Soon, p. 36, fungi on log; p. 53, *Ixora*; p. 84, indigenous people, p. 126, canopy walk; p. 127, Mount Kinabalu; p. 133, *Tropical Evergreen Forests of Malaysia.* **Malaysian Timber Industry Board**, p. 133, *Malaysia: Home of the Evergreens.* **Malaysian Tourism Promotion Board**, p. 127, brochure; p. 130, brochure; p. 133, *Fascinating Adventures* (booklet and brochure). **Manokaran, N.**, p. 28, *keruing* tree. **Mohamed bin Abdul Majid**, p. 42, *Bazzania, Marchantia*; p. 43, *Hypophila, Dawsonia, Bryum, Lopidiun, Macromitrium, Meteorium, Campylopus.* **Mubinas Hanafi**, p. 85, section of *salak*. **Natural History Photographic Agency**, p. 9, boy holding pitcher plant; p. 36, *Cookeina*; p. 124, caterpillars on leaf. **New Straits Times Press (Malaysia) Berhad**, p. 116, Dato' Seri Dr Mahathir Mohamad. **Ong Hean Chooi**, p. 111, *ketupat*; p. 112, *lemang*. **Othman Omar**, p. 110, sowing rice seeds, combine rice harvester, rice mill, husk, polished rice; p. 111, types of rice. **Palm Oil Research Institute of Malaysia**, p. 102, oil palm fruits, tanker; p. 103, crude palm oil products, harvesting oil palm fruits, fruits on wheelbarrow, fungus. **Pan Dong Li**, p. 15, endemic plant genera; p. 17, plant seasons and animal life; p. 42, life cycle of a bryophyte; p. 68, *Macaranga*; p. 112, plants used as offerings; p. 123, giant squirrel; p. 133, ecofriendly tourist activities. **Pang Siew Moi**, p. 27, cut limestone;

p. 38, *Spirogyra, Catenalla*; p. 39, collecting *Sargassum*; drained forest. **Pepper Marketing Board Malaysia**, p. 104, pepper plantation, pepper products. **Photobank**: p. 63, *laksa*; p. 72, lotus pond; p. 73, lotus buds; p. 80, Penang Botanic Gardens; David Muscroft, p. 41, pills. **Picture Library**: David Bowden, p. 15, Gunung Kajang, p. 96, processed tea leaves, p. 107, making rattan furniture; Steve Bristow, p. 89, Chinese medicine man; Chan Chun Keat, p. 16, leafing season; Peter Chan, p. 113, bark jacket; Chin Fah Shin, p. 31, subalpine vegetation; S. K. Chong, pp. 20–1, beach, p. 53, Kuak Forest Reserve, p. 82, chrysanthemums, p. 86, star fruit seedling, p. 107 sorting rattan canes, Iban baskets; Goh Cheng Leong, p. 54, coconuts; Marlane Gueldan, p. 78, cut watermelons; Khoo Kock Guan, p. 126, slipper orchid; Rodney Lai Mun Wai, p. 10, close-up of *tualang* tree; Loke Swee Ying, p. 32, Kuala Lumpur Lake Gardens; Stanley Loo, p. 107, harvesting rattan; Ng Phoe Heng, p. 112, *bak chang*; Nor Azman Shah bin Ali, p. 118, dewdrops on leaf; Kenneth Rubeli, p. 102, oil palm plantation; See Kok Shan, p. 45, potted plants; Geoffrey Smith, p. 96, tea pickers; Song Jin Tek, p. 119, misty rainforest; Tan Tai Peng, p. 122, beach; Teoh Yiew Aun, p. 86, watermelons on lorry, watermelon plants; Teresa Wong, p. 108, flower show; Wong Yew Onn, p. 59, grass; Wong Yoon Keong, p. 31, alpine vegetation, pp. 130–1, Teku Gorge, p. 131, Mount Kinabalu; Yap Kok Sun, p. 10, *tualang* tree in distance, p. 91, nutmegs, p. 96, tea plant, p. 104, threshing pepper berries, drying pepper berries. **Phillipps, Karen**, p. 121, long-tongued bat. **Polunin, Ivan**, p. 138, allamanda. **Pos Malaysia**, p. 83, National Day stamp; p. 84, stamps. **Radin Mohd Noh Saleh**, p. 81, *angsana*; p. 112, tile (bottom). **Raghu Rai**, pp. 94–5, rubber plantation.

# PLANTS

## PATRON

Dato' Seri Dr Mahathir Mohamad


## SPONSORS

*The Encyclopedia of Malaysia* was made possible thanks to the generous and enlightened support of the following organizations:

DRB-HICOM GROUP

GEC-MARCONI PROJECTS (MALAYSIA) SDN BHD

MALAYAN UNITED INDUSTRIES BERHAD

MALAYSIA NATIONAL INSURANCE BERHAD

MINISTRY OF EDUCATION MALAYSIA

PERNAS INTERNATIONAL HOLDINGS BERHAD

PETRONAS BERHAD

RENONG BERHAD

STAR PUBLICATIONS (MALAYSIA) BERHAD

SUNGEIWAY GROUP

TENAGA NASIONAL BERHAD

UNITED OVERSEAS BANK GROUP

YAYASAN ALBUKHARY

YTL CORPORATION BERHAD

## ACKNOWLEDGMENT

*The Encyclopedia of Malaysia* was first conceived by Editions Didier Millet and Datin Paduka Marina Mahathir. The Editorial Advisory Board, made up of distinguished figures drawn from academic and public life, was constituted in March 1994. The project was publicly announced in October that year, and eight months later the first sponsors were in place. By 1996, the structure of the content was agreed; later that year the appointment of Volume Editors and the commissioning of authors were substantially complete, and materials for the work were beginning to flow in. By late 1998, five volumes were completed for publication, and the remaining ten volumes fully commissioned and well under way.

The Publishers are grateful to the following for their contribution during the preparation of the first five volumes:
Dato' Seri Anwar Ibrahim,
who acted as Chairman of the Editorial Advisory Board;
and the following members of the Board:
Tan Sri Dato' Dr Ahmad Mustaffa Babjee
Prof. Dato' Dr Asmah Haji Omar
Puan Azah Aziz
Dr Peter M. Kedit
Dato' Dr T. Marimuthu
Tan Sri Dato' Dr Noordin Sopiee
Tan Sri Datuk Augustine S. H. Ong
Ms Patricia Regis
the late Tan Sri Zain Azraai
Datuk Datin Paduka Zakiah Hanum bt Abdul Hamid

## SERIES EDITORIAL TEAM

PUBLISHER
**Didier Millet**

GENERAL MANAGER
**Charles Orwin**

PROJECT COORDINATOR
**Marina Mahathir**

EDITORIAL DIRECTOR
**Timothy Auger**

PROJECT MANAGER
**Noor Azlina Yunus**

EDITORIAL CONSULTANT
**Peter Schoppert**

EDITORS
**Alice Chee**
**Chuah Guat Eng**
**Elaine Ee**
**Irene Khng**
**Jacinth Lee-Chan**
**Nolly Lim**
**Kay Lyons**
**Premilla Mohanlall**
**Wendy (Khadijah) Moore**
**Alysoun Owen**
**Amita Sarwal**
**Tan Hwee Koon**
**Philip Tatham**
**Sumitra Visvanathan**

DESIGN DIRECTOR
**Tan Seok Lui**

DESIGNERS
**Ahmad Puad bin Aziz**
**Lee Woon Hong**
**Theivanai A/P Nadaraju**
**Felicia Wong**
**Yong Yoke Lian**

PRODUCTION MANAGER
**Sin Kam Cheong**

## VOLUME EDITORIAL TEAM

EDITORS
**Elaine Ee**
**Tan Hwee Koon**

DESIGNER
**Felicia Wong**

ILLUSTRATORS
**Anuar bin Abdul Rahim**
**Atang Fachruroji**
**Chia Boon Kiang**
**Chu Min Foo**
**Julian Davison**
**Bruce Granquist**
**Komang Agus Bagiada**
**Loh Choi Ying**
**Pan Dong Li**
**Studio Satumata**
**Sui Chen Choi**
**Teo Eng Hean**
**U Myo Myint**
**Ujang Suherman**
**Yeap Kok Chien**

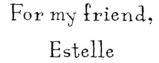

For my friend,
Estelle

First published 2004 by Walker Books Ltd
87 Vauxhall Walk, London SE11 5HJ

2 4 6 8 10 9 7 5 3 1

© 2004 Niamh Sharkey

The right of Niamh Sharkey to be identified as author/illustrator of this work
has been asserted by her in accordance with the Copyright, Designs
and Patents Act 1988

This book has been typeset in Aunt Mildred

Printed in China

British Library Cataloguing in Publication Data:
a catalogue record for this book is available from the British Library

ISBN 0-7445-8373-X (hb)
ISBN 1-84428-523-5 (pb)

www.walkerbooks.co.uk

# Santasaurus

## Niamh Sharkey

WALKER BOOKS
AND SUBSIDIARIES
LONDON · BOSTON · SYDNEY · AUCKLAND

# When the snow began to fall before Christmas, Ollie, Molly and Milo wrote letters to Santasaurus.

Ollie wished for a dinobot.

Molly wished for a dinocycle.

All Milo wanted was to meet Santasaurus and to fly in his sleigh.

When the cold wind blew

through Dinosaur Town,

Ollie, Molly and Milo went

Christmas shopping with Mumosaurus.

"What hustle and bustle and squoosh!"

said Mumosaurus.

Later, Mumosaurus, Dadosaurus, Ollie, Molly and Milo wrapped up presents in fancy paper,

hung up paperchains,

turned on the fairy lights,

made popcorn strings to hang on the tree

and baked sugar-plum cakes

for everyone.

It's Christmas Eve!

Everything is ready for the Dinosaurs' Christmas.
Ollie, Molly and Milo hang up their stockings,
leave milk and cookies for Santasaurus
and carrots for the dinodeer.

Soon everyone
is sleeping ...

except Milo.

Listen! What's that?
Is it the sound of
sleigh-bells ringing?

Milo pops out
from under the covers and
creeps ever so quietly down the stairs.

Who is standing by the Christmas tree?

# SANTASAURUS!

"Ho ho ho, Milo! I was waiting for you."

In the blink of a magic eye,

Milo and Santasaurus

shot up the chimney

to the sleigh on the roof.

They flew up from the house ...

and over Dinosaur Town.

They delivered presents to dinosaur children

all over Dinosaur World.

It was still dark when Santasaurus
brought Milo home.

"Goodnight, dinodeer!" Milo said,

giving each one a carrot.

"Goodnight, Santasaurus,

and thank you for the sleigh ride!"

Milo was back in bed and

fast asleep before you could say

"plum pudding".

"Hurray!" shouted Molly.
"It's Christmas morning!"

Ollie's best present
was a cool dinobot!

Molly got
a smashing dinocycle!

And Milo?

Milo got a miniature sleigh,
eight little dinodeer and a Christmas hat
just like the one Santasaurus wore!

So, were all the dinosaurs happy?
Yesosaurus, they were!
Happy Christmas,
Ollie, Molly and Milo!

Happy Christmas,
Mumosaurus and Dadosaurus!
HAPPY DINOSAURS' CHRISTMAS!